Clingman's Brigade in the Confederacy, 1862–1865

ALSO BY FRANCES H. CASSTEVENS
AND FROM MCFARLAND

*The 28th North Carolina Infantry:
A Civil War History and Roster* (2008)

*Tales from the North and the South: Twenty-Four
Remarkable People and Events of the Civil War* (2007)

*George W. Alexander and Castle Thunder:
A Confederate Prison and Its Commandant* (2004; paperback 2008)

*Edward A. Wild and the African
Brigade in the Civil War* (2003; paperback 2005)

*The Civil War and Yadkin County,
North Carolina* (1997; paperback 2005)

*"Out of the Mouth of Hell":
Civil War Prisons and Escapes* (2005)

Clingman's Brigade in the Confederacy, 1862–1865

Frances H. Casstevens

McFarland & Company, Inc., Publishers
Jefferson, North Carolina, and London

> The present work is a reprint of the illustrated case bound edition of Clingman's Brigade in the Confederacy, 1862–1865, first published in 2002 by McFarland.

LIBRARY OF CONGRESS CATALOGUING-IN-PUBLICATION DATA

Casstevens, Frances Harding.
  Clingman's Brigade in the Confederacy, 1862–1865 / by Frances H. Casstevens.
    p.   cm.
  Includes bibliographical references and index.

  ISBN 978-0-7864-4322-2
  softcover : 50# alkaline paper ∞

  1. Confederate States of America. Army. Clingman's Brigade.
  2. North Carolina — History — Civil War, 1861–1865 — Regimental histories.   3. North Carolina — History — Civil War, 1861–1865 — Campaigns.   4. United States — History — Civil War, 1861–1865 — Regimental histories.   5. United States — History — Civil War, 1861–1865 — Campaigns.   6. Clingman, T. L. (Thomas Lanier), 1812–1897.   7. Generals — Confederate States of America — Biography.   8. Confederate States of America. Army — Biography.   I. Title.
  E547.C625C37   2009
  973.7'456 — dc21   2002006088

British Library cataloguing data are available

©2002 Frances H. Casstevens. All rights reserved

No part of this book may be reproduced or transmitted in any form or by any means, electronic or mechanical, including photocopying or recording, or by any information storage and retrieval system, without permission in writing from the publisher.

Manufactured in the United States of America

On the cover: Fort Fisher, North Carolina, January 1865 (Library of Congress); *inset*— Brigadier General Thomas Lanier Clingman (Department of Cultural Resources, Division of Archives and History, Raleigh, North Carolina).

McFarland & Company, Inc., Publishers
  Box 611, Jefferson, North Carolina 28640
    www.mcfarlandpub.com

To all the descendants
of the members of Clingman's Brigade.
Be proud of your heritage, and know that your
ancestors fought gallantly and with honor.

Acknowledgments

I wish to extend my thanks to my son Danny Casstevens (commander of the Yadkin Gray Eagles, Sons of Confederate Veterans, Camp #1765) for his support; to my son Tim Casstevens, who trudged across some of the major battlefields with me and who shares my interest in the War Between the States and history in general; to my very dear "Yankee" friend Victor Seiders; and to everyone who wants to know the truth about our past.

I would also like to thank the staff of the Yadkin County Public Library, Yadkinville, North Carolina, for their help in finding numerous references.

I am especially grateful to Duke University, Durham, North Carolina, and to the University of North Carolina at Chapel Hill for making available the excellent manuscript and photographic collections they maintain. I also appreciate the Library of Congress making some very priceless photographs available through the Internet. Thanks also to the North Carolina Department of Archives and History for furnishing photographs.

Table of Contents

Acknowledgments   vii

- I. Clingman's Brigade — An Introduction   1
- II. Thomas L. Clingman — The Man   7
- III. Thomas L. Clingman — The Colonel   22
- IV. Battles: 1862–1863   31
- V. Battles: 1864   52
- VI. Battles: 1865   90
- VII. A History of the 8th Regiment   98
- VIII. A History of the 31st Regiment   106
- IX. A History of the 51st Regiment   111
- X. A History of the 61st Regiment   120
- XI. Herocs, Cowards or Fools   131
- XII. Problems of a Brigade Commander   149
- XIII. Evaluation and Summary   166

Appendix A. Clingman's Order Book 1— General Orders Issued by Brigadier General Thomas Lanier Clingman   181

Appendix B. Clingman's Order Book 2 — Specific Orders   191

Appendix C. The Men Who Made Up Clingman's Brigade — Officers   230

Appendix D. Miscellaneous Letters 232
Bibliography 239
Index 249

CHAPTER I

Clingman's Brigade — An Introduction

"It is well that war is so terrible, or we should grow too fond of it."
— General Robert Edward Lee (1807–1870) on seeing a Federal
charge repulsed at Fredericksburg, December 1862

Clingman's Brigade, commanded by Brigadier General Thomas Lanier Clingman, was composed of the 8th, 31st, 51st, and 61st regiments of North Carolina Infantry.[1] This brigade was organized because Major General Gustavus W. Smith, commander of the Department of North Carolina and Southern Virginia, was concerned about the security of the counties of eastern North Carolina. After Roanoke Island and other cities fell to the Federal forces early in 1862, General Smith saw that additional brigades were needed in the eastern counties of North Carolina to prevent further inroads by the Federal troops.[2] Clingman was made a brigadier general and, although he had no formal military training, he had been at the first battle at Manassas on July 21, 1861, and later served as a colonel of the 25th Regiment, North Carolina Troops, which he had formed from men in and around his home near Asheville, North Carolina.[3]

General Robert E. Lee recommended that Clingman be placed in charge of one of the new brigades.[4] On November 11, 1862, Smith agreed with Lee's recommendation and requested that four regiments be sent to the Wilmington area, with Clingman assigned to their command.[5] However, by the end of November, Clingman's brigade was still not complete.[6] Whether complete or not, Clingman's men were soon to see battle, and there had been little time for Clingman to come to know the men assigned to him (see Fig. 1).

Although born in Surry (Yadkin) County, Brigadier General Thomas Lanier Clingman moved from Huntsville, in Surry (now Yadkin) County, North Carolina, to Buncombe County, North Carolina. From his home in Asheville, Clingman explored the Appalachian Mountains extensively. Clingman's Dome in the southern Appalachian Mountains commemorates his efforts.

Thomas L. Clingman — statesman, scientist, and soldier — was "one of the most picturesque, embattled," while at the same time one of the "most colorful and controversial characters North Carolina has produced...."[7] Yet until the publication in 1998 of a book by Thomas E. Jeffrey, entitled *Thomas Lanier Clingman: Fire Eater from the Carolina Mountains*,[8] no complete biographical work had been written about him. Clingman was, however, usually mentioned in most 19th century biographical sketches and in various articles pertaining to the history of North Carolina and the history of the South.[9] His military career, though first as a colonel and later as a brigadier general in the Confederate States Army, received scant attention by his contemporaries and has been practically ignored by later historians. Reports about his brigade as well as the individual regiments in it have not been forthcoming, other than in various works about all of North Carolina's Confederate troops.

Modern biographers and historians have been inclined to focus their attention on Clingman's activities in the political arena and scientific fields.[10] In 1945, one historian ranked Clingman third on a list of outstanding men from Buncombe County, North Carolina, placing him below only Zebulon Baird Vance and David L. Swain, both of whom became governors of the state of North Carolina.[11]

The purpose of this work is to look at the military activities of Clingman's Brigade of North Carolina Infantry, and the individual regiments of the brigade, in order to determine the impact that the Brigade had on various battles or in various defensive positions. The brigade has been both praised and condemned. Clingman's men have been portrayed as soldiers who were "below average with [their] almost unbroken series of defeats from Roanoke Island to Fort Harrison."[12] On the other hand, Clingman's Brigade has, on occasion, also received the highest praise from such men as General Robert F. Hoke,[13] who stated that Clingman's men "did their duty well," and Confederate President Jefferson Davis, who witnessed the assault of Clingman's Brigade at Drewry's Bluff and described it as "the most gallant charge he had ever witnessed."[14] In situations that were unbearable, and could only be held defensively — such as in the trenches at Petersburg, and in the little sand and palmetto fort called Battery Wagner — the men did their duty, gave their lives. On occasions, the lack of men, or the failure of communication or coordination of effort between this brigade and other units, doomed the action to failure, such as at the battle for the Neuse River bridges near Kinston, North Carolina, and at Fort Harrison, Virginia. Much time was spent in doing guard and picket duty, guarding bridges, hunting deserters, and moving from one area to another. Endless days were spent in routine drill, cleaning weapons, writing letters, and trying to make a home for themselves away from home. The men were dedicated, the officers brave and honorable. Yet, they were only human, and as such, made mistakes. They were also blamed for the mistakes of others on several occasions. Whether those mistakes had any bearing on the winning or the losing of a particular battle is doubtful. However, the reputation of the brigade, as created by contemporaries and historians as well, has not been unblemished.

Those who have commented on Clingman's military career are widely diverse in their opinions as to his value as a military officer.[15] Most 19th century historians had little to say about Clingman's war years, although one biographical sketch commented that Clingman served "without special distinction in Eastern North Carolina and Virginia," totally ignoring the many months Clingman spent in South Carolina serving in the defense of Charleston and under fire on Morris Island during the siege of the summer of 1863.[16]

As a lawyer, politician, statesman, scientist, soldier, and entrepreneur, Clingman embraced knowledge and explored the unknown. He was a "firebrand," hot-tempered, and volatile. He evoked strong emotions from those who knew him. He was both admired and despised — envied

Fig. 1. Brigadier General Thomas Lanier Clingman (1); Captain W. H. S. Burgwyn (2); 1st Lieutenant Hal S. Puryear (3), aide-de-camp on Clingman's brigade staff. (Courtesy of Department of Cultural Resources, Division of Archives and History, Raleigh, North Carolina.)

and pitied. He was one of those characters who, if he had died gloriously on the battlefield leading a charge, would have been revered by history. As it was, he lived to an advanced age, and to the point where both mind and body failed him. Therefore, perhaps the long-term value of his contributions in those various areas was diminished.

Douglas S. Freeman, Civil War historian and author, once stated that the place accorded a man in history depends "on care in preserving essential records, and good fortune in having a biographer who uses those records sympathetically...."[17]

This seems to apply to the place in history accorded Brigadier General Thomas Lanier Clingman. While adequate military records exist, there is a paucity of published works concerning the four years Clingman devoted to the cause of the Confederate States Army. Clingman's military accomplishments and those of his brigade have been ignored, and their efforts have gone unrewarded.

Clingman's contemporaries viewed him as ambitious, brash, quick-tempered, outspoken, sometimes comical, and sometimes a pathetic figure. His political enemies did not write favorably about him.

His declining years were marred by mental, physical, and financial deterioration, and may have tarnished his earlier contributions in both politics and war. Was Clingman's personality an advantage or a disadvantage to the brigade? Was Clingman able to utilize his abilities (or overcome his disabilities) and adapt to the military way of life (which was entirely foreign to him), to become an effective Confederate officer? Or was he an incompetent general, who, because of his lack of military training, allowed his men to remain poorly trained, cowardly soldiers who failed to carry out their objectives? Undoubtedly the views of Clingman's contemporaries that were subsequently carried over by modern historians and biographers regarding his value and effectiveness as a brigadier general have also colored how Clingman's Brigade was viewed.

Do those men of Clingman's Brigade deserve to be condemned for dishonorable action, cowardice, failure to obey orders, or do they deserve to receive an "honorable" mention in the annals of military history? Does the reputation of the entire Brigade hinge on actions taken or not taken by individual companies or regiments, or on Clingman and his personality alone? Does the sacrifice of blood shed on the battlefields by the men of the brigade count for naught? Should the heroism of men like McKethan, Burgwyn, and Stedman go unacclaimed and ignored?

In order to understand the brigade, we must understand the situations in which it was placed. We must look at the officers who led the companies and the regiments that comprised the brigade. The performance of the four regiments of the brigade will be examined in detail because the successes or failures of those regiments reflect how the entire brigade is viewed.

Before becoming part of Clingman's Brigade, the individual regiments were under the jurisdiction of the following military districts:

Department of North Carolina (September 1861–January 1862)
District of Albemarle, Department of Norfolk (January–February 1862)
French's Command, Department of North Carolina and Southern Virginia (October–November 1862)[18]

After being transferred, the regiments known as "Clingman's Brigade" were under the jurisdiction of the following military departments:

District of Cape Fear, Department of North Carolina and Southern Virginia (November 1862–1863)
1st Military District of South Carolina, Department of South Carolina, Georgia and Florida (February–May 1863)
Department of North Carolina (May–July 1863)
1st Military District of South Carolina, Department of South Carolina, Georgia and Florida (July–November 1863)
Department of North Carolina (December 1863–May 1864)
Hoke's Division, Department of North Carolina (May–October 1864)
Hoke's Division, Hardee's Corps (March–April 1865)
Hoke's Division, 1st Corps, Army of Tennessee (April 1865)[19]

The regiments and the brigade were transferred as needed, and as the numbers of available Confederate troops dwindled.

The first combat fought by the four regiments of Clingman's Brigade under the brigadier general's command was the battle for the Neuse River Bridge near Goldsboro on December 17, 1862. Shortly after this battle, Clingman's Brigade, together with those of Evans and Pettigrew, were formed into a division under the command of Major General S. G. French.[20]

The brigade was stationed at James Island, Sullivan's Island, and Morris Island around the Charleston Harbor in the spring and summer of 1863. They defended Battery Wagner. Other battles in which the brigade, or parts of it, participated included New Bern and Plymouth in North Carolina, and Drewry's Bluff and Cold Harbor in Virginia — battles that made an impact on the outcome of the war. After Cold Harbor, Clingman's Brigade was stationed in the trenches of Petersburg during the hot summer of 1864, and was instrumental in protecting the lines around Petersburg during the Battle at the Crater on July 30, 1864.

Clingman's Brigade was also involved in the fighting along the Petersburg-Weldon Railroad, and Clingman was wounded at Globe Tavern on August 19, 1864, and was unable to lead his command. The brigade, now under the command of Colonel Hector McKethan, suffered heavy losses on September 30, 1864, in the futile attempt to retake Fort Harrison, Virginia. The remnants of the brigade struggled on until the end of the war, and were on the field at Bentonville, North Carolina, for the final battle. While Clingman's Brigade was not involved in some of the more famous battles — Gettysburg, Vicksburg, the Wilderness, Spotsylvania, Hanover Court House — it was in situations just as dangerous, and as important to the war effort.

The actions of Brigadier General Thomas Lanier Clingman as the commanding officer and the results of those actions had an effect on the achievements and failures of his brigade. In order to understand Clingman and his brigade, we must take a close look at the situations in which they were involved, and examine the countless problems which daily faced the brigadier general. How Clingman dealt with each problem that arose can be seen in his personal order books.[21] These books contain both orders of a general nature from Clingman to the regimental commanders and the troops of his regiment, as well as specific instructions dealing with the problems of individual soldiers.

The orders in these books give a different perspective to life inside the military structure of the Confederate Army. The orders issued at Clingman's command serve to illustrate just how many different kinds of problems were encountered by those men who were given the responsibility of commanding a brigade, and how heavy was the burden placed on their shoulders.

In the end, it is hoped that this work will show that Clingman's Brigade was no better or worse than other brigades, and that its contribution to the war effort was worthwhile. This book is designed to give the reader a different view of the period 1861–1865, by means of photographs of some of the individuals involved and the places in which they fought and died. Diary entries, letters, and official reports are interwoven to paint a picture of a period of courage, perseverance, and daily life of the Confederate soldiers of Clingman's Brigade who endured unbearable hardship while defending their home state of North Carolina, their neighboring states of South Carolina and Virginia, and what was once the Confederate States of America.

Notes

1. W. H. S. Burgwyn, "Clingman's Brigade," in *Histories of the Several Regiments and Battalions from North Carolina in the Great War, 1861–1865, Written by Members of the Respective Commands*, ed. Walter Clark (Goldsboro, N.C.: Nash Brothers, 1901), IV, 480–500. Hereafter cited as Burgwyn, "Clingman's Brigade."

2. *The War of the Rebellion: A Compilation of the Official Records of the Union and Confederate Armies*, XVIII, Series I (Washington: U. S. Govt. Printing Office, 1881), p. 762. These volumes will hereinafter be cited as O.R.

3. Garland S. Ferguson, "Twenty-Fifth Regiment," in Clark, *Histories of the Several Regiments and Battalions from North Carolina in the Great War, 1861–1865, Written by Members of the Respective Commands*, II, pp. 291–291. References to material in Clark's several volumes will hereinafter be cited either by author and title of chapter, or by the abbreviated title of the series as Clark, *Histories of the Several Regiments*.

4. *O.R.*, XIX, Ser. I, Pt. II, p. 689, October 30, 1862, General Robert E. Lee to Major General Gustavus W. Smith.

5. *O.R.*, XVIII, Ser. I, p. 770, November 11, 1862, General G. W. Smith to Major General S. C. French.

6. *O.R.*, XVIII, Ser. I, p. 786, November 26, 1862, General W. H. C. Whiting to Major General S. G. French.

7. Glenn Tucker, "For Want of a Scribe," *North Carolina Historical Review*, XLIII (April 1966), 174–185.

8. Thomas E. Jeffrey, *Thomas Lanier Clingman: Fire Eater from the Carolina Mountains* (Athens, Ga.: The University of Georgia Press, 1998).

9. "Clingman, Thomas Lanier," *The National Cyclopaedia of American Biography*, ed. Lyman Abbott, et al. (New York: James T. White & Co., 1897), VII, p. 200; "Clingman, Thomas Lanier," in *Appleton's Cyclopaedia of American Biography* (New York: D. Appleton & Co., 1887), I, p. 658; Charles Lanman, "Thomas Lanier Clingman," *Biographical Annals of the Civil Government of the United States*, 2nd ed. (New York: J. M. Morrison, 1887), p. 101; and Morton M. Rosenberg, "Thomas Lanier Clingman," in *The Encyclopedia of Southern History*, eds. Avery O. Craven and Dewey W. Granthan, Jr. (Baton Rouge, La.: Louisiana State University Press, 1979), p. 243.

10. John S. Bassett, "The Congressional Career of Thomas L. Clingman," *The Trinity Historical Records*, IV (1900), pp. 48–63; Archibald Henderson, *North Carolina: The Old North State* (Chicago: Lewis Publishing Co.), II, pp. 202, 216; and "Clingman, Thomas Lanier," in *Who Was Who in America: Historical Volume, 1607–1896*, 1967, rev. ed., p. 180.

11. R. C. Lawrence, "General Thomas Clingman," *State*, XII (April 1945), 6.

12. William H. S. Burgwyn, *A Captain's War: The Letters and Diaries of William H. S. Burgwyn, 1861–1865*, Herbert M. Schiller, ed. (Shippensburg, Pa.: White Mane Publishing Co., Inc., 1994), p. xi. Hereafter cited as Burgwyn, *A Captain's War*.

13. *O.R.*, XXXVI, Ser. I, Pt. II, p. 238, "Report of Major General Robert F. Hoke," May 25, 1864; and XXXVI, Ser. I, Pt. II, pp. 236–238.

14. *O.R.*, XXXVI, Ser I., Pt. 2, pp. 236–238, Robert F. Hoke to J. M. Otey, May 24, 1864; E. K. Bryan and E. H. Meadows, "31st Regiment," in Clark, *Histories of the Several Regiments* II, p. 515 (quoting Davis).

15. Richard J. Sommers, *Richmond Redeemed: The Siege of Petersburg* (New York: Doubleday, 1981), p. 116; R. C. Lawrence, "General Thomas Clingman," *State*, XII (April 1945), 6; William E. Rutledge, Jr., *An Illustrated History of Yadkin County, North Carolina, 1850–1965* (Yadkinville, NC: by the author, 1965), p. 28; John H. Wheeler, *Reminiscences and Memories of North Carolina* (1884; rpt. Baltimore: Genealogical Publishing Co., 1966), p. 73; and "Thomas Lanier Clingman," in *Biographical Dictionary of the Confederacy*, ed. John L. Wakelyn (Westport, Conn.: Greenwood Press, 1977), p. 140.

16. H. Thomas Kearney, "Clingman, Thomas Lanier," in *Dictionary of North Carolina Biography*, ed. William S. Powell (Chapel Hill: University of North Carolina Press, 1979), I, no page numbers.

17. Tucker, p. 177.

18. Stewart Sifakis, *Compendium of the Confederate Armies: North Carolina* (New York: Facts on File, 1992), pp. 96–97.

19. Sifakis, pp. 96–97.

20. Order No. 19, Major General G. W. Smith to Thomas L. Clingman, Clingman Papers, Southern Historical Collection, Chapel Hill, North Carolina. Hereinafter cited as Thomas L. Clingman Papers, SHC.

21. Thomas Lanier Clingman Papers, General Orders, Clingman's Brigade, 1862–1864 and Brigade Order Book, 1862–1864, Manuscript Department, Duke University, Durham, North Carolina. Hereinafter cited as Order Book 1 or Order Book 2, respectively.

Chapter II

Thomas L. Clingman — The Man

We can make majors and officers every year, but not scholars.
— Robert Burton (1577–1640)

What sort of man does it take to become a successful commander of a brigade? What were the personality traits necessary to manage thousands of men, to ensure that they did as they were ordered, that they did not disgrace themselves through cowardice or by turning their backs to the enemy and fleeing the field of battle? Some obvious character traits that would be advantageous to a brigade commander are intelligence, leadership qualities, devotion to duty, humility, loyalty, and respect for his men. An officer of superior quality would have to rise above petty differences in order to see the whole picture. He would not succumb to human frailties of greed, jealousy, envy, and spite. The qualities that mark a man as an officer and a gentleman, rather than an incompetent, ineffective military leader, tend to earn the respect of the men who serve under him. Under such leadership, men are often inspired to rise above themselves and give their wholehearted efforts to the cause, even if the war becomes gradually less popular and harder to support as conditions worsen both on the battlefield and at home. Some officers, such as General Robert E. Lee, had the complete confidence of their men. Lee so moved and inspired the men under his command that many would have gladly gone into the jaws of hell out of the love and respect they bore for him.

Did Brigadier General Thomas Lanier Clingman have the character traits that made a successful brigade commander? If his brigade failed, was it because of Clingman himself or was it because of extenuating circumstances beyond his control or beyond the control of the men of his brigade?

One contemporary of Clingman's, Foster A. Sondley, of Asheville, knew the general for "half a century." He credited Clingman as being "courageous," but described him as:

> ...an intrepid man of the most arrogant and aggressive character, greatest self confidence, unlimited assurance, prodigious conceit, stupendous aspiration, immense claims, more than common ability, no considerable attainments of culture, great boastfulness, and much curiosity.[1]

Thomas Lanier Clingman was a complex man of many talents. His exceptional intellectual powers enabled him to achieve many goals in a variety of disciplines: law, politics, science, and military. He was quite distinguished in appearance. While in Congress, he was nicknamed "Handsome Tom." Some saw him as a "strange-looking man."[2] He had a high, broad forehead, a thin, aquiline nose, deep-set piercing eyes, and bushy sideburns.[3] Sometimes he wore a mustache and a beard neatly trimmed.[4] A photograph taken after the war at the Mathew Brady Studio in Washington shows him with a full beard, almost entirely gray (see Fig. 2). His eyes in this photograph seem to reflect great sadness.[5]

Born in the village of Huntsville, Surry County (now Yadkin County), North Carolina, on July 27, 1812, he was the oldest son of a "proud Huntsville family,"[6] Jacob Clingman and wife, Jane Frances Poindexter.[7] The ancestral background of Thomas Lanier Clingman reflects a diversity of nationalities, professions, military involvement, and educational levels. His forebears included an Indian Warrior, three farmers who served as American Revolutionary War soldiers, a clergyman, and a merchant. His heritage[8] was a mixture of English, Norman French, German, Scotch, and Cherokee Indian — a heritage that some believed contributed to his "many excellencies and many peculiarities.[9]

His paternal grandfather, Alexander Clingman, settled in Rowan County, North Carolina, before 1756 and owned land adjacent to the court house in Salisbury.[10] Alexander served in the Continental Army and was taken prisoner at Charleston, South Carolina, when General Benjamin Lincoln surrendered to the British.[11] Shortly after Alexander Clingman's death about 1803,[12] two of his sons, Peter and Jacob, removed from Salisbury to Surry County where they operated a store in the village of Huntsville.[13] The Clingman brothers prospered. By 1812, Peter owned 756 acres of land, and Jacob owned 20.[14] Peter was one of those appointed by the North Carolina Legislature as a commissioner for the town of Huntsville in 1822.[15] The Clingman brothers married the Poindexter sisters: Peter married Ann Poindexter on January 14, 1806,[16] and Jacob married her sister, Jane

Fig. 2. Thomas Lanier Clingman, taken at Mathew Brady Studio, Washington, D.C.

Frances Poindexter, on August 10, 1811.[17] The Poindexter girls, often reported to be "twin" sisters, were not twins. Ann Poindexter was born November 25, 1787, and died January 15, 1815. Her sister Jane, the mother of Brigadier General Thomas L. Clingman, was born November 7, 1789, and died April 12, 1873, according to information from tombstones in the Lanier-Poindexter-Clingman cemetery near the Yadkin River in what is now Forsyth County.[18]

As one of the village merchants, Jacob Clingman was known "for his industry, thrift, and steadfastness of character."[19]

The Poindexter girls were the daughters of Francis Poindexter and wife, Jane Pattillo Lanier. They were the granddaughters of Revolutionary War captain Thomas Poindexter and his second wife, Elizabeth Pledge.[20] The Pledge family is of Welsh extraction,[21] and is closely allied with the Poindexter family. Thomas Lanier Clingman's Norman French ancestry can be traced back for many generations through his mother, Jane Frances Poindexter.[22]

It is through Elizabeth Pledge that Thomas Clingman descends from the legendary Indian chief Donnahoo.[23] Donnahoo may not have been one of the Cherokee Indians, but probably was a member of one of the other tribes that roamed the eastern coast states of Virginia and North and South Carolina. According to family tradition, Chief Donnahoo came to the rescue of some white settlers on the coast of North Carolina during the Tuscarora War, where he met and married a white woman, Mary Wentworth. A daughter of the Indian and Mary Wentworth is believed to have been Elizabeth who married William Pledge. The daughter of William and Elizabeth Pledge, known as Elizabeth "Bettie" Pledge, married Thomas Poindexter. Many descendants hold with the descent from Chief Donnahoo, but others disclaim it.

Perhaps Clingman's most distinguished ancestor was his Scottish great-grandfather, the Reverend Henry Pattillo, the noted Presbyterian minister.[24] Pattillo was an outspoken adversary of the Regulator movement,[25] but later was a delegate to the North Carolina Provincial Convention in August 1775, and was elected chaplain of that body. He was so respected that he was elected chairman of the convention.[26] Like his great-grandson, the Reverend Pattillo was a man of diverse interests. He compiled a public school geography textbook entitled *Geographical Catechism*, and published three of his more noteworthy sermons. At one time he owned 300 acres of land and seven slaves, but by backing a mercantile venture for his oldest son, he lost "every farthing."[27] Financial ruin forced Pattillo to auction all his possessions; however, his parishioners came to his rescue and returned almost everything to him as a gift.[28]

Both of the husbands of Jane Pattillo, Clingman's grandmother, served in the American Revolution. Jane Pattillo married her first husband, Robert Lanier of Williamsboro, on June 12, 1775.[29] Lanier was killed, according to one source, while serving as a colonel in the American forces.[30] Jane Pattillo Lanier then married Francis Poindexter at the home of her parents in Granville County, North Carolina, on May 26, 1786.[31]

Thus, Clingman had some distinguished ancestors to provide inspiration, and of whom he could be proud.

Little is known about Clingman's childhood. Undoubtedly, in the sparsely settled land beyond the Yadkin River, young Tom was exposed to a "love of nature and an interest in the land." He was especially fond of fishing for shad in the Yadkin River.[32] He more than likely learned to ride, shoot, and hunt game, as was common for young men in the South. About 1816, when Tom was four years old, his father died. Jacob Clingman is not listed in the 1820 Surry County census, so he died sometime between 1812 and 1820, and if, as reported, Thomas was four, that would place Jacob's death around 1816, but not later than 1820. Since Thomas, born in 1812, had three younger siblings, a later date for the death of Jacob is possible. Some sources state that Jane took her four small children and moved out of their house near the "Red Store" into the large home of Peter Clingman, known as the "White House."[33] Peter was a widower, his wife Ann having died in 1815. The White House (Fig. 3) is a large, imposing structure, still inhabited. Many of the original features of this house, which was built around 1800, remain, such as hand-blown window panes, hand-crafted mantels, and wrought-iron door hinges. The modern comforts of plumbing and electricity have been added.[34]

Uncle Peter Clingman owned extensive farm acreage, in addition to the store property. He also owned a mill, a still house, a blacksmith shop, and slaves to operate them. He, undoubtedly, played an important part in the molding of the character of Thomas Lanier Clingman.

Peter Clingman was quite well-to-do, and had several children, in addition to his nieces and nephews. However, Peter willed all of his property to his son Francis A. Clingman. Thomas Lanier Clingman was one of three witnesses.[35]

Because Peter Clingman owned and operated a number of businesses, young Tom Clingman was exposed to a variety of occupations. His early education and training was "directed by his mother and uncle, Francis A. Poindexter."[36] Young Tom attended the village school until age 17 years. He is also reported to have attended school in neighboring Iredell County.[37]

Fig. 3. The "White" House, Huntsville, Yadkin County, North Carolina (childhood home of General Clingman). (Courtesy of Lupton Wood.)

Other accounts state simply that he was privately tutored before entering the University of North Carolina as a sophomore.[38]

Peter Stuart Ney, a Rowan and Davie County teacher who died on November 15, 1846, is reported to have spent a winter in the Poindexter home near Huntsville.[39] While there is no evidence to support the theory that Clingman was tutored by Peter Stuart Ney, if Ney did stay at the Poindexter home, he would probably have tutored Tom Clingman as a child. Peter Stuart Ney, reportedly claimed, while under the influence of alcohol, to have been one of Napoleon's most brilliant soldiers, Marshal Michel Ney. Marshal Ney was sent to arrest Napoleon when he escaped from Elba, but the Emperor persuaded Ney to join his cause and Ney was in command of the Imperial Guards at the final battle at Waterloo.[40]

If Peter Ney was, indeed, the famed Marshal Ney, and if he did tutor Clingman, the young man may have heard tales, albeit fictional ones, of the Napoleonic Wars. From his uncle Francis A. Poindexter, who served in the militia during the War of 1812, Thomas L. Clingman may have heard stories of that war also.[41] Clingman more than likely grew up hearing stories of the Revolutionary War skirmish which took place near his home on October 14, 1780, in which 14 Tories and one patriot, Captain Henry Francis, were killed.[42] He would have heard the stories about the British General Lord Cornwallis crossing the Yadkin River at the nearby Shallow Ford in the spring of 1781 in a race to catch American General Nathanael Greene. Once across the river, Cornwallis stopped at "Shallowford," the home of Clingman's grandmother and her first husband, Robert Lanier,[43] before going on to Guilford Court House. There, General Greene and his patriots faced Cornwallis and his Redcoats at the Battle of Guilford Court House, a battle that had a significant bearing on the outcome of the American Revolutionary War.

Young Thomas was "strong in body, mind and will"; he was aggressive and courageous. He enjoyed both athletic activities and reading. He desired to excel in everything he did, and this motivation enabled him to succeed in entering and graduating from the University of North Carolina.[44] After passing an examination, Clingman was admitted in June 1829 to the "Second Class" at the university.[45] At the university, his studies ranged from Greek and Roman history to geometry, astronomy, philosophy, and the principles of civil government.[46] This wide range of study gave him a background for the many fields of endeavor in which he would later excel.

While a student at the university, Clingman became a member of the Dialectic Society. A life-sized portrait of him with his hand outstretched hangs on the walls of the society's quarters, along with those of many others who have contributed to the history of North Carolina.[47] At his graduation three years later in June 1832,[48] Clingman received his first public recognition. His scholastic record had "exceeded all others until his time," and has possibly not been "equaled since."[49] Governor Montford Stokes, who presented the diplomas that year, congratulated Clingman, and commented on his outstanding record: "It discloses that you have stood first in all your classes from your entrance to the hour of graduation, and this is an exceptionally brilliant and studious class; … it augurs well for your future."[50]

David Swain, later governor of North Carolina, entered in his diary in June 1832 that the graduating class "acquitted themselves with much credit, especially young Clingman, of Surry County," and noted that he would probably become "an ornament to the State."[51] Clingman's class, the Class of 1832, did have many men who would become outstanding leaders of the state and nation — men who would become prominent in the United States Congress, and the North Carolina state legislature, and men who would become the military leaders of the Confederacy in the War Between the States.[52]

After finishing his studies at the university, Clingman prepared to pursue a career in law. Since there were no requirements as to the duration of study and no course prerequisites, a young man who wanted to enter the legal profession usually would prepare for the bar examination by "reading Law" under the guidance of a practicing attorney, a process that normally took about two years.[53] In order to prepare and learn enough to pass the bar examination, Clingman moved to Hillsborough to read law in the office of William A. Graham,[54] a young attorney who later became governor of North Carolina, United States senator, and Secretary of the Navy.

However, the years of studying at the university took their toll on Clingman, and in 1833, at age 21, his eyesight failed. A physician prescribed absolute rest. According to family historian Augustus H. Jarratt, Clingman, unable to accept defeat, sat "day after day, with a green silk shade bound closely over his eyes," while his sister Elizabeth read the remainder of the required course material to him. By January 1834, his sight had been restored,[55] and he obtained his Superior Court license to practice law.[56] Elizabeth would later become Mrs. Richard C. Puryear.

Thomas L. Clingman began his practice as an attorney in Surry County where he also became involved in politics. He was elected as a Whig representative from Surry County to the North Carolina legislature in 1835. In 1836 he removed to Asheville where he continued to practice law for many years.[57] By advocating that the Charleston-to-Cincinnati railroad be routed near Asheville, Clingman gained the support of the people of Buncombe County and they elected him to the North Carolina Senate in 1840.[58]

Clingman loved the mountains of North Carolina, and he proclaimed their natural beauty and resources across the nation. According to the 1897 edition of *The National Cyclopaedia of American Biography,* Clingman opened mica mines in Mitchell and Yancey counties, and publicized the existence in the mountains of corundum, zircon, rubies, and other gems.[59] According to the "distinguished Charles Upham Shepard," Clingman is credited as "the discoverer of both diamonds and platinum in North America."[60]

Clingman spent much of his spare time tramping about in the Appalachian Mountains with a compass and sextant, and he measured the heights of many of the peaks in the Appalachians. In 1855 he measured what he believed to be the highest peak east of the Mississippi.[61] That claim led to a dispute with Dr. Elisha Mitchell, a professor at the University of North Carolina. Mitchell, who had taught Clingman at the university, claimed he had discovered the highest peak in 1835.[62] This dispute continued until Mitchell slipped and fell over a precipice into a deep pool and drowned in 1857.[63] As a result of this tragic accident, the highest peak in the Appalachian chain was dubbed "Mount Mitchell." As a consolation prize to Clingman, another high peak is named "Clingman's Dome."

The controversy damaged Clingman's reputation and credibility as an explorer and scientific observer, but did not harm him politically. After serving a single term in the North Carolina legislature, Clingman was elected as a Whig to the United States House of Representatives, where he served from 1843 to 1845, and again from 1847 to 1858. While in Congress, Clingman served as chairman of the Committee on Foreign Affairs.[64] In 1858, North Carolina

Governor Thomas Bragg appointed Clingman to fill the United States Senate seat vacated through the resignation of Asa Biggs. The next session of the North Carolina General Assembly ratified Governor Bragg's action. In 1861, just before the outbreak of the War Between the States, Clingman was duly elected by the North Carolina legislature to serve a full six-year term in the United States Senate.[65]

As a young, eligible bachelor, Clingman enjoyed the social life of Washington, D.C. Always neatly dressed (even in his later years when his clothing was almost threadbare), Clingman was of "handsome and commanding appearance."[66] He was a frequent partygoer, and mingled with such notables as Zebulon Baird Vance, John C. Breckinridge, and Chief Justice Roger B. Taney.[67]

However, Mary Chestnut, an active Southern belle and Washington socialite, had no liking for Clingman. She described him in her diary as "staid and severe of aspect." She noted that even dancing was "a serious business with him." She notes that when a young lady with whom he was dancing insisted on talking, Clingman replied, "Pray withhold all remarks. It puts me out. I cannot do two things at once. If you will talk, I shall have to stop dancing."[68]

As a congressman in the midst of many social activities, Clingman undoubtedly met many women, but he chose never to marry. Although he is reported to have been a "persistent suitor" of the daughter of the owner of Corcoran Gallery of Art in Washington, he was rejected by the young lady. This disappointment was felt so keenly by Clingman that he resolved never to marry. This is in keeping with a remark he reportedly made upon graduation from the University of North Carolina: "Well, I can marry and be a happy man, or not marry and be a great man. I will be a great man."[69] Whether his decision not to marry was made as a young man with high ambitions or as a rejected suitor in Washington is unknown.

Clingman's congressional years were marked by controversy. He took part in nearly all the important debates, and served as chairman of the Committee on Foreign Affairs with much ability. Even as a "rookie," Clingman conducted himself with "great readiness and self-possession."[70] He soon gained a reputation as being outspoken. As antislavery forces attempted to abolish slavery or prevent its extension into the territories, there were many debates in Congress. Clingman believed the Southern states should resist the Wilmot Proviso, which he regarded as a violation of the Constitution.

The Wilmot Proviso was an amendment drafted in 1846 by David Wilmot and presented to the United States House of Representatives during the Mexican War. It was attached to the $2 million appropriation which authorized President Polk to negotiate a territorial settlement with Mexico. The proviso stipulated that slavery would not be allowed in the new territories. The Senate adjourned without voting on the bill. However, in the next session of Congress in 1847, a new bill for $3 million was introduced, and the antislavery amendment was attached to it. The House passed the bill, but the Senate drew up its own version, which excluded the Wilmot Proviso. The controversy caused bitterness between the northern and southern sections of the country, and in the 1848 election, became a political issue.

In a letter published in the *North Carolina Standard*,[71] on November 28, 1849, Clingman, writing in reply to a letter by Senator Henry Foote of Mississippi, urged the Southern states to resist such an attack on slavery as was evidenced in the Wilmot Proviso and that the abolition of slavery in the District of Columbia should be regarded as "an act of tyranny so insulting and so gross as to justify a withdrawal of confidence from such a government."[72]

By 1850, Clingman was regarded as one of the "fire-eaters from the cotton states." When Henry Clay,[73] seeing an intersectional compromise, proposed a series of resolutions in the United States Senate on January 29, 1850, Congressmen from the Southern states aired their views. Clingman paradoxically agreed to the exclusion of slavery from the territories, but opposed any move to prohibit slavery where it already existed.[74] While Clingman believed in the theoretical right of Congress to regulate slavery in the territories, he also saw the necessity of keeping the "balance of power" by making the territories "half slave and half free."[75]

Clingman believed that the South would be in a much better position economically out of the Union; however, he thought that the Southern states would remain in the Union. He advocated trying all possible constitutional and legislative means of compromise, but, failing that, believed armed resistance would be necessary.[76]

Clingman came to hold a position in favor of secession. However, he was the last of the Southern senators to resign his seat. Some of his constituents believed that his policy was "fashioned by personal ambition," and that Clingman thought that if a Southern Confederacy was formed he could gain the office of president.[77]

The secessionists in North Carolina were more prevalent in the eastern counties where there were large rice and cotton plantations worked by large numbers of slaves. Led by Senator Thomas L. Clingman and Governor John W. Ellis, eloquent speeches were delivered at secession rallies.[78]

While Clingman is credited with being the most "ultra–Southern of the North Carolina delegation in Congress," he delivered a speech on January 16, 1861, which, considering the "violent threats then being made by the Southern fire-eaters," was remarkably calm. John Spencer Bassett wrote about Clingman's speech that "It is as if he were convinced of the hopelessness of his cause and were only bent on making a protest for the sake of posterity against a wrong the consummation of which was already fixed by destiny."[79]

Clingman was credited with being a "prolific" writer of speeches.[80] Northerners regarded his speeches in Congress as "mere bluster,"[81] or as being "inconsistent."[82] After the war, Clingman published many of his speeches and writings on some of his scientific discoveries, in a large volume.[83]

In 1851, a newspaper, the *Washington Republican*, saw Clingman as:

> [one] to whom whatever is not extraordinary, is nothing... He is liable to the imputation of seeking notoriety, of doing something extraordinary, and of being restless in the beaten tract ... determined to surprise us by his ultraism if he cannot dazzle us by his oratory.[84]

Clingman's rhetoric did gain him the reputation of being "ultra–Southern," and also gained him many friends among the pro–Southern Democrats. Perhaps the attention he generated also inflated his ego. As a result, he made enemies among the Whigs. William S. Pettigrew, a Whig and planter from Washington County, North Carolina, and later a general in the Confederate Army, saw Clingman as "an immensely great man among the ultras of the South & no doubt has vanity enough for fifty men."[85]

Another who disliked Clingman was fellow Whig congressman and party leader David Outlaw. Outlaw described Clingman in 1849 as "not exactly crazy," but he believed that some of Clingman's "mental balance wheels, necessary to regulate properly the machine, either were absent or out of order." He saw Clingman as "intoxicated with the race of power & popularity."[86] James C. Johnston described Clingman as "gregarious, pompous," and "full to overflowing with himself."[87]

Clingman was often outspoken. This outspokenness brought him to the "field of honor" in 1845 in a bloodless duel with William L. Yancey of Alabama. After both had fired once and missed, the duel was stopped.[88]

Undoubtedly, Clingman relished publicity. He was seen by some as ambitious and ruthless. Some have stated that he wanted to be the "first President of the Southern Confederacy."[89] Even before there was a Confederacy, the *Raleigh Register* criticized Clingman as the "Judas of the Whigs," when he turned to the Democrats, but the *Asheville News* defended him as being an "independent representative courageous enough to buck the 'college of Cardinals.'" The Asheville paper pointed out that Clingman had been wrongly accused by the *Raleigh Register*, and that he was a man who had risen in politics because he placed his principles above those of the party.[90]

Clingman, not unexpectedly, had a higher opinion of himself. He saw himself as the representative of those who had elected him and he justified his actions as representative of the views of those voters.

> For myself, while here as a member [of Congress], I will use my official station to preserve as far as I can the Constitution intact in its letter and spirit and to protect, if possible, from the threatened wrong, those whom I have the honor in part to represent.[91]

The driving forces of Clingman's political career from 1843 to 1852 seem to have been his own ambition and his interest in the development of the mountain areas of North Carolina. These two interests were the basis for his shift from Whig to Democrat, from "a nationalistic policy to what appears to be an extreme pro-slavery position." Those interests took precedence over party loyalty.[92] Clingman had originally joined the Whig Party because that party seemed to represent those ideas that would be beneficial to the voters in western North Carolina, especially since most of the party leaders were chiefly from the western part of the state. From 1836 to 1850, the Whig Party stood for public schools, internal improvements, sound banks and currency, and promotion of industry,[93] all of which would have been of benefit to the people of the western counties. Eventually, however, the party became unresponsive to the needs of the people of North Carolina, and more interested in "economic democracy than in political and social reform."[94] Thus, Clingman became disenchanted with the Whigs and found the Democrats to be the party most likely to advance both his interests and those of his district. In 1852 he supported the Democratic Presidential nominee, Franklin Pierce.

After joining the ranks of the Democrats, Clingman, as a Senator, knew his responsibilities in Congress would be aided by a knowledge of world affairs. To gain that knowledge, he took the "grand tour," and in 1859 spent eight months traveling in Europe. He visited Italy, France, and other countries and observed the great armies of Italy and France.[95] Perhaps his European tour was undertaken to determine how much support for the South could be counted upon should war come. His interest in the armies of Europe may have arisen because he anticipated a conflict. He could not have known that two years after his visit he would need all the military knowledge he could muster.

In the spring of 1861, Clingman was called a "fire-eater" by the editor of the *Weekly Raleigh Register*, who believed that

Clingman did not represent the views of a majority of North Carolinians.[96] Clingman may well have believed that he was acting as the people of North Carolina wished him to act. However, the initial indecision of North Carolina over whether to remain in the Union or in the Confederacy put Clingman in a peculiar position. Events outside North Carolina forced the state to take a stand. In Congress, John J. Crittenden of Kentucky tried several compromise measures, such as prohibiting slavery north of the 30° 30' line of the old Missouri Compromise, which would necessitate a series of Constitutional amendments, and an "unamendable" amendment to guarantee slavery forever. These measures proved unsatisfactory to both North and South. President Abraham Lincoln opposed the compromise measure because it would extend slavery into the southwestern territories. Rejected by the Senate, Crittenden then proposed that the matter be put to the people in a popular referendum.[97] On February 18, 1861, Clingman telegraphed the editor of the Charlotte *Bulletin*: "There is no evidence whatever for Crittenden's proposition. North Carolina must secede or aid Lincoln in making war in the South."[98] Clingman stated his fears in a letter to James W. Osborne of Charlotte, North Carolina. He clearly saw that Lincoln and the majority of the Republican party had already decided that the seceding states were "traitors and rebels" and that there would be no more concessions until those states had been "reduced to obedience, or in fact subjugated...." Clingman wrote that since North Carolina and the South had "declared against this policy of coercion," the only question that remained was whether North Carolina would aid Lincoln in his policy or join the South in "resisting it."[99]

Clingman foresaw the outcome of each choice. If North Carolina remained in the Union, she would not only have to furnish money, but also men in a war against her neighbors. If North Carolina joined the Confederacy "she must, in the end, expect to have slavery abolished by force of arms, and to see the South reduced to the condition of Jamaica or St. Domingo; or ... to a condition of free negro equality."[100] Clingman believed that to submit to Lincoln would lead to civil war and free Negro equality over the South, and he stated that "should North Carolina take a stand for resistance, her influence and that of Virginia, may be sufficient to arrest the purpose of Lincoln and his followers, for they are disinclined to fight a united South, and peace may, in that way be secured."[101]

Clingman did whatever he could while he was still a member of Congress to forestall war before North Carolina left the Union. On March 4, 1861, he introduced a resolution similar to that of Senator Stephen A. Douglas which called for the withdrawal of Federal troops from forts located within the boundary of the Confederacy.[102] While acting in the capacity of a senator from a state that was still in the Union, Clingman voted to expel the members of Congress who represented states that had already seceded. That resolution was tabled by referral to the Judiciary Committee.[103] On March 14, a vote was taken on that resolution, with Clingman voting for it, but it did not carry.

Clearly, Clingman was attempting to "straddle the fence." While keeping the interests of the South in mind, as well as his own career, he continued as a member of Congress as long as he could. He recommended that President Lincoln make a treaty with the states that had already seceded.[104] His actions may have been based on the letters published in the *Raleigh Register* from people across the state, many of whom were pro–Union.[105]

Until the end of the congressional session, Clingman continued to hope that the problems could be resolved by congressional legislation, and that war could be avoided. While he recognized the problem of sectionalism, he believed the solution was only a matter of both sides getting together and reaching a compromise. This may have been somewhat overly optimistic, but compromise legislation had long been used as a delaying tactic to pacify both sides and avoid war. Clingman believed that the North should "submit to the wishes of the South," but he found secession "entirely unsatisfactory" as a means of resolving the differences that had long existed between North and South. In a letter to Honorable James W. Osborne, on February 18, 1861, Clingman stated his views on secession:

> I will not consume my time arguing the question of secession further than to say that, in my judgment, there can be found no warrant for it in the Constitution, and no foundation for it, as derived in any way from that instrument. If a State has a constitutional right to secede, then the Constitution of the United States would be subjected to the will and control of every state in the Union. It could be destroyed at any time by any State.[106]

Whether he thought secession was legal or not, Clingman may have harbored thoughts of a separate nation which included Virginia and North Carolina, both of which were undecided about seceding in the early months of 1861. While he tried every possible legislative means to resolve the differences between North and South, there is some evidence to indicate that in February 1861, Clingman did support the Confederacy and hoped that North Carolina and Virginia would join it in order to avert a war. This was some three months before his home state of North Carolina withdrew from the Union on May 20, 1861.[107] Clingman did not see secession as a remedy for the "grievances of the South." He thought the actions of the cotton states were "unjustifiable and unwise."[108] Those views would seem to contradict the popular opinion that Clingman was a "fire-eater," as he was called in The *Weekly Raleigh Register* in the early part of 1861.[109] Being the true politician that he was, his public and private views may not have been identical, and his stand on the issues changed as events took place and public opinion shifted.

During an extra session of Congress called and held on March 26, 1861, attempts were made on both sides to find some means of averting war. Clingman proposed a resolution with a clause that would have prohibited the President from collecting revenue in the "seceding States." But the resolution was "laid over."[110] This was the last time Clingman spoke as a member of Congress, and he left the Senate on March 28,[111] never to be one of its members again.

When Confederate troops began firing on Fort Sumter in Charleston Harbor on April 12, 1861, Clingman went to Charleston to observe events first hand. Mrs. Mary Chestnut stated that he told her that both Virginia and North Carolina were "arming" to come to the assistance of South Carolina.[112] From Charleston, Clingman telegraphed North Carolina's Governor Ellis and advised him to "take at once the Fayetteville arsenal...." He suggested that North Carolina should assist Governor Letcher of Virginia in taking Norfolk.[113] The take-over of the Federal arsenal at Fayetteville enabled North Carolina to arm its men as soon as they reported for duty and, according to Samuel A. Ashe, "all of these [first] regiments were formed from companies that had been in camp and were well drilled, as well as efficiently officered."[114]

Clingman saw early on the necessity of preparing for the inevitable conflict, and he recognized the importance of controlling the various locations of military stores even before the war got under way.

Although North Carolina was hesitant to leave the Union and join the Confederacy,

Lincoln's call for troops from North Carolina to fight against South Carolina decided the question. On May 6, 1861, the North Carolina legislature sent Clingman as a commissioner to the Confederate government, and he was charged with enrolling the state in the new Southern nation and its war effort. North Carolina Governor John W. Ellis notified Clingman and expressed the sentiments of the state:

> We, reposing special trust and confidence in your integrity and ability, do by these presents appoint you a commissioner to represent the State of North Carolina at the Government of the confederate States of America, in pursuance of the accompanying resolution of the General Assembly of our said State of North Carolina....[115]

Clingman was received by President Davis, who commented that the validity of North Carolina's sentiments was exemplified by her sending one of "such high station and reputation."[116]

Clingman wanted to be in the new Confederate Congress, but he was not chosen at the convention which met on June 18 to elect delegates to represent North Carolina. However, his brother-in-law Richard C. Puryear was chosen to represent the Sixth District.[117]

Again, on August 27, 1861, Clingman was defeated in his bid for a seat in the Confederate Senate by William T. Dortch of Wayne County.[118] President-elect Jefferson Davis spoke at Goldsboro in favor of Dortch, a former speaker of the North Carolina House of Representatives.[119] Thwarted politically, Clingman resorted to other means to promote his interests and those of his district and state. He looked toward the military establishment for a position of authority and prominence.

The War Between the States ended Clingman's political career in both the United States Senate and in the legislative body of the Confederacy. Although he once had been a strong supporter of the Union, he, like many others, came eventually to believe that Southern rights could only be preserved by the establishment of a separate nation. True politician that he was, Clingman went with the flow of popular opinion and sided with his state when it seceded.

Notes

1. Foster A. Sondley, *A History of Buncombe County, North Carolina* (Asheville, N.C.: The Advocate Printing Co., 1930), II, 535; cited also in Tucker, "For Want of a Scribe," p. 180.
2. Thomas E. Jeffrey, *Thomas Lanier Clingman: Fire Eater from the Carolina Mountains* (Athens, Ga.: The University of Georgia Press, 1998), p. 3.
3. Francis T. Miller, ed., *The Photographic History of the Civil War* (New York: Castle Books, 1957), X, p. 281.
4. W. H. S. Burgwyn, "Clingman's Brigade," in *Histories of the Several Regiments and Battalions from North Carolina in the Great War, 1861–1865, Written by Members of the Respective Commands,* ed. Walter Clark (Goldsboro, N.C.: Nash Brothers, 1901), IV, p. 480.
5. Frances H. Casstevens, "Thomas L. Clingman," in *Heritage of Yadkin County, North Carolina,* ed. Frances H. Casstevens (Winston-Salem, N.C.: Hunter Publishing Co., 1981), pp. 173–174.
6. Bill Sharp, "Yadkin County," *The State,* XXXII (Nov. 1964), 14; William Kenneth Boyd, "Thomas Lanier Clingman," in *Dictionary of American Biography* (New York: Charles Scribner's Sons, 1958), IV, p. 220. Some biographical sketches (*Biographical Dictionary of the Confederacy,* p. 139) give Clingman's date of birth as "June" 27, 1812.
7. Melba C. Crosse, comp., *Patillo, Pattillo, Pattullo and Pittillo Families* (Fort Worth, Tex.: American Reference Publishing Co., 1972), p. 262.
8. Lewis Shore Brumfield, *Thomas Lanier Clingman and the Shallow Ford Families* (Yadkinville, N.C.: typescript, privately published, 1989), pp. 1–157.
9. John D. Cameron, "Thomas Lanier Clingman," *University of North Carolina Magazine,* VIII (1889), 251.

10. Rowan County Deeds, Register of Deeds' Office, Salisbury, North Carolina, Deed Book 3, pp. 529–531. Deed dated May 12, 1756, from the Earl of Granville to Peter Arrant on Grant and Crane Creeks, adjoining the Court House lands, the lands of Alexander Clingman, and others.

11. *National Cyclopaedia of American Biography*, VII, p. 199.

12. Mrs. Stahle Linn, Jr., *Abstracts of Wills and Estate Records of Rowan County, North Carolina, 1753–1815 and Tax Lists of 1759 and 1778* (Salisbury, N.C.: by the author, 1980), p. 82. The will of Alexander Clingman, a resident of Rowan County, North Carolina, recorded in Will Book E, p. 234, dated June 19, 1803, stated that Jacob Clingman was his youngest son.

13. Jacob Clingman & Co., Letter Book and Store Account Book, 1816–1821, Clingman Papers, Manuscript Department, Duke University, Durham, North Carolina.

14. Gerald W. Cook, "List of Taxable Property in Surry County, North Carolina, for the Year 1812," in *The Descendants of Claiborne Howard* (Cholon, Republic of Vietnam: by the author, 1960), p. 12.

15. *Laws of North Carolina–1822*, Chapter CX.

16. Crosse, p. 259.

17. Surry County Marriage Register, Register of Deeds' Office, Dobson, North Carolina; and *Raleigh Register* 13 Aug. 1811.

18. Donald W. Stanley, Hazell R. Hartman, and Ann E. Sheek, *Forsyth County, North Carolina, Cemetery Records*, (Winston-Salem, N.C.: Hunter Publishing Co., 1976), II, p. 340.

19. George Wills, "Thomas Lanier Clingman," Charles Van Noppen MS., Duke University, Durham, North Carolina, p. 3.

20. Daughters of the American Revolution, Supplemental Papers of Mary Poindexter Ridings, National Number 43603; *DAR Patriot Index* (Washington, D.C.: National Society Daughters of the American Revolution, 1967), p. 539; and "Marriage Bonds of Goochland County," *William and Mary Quarterly*, Ser. I, VI-VII (1897–1899), 103. Thomas Poindexter married Elizabeth Pledge, daughter of William Pledge, on February 12, 1762, according to the Goochland County, Virginia, marriage register.

21. Cameron, p. 251.

22. "The Poindexter Family," *Virginia Magazine of History and Biography*, XIX (1911), 215–218.

23. Pleasant H. Poindexter, "The Ancestry and Descendants of Thomas and Elizabeth Poindexter," *Yadkin Valley Pilot*, East Bend, N.C., July 6, 1916; Howard Poindexter and Frances H. Casstevens, "The Pledge Family," in *Heritage of Yadkin County*, p. 550; Hattie Poindexter, "George Poindexter (Poingdestre)," in *Heritage of Yadkin County*, pp. 550–551; and Augustus H. Jarratt, Sr., "The Family History," an unpublished manuscript, Yadkin County Public Library, Yadkinville, North Carolina, pp. 1–2.

24. Crosse, p. 239; Jarratt, "The Family History," p. 4; "Henry Pattillo Clingman, M.D.," in *History of North Carolina: Biographies*, VI, ed. R. D. W. Connor (Chicago: Lewis Publishing Co., 1919), p. 152.

25. William L. Saunders, ed., *The Colonial Records of North Carolina*, VII (Raleigh, N.C.: Joseph Daniels, 1886–1890), pp. 814–815, 835.

26. William L. Saunders, ed., *The Colonial Records of North Carolina*, X (Raleigh, N.C.: Joseph Daniels, 1886–1890), p. 191. See also Crosse, p. 241, and Connor, p. 152.

27. *Connecticut Evangelical Magazine*, December, 1800, pp. 232–233, cited in Crosse, p. 242.

28. Crosse, p. 242.

29. Elizabeth H. Hummel, *Hicks' History of Granville County, North Carolina*, I (Oxford, N.C.: Coble Printing Co., 1965), p. 121; and Mary H. Kerr, comp., *Warren County, North Carolina, Records*, I (privately published by the Granville-Warren Committee of the National Society of the Colonial Dames of America in North Carolina, 1967), p. 70.

30. Cameron, p. 251.

31. Frances H. Casstevens, "Jane Pattillo Lanier Poindexter," in *Heritage of Yadkin County, North Carolina*, pp. 535–537.

32. A[ugustus]. H[enry]. J[arratt], "General Thomas L. Clingman," *University of North Carolina Magazine*, New Series XVIII (April 1901), 166. Hereafter cited as J[arratt], "General Thomas L. Clingman."

33. Jarratt, "The Family History," p. 7; and Surry County, North Carolina, Will Book 4, pp. 237–238.

34. Pat Ireson, "Sofley Home Huntsville Landmark," (Jonesville, N.C.) *Yadkin Enterprise*, 13 Aug. 1969, p. 1; and William Seabrook, "The White House—The H. H. Sofley Home," in *Heritage of Yadkin County*, pp. 80–81.

35. Will of Peter Clingman dated October 20, 1835, recorded in Will Book 4, pp. 237–239, Surry County, North Carolina. Thomas L.

Clingman was a witness to his uncle's will. Peter Clingman left his entire estate to his son Francis P. Clingman as his "sole" heir, although he had other living children. He did not leave his nephew Thomas L. Clingman any real or personal property. Since Thomas was not a beneficiary, he could sign Peter's will as a witness.

36. Boyd, pp. 220–221.
37. Wills, p. 3.
38. *National Cyclopaedia of American Biography*, VII, p. 199.
39. Jarratt, "The Family History," p. 27.
40. Carl Cahill, "New Evidence supports Marshal Ney Legend," *State* (December 1987), pp. 30–31.
41. North Carolina, Adjutant General's Department, *Muster Rolls of the Soldiers of the War of 1812: Detached from the Militia of North Carolina in 1812 and 1814* (1851; rpt. Winston-Salem, N.C.: The Barber Printing Co., 1926), p. 115.
42. J. G. Hollingsworth, *History of Surry County or Annals of Northwest North Carolina* (by the author, n.p., 1935), pp. 66–68, 95.
43. Jarratt, "The Family History," pp. 4–5; and Hollingsworth, p. 101.
44. Willis, p. 4.
45. Cameron, p. 251.
46. Kemp P. Battle, *History of the University of North Carolina: From Its Beginnings to the Death of President Swain, 1789–1868*, I (1907; rpt. Spartanburg, S.C.: The Reprint Co., 1974), p. 55.
47. Rutledge, p. 27.
48. *National Cyclopaedia of American Biography*, VII, p. 200.
49. Walter ("Pete") Murphy, "Thomas Lanier Clingman" *State*, XI (2 October 1943), 4.
50. *Ibid.*
51. Wheeler, p. 72.
52. Battle, p. 345.
53. James H. Boykin, *North Carolina in 1861* (New York: Bookman Assoc., 1961), p. 86.
54. *National Cyclopaedia of American Biography*, VII, p. 200.
55. Jarratt, "General Thomas L. Clingman," p. 167.
56. Siegmann, p. 4. According to the Surry County Court Minutes, Clingman was licensed to practice law in the Surry County courts on February 10, 1834.
57. John P. Arthur, *Western North Carolina: A History 1870–1913* (1914; rpt. Spartanburg, SC: The Reprint Co., 1973), p. 384.
58. Foster A. Sondley, "Members of the North Carolina General Assembly," in *A History of Buncombe County* (Asheville, N.C.: Advocate Printing Company, 1930), II, pp. 801–803.
59. *National Cyclopaedia of American Biography*, VII, p. 200.
60. Murphy, p. 4.
61. Cameron, p. 256; and *National Cyclopaedia of American Biography*, VII, 200.
62. Sondley, II, pp. 538–589.
63. S. M. Duggers, *Balsam Groves of the Grandfather Mountain*, cited by Arthur, p. 326, footnote 13.
64. Kearney, p. 200; and Thomas L. Clingman to Charles Lanman, May 32, 1858, Charles Lanman MSS., Duke University, Durham, North Carolina.
65. Cameron, p. 253.
66. R. A. Brock, ed., "The Career of T. L. Clingman," Philadelphia *Times*, 10 October 1896, rpt. in *Southern Historical Society Papers*, XXIV (1896), p. 307.
67. Mrs. J. H. Logan, *Reminiscences of a Soldier's Wife* (New York: Charles Scribner's Sons, 1913), pp. 84–85.
68. Mary Chestnut, *Mary Chestnut's Civil War*, C. Van Woodward, ed. (New Haven: Yale University Press, 1981), p. 50. Hereafter cited as Chestnut Diary.
69. Jane P. Kerr, "Brigadier-General Thomas L. Clingman," *The Trinity Archives*, XII, No. 6 (March, 1899), p. 390, and Wills, p. 6.
70. "Clingman, Thomas Lanier," in *Appleton's Cyclopedia of American Biography*, I, p. 658.
71. *North Carolina Standard* (28 November 1849), quoted in Joseph C. Sitterson, *Secession Movement in North Carolina* (Chapel Hill, N.C.: University of North Carolina Press, 1939), p. 53.
72. Boyd, p. 221.
73. *Ibid.*, pp. 65–66.
74. *Ibid.*, p. 65.
75. *Ibid.*, p. 221.
76. Sitterson, pp. 65–66.
77. Tucker, *Zebulon Vance*, p. 102, quoting from *Vance Papers*, I, p. 74.
78. Eaton, *A History of the Southern Confederacy*, p. 33.
79. John Spencer Bassett, "The Congressional Career of T. L. Clingman," *The Trinity Historical Records*, IV (1900), pp. 61–62, quoted in Sitterson, p. 157.
80. Brock, p. 305.
81. Siegmann, p. 198.

82. *Raleigh Register,* 3 Apr. 1850, cited in Siegmann, p. 85.

83. Thomas L. Clingman, *Selections form the Speeches and Writings of Honorable Thomas L. Clingman of North Carolina with Additions and Explanatory Notes,* 2nd ed. (Raleigh, N.C.: John Nichols, Book and Job Printer, 1878). Hereafter cited as Clingman, *Speeches and Writings.*

84. *Washington Republican,* rpt. in *Raleigh Register,* 4 Apr. 1851.

85. William S. Pettigrew to James C. Johnston, March 14, 1850, cited in Sitterson, p. 66.

86. David Outlaw to wife, December 17, 1849, cited in Siegmann, p. 75.

87. James C. Johnston to William S. Pettigrew, March 6, 1850, cited in Siegmann, p. 79.

88. William L. Yancey, *Memoranda of the Late Affair of Honor Between Honorable T. L. Clingman, of North Carolina, and Honorable W. L. Yancey, of Alabama* (Washington, D.C.: by the author, 1845); Don C. Seitz, *Famous American Duels* (New York: Thomas Y. Crowell, 1929), p. 316; Brock, p. 304; Burton J. Hendrick, *Statesman of the Lost Cause* (Boston: Little, Brown & Co., 1939), p. 142; Robert H. Bartholomew, "Tar Heel Fought Duel with Foe in Congress: Clingman Met Yancey in 1865," Winston-Salem, North Carolina, *Journal & Sentinel,* 29 June 1952; and Sarah Biggs, "Clingman's Dome Named After Dueling Dentist," Winston-Salem, North Carolina, *Journal & Sentinel,* 10 July 1955.

89. *Congressional Globe,* XXIV 2, 1st Session, 32nd Congress, p. 1156, cited in Siegmann, p. 105.

90. *Raleigh Register,* 13 Oct. 1852; *Asheville News,* 28 Oct. 1852.

91. Thomas L. Clingman, "To the Editors of the Republic," in Clingman, *Speeches and Writings,* p. 267.

92. Siegmann, p. 102.

93. Hugh T. Lefler and Albert R. Newsome, *The History of a Southern State: North Carolina,* 3rd ed. (Chapel Hill, N.C.: University of North Carolina Press, 1975), pp. 357, 361.

94. Glyndon G. Van Deusen, "Some Aspects of Whig Thought and Theory in the Jacksonian Period," *American Historical Review* XLIII, No. 2 (January 1958), 318–322, cited in Siegmann, p. 36.

95. Clingman, "Farming and Cookery: Letter to Col. John D. Whitford, Editor, State Agricultural Journal, May 15, 1875," in Clingman, *Speeches and Writings,* p. 87.

96. "Senator Clingman," *Weekly Raleigh Register,* 27 Feb. 1861.

97. John M. Blum, Edmund S. Morgan, et al., *The National Experience,* 3rd ed. (New York: Harcourt Brace Jovanovich, 1973), pp. 321.

98. Clingman, "Telegram to the Editor of the Charlotte Bulletin," in Clingman, *Speeches and Writings,* p. 555.

99. Clingman, "Letter to Hon. Jas. W. Osborne, Feb. 18, 1861," in Clingman, *Speeches and Writings,* p. 554.

100. *Ibid.,* p. 555.

101. *Ibid.,* pp. 554–555.

102. William S. Powell, *A History of Caswell County, 1777–1977* (Durham, N.C.: Moore Publishing, 1977), p. 181.

103. *Congressional Globe, 1860–1861,* pp. 1448–1449, cited in Boykin, p. 130.

104. *Ibid.*

105. Boykin, p. 140.

106. *Congressional Globe, 1860–1861,* pp. 1448–1449, cited in Boykin, p. 130.

107. Clingman, "Letter to Hon. Jas. W. Osborne, Feb. 18, 1861," in Clingman, *Speeches and Writings,* pp. 554–555; Barrett, *The Civil War in North Carolina,* p. 15.

108. *Ibid.,* pp. 554–555.

109. *Weekly Raleigh Register,* 18 Feb. 1861.

110. "Extra Session U.S. Senate," *Weekly Raleigh Register,* 13 Apr. 1861.

111. Chestnut diary, p. 50n.

112. Chestnut diary, p. 50.

113. John W. Ellis, *The Papers of John Willis Ellis,* Nobel J. Tolbert, ed. II (Raleigh, N.C.: State Department of Archives and History, 1964), p. 630.

114. Samuel A'C. Ashe, *History of North Carolina,* II (Raleigh, N.C.: Edwards and Broughton, 1925), p. 637.

115. *O.R.,* I, Ser. IV, p. 289, John W. Ellis to Thomas L. Clingman, May 6, 1861.

116. *O.R.,* I, Ser. IV, p. 308, Jefferson Davis to the Congress of the Confederate States of America, May 10, 1861.

117. Ashe, *History of North Carolina,* II, p. 632.

118. *Weekly Raleigh Register,* 25 Sept. 1861.

119. The Wayne County Historical Association, Inc., and Old Dobbs County Genealogical Society, *The Heritage of Wayne County* (Winston-Salem, N.C.: Hunter Publishing Co., 1982), p. 17.

Chapter III

Thomas L. Clingman — The Colonel

A cock always fights best on his own walk.
— Thomas L. Clingman (1812–1897)

After North Carolina left the union, Clingman had to vacate his seat in the United States Senate. Subsequently, he was passed over as a member of the Confederate Congress, as well as failing to be appointed as one of the first military commanders of the state. Clingman sought another avenue by which to support the Southern cause— that of organizing his own army regiment. Could a 49-year-old former lawyer and politician, amateur explorer and scientist adjust to the military way of life? Could a man who had always thought independently and who had spoken out on issues as he saw them conform to military rules and regulations? The next four years would bring the answers to these questions.

Once North Carolina made the commitment to join the Confederacy, the task of creating an army began. Eventually, North Carolina would furnish 78 full regiments, 20 battalions, numerous companies, and a large number of individuals who served through forces in other states.[1] North Carolina did more than its share in furnishing troops and at best estimate, fully "one-fifth of the total forces of the Confederacy" were North Carolinians.[2]

The work of mobilizing the North Carolina forces was assigned to James G. Martin, Adjutant-General of the state. Martin was a West Point graduate and a veteran of the Mexican War. Under his direction, the state was able to turn over to the Confederacy 40,000 men within a period of seven months.[3]

Although Clingman had no military training, he was well versed in military history, especially the battles fought by the ancient Greeks. He was impressed by the battle of Marathon in which 600 Athenians made "a wide dash against the mass of their enemies." He was to witness military action on a much larger scale many times, beginning with the first major battle of the war.[4] Clingman first saw action as a volunteer aide on the staff of General Joseph E. Johnston during the battle of First Manassas on July 21, 1861,[5] although he had not joined the military establishment and had no official capacity.[6] Clingman viewed the fighting from a horse loaned to him by General Beauregard.[7]

In this first major battle of the war, the Confederates were victorious. There were many casualties on both sides, but it was clearly a win for the South. With the Yankees came many ladies and gentlemen, civilians who had come from Washington to view the action. They, along with the soldiers, fled the battlefield in panic.[8] Referring to the Southern victory at Manassas, Clingman remarked, "A cock always fights best on his own walk."[9]

The task of creating an army of North Carolina troops began by mobilizing and forming volunteer companies. Balis M. Edney informed Governor Ellis from Camp Patton, near Asheville, on June 23, 1861, about a company that was being formed, and stated that they would soon have "one of the finest mountain Regiments of Rifle shooters."[10] This particular regiment became the 25th Regiment, North Carolina Infantry,[11] and was the regiment that would have Colonel Thomas L. Clingman as its commanding officer.

Officially, Clingman's military service dates from August 15, 1861, when he was elected colonel of the 25th Regiment, North Carolina Infantry.[12] This regiment was formed in Asheville on August 15, 1861, and those who enlisted signed up for a 12-month term of service.[13]

Initially, there was no army of North Carolina troops. The affluent leaders of the towns and counties formed companies in communities all over the state and the South. These companies were then grouped into regiments, and the regiments were taken into the service of the Confederate States of America.

Regimental officers were elected by the men in the individual regiments. Clingman was elected colonel over St. Clair Dearing. Dearing, who had formerly been a lieutenant colonel in the United States Army, was elected lieutenant colonel of the 25th Regiment, North Carolina Troops. Henry M. Rutledge, only 22 years old, was elected major.[14] John W. Moore noted in his *Roster of North Carolina Troops in the War Between the States* that he could find "less concerning the officers of this regiment than any in the State's service." He noted that there were no "Field and Staff returns" and that the casualties and promotions of the line officers were all referred to the "Register of Officers," but no register of this regiment was ever made.

The 25th Regiment was composed of ten companies. Company A was made up of Henderson County men; Company B, from Jackson; Company C, from Haywood; Company D, from Cherokee; Company E, from Transylvania; Company F, from Haywood; Company G, from Athens, Georgia, and Clay and Macon Counties of North Carolina; Company H, from Buncombe and Henderson counties; and Company I and K, also from Buncombe County. Each company had a more personalized, localized name.[15] Thus, the 25th Regiment was composed, for the most part, of men from counties located in western North Carolina and northern Georgia in the southern Appalachian Mountains. Many of the men of the 25th Regiment were Clingman's friends and neighbors from his former congressional district.

The officers of the 25th were educated men. Garland Ferguson, the historian for the 25th Regiment, noted that Colonel Clingman was a politician and statesman; Lieutenant-Colonel Dearing was a professional soldier; and Major Rutledge was a civilian with a military education. Ferguson also noted that few of the men in the 25th Regiment were slave owners, and "90 per cent of the men were farmers and farmers' sons, fully 80 per cent home owners, or the sons of farmers who owned their farms." All, except perhaps Lieutenant Colonel Dearing, expected to return to "peaceful pursuits" after the war. Most of the men had been "Union men until after President Lincoln's Proclamation," but they then "acknowledged their allegiance to the State."[16] The men of the 25th were an independent lot, accustomed to freedom of thought and action. But, "under the mild discipline of Colonel [Clingman] and skillful training and accurate drill of the Lieutenant-Colonel," they soon became a "thoroughly drilled and disciplined" regiment.[17] While at Asheville, the regiment was located at "Camp Clingman," established on August 31, 1861.[18]

Clingman had already seen a major battle at Manassas the month before, and its deadly results. He had already formed definite ideas on how troops should perform, and was well aware that well-trained soldiers had the advantage over "raw militia."[19] He believed sincerely in the effectiveness of the "charge," a mode of fighting he thought had been in "disuse in the world for centuries," but which was revived by the Confederates.[20]

The 25th Regiment did not remain in the safety of the mountains very long; soon they were sent to assist in the defense of the coastal areas of both North and South Carolina. The first conflicts in the state of North Carolina occurred on the coast.[21] Control of the sounds and their tributary rivers was vital to supplying the Confederacy. If the enemy gained complete control of the coastal area, they could hinder the imports and exports of goods to and from foreign ports, as well as the movement of supplies over the Weldon Railroad between coastal North Carolina and Richmond.

The 25th Regiment left Asheville on September 18, 1861, and marched to Icard Station below Morganton where they boarded a train for Raleigh.[22] As the troops passed through Salem, North Carolina, the citizens noted that: "Col. Clingman's Regiment from Asheville has gone to the neighborhood of Wilmington."[23] Pausing a few days in Raleigh, the men were issued uniforms before they continued on their way. They arrived in Wilmington on September 29, and were sent to Camp Davis at Mitchell's Sound,[24] where a musket was distributed to each soldier.

There was much apprehension in North Carolina that a Federal expedition was being "fitted out to take possession of some point on the coast...." but that destination proved to be the coast of South Carolina instead.[25] At the time South Carolina seceded, the defenses of Charleston Harbor were a cause for concern. The forts were unmanned and in disrepair.[26] When the Federal fleet attacked Hilton Head Island and Beaufort, South Carolina, Clingman's regiment and others were sent on November 5 to meet the new threat. They did not return to North Carolina for four months, after the capture of New Bern by Federal forces on March 16, 1862.[27]

After the Federal take-over of Hilton Head Island on November 7, 1861,[28] the 25th Regiment was sent by rail to Coosawhatchie, South Carolina, near Port Royal, where it remained for four days at Camp Beauregard. On November 14, the regiment was then ordered to move 11 miles south to Camp Lee near Grahamsville, where it was assigned to "guard the town and cover the roads leading from Boyd's Landing."[29]

Shortly after Clingman's regiment was sent to South Carolina, General Robert E. Lee was placed in command of the department of South Carolina, on November 8, 1861. He remained there until the following March. General Lee established headquarters near Coosawhatchie, and he used this opportunity to become familiar with the topography of the coastal areas. It was on Lee's orders that a line of field works was constructed, and Clingman's regiment was one of those ordered to participate in the construction. One officer who served in that area stated that he had often heard "frequent disparaging remarks as to what these defenses were ever built for." Nonetheless, the works "proved to be well located and quite useful."[30] General Lee reported in November 1861 that the enemy had "complete possession of the water and inland navigations," and that it had captured all the islands on the coast of South Carolina and Georgia. Lee believed that both Savannah and Charleston were threatened because the enemy could "come in his boats within 4 miles of this place."[31]

Clingman's 25th Regiment was positioned to protect vital railroad bridges in case of an attack on the railroad or on Savannah or Charleston. Brigadier General R. S. Ripley, who was in charge of the defense of the Charleston area, described the troops in mid–November as "very raw," requiring severe discipline and constant watching. Ripley believed it would take some time to "make them efficient."[32] Clingman's regiment had been in service since August, only about three months, and were still very inexperienced.

After a line of fortifications was completed from Georgetown to Savannah, further Federal advances in this area were successfully repulsed. General Lee believed that "The people, seeing the Federals repulsed at every point, regained their confidence."[33]

After the line fortifications had been completed, Clingman's regiment was ordered to New Bern, North Carolina, on March 15, 1862. There, they were to assist in the defense of New Bern, which was being threatened by an expedition under General Ambrose E. Burnside. However, the city was taken by the Federal troops on March 14, the day before the 25th Regiment reached it.[34] The unit was assigned to the Second Brigade under the command of General Lawrence O'B. Branch at Kinston. During March and April 1862, Clingman and his regiment were stationed at Camp Ransom, five miles toward New Bern from Kinston.[35]

Thus, after eight months in service, Clingman's 25th Regiment had not been involved in any combat. Undoubtedly, he retained his popularity with his men, who re-elected him colonel in the spring of 1862. The men again had a choice between Dearing and Clingman, but chose Clingman over a man with military training. Dearing was unhappy with the results of the election and resigned. Major Rutledge was elected lieutenant colonel in his place, and Captain S.C. Bryson of Company C was promoted to major. This situation soon changed when Clingman was promoted to brigadier general, and was separated from the mountain men with whom he was most familiar.[36]

Clingman's aspirations and ambition drove him to climb higher and seek advancement within the military structure. Most of the officers appointed to levels higher than regimental commander were men who had been trained at West Point. Many of those generals had fought in the Mexican War. Yet, there were also numerous political generals— men with little or no military training, but with sufficient influence and political connections, such as John C. Breckinridge, Henry A. Wise, John Buchanan Floyd, Robert A. Toombs, and Howell Cobb. For the most part, the officers who commanded North Carolina troops were competent. Samuel A. Ashe, an officer in one of Clingman's regiments and later a historian, noted, perhaps somewhat unrealistically, that the officers of North Carolina were of "superlative merit; the men not only enthusiastic, but disciplined soldiers."[37]

Undoubtedly, it would be a great advantage to have only military leaders who had formal training or experience in military tactics. So, initially, the Confederacy sought United States Army veterans and guaranteed them "at least as high rank" as they had held previously. But volunteer officers were also accepted by companies, and "they were given commands when vacancies occurred or emergencies necessitated them."[38]

Early in the war it was the policy to choose brigadier generals from "the most meritorious of the resigned officers; or when there was reason to hope good results to the service — upon the best of those men the troops had chosen as commanders" during the regimental elections. Much pressure was put on Jefferson Davis, President of the Confederacy, regarding appointments, and the prevailing sentiment was that "these first selections were made with as much judgment and impartiality as the untried state of the army permitted."[39] However, the appointment of generals had to be confirmed by the Confederate Senate. If the Senate was in session, the President made his recommendation to that body, and then the Senate would either confirm or reject the appointment. On a few occasions, the Senate took no action. However, if the Senate was not in session, then the appointment was made first, and the nomination confirmed at the next session.[40]

Clingman approached Thomas Bragg, a former colleague in the Senate and now newly appointed Attorney General of the Confederate government, to ask for a promotion to the rank of brigadier general. Bragg declined to get involved, but Clingman persisted until he had received his commission on May 17, 1862. At the age of 50, he was officially granted his commission on August 4, and assumed command of the District of Pamlico and Cape Fear.[41]

There were 425 individuals who were appointed by the President of the Confederacy to one of the four grades of general: full rank, lieutenant, major, and brigadier. Of those, 169 had some military education, and a total of 272 had previous military training. One hundred twenty-five had been professional soldiers before 1861. Age had little bearing on appointment. Of the brigadier generals, John Henry Winder was 61 years, whereas William Paul Roberts was only 20. There were 70 brigadier generals between the ages of 20 and 29; 138 between 30 and 39; 94 over 40 but less than 50; and 24 from 50 to 59 years of age. The average age of the brigadier generals was 36 years and 3 months. Thus, Clingman was not alone in his age bracket.[42] However, even though he had gained the rank of brigadier general, Clingman's chances of advancing any higher were slim with no military training, education, or experience.

Clingman had done nothing outstanding during his eight months as a colonel of the 25th Regiment. He and his command had done what was required of them, but had not been involved in any engagements with the enemy. When they returned to North Carolina from South Carolina in the spring of 1862, Clingman and the 25th were stationed at Camp Ransom near Kinston.[43] This was soon to end. Four days after receiving his appointment as brigadier general, Clingman was relieved of his responsibilities in the regiment; it was assigned to General Robert Ransom's brigade, and spent most of its service in Virginia.[44] After Clingman was appointed brigadier general, he was ordered to report to General Theophilus H. Holmes, who was in command of the Department of North Carolina.[45]

Clingman's promotion was brought about in part because of the reorganization of the Confederate Army. The first volunteers had signed up for only one year. That term was nearing expiration, and in order to hold on to those trained troops, the Confederate government extended the term of service to three years, or for the duration of the war, whichever came first. At the time of reorganization in 1862, the troops of the various states, except for the militia, were transferred to the Confederate government.[46]

Another factor involved in Clingman's appointment was the withdrawal of some of the North Carolina troops by General Robert E. Lee to aid in the defense of Richmond. New regiments and brigades had to be formed to defend North Carolina, and new commanders were needed for those units. Thus, the opportunity arose for Clingman, as a brigadier general, to command one of the new brigades.[47]

Clingman also used his personal acquaintance with Confederate President Davis. He and Davis had served together in Congress, and Davis was in favor of Clingman's appointment. General Robert E. Lee wrote to North Carolina's Governor, Henry T. Clark, that "The President has determined to appoint General [James G.] Martin and Colonel Clingman brigadier-generals in the Confederate service, which he hopes will be pleasing to Your Excellency and the troops of your State."[48] Thus, it appeared that both Martin's and Clingman's appointments were made not only to pacify the state for the withdrawal of North Carolina troops to aid the Army of Virginia and because of a need for more brigadier generals, but because of the influence of President Jefferson Davis.

There was talk about the promotion of some of President Davis' "pets." Favoritism probably did enter into most of Davis' appointments, and was certainly a source of complaint by those not so chosen. There were hundreds of colonels and brigadier generals and major generals who had fought "hard and successfully all the time" but who were not promoted. Those who grumbled most were men who had not been promoted "all the way from lieutenant-colonel to lieutenant-general," and some were men who had not been in a single battle. Davis was criticized for his failure to promote and utilize men efficiently and for his failure to recognized the fact that "a man could be master of more than one thing." He also let his personal dislikes of some of his best generals, notably Beauregard and Joseph Johnston, interfere with his better judgment in the placement of the most effective man for the job. Some of the best military plans were discarded because Davis did not like the man who had proposed the plan.[49]

Reaction to Clingman's appointment as a brigadier general was mixed. Although Clingman had been promoted before he had been engaged in a single combat, Glenn Tucker attributed his promotion to his "intrepidity" and recklessness in battle, and described him as a "bitter-end" fighter because of his Cherokee blood.[50]

William W. Holden, later governor of North Carolina, who had once said that Clingman was a "novice in military matters," declared that the promotion had come "solely on account of his politics." Conversely, Thomas W. Atkin claimed that Clingman had outstanding ability with "sound practical judgment, quick perception, and cool bravery...." Atkin believed Clingman was qualified for such a "high and responsible position." An article in the *Raleigh State Journal* took the middle ground in stating: "Gen. Clingman has been reproached in times gone by with being ambitious," but believed that "ambition was a necessary ingredient in a successful general." The article further stated, "A noble ambition — the desire to excel — the aspiration to soar — the 'thirst for fame'— constitutes an essential element in the character of military greatness."[51]

The need to satisfy his ambition to excel drove Clingman to exert political pressure, and to call on the friendship of former political allies to gain his appointment. Somehow, despite competition and criticism, and a lack of any formal military training or experience, he achieved his goal of rising in the ranks of the Confederate Army to become a brigadier general, and to be placed in charge of a brigade which came to be called "Clingman's Brigade." Brigades were usually known by the names of their original commanders, and they tended to retain those same names long after the original commanding officer had been replaced.[52] Thus, Clingman's Brigade retained its name until the time of the surrender on May 1, 1865, even though Clingman was not in command of it then,[53] and it was under Colonel Hector McKethan.

Brigades were composed of two or more regiments. The number of men in a brigade was approximately 1,850, but could range higher, depending on the number of regiments and the number of companies in each regiment.[54]

Clingman has been described as "one of the most efficient brigadier-generals in the Confederate service."[55] But he was not without his problems, especially at the beginning of his new position. As a result of a foot injury, he informed Major General Daniel H. Hill on August 7, 1862, that he could not "either ride a horse or walk."[56] Two weeks later, his assistant adjutant general, Edward White, reported that Clingman had been "very much indisposed."[57]

Hill believed Clingman was capable both physically and mentally of handling the job as a brigadier general. He wrote Clingman that there were several independent companies which "from want of discipline" were of no value to the service but "were in great hindrance to effective operation," and suggested that those independent companies should be properly organized and officers elected. Clingman agreed with Hill's' view and suggested Colonel Edward Cantwell, a man of "considerable military experience" and a "gentleman of talent" to command those troops.[58] The next day, Clingman received special Order No. 5 from Hill regarding the formation of his brigade. Instead of being given seasoned troops, Clingman was given "All unattached companies of cavalry and Infantry now serving within the limits of this District."[59] Clingman had grave doubts about some of his regimental commanders, and did not think Colonel Williams "fully qualified for the position" or that the other two colonels were much better.[60] Whatever the condition of his troops and their commanders, Clingman put efforts into the task of building a brigade, and organizing them into a disciplined, effective fighting force — not an easy task by any means.

Brigadier General Thomas Lanier Clingman served for over two years without advancing any further in rank, although he commanded his brigade on the battlefield on many occasions and was the "commanding general" of several territorial divisions. Despite being appointed by President Davis, Clingman did not approve of Davis or his leadership,[61] an opinion that (if known) may have hindered his further promotion. Other factors beyond his control also came into play. Mistakes were made and Clingman's Brigade was incorrectly blamed for losses that were the result of actions or inactions of others, as will be seen in subsequent chapters. The truth of the matter in several instances has yet to be established, and the criticism and ridicule attached to Clingman and Clingman's Brigade continue to stain the memory of the man and his unit.

Notes

1. Aubrey L. Brooks, ed., *The Papers of Walter Clark*, I (Chapel Hill, N.C.: University of North Carolina Press, 1948), p. 502.

2. Louis H. Manarin, and Weymouth J. Jordan, Jr., eds., *North Carolina Troops, 1861–1865: A Roster*, V (Raleigh, N.C.: North Carolina Department of Archives and History, 1975), p. xxi. This complete work is hereafter cited as Manarin and Jordan.

3. J. G. De Roulhac Hamilton, *History of North Carolina* (Chicago, Ill.: The Lewis Publishing Co., 1919), III, p. 7.

4. Thomas L. Clingman, "Speech Delivered at the Charlotte Centennial, May 20, 1875," in Clingman, *Speeches and Writings*, pp. 11–112. Hereafter cited as "Charlotte speech."

5. Burgwyn, p. 480.

6. J[arratt], "General Thomas L. Clingman," p. 169.

7. Thomas L. Clingman, "Floyd's Distribution of Arms in the South," in Clingman, *Speeches and Writings*, p. 512.

8. *Weekly Raleigh Register*, 24 July 1861.
9. J[arratt], "General Thomas L. Clingman," p. 169.
10. Letter from Balis M. Edney to Governor John W. Ellis, June 23, 1861, in John W. Ellis, *The Papers of John Willis Ellis,* p. 869.
11. Ashe, *History of North Carolina*, II, p. 650.
12. John A. Sloan, *North Carolina in the War Between the States* (Washington, D.C.: Rufus H. Darby, 1883), p. iv.
13. Manarin and Jordan, III, p. 350.
14. John W. Moore, *Roster of the North Carolina Troops in the War Between the States* (Raleigh, N.C.: Ashe and Gatling, 1882), II, 323.
15. Garland S. Ferguson, "Twenty-Fifth Regiment," in Clark, *Histories of the Several Regiments and Battalions from North Carolina in the Great War, 1861–1865, Written by Members of the Respective Commands,* II, pp. 291–291; and Louis H. Manarin, compl., *Guide to Military Organizations and Installations in North Carolina 1861–1865* (Raleigh, N.C.: North Carolina Confederate Centennial Commission, 1961), p. 25.
16. Ferguson, p. 293.
17. *Ibid.*
18. Manarin, *Guide to Military Organizations,* p. 2.
19. Thomas L. Clingman, "On the Causes of Mr. Clay's Defeat, Delivered in the House of Representatives, January 6, 1845," in Clingman, *Speeches and Writings,* p. 181.
20. Thomas L. Clingman, "Charlotte Speech," in Clingman, *Speeches and Writings,* pp. 111–112.
21. *O.R.*, IV, Ser. I, pp. 572–579, "Report of Brig. Gen. Richard C. Gatlin, C. S. Army, including operations to March 19, 1862," March 14, 1862.
22. Ferguson, p. 293.
23. *Salem (North Carolina) People's Press,* 4 Oct. 1861.
24. Manarin and Jordan, VII, p. 350.
25. Ashe, *History of North Carolina*, II, p. 665.
26. Davis, I, p. 181.
27. *O.R.*, IV, Ser. I, p. 576, "Report of Brig. Gen. Richard C. Gatlin, C. S. Army, including operations to March 19, 1862," March 14, 1862; Ashe, *History of North Carolina*, II, pp. 665–665; Clark, VII, p. 294; and Manarin and Jordan, VII, p. 350.
28. Daniel Ammen, "Du Pont and the Port Royal Expedition," in Robert U. Johnson and Clarence C. Buel, eds., *Battles and Leaders of the Civil War* (1887; rpt. Secaucus, N.J.: Castle, 1982), I, pp. 687–689.
29. Manarin and Jordan, VII, p. 350.
30. William A. Courtnay, "Fragments of War History Relating to the Coast Defenses of South Carolina 1861–1865 and the Hasty Preparations for the Battle of Honey Hill, November 30, 1864," in *Southern Historical Society Papers,* XXVII (1898), 68.
31. Robert E. Lee, *The Wartime Papers of Robert E. Lee,* eds. Clifford Dowdy and Louis Manarin (Boston, Mass.: Little, Brown and Co., 1961), p. 85.
32. *O.R.*, IV, Ser. I, p. 324, R. S. Ripley to Captain T. A. Washington, November 18, 1861.
33. A. L. Long, *Memoirs of Robert E. Lee: His Military and Personal History Embracing a Large Amount of Information Hitherto Unpublished* (New York: J. M. Stoddart & Co., 1886), pp. 139–140.
34. Manarin and Jordan, III, p. 350.
35. "Field and Staff Muster Rolls," 25th Regiment, North Carolina Troops, Record Group 109, National Archives, Washington, D. C.
36. Ferguson, p. 294.
37. Ashe, *History of North Carolina*, II, p. 637.
38. T. C. DeLeon, *Four Years in Rebel Capitals* (Mobile, Ala.: The Gossip Printing Co., 1890), p. 38.
39. *Ibid.*
40. Ezra J. Warner, *Generals in Gray* (Baton Rouge, La.: Louisiana State University Press, 1959), p. xv.
41. General Order No. 1, August 4, 1862, in Thomas L. Clingman Papers, SHC, cited in Thomas E. J. Kettrey, *Thomas Lanier Clingman: Fire Eater from the Carolina Mountains* (Athens, Ga.: The University of Georgia Press, 1998), p. 168.
42. Warner, pp. xxix, xx, xxv.
43. "Field and Staff Muster Rolls," Thomas L. Clingman, Colonel, 25th Regiment, March and April, 1862, North Carolina Infantry, Record Group 109, National Archives, Washington, D.C.
44. Manarin and Jordan, VII, pp. 350–351.
45. *O.R.*, IX, Ser. I, p. 472, General R. E. Lee to Major General T. H. Holmes, May 13, 1862; and Boatner, p. 596.
46. DeLeon, p. 176.
47. *O.R.*, IX, Ser. I, p. 471, General R. E. Lee to General J. G. Martin, May 8, 1862.
48. *O.R.*, II, Ser. I, Pt. III, p. 512. General Robert E. Lee to Governor Henry T. Clark, May 13, 1862.

49. George C. Eggleston, *Rebel's Recollections*, 5th ed. (Bloomington, Ind.: Indiana University Press, 1959), pp. 168–169.

50. Tucker, p. 180.

51. *Raleigh North Carolina Standard*, 25 September 1861, 21 May 1862; *Asheville News*, 29 May 1862; communication from "North Carolina" (from *Raleigh State Journal*), in *Asheville News*, 14 August 1862, cited in Jeffrey, p. 168.

52. Boatner, p. 611.

53. Burgwyn, "Clingman's Brigade," p. 498.

54. Walter Clark, "Brigade Organization," in Clark, *Histories of the Several Regiments*, IV, pp. 435–436.

55. Bassett, p. 63.

56. *O.R.*, IX, Ser. I, pp. 476–477, Brigadier General T. L. Clingman to Major General D. H. Hill, August 7, 1862.

57. Edward White, assistant adjutant general on Clingman's staff, to Colonel C. Leventhorpe, August 17, 1862, in Thomas L. Clingman Papers, SHC.

58. General D. H. Hill to Thomas L. Clingman, August 12, 1862, Thomas L. Clingman Papers, SHC.

59. Special Order No. 5, August 13, 1862, Thomas L. Clingman Papers, SHC.

60. Thomas L. Clingman to D. H. Hill, August 7, 1862, Thomas L. Clingman Papers, SHC; *O. R.*, IX, Ser. I, pp. 476–477.

61. J[arratt], "General Thomas L. Clingman," p. 170.

Chapter IV

Battles: 1862–1863

Hell can't be worse than Battery Wagner.
— Private John Harleston

Picket duty was the first task assigned to the men of the four regiments once they became part of Clingman's Brigade. They were stationed near Kinston, North Carolina, during the months of October and November 1862, then moved to Wilmington and stationed at Camp Whiting. In December, the Brigade was ordered to Goldsboro to oppose Union General Foster's move on that town.

Neuse River Bridge, Goldsboro, North Carolina, December 17, 1862

After the Burnside Expedition in the spring of 1862, which resulted in the capture of several inland cities on the coast of North Carolina, the Federals halted their operations in eastern North Carolina temporarily. Union General John G. Foster was left at New Bern with a force of Federal troops large enough to take Goldsboro.[1]

With a force of 5,000 men, Foster began to move on November 2, 1862, from Washington, North Carolina, toward Tarboro. Several small engagements occurred, but after the Federals failed to capture Tarboro, they returned to Plymouth and then to New Bern.[2]

General Foster did not remain idle long before starting to carry out plans to capture Goldsboro, destroy the railroad, and cut off communications with points farther south. Goldsboro is situated at the junction of the North Carolina Atlantic and Wilmington and Weldon Railroads. On December 11, Foster, now with a force of 10,000 infantry, 40 pieces of artillery, and 640 cavalry, began to move toward his destination — the railroad bridge over the Neuse River between Goldsboro and Dudley Station (later called Everittsville).[3] Fighting occurred at Kinston and at White Hall.[4] The Federal troops forced the Confederate troops back at every stage.

When Kinston fell to Union troops on December 14, panic seized the people of Goldsboro. Defenses were thrown up at White Hall on the south side of the Neuse River, and there Confederate troops under Brigadier General Nathan G. Evans clashed with Foster's men on December 16. Evans faced the enemy at White Hall with four regiments, among them the 61st Regiment of Clingman's Brigade, under the direction of Colonel Radcliffe.[5] Unable to withstand the constant barrage of fire, the Confederates withdrew to Goldsboro on the north side of the river.

Part of Foster's men were engaged

with Evans and captured 400 of Evans' men, while another detachment of Federal troops moved toward Mount Olive Station. The main body of Foster's troops moved on toward Goldsboro and by December 17 they had reached the railroad only a few miles from the town, but were still on the south side of the river.[6] The Federal troops cut the railroad tracks and burned the bridge over the Goshen Swamp to prevent Confederate reinforcements from reaching Goldsboro. The Federal detachment that had raided Mount Olive then moved to Dudley Station where it destroyed railroad track, burned the water tank, and demolished other equipment. The northerners then attempted to move on to Goldsboro by way of the "covered bridge" carrying the road over the Neuse River. However, they encountered resistance from the Confederates guarding the railroad bridge over the Neuse.[7]

That crossing was guarded by Clingman with a portion of his brigade (the 8th and 51st regiments), and the 52nd North Carolina Regiment. This engagement near Goldsboro on December 17, 1862, was the first actual combat in which Clingman and his new brigade were participants. There had been little time to train and drill the men assigned to him before they were called upon to defend the Neuse River Bridge from the advance of Federal general John G. Foster and his troops. Clingman also had on hand the 10th Artillery, and one company of the 40th Artillery who were acting as infantry, plus Starr's Battery, commanded by Colonel S. D. Pool.[8]

Two bridges spanned the Neuse River between Dudley and Goldsboro — a railroad bridge and a "covered" county road bridge, which was about a quarter of a mile west of the railroad bridge.[9] Here, too, the Federals split their forces. One column advanced northward along the railroad toward the railroad bridge, and a second column moved up the White Hall road. Clingman was ordered to "form his command with two pieces of artillery obliquely across the county road," so as to cover the head of the railroad bridge. A steady bombardment was launched on this bridge by the enemy.[10]

Clingman's job was to hold both bridges, but his force was insufficient to defend even one of them against the larger number of Federal troops. When he arrived at the railroad bridge on December 16, he positioned the 8th Regiment about 1½ miles south of the railroad and waited. With the arrival of the 51st and 52nd regiments, he placed one regiment in front of the county road bridge and another between the two bridges.[11] As the main body of Foster's troops approached on December 17, two of the regiments and two pieces of artillery were moved along the county road, and the 51st and 52nd regiments were moved to a position down the riverbank to within 300 yards of the enemy's right flank. Clingman ordered his men to lie down, "to make no reply to the enemy, and no attempt to pass the open field between them and the enemy" until the enemy attack began on the right. He determined that the Federals were in position on the south side of the river for about 1½ miles along the railroad, and were protected by the high railroad embankment in front of them. When firing began, the 51st and 52nd, stationed on the southwest side of the railroad bridge, were to move forward and carry the embankment behind which the enemy were positioned.[12] However, the Federal attack centered on the 51st and 52nd regiments and neither was able to hold its position. They fell back in confusion across the county road bridge, and left the railroad bridge undefended.[13] Clingman informed Lieutenant Colonel W. H. Stevens, chief engineer on General G. W. Smith's staff, that his men "would not stay at the railroad bridge," and asked for advice about crossing the county road bridge. Stevens advised Clingman that he had better cross the bridge if the "men would not stand." Starr's Battery (13th Battalion), had their guns placed in position to fire at the railroad bridge, and they continued firing until all the Confederates had crossed the bridge from the south bank of the river. Starr's Battery did not, however, prevent two of the Federal soldiers from getting on the railroad bridge and setting it on fire.[14]

In the confusion, when the 52nd Regiment retreated from the railroad bridge, they were fired upon by the 51st Regiment, who mistook them for the enemy. After the retreat, Clingman rejoined the two regiments and led them along the county road and across an open field. There, he formed them into a line of battle facing the enemy and the railroad embankment. They then advanced toward the railroad, only to find the enemy had abandoned it.[15] The two regiments were under heavy artillery fire from the Federal guns. Clingman took two cannon from Starr's Battery in an effort to attack the enemy's flank.[16]

After conducting the 51st and 52nd regiments down the river to a safe position, about 300 yards from the enemy, Clingman returned to the 8th and 61st regiments (who had arrived in the afternoon)[17] as they moved down the county road toward the enemy's right. Before Clingman had reached his desired position, General Nathan G. Evans and the 23rd South Carolina Regiment and Holcombe's Legion arrived. Evans ordered an immediate advance, disregarding Clingman's order for the 51st and 52nd regiments to wait until he could bring the men around for the flank attack. Someone suggested that Evans should wait until Starr's Battery had reached its position, otherwise Clingman's plan would "result in disaster," but Evans replied: "I rank Clingman; move forward at once; I will support you with the Holcombe Legion." The men had to obey Evans, and so advanced to the railroad embankment. The enemy retreated to higher ground, where they drew up in two lines about 100 to 200 yards apart, and about 400 yards from Clingman's men. The Confederates rushed forward with a yell, but were met with grape and canister from nine pieces of Federal artillery. The Confederates only succeeded in reaching a ditch midway and "sank into it." Evans' men reached the railroad, but retreated. Meanwhile, Clingman and the 8th and 61st had reached the enemy's left flank and opened fire. However, it was too late to renew the frontal attack.[18]

As darkness approached, the Federal troops retreated,[19] and withdrew as suddenly as they had come. One source credits the withdrawal to a lack of ammunition. Had the Confederates known this, the results of the engagement might have been different, and Clingman and his men might have presented the South with a victory.[20] The mix-up at the Neuse River Bridge was the result of the tardiness of General Evans in supporting Clingman's men. Evans, who had been defeated at White Hall, had retreated to Goldsboro. He had been informed of Clingman's position, and advised to go there by rail as soon as possible.[21] Evans was delayed by problems encountered in clearing the railroad tracks and of watering the train engines. The cars were, therefore, delayed until after 11 o'clock, by which time Clingman had been forced to withdraw. When Evans' men did arrive after the railroad bridge had been set on fire, they were forced to cross the river by the county road bridge, which added to their delay.[22]

The *Raleigh Register* described the battle as an "artillery duel" and praised Clingman's Brigade for forcing the enemy to "skeddadle." The entire Confederate loss, according to the paper, "did not exceed 200." The paper did admit, however, that the Yankees succeeded in tearing up miles of railroad track and destroying two bridges, in addition to numerous "acts of murder and incendiarism," during the course of the expedition.[23]

Colonel Allen, commander of the 51st Regiment, resigned, probably because of the error in firing on the men of the 52nd Regiment. He was replaced by Hector McKethan.[24] Clingman learned that the North Carolina legislature had passed a resolution asking for reports and other information on the "attack on the Railroad at Goldsboro." He also learned, and he stated in a letter to Governor Vance, that "certain members of the Legislature and others at Raleigh were censuring me [for] allowing the Bridges at Goldsboro to be burnt by the enemy...." He then tried to obtain permission from General Smith, the Secretary of War, to publish his report, but that permission was denied. Clingman emphatically stated in defense of his men that the "troops under my command made the attack on the enemy at Goldsboro which caused them to retreat ... tho up [until] that time they had steadily advanced, it is but an act of simple justice to them that all the facts should be known."[25] The 51st and 52nd regiments had taken the brunt of the Federal attack, and were unable to hold their positions. They fell back across the county bridge about a quarter of a mile from the railroad bridge. As these regiments retreated, the 23rd New York Battery advanced and set fire to the railroad bridge. Foster let loose all of his artillery to prevent the Confederates from saving the bridge. He then marched off to New Bern, leaving Colonel H. C. Lee to bring up the rear. The Confederates were able to approach Lee's brigade, and the day ended with this "heroic little charge."[26]

The 61st Regiment and Evans' Brigade arrived on the field in time for the afternoon fighting. However, as soon as General Evans was on the scene, he took over command from Clingman,[27] which resulted in confusion, and since he was late, the bridge was lost. Evans disregarded Clingman's order for the 51st and 52nd regiments to wait until he could bring the men around for the flank attack. Without waiting for Starr's Battery to get into position, Evans ordered the troops to move forward at once.[28]

Union General Foster reported that the expedition was "a perfect success," an opinion not shared by some of his soldiers.[29] Mrs. Catherine Edmonston noted in her diary that as the enemy retreated from Goldsboro they committed "the most terrible excesses." Their retreat could be followed by a "column of smoke rising from the houses and property" they destroyed along their route. She also noted that the railroad bridges on the Wilmington and Weldon Railroad had been burned, and tracks torn up for several miles.[30] The damage to the railroad bridge was only temporary, and General Smith reported that it would soon be restored to its "former condition."[31]

The engagement at the Neuse River bridge near Goldsboro involved the Union 1st, 2nd, and 3rd brigades of the First Division and Wessell's Brigade of Peck's Division, Department of North Carolina, and the Confederate brigades of Robertson, Clingman, and Evans. Losses were: Union — 90 killed, 478 wounded; Confederate — 71 killed, 268 wounded, 400 missing, for the period December 12–18.[32] Total losses to the North Carolina troops were 40 killed and 177 wounded.[33] Overall, the Confederates sustained fewer casualties in the battle, probably because their numbers were fewer to begin with.

Shortly after the Neuse River Bridge battle, Clingman's Brigade,[34] together with those of Evans and Pettigrew, were formed into a division under the command of Major General S. G. French.[35] The action at the Neuse River Bridge has not been regarded as important by either historians or contemporaries. It was, however, a baptism of fire for the newly formed brigade of Thomas L. Clingman.

General Robert E. Lee wrote President Jefferson Davis on January 13, 1863, that the movement of the enemy in North Carolina had only been a ploy to draw troops away from Virginia.[36] Lee was more concerned with the situation in Virginia than that at Wilmington, North Carolina, although he believed Wilmington would be the site of the next Federal assault. Lee also believed that there would be no action against Charleston until Wilmington was taken, and thus General P. G. T. Beauregard would be able to "fight them at both points."[37] Lee was mistaken. Fighting soon commenced at Charleston, and Clingman's Brigade was to play a major role in the defense of that city, long before Wilmington became endangered.

In February 1863, Clingman's Brigade was transferred to Charleston, South Carolina, and were encamped on James Island, on the south side of Charleston Harbor. Because of a lull in the fighting near Charleston, Clingman's Brigade was returned in May 1863 to Wilmington, North Carolina, where they camped in the "large oak grove near old Topsail Sound," called "Camp Ashe."[38] However, the lull was short-lived, and the brigade was ordered back to Charleston in July 1863 to take part in the defense of the city and the fortifications in the harbor.[39]

Battery Wagner, Morris Island, Charleston Harbor, South Carolina, July 10–September 6, 1863

As the war progressed, Confederate General P. G. T. Beauregard, the Confederate government, and the town council of Charleston were all determined not to allow Charleston to fall into Yankee hands as had New Orleans on April 25, 1862. Beauregard's official orders were to "allow Charleston to be laid in ashes sooner than surrender it." In early June of 1863, Beauregard did not think such a fate was imminent.[40]

Beauregard was wrong, however, and intense military activity conducted by the Federal land and naval forces concentrated on Morris Island in Charleston Harbor beginning in early July and continuing throughout the summer of 1863. This assault on Morris Island was undertaken because the Federal troops wanted to capture the city of Charleston, South Carolina, the hated "cradle of Secession." The bombardment of the Federal-controlled Fort Sumter by Confederate forces firing from other forts in Charleston Harbor had been the spark that triggered the War Between the States on April 12, 1861.

Morris Island was the key to the capture of Fort Sumter and thus to Charleston. A little three-mile strip of sand, Morris Island lies on the south side of the harbor at Charleston, only about 2,500 yards from Fort Sumter. Its main fortification, Battery Wagner, was only about 2,600 yards from Fort Sumter (Fig. 4). Once Battery Wagner was captured, the Federal gunners would be able to destroy Fort Sumter. Fort Sumter, which sits in the middle of the harbor, guarded the approach to Charleston from the Atlantic Ocean. When the Federal forces were again in control of the fort,

Fig. 4. Parapet of Fort Sumter looking toward Morris Island, 1865. (Library of Congress)

their fleet would be able to enter the harbor, slip by the other Confederate batteries still on James and Sullivan's islands, and reach the city of Charleston.[41]

Morris Island was defended by two little batteries—Battery Wagner and Battery Gregg—on its northern tip (Fig. 5). By 1863, the upper portion of Morris Island was treeless. Part of the island had been used as a quarantine station and burial

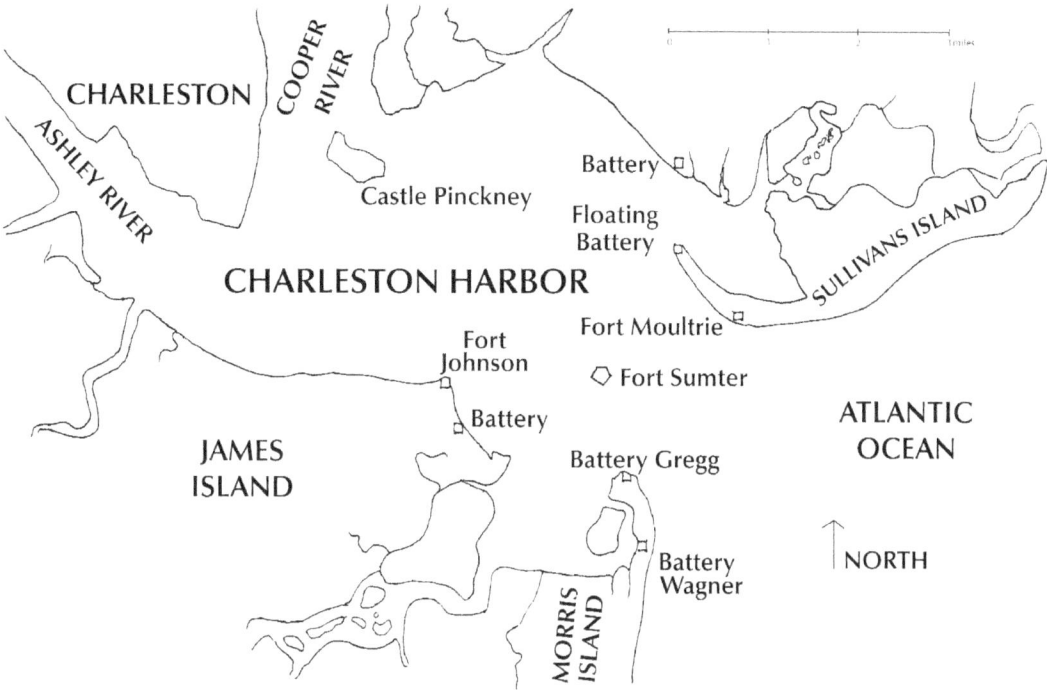

Fig. 5. Sketch of Charleston Harbor showing various forts. (Artwork courtesy of Danny Casstevens.)

ground. Battery (Fort) Wagner, named in honor of Lieutenant Colonel Thomas M. Wagner, was built across the width of the island at its narrowest part, a distance of about 280 yards. On the sea side of Battery Wagner, there was a bomb proof magazine 20 by 20 feet, which protected the three guns from land fire. Behind the sea face, another bomb proof shelter had been constructed. It measured 30 by 130 feet, and could shelter 900 men during a bombardment if they were "standing elbow to elbow and face to back."[42] This area was reduced when about a third of it had to be used for a hospital. Usually, there were between 800 to 900 men confined within the bomb proof for five days and nights.[43] Still under construction in the summer of 1863, Battery Wagner was made entirely of sand, and lined with palmetto wood, because palmetto wood does not splinter. The fort itself measured 630 by 275 feet.[44] A marsh lay about 250 yards in front of the little fort, and a sandy ridge lay just beyond that.[45]

The northern tip of Morris Island, Cummings Point, was defended by Battery Gregg, about three quarters of a mile north of Battery Wagner. Battery Gregg was named in honor of Brigadier General Maxey Gregg. Here, guns of the heaviest caliber were situated. At the time of the Federal assault in July 1863, Battery Wagner was armed with two heavy guns which faced the sea, and 12 or more guns of lighter caliber which faced south and west.[46]

Shortly before the Federal offensive began, British lieutenant colonel James Arthur Lyon Fremantle of the Coldstream Guards arrived in Charleston and visited the island. On June 11, 1863, he wrote in his diary:

> Morris Island is a miserable, low, sandy desert, and at its further extremity there is a range of low sand hills, which form admirable natural parapets. About ten

guns and mortars were placed behind them, and two companies of regular artillery were stationed at this point under the command of Captain Mitchell.... He told me he expected to be able to open fire in a day or two upon the Yankees in Folly Island and Little Folly. He expressed a hope that a few shells might drive them out from Little Folly, which is only distant 600 yards from his guns. The enemy's large batteries are on Folly Island, 3400 yards off, but within range of Captain Mitchell's rifled artillery, one of which was a twelve-pounder Whitworth.[47]

There were two approaches available to the Federal troops to capture Charleston: (1) an amphibious landing on one of the islands or upon one of the inlets to the south, and then to approach Charleston from the rear; or (2) through the harbor for a "quick decision." The former method had already been tried twice, in 1862 and again in April 1863. Since those earlier failed attempts, the Confederates had greatly strengthened their harbor defenses.[48] By the summer of 1863, a new Federal offensive utilizing both land and water had been able to secure a foothold on Folly Island. The next objective was to take the southern end of Morris Island. Once entrenched on Morris Island, the Federals could lay siege to Battery Wagner on the north end of the island.

The Federal assault was assigned to U.S. Army Major General Quincy Gillmore (Fig. 6) and U.S. Navy Admiral John Adolph Dahlgren. By mid June, Gillmore had arrived in South Carolina to lead the attack. A West Point graduate, Gillmore had been chosen because he was an expert in siege operations. Gillmore had 15,000 Federal troops at his disposal for the attack.[49] The first attack was launched on July 10, when General George C. Strong led his brigade from Folly Island. These troops gained a foothold on the southern part of Morris Island. The next day, Strong lost 339 men when he attempted to take Battery Wagner, which was defended by 1,200 Confederates. Confederate casualties that day were only 12.[50] A force of 2,000 Federal troops landed on the southern tip of Morris Island, and from this position the Federals attempted to capture Battery Wagner using the standard, time-tried siege techniques. The siege continued for 58 unbearably hot July and August days and nights.[51]

Beauregard anticipated Gillmore's plan,[52] but he still believed Charleston could avoid capture even if the harbor islands were taken. However, Beauregard's forces had been diminished by the Federal assault in April of 1863, and had been further diminished when various regiments were ordered to other states.[53] When the Federal offensive aimed at Battery Wagner began on July 10, Beauregard counted a total fighting force of 5,841—2,906 on James Island; 927 on Morris Island; 1,158 on Sullivan's Island; and 850 in the city of Charleston.[54]

Private John Harleston, of the Charleston Light Dragoons, Company H, 4th South Carolina Cavalry, noted upon being evacuated from the little fort on Morris Island: "*Hell* can't be worse than Battery Wagner."[55] Harleston, a courier between Batteries Wagner and Gregg, was asked: "What was the tightest place you were in during the Civil War?" He replied:

> Battery Wagner on Morris Island, and I have been in many tight places: as a prisoner on U.S. vessels, in the Tombs prison in New York, in Fort Lafayette, in Fort Delaware, and in the Bull Pens of Logan's Corps, in North Carolina, and the Bombardment and defense of Fort Sumter, and in numerous other places, but of *all*, the last six days before Battery Wagner was evacuated, was the worst.[56]

Henry J. Clifton of the 21st South Carolina Regiment wrote to his parents, "Battery Wagner is one of the worst dreaded places in the south." He described how every soldier he knew would "almost as soon die as to start there." Speaking from firsthand experience, Clifton remarked, "We are in danger from the time we start until we get back. Our shells do us almost as much harm as the Yankees.... [O]ur men shell at night and lose the range very often and shell us."[57]

Although undoubtedly some of the hardest fighting during the entire war, the battle for Morris Island and the siege of Battery Wagner have been overshadowed by two other major Confederate defeats in July 1863: the defeat of Lee's Army at Gettysburg, July 1–3, and the capture of Vicksburg, Mississippi, on July 4.

When the 31st and 61st Regiments of Clingman's Brigade returned to Charleston on July 12, 1863, from Wilmington, North Carolina, Captain Nathan Ramsey of the 61st described the move as being cast "Out of Paradise into Hell."[58] The men of Clingman's Brigade were initially quartered on James Island, which they described as a "little Sahara, with plenty of wind; rolling and twisting clouds of sand, millions of black gnats, and a very scanty supply of devilish poor beef." Water was obtained by sinking holes in the sand, but it had an unpleasant taste. While there was a good well at nearby Fort Pemberton, "no Tar Heel was allowed to sample that water. The men from North Carolina regiments also complained of the high prices for food charged in Charleston, and that their money was refused at "the post office, in the market, in the stores and on the streets."[59] They welcomed the move to the north side of the harbor to Sullivan's Island.[60] But of all the places in and around Charleston, Morris Island was beyond compare to anything they had ever seen before or were ever to encounter again.

On July 10, the heavy artillery on Folly Island unmercifully bombarded the Confederate fortifications on Morris Island.[61] This Federal assault was repulsed by the Confederates, but heavy fire from Federal guns forced the Confederates to abandon the southern part of Morris Island.[62]

Fig. 6. Major General Quincy A. Gillmore, in charge of Federal assault on Morris Island, for which he was promoted on July 10, 1863. Brady National Photographic Art Gallery, Washington, D.C. (Library of Congress)

Once the Federals had made a "lodgement" on the lower end of Morris Island, General Beauregard initially thought that the enemy could be driven off, with the help of Clingman's Brigade and other reinforcements. This had also been suggested by General Clingman.[63] Shortly after Clingman's arrival in Charleston, General Beauregard called a conference to discuss how best to recapture the ground lost on Morris Island. Eventually it was decided that such an effort would be impractical. However, Battery Wagner was to be held at all costs for the present, while new batteries were built on James Island and fortifications elsewhere were strengthened.[64] Since he had not had a chance to "examine the ground," Clingman went along with the views of the other generals.[65]

Clingman and the other officers in charge of Battery Wagner held their men in constant readiness to repulse any attack.[66] Conditions were so bad that even the commanding officers were frequently changed. Generals William Booth Taliaferro, Johnson Hagood, and A. H. Colquitt, and Colonels George P. Harrison, R. F. Graham, and L. M. Keith, as well as Brigadier General Thomas L. Clingman, each took his turn as commander, generally serving about five days.[67] One of Clingman's regiments was always at the little fort.[68]

Private John Harleston described the conditions the men had to endure:

> The water supply obtained from barrels sunk in the sand soon became unfit to use. Dead bodies were all around, and the water smelt and tasted of them, and was half salt anyhow. A limited supply was brought from the city, but this was kept for the wounded. There were some of the wells some distance below Wagner that were better but one had to expose himself to reach them.[69]

In addition to gnats, mosquitoes pestered the soldiers, and flies swarmed by the thousands, feeding on decaying flesh and the refuse of men and war. The sun blazed down relentlessly. The constant roar of cannon and rifles became the normal sounds both day and night.

July 18, 1863

The fight to gain control of Battery (Fort) Wagner, led in part by a regiment of black troops—the 54th Massachusetts—has been accurately portrayed in the motion picture *Glory*. Neither the Confederates defending the fort nor the Federal troops attacking that day found any "Glory," but the men from both sides got a glimpse into "Hell."

On July 18, 1863, the second major Federal assault on Battery Wagner was launched, using infantry as well as long-range artillery from both land and sea. The little fort was bombarded by 26 rifled guns and 10 siege mortars. At dusk, there began an assault directed by Truman Seymour with brigades of George Strong and H. S. Putnam of the Federal X Corps. The assault was led by Colonel R. G. Shaw and his black troops of the 54th Massachusetts.[70]

Confederate General William Booth Taliaferro, of Virginia, in charge of Battery Wagner that day, estimated that "nine hundred shot and shell were thrown in and against the battery during the eleven hours that the bombardment lasted."[71] General Taliaferro, a veteran of the Mexican War and a commander of a militia company at Harpers Ferry after the John Brown raid, was commissioned a Colonel in the Confederate Army and had served under Jackson in the Shenandoah Valley. He had seen action at Winchester, Port Republic, and Cedar Mountain, in addition to Second Bull Run, and Fredericksburg. He is described as "six feet tall and full-bearded ... by tradition and character, a Virginia gentleman and leader."[72]

During that doomed attack, as night approached on July 18, the Federal bombardment increased, and the Union troops moved forward under that cover and the approaching darkness to launch the attack. The Federal troops were met with a shower of grape shot and cannister from the guns within Battery (Fort) Wagner launched by the men of the Charleston Battalion and the 51st Regiment of Clingman's Brigade. The Confederates fired point blank at the men of the 54th Massachusetts as they ran down the narrow strip of land toward a ditch. The fort defenders maintained their positions, and were able to drive the enemy back.[73]

The frontal assault by 6,000 Federal troops was headed by the 54th Massachusetts, which included two of the sons of Frederick Douglass.[74] Union General George C. Strong was wounded while leading the charge against Battery Wagner, and died 12 days later.[75]

More than half of the 600-man regiment, including Colonel Robert G. Shaw, were either killed or wounded. Only one of the six Federal regimental commanders was not killed or wounded.[76]

A drama was being enacted inside the little sand fort as well. On the left of the work, the 31st North Carolina were supposed to occupy the parapets, but they, according to General Taliaferro, "ingloriously deserted the ramparts," and as a result, the Union soldiers rushed forward, entered the ditch, and climbed the fort walls on the left of the salient, and occupied it. General Taliaferro directed his Lieutenant Colonel Gaillard to keep up a heavy fire, and to aim the field pieces on the left of the fort to prevent the enemy from being supported. The majority of the Federal forces in front of Battery Wagner suffered heavy casualties within the range of the Confederate guns. In order to dislodge the enemy, Taliaferro called for volunteers. This call was answered immediately by Major J. H. McDonald of the 51st Regiment and Captain Ryan of the Charleston Battalion. Taliaferro chose Ryan's men to charge the salient, but in the advance, Captain Ryan was killed and his men faltered. The men of the 51st Regiment kept up a steady fire on the enemy, and inflicted heavy casualties. Taliaferro estimated the Federals lost 2,000 men killed, wounded or prisoners, and thought the numbers might have been higher.[77] The failure of the men of the 31st Regiment to obey orders almost resulted in the loss of the little fort by allowing the enemy to gain the ditch in front of Battery Wagner. Luckily, the Federals were dislodged and driven back by the quick action of soldiers of Clingman's 51st Regiment, who had answered General Taliaferro's call for volunteers.[78]

The assault on July 18 was disastrous for the Federal troops. Confederate General Beauregard estimated that they must have sustained 3,000 losses—those dead, wounded, or prisoners. The next day, the bodies of 800 Federal soldiers were buried in front of Battery Wagner. Confederate losses on July 18 were 175 killed and 40 wounded.[79] Others[80] estimate casualties on July 18 as:

Federals engaged = 5,264; casualties 1,515

Confederates engaged = 1,785; casualties 174

The flag of the 51st Regiment which was mounted on top of Battery Wagner the night of July 18 was torn badly by enemy gunfire. Colonel Hector McKethan requested a new flag for the regiment.[81]

First Lieutenant E. K. Bryan, of Clingman's 31st Regiment, gave a graphic description of the carnage of July 18, 1863:

> Blood, mud, water, brains and human hair matted together; men lying in every possible attitude, with every conceivable expression on their countenances; their

limbs bent into unnatural shapes by the fall of twenty or more feet, the fingers rigid and outstretched as if they had clutched at the earth to save themselves; pale, beseeching faces, looking out from among the ghastly corpses, with moans and cries for help and water and dying gasps and death struggles. In the salient and on the ramparts they lay heaped and pent up, in some places, three deep.[82]

The conditions on Morris Island and in the little sand fort of Battery Wagner were almost unbearable. Smoke from exploding artillery shells filled the air, almost blocking out the sun. Projectiles from land and sea whistled and exploded in the air and on land, sending huge sprays of sand and anything buried in it high into the sky. The noise was deafening, but occasionally the screams of wounded men could be heard echoing across the hot sand. The odor of blood, sweat, decomposing flesh, and gunpowder combined to make a deadly perfume.

Arthur Ford, observing the battle from three quarters of a mile away, described it graphically:

> At daylight the bombardment of the fort began, and continued without a minute's cessation all day. Occasionally as many as four shells were observed in the air at the same time. The fort itself was enveloped in a dense black pall of smoke from bursting shells, and at times was completely hidden.[83]

Charleston, South Carolina, was, as usual, unbearably hot during the summer months, and the blazing sun reflecting on the white sand intensified the heat. To make matters worse, the Confederates in Battery Wagner were jam-packed into the bombproof shelter during the bombardments. The stench of decomposing bodies of men and horses hung in the air, an odor increased by barrels of putrid meat that had been thrown on the beach. Frequently, corpses of soldiers that had been buried were disinterred by shells from the big guns. "The water in the shallow wells became so contaminated by dead bodies that it was unfit to drink."[84]

The men at Battery Wagner were exposed to enemy fire both from land and sea. While under fire, they tried to remain under the cover of the battery or in pits dug into the sand hills. Even when they were not under fire, there was no time to rest or relax, because the damage to the fort had to be repaired. Moreover, as they made those repairs, there was the ever-present danger of being shot by sharpshooters.[85]

The contest for control of Morris Island became one of endurance. Battery Wagner was shelled continuously day and night. Each day, the Federal fleet sailed in close to the island and bombarded the little fort with heavy naval guns. This bombardment was so heavy and so constant that the men defending the garrison had to be relieved every five days.[86]

Even while stationed across the harbor on Sullivan's Island, Clingman's men could not relax. Clingman received orders on July 19 that "at least 750 infantry" should be kept in "readiness to embark for Morris Island at a moment's notice."[87] A routine was established by which a force of about 500 men was kept in the fort during the day, while the rest withdrew to the sand hills and "rat holes."[88]

On August 23, 1863, Clingman reported to Captain W. F. Nance that the enemy's ironclad monitors had come into Charleston Harbor between Fort Moultrie and Battery Gregg and opened fire on Fort Sumter. He also reported that one of the enemy ships was very close to Sullivan's Island, and that his guns had fired at the ship (Fig. 7). He believed the enemy's ship had

Fig. 7. Guns at Fort Marshall on Sullivan's Island, South Carolina, 1865. (Library of Congress)

been damaged by repeated hits, but their aim was hindered by the distance and by a heavy fog.[89]

Enemy monitors again entered the harbor on August 26. But Clingman's men also fired on one of the Confederate ships by mistake. The steamer *Sumter,* hit by fire from Sullivan's Island, ran aground on a shoal and sank. Clingman declined any blame in the matter, and said that the captain of the *Sumter* should have alerted the artillery on Sullivan's Island. Clingman suggested that in the future a "small boat or two" be stationed "opposite Cumming's Point to give notice of the approach of the enemy's vessels by rockets, or other signals," so that his artillerists would know when to fire, to avoid such "unfortunate occurrences in the future."[90]

The siege continued and little by little

the Federals advanced under the cover of a series of entrenchments and by use of zigzag lines. By August 26, the Federal troops were just 25 yards away from the rifle pits in front of Battery Wagner. Just after 7 o'clock P.M., the Federals launched a heavy attack,[91] and the 61st North Carolina and the 54th Georgia had to abandon their rifle pits on the ridge that separated the battery from the Federal line.[92]

General Gillmore continued his siege operations against Battery Wagner until September 6. By that date, his Federal troops had reached the ditch in front of the fort, and an all-out assault was ordered to take place the next day.

With the Federals entrenched only about 100 feet away from Battery Wagner, it was now apparent that Morris Island could not be held, and the little fort would have to be abandoned. Beauregard had completed his "interior lines" for the defense of Charleston, and he believed that Charleston was secure. Although his men had held the fort with almost "superhuman energy and pluck," Beauregard ordered them to evacuate on the night of September 6.[93] The next morning, the Federal troops were amazed to find that Battery Wagner as well as Battery Gregg had been abandoned.[94] (See Fig. 8.)

Many have described the action for

Fig. 8. Interior of fort on Morris Island, with Federal gun crews and mortars aimed at Fort Sumter, 1865. Sam A. Cooley, photographer. (Library of Congress)

Morris Island as some of the most terrific fighting of the entire war. While the numbers of men engaged were not nearly as great as those in the battles at Gettysburg, Spottsylvania or Cold Harbor, the "fierce fighting and heroism at [Battery] Wagner was not excelled upon any battlefield in the war."[95]

The Union forces sustained 214 losses for every 1,000 men engaged.[96] Out of a total 5,264 Federal soldiers engaged, casualties were 1,515, compared to 174 Confederate casualties from among 1,785 men.[97] Losses in Clingman's Brigade were 21 men killed and 80 wounded from the 8th, 51st and 61st regiments.[98] The 31st Regiment, which had failed to man the parapets on July 18, suffered seven killed, 31 wounded, and one missing.[99] North Carolina historian Ashe believed that of all the Confederate men lost on Morris Island, half of them were members of Clingman's Brigade.[100]

Fig. 9. Charleston, South Carolina. View of ruined buildings through porch of the Circular Church, 150 Meeting Street, taken in April 1865. (Library of Congress)

Even though Morris Island was eventually lost, the city of Charleston was able to hold out until the closing months of the war, and it was eventually almost destroyed (Fig. 9). That destruction was delayed as long as the Confederates held Morris Island. However, with the loss of Morris Island, the role of Charleston "as a Confederate port" was essentially over. The Federals thereafter used Morris Island as a base to continue their shelling of Fort Sumter and the city of Charleston.[101] (See Fig. 10.)

Clingman and his men continued to

Fig. 10. Site of night attack on Fort Sumter, September 8, 1863, after the Battery Wagner was abandoned to the Federal forces; taken in 1865. (Library of Congress)

defend Sullivan's Island and helped prevent Federal ships from gaining access to Charleston by water. They remained in the harbor defense until November 27, 1863, when President Davis ordered Clingman to move his brigade immediately to the vicinity of Tarboro, North Carolina, where a Federal attack was expected.[102] The next day, November 28, Clingman's Brigade, consisting of only 1,810 "effective" men, returned to North Carolina.[103] At last, those horrible days were behind them.

When the situation in Virginia worsened, Clingman and his brigade were ordered first to Kinston, North Carolina, then on to Virginia, to Petersburg.[104] They arrived in Petersburg on December 14, 1863, and camped near the city.[105] Clingman then arrived with the men of the 61st Regiment, and the 51st Regiment soon followed,[106] but in response to a request by General Whiting, President Jefferson Davis ordered Clingman's Brigade back to Goldsboro. Davis' wishes were relayed "verbally" to General Pickett, who believed the enemy were contemplating a move on Suffolk, Virginia, instead of toward Goldsboro as Whiting feared.[107] On December 28, the 8th and 31st Regiments were ordered to be ready to "move at a moment's warning."[108]

Thus, Clingman and his men ended the long, hard year of 1863. The regiments had endured great hardships on Morris Island, and performed bravely. Clingman and his men had been placed in one of the worst situations of the entire war, and they

Fig. 11. Columbiad cannon inside Fort Sumter, as seen in October 2000. (Courtesy of Carl D. Casstevens.)

had endured, although they had suffered many casualties and lost many fine men and officers. Yet, the upcoming year of 1864 would prove to be as bad or worse when Clingman's Brigade became part of Robert F. Hoke's Division in Robert E. Lee's Army of Northern Virginia.[109]

Today, nothing remains of the little sand fort known as Battery Wagner. Were it not for the motion picture *Glory*, the struggle for Battery Wagner might have been entirely forgotten by the general public. The notes of a spirited little polka written in 1863 entitled "Battery Wagner" have faded away. Conversely, Fort Sumter, where it all began, has become a major tourist attraction. Standing on the parapets of Fort Sumter, one can gaze at the site of Battery Wagner on Morris Island across the blue water of the harbor and wonder how it was in July of 1863 when men in Blue met men in Gray. From the quiet serenity that exists today, it is hard to imagine the air thick with smoke, and the sound of gunfire from thousands of rifles combined with the boom of the cannons from the Federal ironclads that drowned out the cries of the wounded and dying.

Notes

1. Barrett, pp. 128–131.
2. *Ibid.*, pp. 137–139.
3. Barrett, p. 139; and Wayne County Historical Association, Inc., and the Old Dobbs County Genealogical Society, "First Dudley," in *Heritage of Wayne County, North Carolina* (Winston-Salem, NC: Hunter Publishing Co., 1982), p. 12.
4. W. W. Howe, *Kinston, Whitehall and Goldsboro* (New York: W. W. Howe, 1980), pp. 31–34.
5. *O.R.*, XVIII, Ser. I, p. 112, General N. G. Evans to General S. Cooper; John B. Jones, *Rebel War Clerk's Diary* I, ed. Howard Swiggett (1866; rpt. New York: Old Hickory Bookshop, 1935), p. 214; Barrett, pp. 145–146; and "The Civil War," in *Heritage of Wayne County*, p. 17.
6. Barrett, p. 145.
7. "Garrard's Raid on Mount Olive," in *Heritage of Wayne County*, p. 17.
8. Barrett, pp. 140–146.
9. "The Civil War," in *Heritage of Wayne County*, p. 17.
10. *O.R.*, XVIII, Ser. I, pp. 110–111, Lieutenant Colonel W. H. Stevens, "Report of Operations, December 16–17, 1862," dated December 19, 1862.
11. Manarin and Jordan, IV, pp. 515–516. Neither the regimental history of the 61st Regiment nor John G. Barrett in his *The Civil War in North Carolina*, pp. 145–147, places the 61st Regiment at the Neuse River railroad bridge with General Clingman until late in the afternoon of December 17, 1862. Clingman mentions Devane and the 61st, but he may have more correctly meant a portion of the 61st Regiment or the 40th Regiment. See *O.R.*, XVIII, Ser. I, pp. 117–119 for Brigadier General Clingman's report of the action.
12. *O.R.*, XVIII, Ser. I, pp. 117–119, "Report of Brig. Gen. Thomas L. Clingman, December 21, 1862"; T. C. Moore, "Tenth Regiment, First Artillery, Co. I," in Clark, *Histories of the Several Regiments*, I, p. 519; and Manarin and Jordan, IV, pp. 516–517.
13. Barrett, p. 147; *O. R.*, XVIII, Ser. I, pp. 129–121, "Report No. 38," Stephen D. Poole; and Moore, "Tenth Regiment," p. 519.
14. *O.R.*, XVIII, Ser. I, pp. 110–111, Lieutenant Colonel W. H. Stevens, "Report of Operations, December 16–17, 1862"; and *O.R.*, XVIII, Ser. I, pp. 129–131.
15. *O.R.*, XVIII, Ser. I, pp. 117–119; Manarin and Jordan, IV, pp. 516–517.
16. *O.R.*, XVIII, Ser. I, pp. 117–119; Manarin and Jordan, IV, pp. 516–517; and John H. Robinson, "Fifty-Second Regiment," in Clark, *Histories of the Several Regiments*, III, pp. 229–232.
17. Manarin and Jordan, IV, pp. 515–516. Neither the regimental history of the 61st Regiment nor John G. Barrett in his *The Civil War in North Carolina*, pp. 145–147, places the 61st Regiment at the Neuse River railroad bridge with General Clingman until late in the afternoon of December 17, 1862.
18. Robinson, "Fifty-Second Regiment," pp. 229–232; and Ashe, *History of North Carolina*, II, pp. 791–792.
19. *Ibid.*
20. "Garrard's Raid on Mount Olive Station," p. 17.
21. *O.R.*, XVIII, Ser. I, pp. 109–110; Major General G. W. Smith to General S. Cooper,

December 29, 1862; and *O.R.*, XVIII, Ser. I, pp. 110 –111, Lt. Col. W. H. Stevens to Major General Gustavus W. Smith, December 29, 1862.

22. *O.R.*, XVIII, Ser. I, pp. 109–110, Major General G. W. Smith to General S. G. French, December 16, 1862.

23. *Raleigh Register*, 23 December 1862.

24. A. A. McKethan, "Fifty-First Regiment," in Clark, *Histories of the Several Regiments*, II, pp. 204–205.

25. T. L. Clingman to Governor Zebulon B. Vance, January 28, 1863, Vance Papers, North Carolina Department of Archives and History, Raleigh, North Carolina.

26. Barrett, p. 147.

27. *Ibid.*

28. Robinson, "Fifty-Second Regiment," pp. 229–232; and Ashe, *History of North Carolina*, II, pp. 791–792.

29. Barrett, p. 147.

30. Edmondston, p. 321.

31. *O.R.*, XVIII, Ser. I, pp. 109–110, Major General G. W. Smith to General S. G. French, December 16, 1862.

32. Francis Trevelyan Miller, ed. *The Photographic History of the Civil War* (New York: Castle Books, 1957), II, pp. 327–328; *O.R.*, XVIII, Ser. I, p. 60, "No. 2, Return of Casualties in the Union forces"—this report encompassed losses in skirmishes on the Kinston Road, December 11–12, 1862, on Southwest Creek, December 13–14, 1862, Kinston, December 14, 1862, White Hall, December 16, 1862, and Thompson's Bridge and Goldsboro Bridge, December 17, 1862.

33. *O.R.*, XVIII, Ser. I, pp. 109–110, Major General G. W. Smith to General S. G. French, December 16, 1862.

34. *O.R.*, XVIII, Ser. I, p. 809, "Abstract of Field Report of the Troops of the District of the Cape Fear, commanded by Brig. Gen. W. H. C. Whiting, for December, 1862."

35. Order No. 19, Major General G. W. Smith to Thomas L. Clingman, Clingman Papers, SHC.

36. Long, pp. 569–570.

37. *Ibid.*, p. 570, Robert E. Lee to Jefferson Davis.

38. *Ibid.*, p. 484.

39. *Ibid.*, p. 485.

40. *Ibid.*, 159.

41. Quincy A. Gillmore. "The Army Before Charleston in 1865," *Battles and Leaders of the Civil War* (hereinafter referred to as *Battles and Leaders*), Vol. IV, Robert U. Johnson and Clarence C. Buel, eds. (1887 rpt. Secacus, N.J.: Castle, 1982), p. 55.

42. E. K. Bryan and E. K. Meadows, "Defense of Fort Wagner, Morris Island, 8 July, 1863," Walter Clark, ed., *History of the Several Regiments*, vol. 5, p. 162.

43. John Harleston, "Battery Wagner on Morris Island," *South Carolina Historical Magazine*, 57 (January 1956), p. 6.

44. E. Milby Burton, *The Siege of Charleston, 1861–1865* (Columbia, S.C.: University of South Carolina Press, 1970), pp. 151–153.

45. Robert C. Gilchrist, "Confederate Defenses of Morris Island," in *Charleston Year Book, 1884* (Charleston, S.C.: City of Charleston, South Carolina, 1884), p. 356.

46. Clement Evans, *Confederate Military History* (Atlanta: Confederate Publishing Co., 1899), V, 225.

47. Walter Lord, ed., *The Fremantle Diary, being the Journal of Lieutenant Colonel James Arthur Lyon Fremantle, Coldstream Guards, on his Three Months in the Southern States.* (Boston: Little, Brown and Company, 1954), p. 149.

48. Shelby Foot, *The Civil War: A Narrative* (New York: Random House, 1958), II, p. 222.

49. *Ibid.*, p. 696.

50. Boatner, pp. 300–301.

51. Charles Girard, *Visit to Confederate States in 1863: Memoirs Addressed to Napoleon III*, trans. William S. Hoole (1864; rpt. Tuscaloosa, Ala.: Confederate Publishing Co., 1962), pp. 43–44.

52. G. T. Beauregard, "The Defense of Charleston," Robert Underwood Johnson and Clarence Clough Buel, eds., *Battles and Leaders of the Civil War*, vol. IV (1888; reprint, Secaucus, N.J.: Castle, 1982), p. 14.

53. *Ibid.*, p. 13.

54. *Ibid.*, footnote, p. 14.

55. Harleston, p. 13.

56. *Ibid.*, 1–2.

57. Henry J. Clifton to his father and mother, September 1, 1863, John L. Clifton Papers, cited in Manarin and Jordan, XIV, p. 610, footnote 49.

58. N. A. Ramsey, "Sixty-First Regiment," *Histories of the Several Regiments and Battalions from North Carolina in the Great War, 1861–1865, Written by Members of the Respective Command* (hereinafter cited as *Histories of the Several Regiments*), vol. 3, Walter Clark, ed. (Goldsboro, NC: Nash Brothers, 1901), p. 510.

59. *Ibid.*, p. 510.
60. *Ibid.*, p. 510.
61. Edward Pollard, *The Lost Cause: A New Southern History of the War of the Confederates* (New York: E. B. Treat & Co., 1867), pp. 430–431.
62. Girard, *Visit to Confederate States in 1863: Memoirs Addressed to Napoleon III*, pp. 43–44.
63. Ashe, *History of North Carolina*, II, p. 832.
64. Beauregard, "The Defense of Charleston," p. 15.
65. *O.R.*, XXVIII, Ser. I, Pt. I, pp. 60–62, "Addenda No. 2," Brig. Gen. Thomas Jordan, July 12, 1863.
66. *O.R.*, XXVIII, Ser. I, Pt. II, p. 204, Special Orders, No. 249, Wm. F. Nance, A.A.G., July 16, 1863.
67. Bryan and Meadows, p. 167.
68. Ashe, *History of North Carolina*, II, p. 832.
69. Harleston, "Battery Wagner on Morris Island, 1863," pp. 5–6.
70. Boatner, pp. 300–301.
71. Beauregard, "The Defense of Charleston," p. 16.
72. Boatner, pp. 825–826.
73 *O.R.*, XXVIII, Ser. I, Pt. I, pp. 418–419, General William Booth Taliaferro to W. T. Nance, report on Battery Wagner, July 18, 1863.
74. Clint Johnson, *Touring the Carolinas' Civil War Sites* (Winston-Salem, N.C.: John F. Blair, Publisher), 1996, p. 253.
75. Boatner, *The Civil War Dictionary*, pp. 811–812.
76. *Ibid.*, p. 301.
77. *O.R.*, XXVIII, Ser. I, Pt. I, pp. 418–419, General William Booth Taliaferro to W. T. Nance, report on Battery Wagner, July 18, 1863.
78. *O.R.*, XXVIII, Ser. I, Pt. I, pp. 417–418, General William B. Taliaferro to W. T. Nance, report on Battery Wagner, July 18, 1863.
79. Beauregard, "The Defense of Charleston," p. 16.
80. Boatner, p. 301.
81. Colonel Hector McKethan to Captain Edward White, September 29, 1863, Thomas Lanier Clingman Papers, SHC.
82. Bryan and Meadows, "Defense of Fort Wagner," pp. 165–166.
83. Arthur Peronneau Ford and Marion Johnstone Ford, *Life in the Confederate Army, Being Personal Experiences of a Private Soldier in the Confederate Army; and Some Experiences and Sketches of Southern Life* (New York: The Neale Publishing Company, 1905), pp. 18–19. Electronic edition. UNC-CH, Documenting the American South. Call number C97073 F691.1905 (North Carolina Collection, UNC-CH) online: docsouth.unc.edu/ford/ford.html.
84. *Ibid.*
85. H. T. J. Ludwig, "Eighth Regiment," *Histories of the Several Regiments*, vol. II, pp. 392–395.
86. Fitzgerald Ross, *Cities and Camps of Confederate States*, Richard B. Harwell, ed. (1865; rpt. Urbana, Ill.: University of Illinois Press, 1958), p. 99.
87. *O.R.*, XXVIII, Ser. I, Pt. II, p. 209, Thomas Jordan, chief of staff to Brigadier-General Clingman, Charleston, S.C., July 19, 1863, 1:30 A.M.
88. Burton, *The Siege of Charleston, 1861–1865*, p. 172.
89. *O.R.*, XXVIII, Ser. I, Pt. I, p. 671, Thomas L. Clingman to Capt. W. F. Nance, Sullivan's Island, August 23, 1863.
90. *O.R.*, XXVIII, Ser. I, Pt. I, p. 704, T. L. Clingman to Capt. W. F. Nance, Sullivan's Island, S.C., August 31, 1863.
91. Ashe, *History of North Carolina*, II, p. 832.
92. Gilchrist, pp. 385–386.
93. Beauregard, "The Defense of Charleston," p. 18.
94. Samuel A'C. Ashe, "Life at Fort Wagner," in *Confederate Veteran*, XXXV (1927), 255–256.
95. Burton, p. 151.
96. Thomas L. Livermore, *Numbers and Losses in the Civil War* (Bloomington, Ind.: Indiana University Press, 1957), p. 75.
97. Boatner, *The Civil War Dictionary*, p. 301.
98. Robert C. Gilchrist, "Confederate Defenses of Morris Island," in *Charleston Year Book 1884* (Charleston, S.C.: City of Charleston, South Carolina, 1884), p. 401.
99. Manarin and Jordan, VIII, p. 427; and Bryan and Meadows, "Thirty-First Regiment," p. 514.
100. Ashe, *History of North Carolina*, II, p. 832.
101. Walter Lord, ed., *The Fremantle Diary, being the Journal of Lieutenant Colonel James Arthur Lyon Fremantle, Coldstream Guards, on his Three Months in the Southern States* (Boston: Little, Brown and Company, 1954), p. 284.
102. *O.R.*, XXVIII, Ser. I, Pt. II, p. 527, Brigadier General R. S. Ripley to Brigadier

General Thomas Jordan, November 27, 1863; *O.R.*, XXVIII, Ser. I, Pt. I, p. 113, General G. T. Beauregard, Endorsement No. 2, November 28, 1863; *O.R.*, XXVIII, Ser. I, Pt. I, p. 528, Brigadier General Thomas Jordan to Brigadier General R. S. Ripley, November 28, 1863; and *O.R.*, XXIX, Ser. I, Pt. II, p. 860, General George Pickett to General Samuel Cooper, December 4, 1863.

103. *O.R.*, XXVIII, Ser. I, Pt. I, p. 113, General G. T. Beauregard to W. S. Walker, November 28, 1863; and *O. R.*, XXIV, Ser. I, Pt. II, pp. 906–907.

104. Edward White to Col. Hector McKethan, December 11, 1863, Order Book 2.

105. *Ibid.*; Burgwyn, "Clingman's Brigade," p. 486.

106. Burgwyn, "Clingman's Brigade," p. 486; Edward White to Col. James D. Radcliffe, December 12, 1863, Order Book 2.

107. *O.R.*, XXIX, Ser. I, Pt. II, pp. 899–893, W. H. C. Whiting to Samuel Cooper, December 28, 1863.

108. Edward White to Cols. J. V. Jordan and Whitson, December 28, 1863, Order Book 2.

109. Moore, IV, p. 7.

Chapter V

Battles: 1864

I propose to fight it out on this line, if it takes all summer.
— General Ulysses S. Grant (1822–1885) from Dispatch to Washington, before Spotsylvania Court House, May 11, 1864.

On January 23, 1864, the 31st Regiment was sent from Petersburg, Virginia, to Ivor Station on the Blackwater River just southeast of Petersburg. Three of its companies were sent to Smithfield on the James River.[1] Clingman wished to remain with Lee's Army rather than return to North Carolina. General George Pickett, knowing Clingman's wishes, advised that no North Carolina troops be sent to their home state at present because of the internal division there. Pickett suggested that the "presence of other men whom we could depend on might be of infinite service in case of internal trouble."[2] Conditions in eastern North Carolina were described as "deplorable" by the close of 1863 and early in 1864. There were frequent incursions by the enemy, which resulted in much property destruction. Union sympathizers, called "Buffaloes," hid out in the swamps and terrorized the countryside. Late in January 1864, General Pickett was sent to North Carolina to capture the Federal garrison at New Bern. Clingman's Brigade was ordered to leave Virginia and to take part in the attack as part of a Confederate force of 12,700 men, excluding officers.[3]

New Bern Expedition, January 28–February 10, 1864

Lee's army badly needed supplies from eastern North Carolina, and Lee had suggested that an attempt be made to drive the Federals from New Bern. President Davis approved, but wanted Lee to lead the attack. Lee declined and suggested Brigadier General Robert F. Hoke (Fig. 12), because Hoke knew the area. Hoke developed a plan of action.[4] Since Hoke was only a brigadier general, Lee selected Major General George E. Pickett to lead the attack. Pickett was the only officer of rank that could be spared from Virginia. This proved to be an unfortunate arrangement.[5]

New Bern was defended on land by a line of entrenchments which ran from the Neuse River to the Trent River. A redoubt near the Trent gave the city protection from the flank, and three or four gunboats on the Neuse protected the city from attack by water.[6]

In his orders to Pickett, Lee stressed the advantage to be gained in a surprise attack, and suggested that nothing should be sent by telegraph that would disclose their pur-

Fig. 12. Major General Robert F. Hoke. (Courtesy of the North Carolina Division of Archives and History, Raleigh, North Carolina.)

pose to the enemy. Lee thought it equally important to keep their plans from the citizens as well. Hoke, in turn, was ordered to give out false information that he and his men were going to "arrest deserters and recruit [men for] their diminished regiments."[7]

A large Confederate force of about 13,000 men and 14 navy cutters,[8] which included the brigades of Random, Clingman, and Hoke, were concentrated at Kinston. The plan, drawn up by Hoke and approved by Lee, was forwarded to Pickett. Pickett discarded Hoke's plan and silenced the young brigadier general by threatening to have him arrested and court-martialed.[9] Pickett's plan was, however, basically the same as that suggested by Hoke, which utilized the brigades of Barton, Kemper, and three regiments of Ransom's plus cavalry to cross the Trent River and proceed south to Brice's Creek below New Bern. After crossing the creek he was to capture the forts along the Neuse and Trent Rivers and enter New Bern by the railroad bridge. Another column headed by Colonel James Dearing of the 15th and 17th Virginia, and Colonel J. N. Whitford's regiment, plus artillery and cavalry, were to move down on the north side of the Neuse and capture Fort Anderson at Barrington Ferry. Hoke and Pickett and the rest of the troops planned to move between the Trent and the Neuse and surprise the troops at Batchelder's Creek. They planned to silence the guns in the fort and batteries near the Neuse River, and enter the town from that direction. Success depended on a coordinated, simultaneous attack from the three different directions.[10] Barton, Kemper, and part of Ransom's brigade were to move south of the Trent River and attack the enemy behind Brice's Creek, take the railroad bridge, and the forts along the Neuse and Trent rivers, then enter new Bern with artillery and 600 cavalry. These actions were necessary to prevent reinforcements from entering New Bern from Morehead City. Three of Ransom's regiments were to cross the Trent River and take the works in front of the town, to prevent the enemy from being reinforced either by land or water. Colonel James Dearing, commanding Colonel J. N. Whitford's regiment, with 300 cavalry and three pieces of artillery, was to take a position on the north side of the Neuse River, and capture Fort Anderson. The plan was to surprise the enemy and attack the town.[11] Without the element of surprise or the success of any of the various tasks, the plan would fail.

In addition to the land forces, naval commander John Taylor Wood, President Davis' own personal aide, was selected to create a diversion on the Neuse River, and destroy any Federal gunboats he encountered.[12] The attack was to be made Monday morning, simultaneously from the various directions.

The expedition led by Pickett and Hoke left Kinston on January 20, and a ten-day period of "disjointed and ineffective battles and skirmishes" followed.[13] They proceeded "under forced marches" and bivouacked the night of January 31 at Steven's Fork, about ten miles from New Bern and two miles from a Federal outpost which guarded the crossing over Batchelder's Creek. The men camped "without fires until about 1:00 A.M.," and then resumed their march, hoping to reach Batchelder's Creek before the bridge over it could be destroyed. But the firing of the pickets warned the enemy, and when Hoke and his men arrived, the bridge had been destroyed, and the enemy was "strongly entrenched." Hoke halted the advance until daylight. The next morning his men threw some trees across the creek and two regiments crossed. These regiments were to keep the Federal troops occupied so that the bridge could be repaired, but the enemy received reinforcements and made a strong resistance. The Confederates, however, eventually succeeded in routing the Federals.[14]

Captain William H. S. Burgwyn described the action at Batchelder' Creek and New Bern. On Sunday, January 31, 1864, the brigade started out for New Bern about sunrise, and marched to within ten miles of the city, where they halted for the night. The next day (February 1, 1864), the Confederates were attacked:

> About 2:00 a.m., we recommenced our march so as to arrive at New Berne about daybreak or sunrise. About 3:15 A.M. we attacked the enemy outposts at Batchelder's Creek and lost Colonel [Henry M.] Shaw of the 8th North Carolina, one of the very best colonels in service, though we only had about a hundred and fifty men at the crossing owing to the dense fog and mist and did not force a crossing. At about 7:00 A.M. General Hoke immediately on crossing pushed his men forward as fast as they could go intending to reach the railroad in time to cut it and also cut off the enemy's camp at Deep Gully and a train with all included cars attached but the troops being very much exhausted they only came in view of the train so it passed with the iron clad car and about four hundred Yankees. Our brigade was there put in advance and we marched down the country road till we came in view of New Berne. General Clingman's brigade followed after General Hoke's but at Batchelder's Creek he marched cross the country to the railroad to cut off the enemy's force camp[ed] at Deep Gully. After arriving in sight of New Berne we remained quiet for some time but about 2:00 P.M. we moved about a mile from the road to the right and made a demonstration in front of a body of cavalry that were maneuvering on the Trent Road so arrived in about one-half mile from there and formed in line of battle as they had the appearance of preparing to charge us which they attempted but the fire of our skirmishers alone drove them back. They then fired some five or six shots from a light field piece one of which shots a shell exploded and three shrapnel balls and a piece of the shell struck General Clingman but having hit the sand before striking home he was only bruised. About 5:00 P.M. we returned to the railroad three miles from New Berne and bivouacked for the night.[15]

One major casualty at Batchelder's Creek was the death of Colonel Henry M.

Shaw, commander of Clingman's 8th Regiment. Clingman, who rode beside Shaw, escaped injury.[16]

Timing was everything. Brigadier General Hoke had expected the enemy to move their troops westward on the train to his rear and away from New Bern. Had they done so, he had planned to move quickly toward the city, cut the railroad, capture the train, and move his men by rail to the city. This plan miscarried, and Hoke's forces (including some of Clingman's Brigade) missed the train by five minutes.[17] The enemy, warned by telegraph of Hoke's approach, rushed the train back to New Bern.[18]

As the Union troops escaped on the train, they fired at the Confederates with a "heavy piece of ordnance" mounted on an iron-clad car attached to the rear of the train. The Confederates did succeed in capturing a number of the enemy who had failed to board the train, and were attempting to escape on foot. Later in the day, Clingman's Brigade dispersed a cavalry command near New Bern.[19]

Knowledge of the terrain was also vital. Clingman was then ordered to cross the road to the Trent River to prevent the enemy from advancing from Deep Gully, south of New Bern, and to take up all stragglers. However, not knowing the country, he failed to reach the road, and thus allowed 500 Federal infantry and 400 cavalry to enter the town, according to Pickett's report.[20]

Pickett then ordered Clingman's Brigade to advance to support Hoke's men. When Clingman was within almost a mile of New Bern, his command diverged to the right, parallel with the enemy fortifications. The enemy was not encountered until they were within "six or eight hundred yards of the Trent road." At this point, a regiment of enemy cavalry, supported by some field artillery, appeared and charged Clingman's men. The charge was repulsed by his skirmishers, but then the Confederates were fired upon by the artillery. Clingman instructed his men to lie down and "little or no injury was sustained" by them. Repeated charges by the enemy were repulsed, and Clingman believed that if Hoke, nearly a mile to the rear, could bring up reinforcements, the attackers could be driven back within the fortifications of New Bern. After conferring with Clingman, Hoke returned to his men for that purpose. However, Clingman waited nearly an hour without hearing from Hoke, and finally gave up any hope of receiving reinforcements from him. In desperation, Clingman sent two of his staff officers to see if some artillery could be brought up from Hoke's position. While he waited, Clingman's men were bombarded by heavy artillery from Fort Totten, three-quarters of a mile away. Fort Totten was armed with 15 large-caliber guns. After almost three hours, Clingman was finally told that the artillery could not be brought to his assistance, and Hoke did not advance with his brigade. Clingman was forced to order his men to retire "slowly by sections" to a new position, so that they could repel any further attacks by the enemy's cavalry.[21]

In the meantime, Confederate naval commander Wood had failed on January 31 to find any gunboats on the Neuse River. Colonel Dearing had found Fort Anderson too strong to attack, and Barton's cavalry also failed to cut the railroad or telegraph lines.[22]

Knowing none of this, Pickett, Hoke, and Clingman continued on to New Bern, where they found the city had been heavily reinforced, and that Federal gunboats were shelling the attacking Confederate forces. During the bombardment, Clingman was hit by several pieces of shrapnel, but was "only bruised."[23] Hoke learned that several trains of reinforcements had arrived to assist the Federal forces in New

Bern. He then knew that Barton had failed to carry out his tasks.[24]

For a time, Pickett could not decide to attack the fortifications of the city. He called for a council of war, in which Clingman proposed that they demand an "unconditional surrender" from the Federal garrison. If this was refused, Clingman advised an immediate assault. He was overruled and nothing further was done. The Confederate troops "lay on their arms" all night, and quietly withdrew to Kinston early the next morning and throughout the next day.[25]

Burgwyn believed that the attack on New Bern did not occur because General Barton did not attack New Bern from his side of the Trent River. Barton said he could not attack New Bern because he was unable to take the works on the opposite side of Brice's Creek. According to Burgwyn, General Pickett got in touch with General Barton, and then ordered Clingman's Brigade to fall back, which they did the next day, to the Kinston side of Core Creek, about 13 miles from New Bern.[26]

The casualties of this expedition were relatively small. The Federals lost about 100 men, either killed or wounded, and 13 officers and 284 privates were captured by the Confederates, along with several artillery pieces, small arms, wagons, and animals. The Confederates lost about 45 men, either killed or wounded. The only major success was the sinking of the Federal gunboat *Underwriter* by Commander Wood.[27]

When Hoke invested New Bern, he delayed his attack for the arrival of the *Albemarle*. After the heavy firing began, however, Hoke knew the Confederate ram had been engaged in battle. He was ordered to leave New Bern and to move to Virginia, which he did not do until he tried a *coup de main* and summoned the garrison to surrender. Those in the garrison wanted four hours to consider his demand, but unfortunately they discovered before the time was up that Hoke and his men did not have time to force them to surrender, or give them another "Hoke ache" (hoe cake). He did, however, cut communication with Morehead City, and had the *Albemarle* not been attacked, New Bern probably would have been taken before Hoke was ordered to Richmond, since the enemy force was a small one.[28]

Plymouth, North Carolina, April 17–20, 1864

A plan was devised by Confederate general Braxton Bragg to reclaim the town of Plymouth, which had been captured during the Burnside Expedition in April 1862.[29] During April 1864, the 8th Regiment of Clingman's Brigade was ordered to report to Brigadier General Ransom at Weldon, North Carolina,[30] for an attempt to retake Plymouth, North Carolina. The 8th Regiment joined with Hoke's and Terry's Virginia Brigades, and the 43rd North Carolina Regiment. They were supported by the ironclad ram *Albemarle* under the command of Captain James W. Cooke of the Confederate Navy.[31] In order to assist the land forces, the ram had been ordered to move up the river to Halifax. This vessel had armor made from railroad iron rails, spiked down upon heavy oak timbers. It had been built at Edwards's Ferry on Mr. William R. Smith's plantation, by his son, Peter E. Smith, and Gilbert Elliott.[32]

The attack was begun by Hoke at 4 P.M. on April 17. The Federal garrison, under the command of Union general H. W. Wessells, was composed of four infantry regiments, plus artillery and cavalry. The *Albemarle* sank the Federal boat *Smithfield* on the 19th, and disabled the *Miami*. Hoke surrounded the town, and with a combination of attacks by infantry, artillery, and the ram, bought the action to a close on April 20.[33]

Fourteen-year-old Joseph Blunt Cheshire witnessed the fighting at Plymouth, from his home:

> I could hear the booming of the cannon in the early morning, when I went out to the stable to feed my father's horse. I had heard the cheering of the regiments as they marched by night through the streets of Tarborough on their way to Plymouth; and afterwards I saw the two or three thousand prisoners captured at Plymouth, as they passed through on their way to Salisbury...."[34]

In 1885, while both Cheshire and Hoke were traveling from Raleigh by train, Cheshire took the opportunity to question the general. Hoke, " a modest man," did not like to brag on his own exploits. Cheshire persisted, and eventually got him to talk about the battle. Hoke told him of the need to bring food to the Army of Northern Virginia, and that food invariably came from eastern North Carolina, and was transported over the Wilmington-Weldon-Petersburg Railroad. Plymouth, after its capture by the Federal troops, became a supply depot for the Federal Government. "Great quantities of food, ammunition, and military material of all kinds were being collected to an extent which suggested the inauguration of some great movement from that base." The Confederates discovered that the Federals proposed to move a large force "from Plymouth up the Roanoke River to capture Weldon, and thus cut the line between eastern North Carolina and Richmond and deprive General Lee of supplies of food for his army." The capture of the Weldon railroad by the Federal forces would have been "fatal to the South."[35]

Clingman did not accompany the troops to Plymouth but was ordered to make a reconnaissance toward Suffolk, Virginia, to obtain information on enemy positions and troop movements. From Ivor Station he reported that the Yankees there did not number over 5,000.[36]

President Davis sent for General Hoke and told him that he had been selected to lead the land forces, which were to be composed of his own brigade, and the brigade of General Matt W. Ransom. Davis impressed upon Hoke the need for "rapid movement and a prompt attack." Hoke assured Davis that "if he should command the expedition, the attack would be made at the first moment possible."[37] In a footnote, Cheshire notes that General Hoke going into battle reminded some generals of Stonewall Jackson. Hoke was reported to bring his men "into action with extraordinary rapidity; that, almost before it was apparent what they proposed to do, it had been done."[38]

To ensure success, Hoke told Davis that it was necessary that the *Albemarle* cooperate and coordinate the attack with his land forces. Although the ship was under the command of the Navy Department, Hoke wisely convinced Davis that it was necessary that Cooke be instructed to take orders from him, rather than the Navy. So, when Hoke's men were proceeding to march to Plymouth, Hoke sent word to Captain Cooke, and asked when the ship would be ready. Cooke replied that it would be about three weeks, and Hoke then directed Cooke to "proceed down the Roanoke" with the *Albemarle* on a specific day, and to cooperate with the land forces in the attack on Plymouth. Cooke was agreeable, and declared he would start out down the river on the day named, "*ready or not ready.*"[39] As a result, the *Albemarle* set forth on the specified day, with defensive armor on "one side only," and insufficient coal supplies for fuel, so that they had to burn "bacon to make steam."[40]

The *Albemarle* rammed and sank

some Federal gunboats, and chased others from the area around Plymouth back into the sound. She aimed her guns on the town, and helped bring about the surrender and capture of several thousand prisoners, plus "immense stores of food and valuable supplies of all kinds."[41]

The 8th Regiment of Clingman's brigade waited in front of one of the forts at Plymouth, "rushed upon the works, leaped into the ditch surrounding the fortifications and attempted to scale the walls." They were driven out of the ditch by hand grenades thrown from inside the fort by the enemy. They then attempted to "force the palisades," which had "loop-holes" from which the Union soldiers could fire their guns at the attacking Confederates. Many of the men of the 8th Regiment were "shot through the head." When the enemy inside withdrew their guns to reload, the Confederates outside had gotten so close they could thrust their own guns into those same holes and fire inside at the enemy.[42] The 8th Regiment moved around the fort to a gate at the rear. The gate burst open, and the regiment rushed in and those inside the fort surrendered.[43]

Another fort still remained in possession of the Yankees. The 8th Regiment then "formed and attempted to storm" Fort William. The men charged up to the ditch, but found they could not go any farther. They had two choices: either fall back or surrender. They decided to fall back, and when they did, they were fired upon by the enemy; many of the men were killed or wounded. The 8th Regiment lost 154 men killed or wounded, about a third of its entire force.[44] The Federals lost 2,834 men, including prisoners, plus a large amount of supplies.[45]

The Confederate raid on Plymouth was carried out successfully, and a grateful President Jefferson Davis promoted its leader, Brigadier General Robert F. Hoke, to major general on the field.[46] Congress confirmed Hoke's promotion and his commission bore the date of the victory at Plymouth — April 20, 1864. General Robert E. Lee wrote to President Jefferson Davis: "I am very glad of general Hoke's promotion, though sorry to lose him, unless he can be sent to me with a division."[47]

Hoke, born in 1837 at Lincolnton, North Carolina, was educated at the Kentucky Military Institute. He entered the service of the Confederacy in April 1861 as a member of Company K, 1st Regiment, and was immediately commissioned a second lieutenant. After being promoted to captain, Hoke was known for his "coolness, judgment and efficiency," a reputation gained during the battle of Big Bethel. After the reorganization of the State's troops in 1862, Hoke was commissioned "lieutenant-colonel" of the 33rd Regiment. In the battle at New Bern on March 14, 1862, he was "distinguished for gallantry." Hoke subsequently took command of the regiment, and participated as a part of Branch's Brigade in Virginia during the battles of Hanover Court House, Mechanicsville, Gaines' Mill, Frayser's Farm, and Malvern Hill.[48]

After being assigned to command the 21st Regiment of Trimble's Brigade, a part of Early's Division, Hoke was in command at the battle of Fredericksburg and was praised by both Early and Thomas J. "Stonewall" Jackson. Hoke had been wounded at Chancellorsville on May 4, so he was not involved in the fighting at Gettysburg. He had recovered enough to report to General George Pickett at Petersburg for duty in January 1864.[49]

Drewry's Bluff, May 4–16, 1864 (Including Port Walthall Junction, Swift Creek, and Bermuda Hundred Line)[50]

During the first week in May, Federal forces under General U. S. Grant set out to crush Lee's Army and capture Richmond, Virginia. Grant had 130,000 men, while Lee had only half that number. The two armies fought almost daily, but Grant still found the Confederate army between him and Richmond. Grant then decided on a new plan of attack and determined, by laying siege to Petersburg and cutting the railroad connections to the south, to starve the Confederates into submission.[51] He sent a 30,000-man force under the command of General Benjamin F. Butler to City Point near Petersburg to destroy the railroad connections between Petersburg and Richmond. Grant's plan was to continue his own movement against Lee's army, and move on to Richmond by the northeast. He also sent other Federal forces to Petersburg, and then to move on to take Richmond from the southeast. After moving up the James River by boat and embarking at City Point, Butler's army was set to capture Petersburg and move on to Richmond.[52] On May 4, the Federals had occupied both City Point and Bermuda Hundred.[53] While Butler was instructed to entrench at City Point, Grant left further movement to Butler's discretion, as long as he captured Petersburg and moved toward Richmond, his main objective.[54]

Many of the Confederate commanders were alarmed at the situation. Pickett, in charge at Petersburg, repeatedly requested reinforcements, especially when he observed the Federals landing at City Point. At that time, Petersburg was defended by only one regiment of Clingman's men, in addition to the "city battalion, and the militia."[55] Had Butler (Fig. 13) moved immediately on Petersburg, he could have easily captured the city while Lee was occupied holding off Grant's massive army at the Wilderness (May 5–7, 1864) and Spotsylvania (May 8–18).[56]

Fig. 13. Union General Benjamin F. Butler, who was "bottled up" at Bermuda Hundred; taken between 1860 and 1865. Brady National Photographic Art Gallery, Washington, D.C. (Library of Congress)

The first two weeks of May saw action at Drewry's Bluff on the James River just below Richmond. President Davis had placed all of the region south of Richmond under the command of General G. T. Beauregard, and he was given some troops from the Richmond garrison. Beauregard also sent for reinforcements from South Carolina, and sent for Major General Robert F. Hoke in North Carolina.[57] Beauregard replaced General George E. Pickett as area commander, but before Beauregard arrived in Petersburg, Pickett learned that Butler was nearby. At the time, Petersburg was short of defenders, with only one regiment, the Washington Artillery of 21 guns, and the City Battalion of Petersburg, plus some militia.

To meet Butler's threat, Clingman's Brigade, already on the railroad cars traveling from Petersburg to Suffolk on May 3, was called back to Petersburg.[58] Hagood arrived after a day on May 6, and by daylight the next morning, there were 2,668 Confederate infantry at Port Walthall Junction facing Butler's Union troops. Confederate general D. H. Hill was sent to advise Hagood and Johnson.

As part of his overall strategy, Union general U. S. Grant had ordered Butler to move his Army of the James against Richmond from the south side of the James River. Butler was reinforced by Gillmore's X Corps from South Carolina and, with a force of 36,000 men, including Major General William P. Smith's XVIII Corps, moved up the James River. Grant ordered Butler to take City Point and entrench, but Richmond was to remain the main objective. However, Grant left the details up to Butler, and Butler "botched the job." Instead of setting up a base at City Point, as Grant had instructed, Butler concentrated his forces at Bermuda Hundred, a 25-square-mile peninsula. At Bermuda Hundred, Butler wasted three days building entrenchments across the narrow neck of the peninsula. He also rejected recommendations from his commanders to cross the Appomattox and take Petersburg from the east.[59]

A few Confederate troops were dispatched from Petersburg to meet Butler's advance.[60] Clingman and the 51st Regiment had been guarding the railroad from Petersburg to Suffolk, and were part of those troops sent to meet Butler. On May 5, together with a battery of artillery, they marched out to meet the Federals advancing from Bermuda Hundred. Clingman's men took their positions at Port Walthall Junction at about 5 p.m., and they were to be reinforced by Hagood's Brigade.[61]

Before Hagood's Brigade could arrive, Ransom also ordered Brigadier General Bushrod Johnson to assist in stopping the enemy.[62] These units arrived that night.[63] On May 6, the enemy attacked and drove the Confederates from their position. On May 7, Clingman received orders to return to Petersburg to meet the approaching enemy along the City Point Road. On May 9, Clingman's men, Hoke's Brigade, and Sturdivant's artillery made a "reconnaissance on the City Point Road," and halted at the enemy picket lines. Then they returned to their entrenchments. On May 10, Clingman was ordered to report with his brigade to the Richmond Turnpike to join Hoke. It was at this point that Clingman's Brigade officially became part of Hoke's Division, from which the Brigade was never separated during the remainder of the war.[64]

Port Walthall Junction — May 6–7, 1864[65]

Instead of moving immediately on Petersburg, Butler wasted three days constructing entrenchments at Bermuda Hundred.[66] This gave the Confederates time to shift troops to meet him. Butler entrenched himself on the narrow neck of land between the James and Appomattox rivers and sent out a brigade to destroy the Richmond-Petersburg railroad at Walthall Junction, six miles from Petersburg and below Richmond, in an attempt to cut communications between Richmond and Petersburg.[67] The Confederates moved as well, and a few companies of Hagood's Brigade left Petersburg. When they arrived at Walthall Junction, they saw the Federal troops advancing. After a short battle, the Federals retired. The 51st North Carolina, led by Clingman, arrived on the scene, and Bushrod Johnson came down from Drewry's Bluff with 1,100 men. The fighting renewed on May 7, and the Federal force was driven off. Clingman and his men were recalled to Petersburg on May 7 to meet the enemy advancing from City Point. On May 9, Clingman's brigade and another brigade made a "reconnaissance: on the City Point road."[68]

In the fighting at Walthall Junction, the Federals lost 289 men; the Confederates lost 184.[69]

Swift Creek — May 9, 1864[70]

The breastworks at Swift Creek were defended by 1,100 of Johnson's men, 2,400 of Hagood's and Clingman's 51st Regiment, which probably consisted of fewer than 500 men, supported by 18 pieces of field artillery. When Butler moved his army to Swift Creek, "a rapid artillery engagement ensued," and the fighting continued into the night.[71]

On May 9, McKethan's 51st Regiment of Clingman's Brigade guarded the railroad bridge, and Tilman's Brigade guarded Level Ford on the Appomattox River. Confederate artillery was in place. The Confederates occupied Fort Clifton, and drove off enemy gunboats.[72] A movement by Butler toward the breastworks at Swift Creek on May 9 was blocked by Johnson's and Hagood's troops, and Clingman's 51st Regiment under Colonel Hector McKethan—a force of about 4,000 infantry. After an artillery engagement, the fight continued into the night of May 9 with Butler massed in front of the Confederate works. Clingman's Brigade was positioned to the left of the Confederate artillery. The next day was spent in watching and firing at the enemy. On May 11, the battle resumed and the enemy were driven from the Confederate front by afternoon. On May 12, Confederate artillery and infantry moved down the turnpike to Bermuda Hundred.[73]

Butler, having discarded a proposal by Gillmore and Smith to use a pontoon bridge to move a large force cross the Appomattox River, decided instead to move cautiously toward Petersburg. He was halted at Swift Creek by a small Confederate force, and he quickly withdrew on May 10 to Bermuda Hundred.[74]

Butler had intended to cross Swift Creek on May 10 and go on to capture Petersburg. However, the action at Swift Creek stopped Butler from taking Petersburg, and when he withdrew, the Confederates were able to transfer troops to Drewry's Bluff in the defense of Richmond.[75]

Participants in the action at Swift Creek on May 9–10, 1864, were the Federal X and XVIII corps of the Army of the James, against the troops under Beauregard's command. The Union forces sustained casualties of 90 killed, 400 wounded; Confederate casualties were 500 wounded and missing.[76]

Drewry's Bluff, May 12–16, 1864[77]

The fighting at Drewry's Bluff pitted Union general Benjamin F. Butler, commanding the Army of the James with superior numbers, against Confederate general Pierre G. T. Beauregard.[78] Drewry's Bluff, only about eight miles below Richmond, is a high bluff above the James River. It is a strategic point from which the Confederates could keep Federal boats from coming up the James River to attack Richmond. It was protected by a line of works that ran westward from Fort Darling, on the south side of the James River at Drewry's Bluff, across the Richmond and Petersburg turnpike, and continued on westward across the Petersburg-Richmond railroad, which ran parallel to the turnpike. Another line of works extended from Fort Stephens east of the turnpike, and branched off from it to the southwest, to a point near the railroad.[79]

With Butler back at Bermuda Hundred, Beauregard ordered Hoke to move six brigades to Drewry's Bluff. Beauregard himself went to Drewry's Bluff and left Petersburg in the hands of General Whiting with only a small force. At Drewry's Bluff, Hoke's Division took a position on the outer line of breastworks, between the railroad and the turnpike on the far west side of the line of breastworks. On May 12, the fighting began when Ransom's Brigade (part of Hoke's Division) was attacked from the rear by the enemy who had gotten between them and Colquitt's Brigade.[80]

May 12, 1864

On May 12, Butler decided to move on Drewry's Bluff, and advanced the corps of Smith and Gillmore. Other Federal units did not participate. Hinks' division stayed at City Point, and Ames's division was moved to Walthall Junction. Kautz's cavalry carried out a raid on the railroads around Richmond. Federal gunboats also moved up the James River to Chaffin's Bluff.

After Beauregard arrived at Drewry's Bluff on May 13, he ordered an early morning attack. When the signal was given, the men of Clingman's Brigade went over the breastworks, crossed the ditch in front, and advanced to meet the enemy under heavy fire. Clingman's Brigade penetrated the enemy lines, but found they were unsupported, and were being fired upon by the enemy from the rear and on both flanks. However, they held their ground, and when Butler withdrew, they followed him to his entrenchments at Bermuda Hundred.[81]

May 13–15, 1864

On May 13, 14, and 15, Clingman's Brigade encountered sharp skirmishing and were forced back behind the inner line of entrenchments. Pickets, placed in pits about 150 yards in advance of Hoke's position, were under heavy fire, and could only be relieved at night. The 8th Regiment of Clingman's Brigade sustained several casualties. Captain. T. J. Jarvis, later Governor of North Carolina, United States senator, and minister to Brazil, received a wound to his right arm while on the picket line. Captain Junius N. Ramsey was wounded while mounting the breastworks. Ramsey had been in the war since the firing at Fort Sumter began in April of 1861. Ramsey is credited with having "fired the second cannon that was aimed at the fort [Fort Sumter] in the bombardment."[82]

Captain Burgwyn described in his diary on Friday, May 13, 1864, how "our lines fell back to the inner line of entrenchments around Drewry's Bluff about three-fourth mile in rear of the first." Because of the skirmishing, the brigade suffered some losses. The enemy had a distinct advantage by being in some thick woods, and were able to approach the "sharpshooters" undetected.[83]

May 14, 1864

Heavy fighting continued through the next two days. On May 14, Clingman's Brigade "skirmished all day" and lost about "one-fourth killed and wounded" of those engaged in the fighting. They were under artillery fire from the enemy as well. The picket lines, which had earlier been driven back about 150 yards, were "advanced" and "pits dug for the men."[84]

May 15, 1864

The next day, May 15, the skirmishing continued, but Clingman did not lose as many men as on the previous days because the men were in the "rifle pits."[85] On May 15, President Davis arrived and ordered Beauregard to assault the enemy on May 16. Beauregard protested because of the disparity in numbers and because the Yankees were behind breastworks. The Union force had been estimated at 17,000, and the Confederates at 10,800. The Confederate army was composed mainly of Hoke's Division, which included the brigades of Corse, Barton, Johnson, Hagood, Colquitt, and Clingman.[86] Beauregard wanted Lee to fall back toward Richmond, and to send 10,000 men to assist at Drewry's Bluff. That would have given Beauregard a total of about 25,000 effectives. In addition, Beauregard wanted Whiting moved from Walthall Junction to attack Butler's rear. Beauregard also planned to attack Butler's right flank and cut him off from his base at Bermuda Hundred on May 15. As an alternative plan, Beauregard proposed to move his troops across the river and attack Grant's left flank while Lee attacked Grant's front. However, President Davis disagreed with both plans.[87] Beauregard had no choice but to begin a full-scale assault, as ordered by Davis, on May 16, without the help of Lee's 10,000 men.[88]

The Confederate offensive began as planned. By six in the morning, Ransom's men had carried the enemy's breastworks and captured over 500 prisoners. By 6:30 a.m., Colquitt's Brigade was sent to reinforce Ransom. Ransom, misinformed that the enemy was driving in Hoke's left line, sent a regiment to Hoke's assistance until a reserve brigade could come up. The ensuing confusion necessitated a change in the original plan, and eventually Beauregard ordered Ransom to halt his men where they were.[89]

Hoke's Division was heavily engaged, but had not been driven back, and the reserves were ordered in. Clingman's 8th Regiment moved forward to charge.[90]

As soon as the order was received to charge, Captain Burgwyn jumped up on the parapet, waved his hat and "yelled with all my might as soon as I could cross the ditch in front." He ran ahead of his regiment, waving his hat, and urging them to follow and "nobly did they come though the enemy's sharpshooters fired as fast as possible from rifles that shot seven times in succession…." There was much confusion and disorganization, but even through thick underbrush "not a man faltered."[91] (There is additional information on Burgwyn's role in the fight at Drewry's Bluff in Chapter XI, *Heroes, Cowards or Fools*.)

On the right of the battle line, Hoke had pushed his skirmishers forward and used his artillery.[92] Two regiments of Clingman's Brigade were ordered to reinforce Johnson's Tennessee troops on their left, but they failed to drive the enemy entirely from their positions because of the larger numbers of men positioned behind "strong entrenchments."[93] Beauregard then ordered Hoke to relieve his right center with those men on his right, and Hoke ordered up Clingman's remaining regiments and Corse's whole brigade.[94]

Butler's planned attack on May 15 was canceled because his men were involved in "defensive measures" and he had no troops left to mount an attack. Beauregard quickly gathered 10 brigades into three divisions and prepared to attack, hoping to totally defeat Butler's Union troops. At 4:45 A.M. on May 16, the four brigades of Ransom's Division attacked the Federal right. The Confederate troops of Gracie and Lewis advanced, followed closely behind by those of Terry and Fry. Within an hour, they had overpowered the Union forces of Heckman's Brigade, and captured Heckman, together with five stands of colors and about 400 prisoners. However, Ransom's Brigade had suffered heavy casualties and run low on ammunition, and his troops had become disorganized in the fog. Union generals Weitzel and Brooks repulsed the Confederate frontal attacks in the center. On the opposite flank, Hoke's attack was delayed by the fog until about 6:30 A.M. Then with Johnson Hagood's men on the left, Bushrod Johnson advanced and gained some ground along Gillmore's front. Corse and Clingman's Confederate brigades advanced on the extreme right, but they had to be called back when a gap opened in the lines between them and Bushrod Johnson's men. Johnson then came under heavy fire on his right flank and had to be reinforced. After some very confused fighting, Butler withdrew his forces to prevent them being cut off by Ransom's. By 10 A.M., Beauregard had used up all his reserve forces, Hoke was still under attack, and Ransom did not believe he could continue to advance his men. The activity at Drewry's Bluff almost wiped out Ransom's Division, but it reformed on the turnpike, and Colonel R. H. Keeble was put in command temporarily. They remained there until ordered to "close up on General Clingman." By this time, the fighting was over.[95]

At the time, Butler did not recognize that his position at Bermuda Hundred was one from which he would be unable to move. Surrounded on three sides by water (the Appomattox and James Rivers), his only avenue of movement was effectively blocked by the Confederates. He advised officials in Washington that he and his forces had landed, entrenched, and destroyed many miles of railroad, and he bragged that he was in a position to hold out against the "whole of Lee's Army."[96] This was true, of course, but while in his secure, defensive position, Butler was unable to carry out Grant's orders to move against Richmond.[97]

The Confederates tightened their lines and sent reinforcements to Lee. Hoke's Division became temporarily a part of Lee's Army of Northern Virginia.[98]

A division was composed of three or four brigades, commanded by a major general, and it, together with cavalry and artillery, formed a complete fighting unit. As part of a division, the movements of Clingman and his men are sometimes hard to determine. Some official reports mention "Hoke's Division" but omit the names of the individual brigades or brigade commanders involved.

Drewry's Bluff, Virginia, May 16–20, 1864

Hoke's Division was outside the "intermediate line of entrenchments" around Drewry's Bluff, and between that line and the outer line of entrenchments occupied by the enemy.[99]

Colonel Hector McKethan, commander of Clingman's 51st Regiment, said of the action on May 16 that, after the order came to mount the works and charge the enemy, his men did so "over ground strewn with fallen trees … but pressed forward carrying line after line of the enemy until we had them in full retreat...."[100]

The enemy was forced to give way, but a gap was left between the troops on Clingman's left and his own command. This forced him to fall back to prevent a flank movement, which would have isolated Corse. Corse, in turn, retreated. After his retreat, neither Corse's nor Clingman's men participated much in the events that day, although "both were afterward marched again to the front and gave evidence of their readiness to perform any duty...."[101]

The early morning fog on the 16th of May had made it difficult to distinguish friend from foe, and the action resulted in great slaughter.[102] By 4 o'clock in the afternoon, Beauregard reported that the enemy had been driven back, and a general advance was ordered involving all Confederate forces. Corse's and Clingman's men were moved to a line of works on a hill west of the railroad.[103]

On May 16, the Confederate forces under Beauregard attacked Butler's troops. The action was "sharp and decisive. Butler was forced back to his entrenchments, and withdrew to Bermuda Hundred.[104] Beauregard followed by the next day and, with the brigades of Gracie, Corse, Clingman, Hoke, Walker, Hunton, Ransom, Barton, Hagood, Kemper and Martin, plus those forces of Wise in place in front of Butler's entrenchments,[105] Butler's entire Army of the James was "completely shut off from further operations against Richmond as if it had been in a bottle strongly corked," a phrase attributed to General U.S. Grant. The epithet "Bottled-Up Butler" followed Benjamin F. Butler the rest of his life.[106]

The Confederates were eventually able to form a line of battle on the dirt road between Richmond and Petersburg and to move forward to occupy the enemy's first line of entrenchments. Clingman's Brigade, together with the 44th Tennessee Regiment, moved to support Captain Martin's artillery, which engaged the enemy on the second day of fighting.[107]

The fighting at Drewry's Bluff lasted three days. During the third day, Clingman's Brigade encountered some sharp skirmishing and were forced back to the inner line of entrenchments. Pickets were placed in pits 150 yards in advance of Hoke's Division, and they came under such heavy fire that they could only be relieved at night. Several men of the 8th Regiment were wounded.[108]

The statistics for the fighting from May 12 to 16 are large. Of the 15,800 soldiers of the Army of the James, commanded by General Butler, 390 were killed, 2,380 wounded, and 1,390 missing. Of the estimated 18,025 Confederates of General Beauregard, 400 were killed, 2,000 wounded, and 354 missing.[109]

Beauregard reported that five pieces of artillery, five stands of colors, and 1,400 prisoners had been taken at Drewry's Bluff.[110] Corse and Clingman's combined losses were 394.[111] Clingman's Brigade lost 30 men killed, 184 wounded, and 23 missing for a total of 237.[112] The 51st Regiment of Clingman's Brigade lost about 119 men, and the 31st about 70, on May 16th alone.[113]

Bermuda Hundred May 17–June 14, 1864[114]

After the Confederate victory at Drewry's Bluff, Union General Butler withdrew his X and XVIII Corps to Bermuda Hundred. His troops were almost immediately "bottled up" by Confederate earthworks.[115]

Union brigadier general Edward W. Hinks reported on May 18, 1864, from City Point, that "Clingman's Brigade, three regiments of infantry, and a battery of six guns came down from Petersburg to within 2 miles of the [Federal] works at City Point, and returned by the river road."[116]

Ware Bottom Church, May 20, 1864

In front of Butler's entrenchment at Bermuda Hundred, the 85th Pennsylvania and the 39th Illinois had a skirmish with Confederates. That same day, the rifle pits of Ames and Terry were captured by the Confederates. Howell's Brigade of Union troops was reinforced by the 6th Connecticut and the positions were regained,[117] but the Federals lost 702 killed and wounded. The estimated Confederate losses were 700 killed, wounded and missing.[118]

Second Battle of Cold Harbor, Virginia, May 31, June 1–3, 1864

May 31, 1864

U. S. Grant had decided to "end things," and he amassed his troops for a major assault on Lee's army. The Second Battle of Cold Harbor was the next major battle after the Wilderness. Like other major battle sites, Cold Harbor was not even a town, but a meeting place of several roads of strategic importance to the Federal army. At "Old" Cold Harbor there was a tavern, a well, one or two houses, and a blacksmith shop. This site was behind Confederate lines during the first battle on June 26–28, 1862.

In the second battle at Cold Harbor in June 1864, the lines were reversed. The crossroads at "Old" Cold Harbor where Clingman's Brigade and Fitzhugh Lee's cavalry attempted to drive Federal general Phil Sheridan away remained in Union hands. The major fighting took place several hundred yards south near a crossroads called "New" Cold Harbor.[119] This second battle, although fought over much of the same ground as the first, also saw minor engagements at Gaines' Mill, Salem Church, and Hawes' Shop.[120]

The South did not have the men to replace the men lost at the Battle of the Wilderness. General Lee, therefore, began to make all possible efforts to save the lives of men,[121] and preferred to fight from behind entrenchments and fortifications. However, the Confederates put every available man into the lines at Cold Harbor. A deserter reported to Union Colonel George H. Sharpe that "all business had ceased in Richmond, that stores, shops and government departments were closed" so that men could be spared for battle. Sharpe also noted that he knew Confederate commander Beauregard had 12 brigades positioned in front of General Butler at Bermuda Hundred, which included Hagood's and Evans' South Carolina brigades, and Martin's and Clingman's North Carolina brigades.[122]

At the time of the Second Battle of Cold Harbor, Clingman's Brigade consisted of 122 officers and 1,433 men, for an aggregate present of 1,596. The total of men both present and absent was 2,900.[123] Clingman's regimental commanders were Colonel J. R. Murchison (8th), Lieutenant Colonel C. W. Knight (31st), Colonel Hector McKethan (51st), and Colonel J. D. Radcliffe (61st).[124]

According to Grant's marching plan, the various corps of the Army of the Potomac moved out from the banks of the North Anna on the night of May 26, 1864.

Fig. 14. Bones of soldiers killed at Cold Harbor, Virginia, being collected for burial. Photo taken in April 1865. John Reekie, photographer. (Library of Congress)

Lee responded quickly, and early on the morning of May 27th, set his force in motion. On May 31, Union general Sheridan's cavalry reached "Old" Cold Harbor. He had been ordered by U. S. general George Gordon Meade to "hold at all hazards."[125] Grant's plan was to launch a two-pronged attack on the Confederate lines.[126]

Hoke's Division had been ordered to Cold Harbor by way of Richmond. They were to march to Mechanicsville and stop there.[127] On May 30, 1864, Hoke's Division numbered 7,656 men. The troops were seasoned and were a much needed addition to Lee's Army of Northern Virginia.[128] Assistant Adjutant General W. H. Taylor directed Major General R. H. Anderson to see that "every man fit for duty" be present for the upcoming battle. He advised Anderson to cooperate with Major General Robert F. Hoke.[129] Major General W. H. F ("Fitz") Lee reported at 3:15 P.M. on May 31, from "Old" Cold Harbor, that enemy cavalry were advancing. Clingman's Brigade left the trenches at Bermuda Hundred about 2 o'clock on the morning of May 31. Clingman's men "halted between Gaines' Mill and Mechanicsville," about two miles from Old Cold Harbor. Major General Fitz Lee wanted General R. E. Lee to order Clingman's Brigade to "assist in securing this place ['Old' Cold Harbor]."[130] A few miles from Lee's headquarters, Clingman received orders to proceed by way of Mechanicsville and Gaines' Mill to Old Cold Harbor to support Fitzhugh Lee's cavalry.[131] After moving about two or three miles beyond Mechanicsville, Clingman received an order from Hoke to await further orders. When, after three hours, he had received no further orders, Clingman proceeded to Cold Harbor "to take a position to the left of the main body of cavalry." He placed the 31st Regiment on the right, the 8th in the center and the 51st on the left.[132]

Lee had positioned his army with Hoke's Division on the right near Cold Harbor. Next were portions of Longstreet's Corps—Kershaw, Pickett and Field. In the center were Ewell's Corps under Early, and Early's Division under Ramseur. A. P. Hill held the left part of the line. From North Carolina were the brigades of Martin, Clingman, Grimes, and Ramseur (now Cox), Johnston, Cooke, Kirkland (now under MacRae), Lane, Scales, and Hoke. With other portions of various regiments, the men from North Carolina were present in a total of 43 regiments of infantry, three of cavalry, and four batteries of artillery.[133]

When Clingman arrived with his brigade, he was ordered by Hoke to take a position to the left of that occupied by the cavalry. Hoke ordered the 51st Regiment to move forward and to the left about 400–500 yards to support part of the cavalry, who had dismounted and were acting as infantry, and to engage the enemy. Clingman, himself, led the regiment and put it in position at the "most exposed and dangerous part" of his line. He remained there with the men of the 51st as they came under heavy artillery and musket fire. After they had been fighting for some time, the cavalry on the left gave way, and "the enemy's advance then enabled them to annoy us a good deal by their fire on the left flank of our position…." Trouble began when two companies from the 51st Regiment on the left, "owing to the misconduct of their commander, Captain _____, failed to drive the enemy back there." Clingman tried to save the day, and ordered the captain three times to "open on them, yet he failed to do so, but kept his men lying down in the road about one hundred and fifty yards on my left."[134]

After the cavalry on Clingman's right gave way and moved to his rear, he saw that he would soon be surrounded. Clingman knew that the enemy would quickly pass on both sides, and he ordered Colonel McKethan to fall back a few hundred yards to the fence. Clingman sent for his other two regiments to advance to the fence, and as he attempted to show each of the regiments where they should position themselves, he was slightly wounded by a shell which "took away the front of my hat and slightly wounded my forehead." He was stunned for a moment, but not disabled. A few soldiers of the 51st and 8th regiments of his brigade were captured, but overall losses were less than 100. Clingman's assistant adjutant general, Edward White, was "severely wounded by a shell" while he was in the line with the 8th Regiment. The three regiments were reinforced about dark by the 61st Regiment, led by Colonel J. D. Radcliffe, and also by General Colquitt's Brigade.[135]

As a result of the attack by Union general Tolbert on "Fitz" Lee's cavalry and one brigade of Hoke's Division (Clingman's), the Confederates were driven from their position at "Old" Cold Harbor. A report by Federal general Phil Sheridan stated that "about half a regiment and 15 of Clingman's infantry" were captured.[136] Sheridan held his position until the next day, after being reinforced by General Wright,[137] and "routed" Clingman's Brigade, along with Fitzhugh Lee's cavalry, and took several prisoners. A Union officer reported there were "many rebel dead and wounded on the field."[138] Sheridan corrected an earlier report of the battle to say that 61 of Clingman's men, "instead of 15," had been captured.[139]

June 1, 1864

Early on the morning of June 1, Clingman withdrew his men about 200 yards to a position selected by General Hoke. Clingman's left rested at the "bank of a branch," and his right joined the units of General Colquitt. Kershaw's Brigade was on a hill to the left of Clingman, with a gap between members of Kershaw's and Clingman's men of about 75 yards. Clingman expressed the concern to one of Kershaw's brigade that Kershaw needed to extend his lines to the branch to join with Clingman's. Clingman decided that he would see about closing the gap with his men, but was informed by General Hoke that "this was unnecessary, as General Hagood's brigade would be stationed in front of my left and cover this interval." Hagood's Brigade took a position about 15 yards in front of Clingman's line, "so that his right regiment was in front of the left regiment of my brigade," and the rest of Hagood's men were in front of General Kershaw's position.[140]

The 61st Regiment was placed on the left of Clingman's line, then the 31st, then the 51st, and the left was held by the 8th Regiment. The men worked to dig out entrenchments with their bare hands, fence rails, and their bayonets. After 1 o'clock, Clingman inspected the lines of Hagood's men, but by 3 o'clock Hagood's Brigade had been ordered by Major General Hoke to move to the right, without Clingman's knowledge. General Hagood later told Clingman that he had "notified General Kershaw of his movement, but [Kershaw] gave [Clingman] no notice." So, Clingman, unaware that Hagood's men had moved, was at a disadvantage when the enemy rained heavy artillery fire down on them, and their infantry advanced. Hearing firing to his left where Kershaw's Brigade was placed, Clingman believed the enemy had made only a "feint in that direction, whereas, in fact, ... this brigade [Kershaw's] fled precipitately from the field after discharging their muskets." Clingman thought the greatest danger was to his left where the woods were thick, so he took a position near his 51st Regiment. Shortly, men were seen advancing through the trees, about 150 yards away, and Clingman ordered his troops not to fire, because he believed the approaching men were part of General Hagood's Brigade.[141]

Clingman described the bitter battle in detail:

> As soon as their true character was ascertained, we opened on them. They were then in line of battle and about one hundred yards distant. Though the places of those in front were for a time supplied by fresh troops, they ultimately gave way and were driven back out of sight. I ordered my men to stop firing to allow the smoke to be dissipated. Immediately in my front for seventy or eighty yards the ground slightly descended, then rose up into the slope of the hill. But a little to the left where the branch came down the ravine was continuous. Along this depression a large column of the enemy following their lines of battle advanced without being observed by us. As soon as they were drawn in the bottom they changed their route somewhat, inclining toward our right. They were in this manner brought up directly in front of the left of the Fifty-first where I was standing. After I had ordered the firing to cease and the smoke had partially been dissipated, I directed there should be no firing until the enemy should be seen again.
>
> As the hill where the enemy's line of battle had been, in our front, was much elevated above us, we did not from our position behind our hastily made earthworks, observe the low ground in front and to the left. On my repeating the order to look out for the approach of the enemy, Captain Fred. R. Blake, of my staff, who was just by my side on the right, elevated himself so as to overlook the heads of our men, who after loading their guns, were in a stooping position, [and] suddenly exclaimed: "Here they are, as thick as they can be!"[142]

About 30 of the enemy, in new blue uniforms, "marching at a quick-step" approached to within 8 or 10 paces of Clingman and his men. Clingman's Brigade made short work of these new recruits, who had never been in battle. The raw troops of the enemy had been given orders "not to fire a gun or to cheer until they had carried our works." Clingman ordered his men to redirect their fire: "Aim low and aim well!" The firing from Clingman's men "knocked down the front ranks of the [enemy's] column, while the oblique fire along the right and left cut down the men rapidly all along the column towards the rear." In a few minutes, "the whole column either acting under orders, or from panic, lay down." This was not advantageous, to say the least, because Clingman's seasoned troops continued to fire, reload, and fire again into the enemy lying on the ground. "The officers fired their repeaters, while such as had none occasionally borrowed muskets from privates and discharged them at particular individuals." Soon it was impossible to distinguish the living from the dead, and after about 15 or 20 rounds had been fired, Clingman ordered a halt to the firing. When the shooting stopped, a few of the surviving enemy rose, and "fled to the rear," but were shot as they attempted to escape.[143]

On the right of Clingman's line, the 61st Regiment held off an attack on their lines, and a large number were killed because they were not able to approach through the woods. Heavy underbrush lay in front of the 31st Regiment, but they repulsed the enemy. However, under cover of smoke and the thick woods, the enemy managed to get in position to attack both Clingman's left flank and the rear. The Federal soldiers, at a distance of 50 yards from the 8th Regiment, opened fire on the backs of the men of the 8th. The 8th Regiment "faced about, and with the left of the Fifty-first, endeavored to keep up the contest." The soldiers of Clingman's regiment were falling fast, and he ordered Lieutenant Colonel Murchison to "withdraw the survivors so as to form a new line of battle perpendicular to the first one, extending from the right of the Fifty-first to our rear." In this position, those of the 8th and 51st who had survived the surprise attack "held their ground for some time against the greatly superior forces of the enemy. Clingman then ordered the men of the 31st Regiment out of the entrenchments to join the 8th and the 51st. Together, the men of the three regiments charged the enemy and drove them back, and were able to reoccupy their original line temporarily, but were forced to fall back.[144]

While attempting to get the men into a new line, Clingman was informed that Colonel Murchison had been killed in the trench, by an enemy ball to the head. Clingman had spoken to the man just a few minutes earlier.[145]

Reassessing the situation, Clingman determined that there were no troops in their front, and he ordered Colonel Radcliffe to move his regiment out of the trenches to aid in the next attack. Afterwards, Clingman learned that Radcliffe, with the biggest part of his regiment, "did not obey this order and stayed in the trench." Clingman soon noticed their delay in moving, and he ordered Radcliffe and his men to form a new line of battle on the right. Lieutenant Colonel Devane took part of the regiment. In the meantime, Colonel Zachary of Colquitt's Brigade and five companies of the 27th Georgia Regiment arrived and charged together with Clingman's men in a battle that lasted for several hours until after sunset. The day ended with the enemy driven back and Clingman's Brigade occupying their original line from earlier in the day. Captain Henderson of the 8th Regiment had been killed in the last charge of the day.[146]

Clingman's Brigade received orders from General Hoke that night to "vacate" their lines, because the Confederate brigade under Hunton was moving up to occupy the ground. Clingman wanted to hold his position until Hunton's men arrived to prevent the enemy from gaining the ground, but he was told to "withdraw at once, as the other brigade was approaching, and confusion might be produced." So, Clingman reluctantly moved his men 150 yards to the left. As it turned out, Hunton's Brigade did not arrive until the next morning, and as Clingman had feared, the enemy had extended their lines to "within twenty or thirty yards of my left, being protected by a little elevation of the ground between us."[147]

A Virginia regiment moved up to take a position at right angles to Clingman's left. Troops were seen moving toward the Confederate line from the left. Thinking they were part of Hunton's command, Clingman called to them. Some of his officers thought that the approaching men were their own pickets, but Clingman replied, "We have no pickets out." By this time, the approaching force was only about 10 feet from the line, "but just as near as they could get by reason of the slight work thrown up high enough to cover a man to the hips." Clingman shouted, "Speak or you will be fired into." When he received no answer, he ordered his men to fire, and he barely escaped being shot by his own men, by falling to the ground as the muskets of his Confederates were discharged all around him. After a few rounds, the enemy left, having failed in their attempt to move up "silently to occupy a still larger share of our original line." The two forces were separated during the night by less than 50 yards.[148]

The fighting on June 1 also saw the loss of Captains Blake and Burgwyn, both wounded, in addition to Captain White. Clingman was, therefore, left "without a single staff officer present."[149]

June 2, 1864

On June 2, there was skirmishing but no major battle.

June 3, 1864

On Friday, June 3, the Federal forces made an attack at several points along the Confederate lines, although not heavily in front of Clingman's position. However, the right part of his line and the lines of General Colquitt's Brigade were engaged. Federal losses this day were heavy, and there was "no further attempt by them, except by slow approaches."[150]

Many veterans, historians, students and authorities on military history agree that the fighting at the Second Battle of Cold Harbor in front of General Hoke's (including General Clingman's) lines constituted perhaps one the greatest slaughters of the entire war.[151]

The fighting at Second Cold Harbor in Virginia was so intense Union General Ulysses S. Grant (Fig. 15) commented in his memoirs: "Cold Harbor is, I think, the only battle I ever fought that I would not fight over again under the circumstances. I have always regretted that the last assault at Cold Harbor was ever made." He concluded that "no advantage whatever was gained to compensate for the heavy loss we sustained. Indeed, the advantages other than those of relative losses, were on the Confederate side." Following that battle, Grant observed that his men no longer wished to fight "one Confederate to five Yanks."[152] Indeed, Fox estimates that over the 12-day period of June 1 to June 12, which included several peripheral battles at Gaines' Mill, Salem Church, and Hawes Shop, the Union Army—consisting of the II, V, VI, XI and XVIII Corps, and Sheridan's Cavalry—lost 1,844 killed, 9,077 wounded, and 1,816 missing (for a total of 12,737).[153] Confederate losses in the Army of Northern Virginia were fewer, Miller

Fig. 15. Major General Ulysses S. Grant, taken at Brady National Photographic Art Gallery, Washington, D. C. (Library of Congress)

federacy's spirits and hope for success. It proved, however, that the South would have to continue to take a defensive stance. As a result, Grant "changed his whole plan of operations, and instigated the siege of Petersburg, a siege that was to continue for a full year."[157]

Accusations that on June 1, the lines held by Clingman's and Wofford's brigades of Kershaw's Division were badly broken were denied by Clingman.[158]

Petersburg, Virginia, June 1864–April 1865

Petersburg, lying south of the Appomattox River, was a key element in the defense of Richmond, as well as a vital link with the states to the south. The defenses at Petersburg were composed of a heavy line of "redans" connected by a line of rifle-trenches, which could accommodate 25,000 men.[159] The Petersburg Campaign launched by Grant began in June 1864 and continued until May 1865.[160]

estimated, with 1,200 killed and wounded, and 500 missing.[154] Lee estimated losses at 20,000, with Grant loosing three times as many, or about 60,000.[155]

Historian Clement Eaton described Cold Harbor as the "most violent fighting of the campaign." The charge ordered by Grant against the Confederate entrenchments led to a "horrible slaughter." Eaton estimates Federal casualties at 55,000 men lost to "death, wounds, disease, and desertion."[156]

General Robert Lee saw the battle of Cold Harbor as one that raised the Con-

Union commander U. S. Grant waited ten days after the fighting at Cold Harbor before moving to Petersburg. He intended to take the city by storm, but after three days of intense fighting, the contest settled down to regular siege tactics.[161]

With most of the Confederates massed at Drewry's Bluff and Bermuda Hundred, Petersburg was left in a vulnerable position. General Beauregard began to worry that the city did not have enough men to save it from a Federal attack. He sincerely believed that at least 25,000 men were needed to protect the vast network of

Fig. 16. Interior of Confederate works at Petersburg, Virginia, taken April 3, 1865. (Library of Congress)

trenches and fortifications around the city.[162] Beauregard ordered a withdrawal of troops from the lines at Bermuda Hundred for the defense of Petersburg. He also ordered Clingman's Brigade to take a train from Port Walthall Junction.[163] On June 15, four of Hoke's brigades moved from Drewry's Bluff to Petersburg in a forced march. At Chester Station, railroad cars were available to take some of the men on to Petersburg. Additional trains arrived to pick up the remainder of Hagood's and Colquitt's brigades, but Clingman's and Martin's men were forced to travel on foot "by the shortest cut, through fields and dirt roads."[164]

The Federals were in position in front of Petersburg with 22,000 men before Confederate commander Beauregard could get troops moved there from other places. Until those reinforcements arrived, Petersburg was weakly defended by Wise's Brigade, some detached infantry, the local militia, and Dearing's cavalry, a force of about 2,200.[165] Thus, when the Federal assault on Petersburg began, Beauregard's

2,200 men faced Smith's attacking force of 20,000.[166]

June 15, 1864

An assault along the whole Confederate line at Petersburg was launched by Smith's Federal forces at 7:30 P.M. They seemed destined to succeed, when, relieved by General Hancock's troops, Smith called his men to a halt and the assault was called off until morning. This was a tactical error, because when Hoke and Bushrod Johnson and their men arrived, they established a new line to the rear of the last redan.[167]

June 16, 1864

Martin's and Clingman's men arrived in the city about midnight. Late the next day, on June 16, the Union batteries began a heavy assault on the Confederate lines. Two attacks were made on Clingman's position, "both of which were repulsed." The brigades of Clingman and Martin

Fig. 17. Confederate fortifications at Petersburg, Virginia, with chevaux-de-frise beyond, 1865. (Library of Congress)

were used to close a breach in Wise's line.[168] Wise had abandoned his position "in panic without firing a gun," leaving his works unprotected. The Federals repeated their charge several more times, but were repulsed each time. With the coming of darkness, the Federal troops captured the abandoned works and began firing from a closer position. Clingman ordered Burgwyn to "go down the line and detail every third man and form them in front of that position of our works in possession of the enemy." This was done and the fighting continued, somewhat unequally, until Ransom's Brigade arrived. With those reinforcements, the Confederates were able to retake the lost position. A Petersburg newspaper reported, however, that "Hoke's division stood last night like a rock wall and saved the city. They may be overrun, but no power on earth can drive them from a position." Clingman's aide, Hal Puryear, showed the paper to General Hoke, who remarked, "They should have said Clingman's Brigade, for no other troops of my command were engaged.[169]

June 17, 1864

The heavy fighting on June 16 pitted 70,000 Union troops against 10,000 Confederates, who had been reinforced. On June 17, after a series of assaults and countercharges, the Confederate lines were pierced. But Gracie's men suddenly appeared, "leaped over the works, and captured over 1500 prisoners, and drove the enemy pell-mell from the disputed point." The fighting that day continued until nearly midnight.[170]

Heavy fighting resumed and pickets from Clingman's 8th Regiment were driven inside the lines as the Federals advanced. The fighting began early and continued through the afternoon. About 5 o'clock, the enemy massed men along the front, and Clingman's men saw that another heavy assault was about to take place. It came about dark, and the Union forces succeeded in breaching the line to the right of the 8th Regiment. Beauregard ordered Hoke's Division to drive the enemy out, and the men obeyed to quickly reestablish their lines. After several hours of fighting the enemy retired.[171]

An English aristocrat, Francis Charles Lawley, described the fighting on June 17 at Petersburg as: "heavy assaults and fearful slaughters." He noted that the Confederates were so secure in their entrenchments that it was difficult to realize when walking down the streets of Petersburg that a besieging army of 100,000 Union troops lay only a few miles away.[172] He noted the enthusiasm of the Confederate troops and the difficulty some of their officers had in keeping the men from "rushing at the breastworks in front of them" to attack the enemy.[173]

Heavy fighting continued over the next four days, and the Union army lost 10,000 men.[174] Eventually, the assault at Petersburg settled down to regular siege warfare as the Federal forces continued their efforts to breach the line of trenches that almost encircled the city. To counteract these tactics and to forestall penetration of the Confederate lines, Beauregard ordered his men to fall back to a shorter line in the rear of the original lines.[175] This line held for months until the fortifications were abandoned in March 1865, near the end of the war.[176]

Initially, the defending units at Petersburg had been mixed up but were soon stationed by brigades. Clingman's Brigade was positioned west of the Charles City road, near the Appomattox River, where they suffered from the gunfire of Federals nearby. The lines of the two armies at this point were so close that the men of the opposing forces could talk to each other and swap tobacco, newspapers, and other items.[177]

Casualties at Petersburg from June 15 to 19 were Union killed, 1688; wounded, 8513; and missing, 1,185. Estimates of Confederate losses for the same period were 5,000 killed, wounded, and missing combined.[178]

Petersburg Mine Assault (The Crater)— July 30, 1864[179]

The idea to build a mine under the Confederate works and trenches around Petersburg was conceived by Union officer and former mining engineer Lt. Col. Henry Pleasants, of the 48th Pennsylvania. His regiment, composed mostly of coal miners, was positioned opposite Elliott's Salient. Pleasants pitched his idea to Burnside and it was approved by Grant. The mine was begun on June 25 and completed on July 23. The final length was 511 feet which extended 20 feet under the Confederate battery at the salient. It also had two lateral galleries which ran 75 feet under the Confederate trenches. The tunnel was 5 feet in height, and 4½ feet wide at the bottom and 2 feet wide at the top. Ventilation was achieved by a fire in a chimney near the entrance which drew stale air out of the mine.

Grant was never "enthusiastic" about the project, mainly because its location did not provide a "tactical exploitation" once the explosion was detonated. However, the plan was devised for Burnside's IX Corps to attack through the gap that would open up once the explosion occurred. Burnside selected his "colored division" for the initial assault. By July 18, Ferrero's division was brought up and its colored soldiers "given special training for the assault." Meade did not approve of the use of the colored troops and thought that there could be political "repercussions" if anything went wrong. He suggested a division of all white troops be used instead. Therefore, Burnside had his three division commanders "draw straws" to see which one of them would lead the assault. Ledlie's 1st Division got the short straw. In addition, Burnside neglected to make sure that the passageway through his own parapets was clear so that his forces could move unhindered by abatis. The Federal mine, completed on July 23, was filled with 8,000 pounds of explosive powder.[180] The Confederates learned of the operation about the first of July when they heard the "sound of pick axes digging, far underground." They dug a countershaft of their own with deep side trenches in order to determine the position of the Federal shaft.[181] Beauregard ordered construction of entrenchments across the neck of the salient and added additional heavy mortars there to thwart any attack.[182]

The Confederate engineers probed in various places but were never quite able to determine the exact location of the enemy tunnel. According to a Confederate deserter, one of their countermines was begun about 30 yards behind the Confederate works held by Clingman's men. This tunnel ran toward the Federal lines, then made a turn to the right. It was constructed by "boring holes in the earth" with a boring "tool." A row of holes about ten feet apart served as "listening galleries," to help the Confederates locate the Federal mine.[183]

However, the countermine was extensive. It measured over 368 feet by July 29. Hoke was given a section to maintain, and the "miners" of Clingman's Brigade were ordered to report to him. The work continued even after the explosion of the Federal mine, and both men and officers were detailed to dig.[184]

The explosion in the Federal mine was set for 3:30 A.M. on the morning of

July 30, but the fuse failed to ignite the powder. At 4:15, two Federal soldiers entered the tunnel and relit the fuse. The fuse ignited the powder this time, and the explosion occurred at 4:45 on July 30, 1864. It created a crater 170 feet long, 60 to 80 feet wide, and 30 feet deep. The blast was heard for miles, shaking the earth and awakening sleeping Confederates. An immense mass of earth was thrown hundreds of feet into the air.[185] Thousands of Yankees, including Negro troops, rushed into the crater, hoping to take the Confederate lines at the point where the explosion had created a breach.[186] At first the men on both sides were paralyzed by the shock of the explosion, but the Confederates soon rallied and prevented the Federals from overrunning their lines.[187] Confederate artillery began shelling the Union soldiers in the crater. Lee ordered men transferred from the trenches above and below the crater to form in a ravine about two hundred yards to the rear. Word passed up and down the lines to hold the Confederate attack until the Yankees began climbing out of the crater and then to "slaughter them." The Confederate line had to be reestablished at all costs. The Federal soldiers began climbing "out of the hole about 9 in the morning," and began running toward the opening in the Confederate lines. As they did, the Confederates sprang up, and the Federal assault was crushed.[188] The situation was so critical that General Lee came down on his horse, Traveler, to watch the Confederates repulse the attack.[189]

The Federal mine had been constructed under the Confederate lines at Bushrod Johnson's position. When the explosion occurred, the only Confederate divisions in the trenches were those of Hoke and Johnson.[190] Clingman's 8th and 61st Regiments were among those who assisted in repulsing the enemy during three successive attempts to take the Confederate lines after the explosion.[191] By noon, the battle of the crater was over, and the Confederates had reestablished their defensive line.[192]

According to the National Park Service, when the mine exploded on July 30, 1864, 278 Confederates were killed or wounded; nine companies of the 129th and 22nd South Carolina were "blown into the air."[193]

The estimated number of Federals engaged was 20,708[194] with 3,798 lost.[195] The estimated number of Confederates engaged was 11,466. Losses from Colquitt's and Johnson's division were 1,182; losses from Mahone's division and the 61st N.C. were not recorded. The National Park Service pamphlet on Petersburg gives an estimate of the total Confederate casualties at about 1,500.

The Federals lost a tremendous number of men in their attempt to blast through the Confederate lines, and were no closer to taking Petersburg than they had been before.[196] Confederate officers, who had seen "on horror's head horrors accumulated," were quoted in the London *Times* as saying, "their eyes had rested on no such other scene" as the "ghastly hole, into which wounded, dead, and shrieking men had together been thrust, a scene ... which baffled description."[197]

The explosion of the mine was somewhat of a Pyrrhic victory, because the losses of Federal troops were tremendous. In addition, the Federal assault failed to take the Confederate lines because of the lack of organization of the Federal troops and the difficulty the men had in getting across the hole left by the explosion. Lee and his generals absorbed the "frightful shock of the surprise explosion," and restored order among their "panic-stricken troops," in time to prevent the Union troops from "swarming through a gap nearly four hundred yards wide." Union casualties were twice those of the Confederates. This battle this day was a Confederate victory, and Petersburg was saved, for a time.[198]

Clingman and his men served in the trenches through June, July and most of August—the hottest months of the year. He and his men practically lived in the ground. They "walked in the ditches, ate in ditches and slept in pits." By June 25, Clingman and his men had spent 50 days in trenches, which included the time spent at Drewry's Bluff, Cold Harbor, Bermuda Hundred, and Petersburg.[199] There was no time to rest. Every day was devoted to surviving the fire on the trenches from the enemy batteries in front of the lines and from heavy mortars farther back.[200] At night, every Confederate soldier was detailed to either guard duty or to labor with pick and spade repairing works knocked down during the day."[201]

Trench warfare is, at best, extremely trying, and in the blazing sun of the summer of 1864, conditions at Petersburg were almost unbearable. It was necessary to rotate the troops every three days. The heat only added to other problems, such as poor sanitary conditions.[202] The men had to remain down in the trenches, because to expose one's head above the trenches was tempting a quick death. Sometimes soldiers would put their hats "on the end of their bayonets or ramrods" and raise them in the air. Within moments the hats were "perforated with bullets from Yankee sharpshooters."[203]

There was no shelter from either rain or sun, and there were casualties every day from enemy bombardment. Diseases, such as malaria, diarrhea, and scurvy, debilitated men and officers alike. There was no coffee, sugar or vegetables, and food could not be cooked in the trenches, but had to be carried "on the shoulders of men from the cook yards some miles in the rear." Rations consisted of "one pound of pork and three pounds of meal for three days" per man. Even under those conditions, while at Petersburg, the North Carolina troops behaved "admirably."[204]

In the end, though, but Union general Grant would not give up, and the siege of Petersburg continued. The firing from Federal sharpshooters and the bombardment from heavy artillery was nearly incessant. As a result, the number of Confederate troops decreased daily.[205] However, the Confederates managed to hold on to their position, but were kept on the defensive. They had no hope of defeating the attacking force of Grant's army. All that could be hoped for was to "delay the final assault."[206] The remainder of the summer was spent by the troops at Petersburg constructing new works and strengthening old ones.[207]

Sporadic fighting continued at Petersburg. Five prisoners from Colquitt's and Clingman's brigades captured by the Union forces reported that "Clingman was relieved in the trenches by Ransom's brigade at 10 o'clock this morning [August 9, 1864]." They also reported that a charge on the "left flank of the Fifth Corps" was made in the afternoon by Mahone's, Colquitt's and Clingman's brigades. According to the prisoners, their former Confederate associates had managed to drive the Federal skirmish line back and "were still advancing."[208] An almost identical report, only dated August 19, 1864 (instead of August 9), and directed to Major General Humphreys, adds that they "marched down the railroad."[209] The Confederates would soon be engaged in very heavy fighting along the Weldon Railroad south of Petersburg.

While the Federal troops continued to assail the fortifications at Petersburg, they also extended their lines and stepped up their attempts to cut rail communications between Petersburg and North Carolina. The Petersburg-Weldon Railroad was an important supply line for the Confederate armies in Virginia. As Grant extended his lines south from Petersburg, Lee had to do likewise to protect the Weldon railroad.[210] With both sides moving southward, a conflict was inevitable. On August 19, an assault on the railroad about three miles from Petersburg by the Union Fifty Corps was met by Confederates under General A.P. Hill.[211] The battle near the Globe Tavern was to have a devastating effect on Clingman as well as Clingman's Brigade.

August 14–15, 1864

After the failure of the Federal mine to breach the Confederate lines at Petersburg, Union general Hancock carried the Federal efforts to the north side of the James River at Deep Bottom Run, in an attempt to extend the Federal lines farther west and to cut communications with Petersburg. On August 14–15, the Federal troops of Warren's V Corps moved out of the trenches at Petersburg to gain a position south of that city on the Weldon Railroad near Globe Tavern. The Federal troops were ordered to destroy railroad track as far south as possible. Federal brigadier general Samuel Perkins Spear's cavalry brigade was attached to Warren's Corps.

The action began with a Federal assault by Major General Winfield Scott Hancock on the Confederate works at Deep Bottom, and this was followed almost immediately by an assault on the Weldon Railroad by the Federal forces. The Confederates' line was weakened at Petersburg and the surrounding entrenchments by their having to send troops to oppose Hancock at Deep Bottom. Union General Governor Kemble Warren led the attack on the railroad. The Weldon Railroad was a vital communication link, but it "was not as vital as the railroad from Danville, which was the main avenue to the fertile grain districts of the South."[212]

Globe Tavern, Virginia, and the Weldon Railroad, August 18–21, 1864[213]

The battles that were fought during this three-day period — August 18–21, 1864 — are also referred to as the Weldon Railroad and Six Mile House, and all are considered a part of the Petersburg campaign.

On August 18, when Warren reached the railroad, his only opposition was Dearing's Cavalry Brigade. Griffin's Division stopped on the west side of the track and began destroying the rails. Ayers's division moved north along the railroad and Crawford's division formed on his right (east). Cutler's division remained to the rear in reserve.

The weather was extremely hot and rainy, and the area was thickly wooded, making visibility poor. Confederates retaliated promptly as Heth attacked Ayers's left flank about 2 P.M., and was able to drive Dushane's Brigade back. Ayers pulled back initially, but then counterattacked. Federal losses on August 18 were 936.[214]

August 19, 1864

Federal general Hartranft encountered Confederate troops advancing through some woods who were believed to have been Clingman's men. The Confederates had "penetrated about 600 yards in the right and rear of Crawford's works, and through a corn-field, giving them full view of the space around Globe Tavern," and thus all the Federal troop movements. Hartranft moved his right regiment forward, and drove the Confederates through the woods and into the field, and captured a large number. However, the Confederates regrouped in the corn field and advanced, only to meet heavy fire from the Federals. They retreated, and rallied, and advanced again to within 75 yards of the Federal troops.[215]

The fighting continued along the Federal right. Colquitt attacked the Union troops of Hartranft and White, and was repulsed. Confederate general Beauregard telegraphed General Lee that "Colquitt and Clingman, in advancing through the thick undergrowth, lost their organizations, and were ordered to their camps to rally them."[216] The Federals were ordered to "attack and recapture the lost rifle-pits yet remaining in the enemy's hands," and White began to drive Colquitt back. The Confederate rifle pits were retaken, and "rows of muskets in stacks" were captured by the Federals. Confederate general Heth made two attempts to break the lines in front of Union general Ayres, but Ayres held, although he "lost some prisoners as well as a flag." About dark, Heth made another assault, but the Federals had been reinforced, of which he was unaware, and the gallant charge of Heth and his Confederate troops was repulsed.[217] Confederate general W. H. F. Lee tried to turn the Federal flank, but instead, was driven by Union brigadier general Samuel P. Spear's cavalry nearly to Ream's Station,[218] where fighting would continue a few days later. The Union troops celebrated, and Warren thanked his IX Corps for saving the day. General Meade telegraphed to congratulate Warren and his men on their "success."[219]

General Clingman's Brigade took part in Mahone's and Heth's attack on Warren's Corps on the 19th of August, 1864. Lieutenant General A. P. Hill reported that the enemy had been attacked at 4 o'clock by the brigades of Davis and Walker, under Heth, and the brigades of Colquitt, Clingman, and Mahone, under Major General Mahone. They succeeded in capturing about 2,700 Federal prisoners.[220]

In this engagement, General Clingman was severely wounded in the leg,[221] so that his return to the Army at all was "doubtful."[222] The word spread quickly and a few days later, the Union commander, Lieutenant General U. S. Grant, reported the rumors circulating that W.H. F. Lee had been "mortally wounded," and "General Clingman" was "losing a leg," and "General Sanders killed."[223] The Federal forces suffered considerable losses, but eventually succeeded in taking and holding the railroad line. The Confederates needed to recapture the railroad, and thus Lee ordered the assault on Warren's lines.[224]

On the previous day (August 18), Grant's left under Warren's command had been defeated, but they had held their position. The fighting on the 19th was more severe, and Warren reported that he had lost 4,455 killed, wounded or missing.[225]

August 20–21, 1864

During the night of August 20–21, Lee withdrew most of the troops from north of the James to help reinforce Hill, and Grant sent the rest of Hancock's corps to reinforce Warren.

With skirmishing having continued on August 20, on August 21, Hill launched an attack on Warren's new position, but gained no ground.

Federal reports of the action around the Globe Tavern, as gleaned from a Confederate deserter, said that the Confederate troops were positioned in front of the Union V Corps, beginning with the brigades of Mahone, Harris, Perrin, Wright, Colquitt, Clingman, Fry, and Davis. Ransom's brigade had relieved Clingman's, and Cooke's and Kirkland's men were in the trenches on August 20, 1864.[226]

Casualties, as estimated by Livermore, for the fighting of August 19 to 21, were[227]:

Federals engaged = 20,289, 1,303 killed, wounded, 3,152 missing

Confederates engaged = 14,787, 1,200 killed, wounded, 419 missing

For the three-day period, Orlando Willcox estimated 251 Union soldiers killed, 1,148 wounded, and 2,879 missing, most of whom were captured by the Confederates. Confederate general Hill lost at least 2,339, with approximately 1,200 killed, 720 wounded, and 419 missing.[228]

This attack on Grant's lines was deemed a Confederate victory. Clingman's men took three times as many prisoners as they had men in the field.[229] Overall, the Confederates captured 2,500 prisoners. Yet, the Confederates did not drive the enemy away from the railroad. The Federal forces then turned their attention further south along the railroad line and attacked at Reams's Station. Hancock's troops were moved up to a position behind Warren, and ordered to destroy a portion of the railroad. On August 25, the Federal forces encountered the Confederates A. P. Hill, Wilcox, Heth, and Mahone. The ensuing heated battled resulted in the breach of the enemy lines by Heth, and one line of breastworks was carried by the Confederates under General Hampton. Confederate losses were 720 men killed, wounded or missing, but Warren still held the Weldon Railroad.[230]

Fort Harrison, Virginia, September 29–30, 1864

The action now shifted north of the James River. General Benjamin Butler, with the corps of Birney and Ord, moved up the river to attack a strong fortification and entrenchments near Chapin's farm known as Fort Harrison. Some of Butler's men moved up on the Newmarket Road, and an engagement occurred there. On September 28, though, the Federals sent a column to surprise the fort, and the Confederates there surrendered after "a very feeble resistance on the part of the artillery," even while Confederate forces were moving to support the men inside the fort and prevent its capture. The capture of Fort Harrison was the one real success achieved by Butler.[231]

The loss of Fort Harrison to the Federal forces was a serious one because the structure occupied a commanding position below Drewry's Bluff and constituted the main defense of that part of the Confederate defensive lines. Confederate forces would have to be moved from Petersburg to retake this vital fort, which was just 8 miles south of Richmond and situated on the north side of the James River near Chaffin's Bluff.[232]

Along with Brigadier General Edward Porter Alexander's artillery, Hoke began moving men from the trenches of Petersburg on September 29. Lee ordered a pontoon bridge constructed across the James River. Clingman's Brigade, at the rear of the division, arrived at 10 P.M., even as the Federals continuously reinforced Fort Harrison.[233] General Charles W. Field was in favor of attacking immediately, before the Federals could send reinforcements to the fort. He was overruled, and the attack did not begin until the next day, September 30. The brigades of Anderson, Bratton, and Law of Field's Division were to make the assault, while Hoke was to attack on the other side. Hoke took advantage of a ravine to move his men to within two or three hundred yards of the fort.[234]

Clingman's Brigade was part of Hoke's Division of 12, 298 men.[235] With Clingman unable to lead his brigade because of his leg wound, Hector McKethan, the experienced colonel of the 51st Regiment, was put in charge of the brigade. Clingman's brigade was in the thick of the fight to retake Fort Harrison from the Federal forces.

General Lee had wanted a night attack on the fort, before the enemy could be

Fig. 18. Federal soldiers in front of bombproof headquarters inside Fort Burnham, formerly Confederate Fort Harrison, Virginia, taken between 1860 and 1865. (Library of Congress)

so firmly entrenched. However, this was not possible because all the troops had not arrived. Once all the Confederate forces were in place in front of Fort Harrison, an attack was ordered on the morning of September 30. Lee had about 16,000 men, but the Federals under Butler had 21,000.[236]

To attack the fort, Hoke's and Field's men, including Clingman's Brigade, would have to cross an open field guarded by Federal forces situated behind a rail fence. In order to storm the fort, the Federal skirmish line would have to be broken. Also in the path were sharp wooden spikes and stakes in front of the works. In addition, the Federal troops were supplied with Spencer repeating rifles. Hoke did not relish the upcoming battle. He tried to convince Lee that an attack would be "impracticable," and "would result only in loss of life without accomplishing any good end." A better plan, Hoke reasoned, was to construct a new line of defenses near where Hoke's Division was positioned, about 200 yards from the fort.[237] Officers of Clingman's Brigade agreed. Second Lieutenant A. A. McKethan of the 51st Regiment stated: "To have attempted its recapture under the circumstances was a mistake, and as carried out a terrible blunder on the part of some one...."[238] Colonel Hector McKethan, in charge of Clingman's Brigade at this time, and other officers on the field protested against the assault, because they saw that it was impossible for it to succeed, and that there would be heavy losses.[239]

The action did not go according to plan. "Anderson's men being put in motion merely to adjust the line, misunderstood the orders of their commander, leaped the breastworks of the enemy, rushed forward with a yell, and were soon past control." This forced the other brigades to move. General Hoke, who had not received the agreed-upon signal to begin, did not move. The enemy then were able to concentrate their fire on Field's Division. The main attack failed to take the fort, and Butler remained entrenched in a stronghold very close to Richmond.[240]

Captain William H. S. Burgwyn wrote extensively in his diary about the fight at Fort Harrison. He was among those captured and taken as a prisoner to City Point. His diary entry for Friday, September 30, 1864, describes how the brigade moved up early in the morning at 6 A.M. to the entrenchments, and waited until about noon to take a position from which they could charge the "enemy out of the works he had captured from us yesterday [Fort Harrison]." By 2 P.M. the Confederate artillery had begun to fire on the fort, and Clingman's Brigade, now under McKethan, began their charge from their location on the front left. Behind McKethan's men were General Colquitt's Brigade, who were to "act as our support," and all the line was to charge "simultaneously." Burgwyn states that as soon as they saw General Field's Division charge, and then driven back, "word came for our brigade to go forward." Burgwyn had been ordered by Major James M. Adams to "take charge of a line of skirmishers in the rear" to keep them moving forward, and he charged along with the brigade. "We started slowly up the hill till we came on top then with a yell we started on the charge." Burgwyn, along with the 31st North Carolina, was ordered to move towards the right by Colonel McKethan, "as he did not know how it would do" under the command of the new regimental commander, Colonel Caleb B. Hobson. They immediately ran into trouble.

> As we started the whole Yankee line opened on us in plain view and about four hundred yards and as I after found the Yankees had massed their troops in the works right in our front having virtually vacated the works to their left and I suppose they were three lines deep behind their works and as they were all armed with seven shooters the fire was awful.
> By the time we got [with]in about seventy yards of their works our line was entirely broken not from any falling back but literally from the men being cut down by piles [sic] by the brigade's fire and our support, Colquitt's Brigade, having returned behind the hill being appalled at the sight of the mortality and fire. What remained of our brigade lay down on the ground somewhat protected by an undulation between the hill from where we started and the hill [where] the enemy were.... From the time we lay down about 3:00 P.M. until dusk there we lay about seventy yards from the enemy line, some entirely exposed and some shielded from view by some weeds and grass, but all entirely at the mercy of the enemy....[241]

About dark, the enemy within Fort Harrison sent out a line of skirmishers and captured all the Confederates who had not surrendered, including Captain Burgwyn.

Writing to Clingman, Colonel Hector McKethan was proud to report that he had been told by officers at the scene that they had "never seen men advance more gallantly under such a murderous fire."[242] He gave the grim statistics to the General: "while charging unsupported over an open field, a distance of full 450 yards, we took into the fight 848 men and 63 officers. Of that number but 18 officers and 366 men came out unhurt."[243]

"The brigade is literally cut to pieces," the sole surviving officer of the 31st Regiment declared. About 122 men had been killed. Three of the four regimental commanders had been killed, and 27 of 40 company commanders were among the casualties. Approximately 122 men were killed out of the brigade, and 203 captured. All eight flags of McKethan's (Clingman's) Brigade were lost, plus the two of the 6th South Carolina. A few flags were destroyed by their own men.[244]

McKethan reported casualties as 16 known dead, 220 wounded, and 291 missing.[245] Most of Clingman's experienced regimental and brigade officers had already been either killed or wounded, and the fight at Fort Harrison further depleted their ranks. Other, less experienced men had to take command. Major Rufus A. Barrier became commander of the 8th Regiment, and Major Henry Harding took command of the 61st.[246] Yet, in spite of all, Colonel McKethan reported to General Clingman on December 6, 1864, that there were still 1,100 men of Clingman's brigade who were "present and are comfortably quartered."[247]

W.H.S. Burwgyn saw the failure to take the works at Fort Harrison as a result of Field's Division failing to "drive the enemy or turn their right flank and to General Kirkland's and Hagood's Brigades not charging on the right and to Colquitt's Brigade not supporting us." Burgwyn estimates that his brigade, Clingman's, lost "at least two-thirds killed, wounded, and prisoners, and I fear three-fourths."[248] Certainly, Clingman's Brigade lost many more than other regiments at the site.

Notes

1. Bryan and Meadows, "Thirty-First Regiment," p. 515.
2. *O.R.*, XXXIII, Ser. I, p. 107, General George Pickett to General Samuel Cooper, January 8, 1864.
3. D. H. Hill, Jr. *Confederate Military History: North Carolina*, Evans, ed. IV, pp. 218–219; and *O.R.*, XXXIII, Ser. I, p. 1201, "Abstract from return of the Department of North Carolina, Maj. Gen. George E. Pickett, C. S. Army, commanding, for the month of February, 1864, headquarters Petersburg, Va."
4. Marshall Williams, "Fifty-Fourth Regiment," in Clark, *Histories of the Several Regiments*, III, p. 273.
5. R. D. W. Connor, *North Carolina: Rebuilding an Ancient Commonwealth*, II (1928), p. 246; Hamilton, II, p. 23; and Long, p. 639.
6. Barrett, p. 202.
7. Long, p. 640.
8. Barrett, p. 203.
9. Connor, *North Carolina: Rebuilding an Ancient Commonwealth*, II, pp. 246–247.
10. Barrett, pp. 203–204.
11. George Pickett, "Report of General Pickett," *Southern Historical Society Papers*, IX, No. 1 (Jan. 1881), 1; Long, p. 639; and Barrett, p. 203.
12. Barrett, p. 203.
13. Connor, *North Carolina: Rebuilding an Ancient Commonwealth*, II, p. 247.
14. Barrett, p. 204.
15. Burgwyn, *A Captain's War*, p. 119.
16. Burgwyn, "Clingman's Brigade," p. 486.
17. Barrett, p. 204.
18. *O.R.*, XXXIII, Ser. I, p. 96, "No. 13, Report of Brig. Gen. Robert F. Hoke," February 8, 1864; also cited in Barrett, p. 204.
19. Burgwyn, "Clingman's Brigade," p. 487.
20. Pickett, p. 4.
21. Thomas L. Clingman to George Pickett, March 17, 1864, Order Book 2.

22. Pickett, p. 4.
23. Burgwyn, "Clingman's Brigade," p. 487.
24. Pickett, p. 4.
25. Burgwyn, "Clingman's Brigade," p. 487.
26. Burgwyn, *A Captain's War*, p. 120.
27. Barrett, pp. 208–211.
28. Catherine Edmondston, May 14, 1864, p. 559.
29. Boatner, p. 108.
30. *O.R.*, LI, Ser. I, Pt. II, p. 857, General Braxton Bragg to Maj. Gen. G. E. Pickett, April 12, 1864; and *O.R.*, LI, Ser. I, Pt. II, p. 862, Major General G. E. Pickett to General Braxton Bragg, April 14, 1864.
31. William H. S. Burgwyn, "Thirty-Fifth Regiment," in Clark, *History of the Several Regiments*, II, p. 616.
32. Joseph Blunt Cheshire, *Nonnula* (Chapel Hill, N.C.: University of North Carolina Press, 1930), p. 145.
33. Boatner, p. 656.
34. Cheshire, pp. 143–144.
35. Cheshire, pp. 144–145.
36. *O.R.*, LI, Ser. I, Pt. II, p. 866, Brig. Gen. T. L. Clingman to General Braxton Bragg, April 18, 1864.
37. Cheshire, p. 146.
38. Cheshire, p. 146, footnote 1.
39. Cheshire, pp. 147–148.
40. Cheshire, p. 148.
41. *Ibid*.
42. Ludwig, "Eighth Regiment," p. 400.
43. *Ibid*.
44. *Ibid*., p. 401.
45. Boatner, p. 656.
46. Burgwyn, "Thirty-Fifth Regiment, pp. 616–619; Burgwyn, "Clingman's Brigade," pp. 488–489; Dunbar Rowlan, *Jefferson Davis, Constitutionalist* (Jackson, Miss.: Mississippi Department of Archives and History, 1923), VII, p. 233.
47. Hill, IV, pp. 318–319.
48. Hill, IV, p. 317.
49. Hill, IV, p. 318.
50. Boatner, pp. 247–249.
51. C. F. R. Henderson, *The Civil War: A Soldier's View*. Ed. Jay Luvaas (Chicago: University of Chicago Press, 1958), p. 196.
52. Davis, p. 428.
53. Pollard, p. 523.
54. R. Earnest Dupuy and Trevor N. Dupuy, *Compact History of the Civil War* (New York: Hawthorn Books, 1960), p. 207.
55. *O.R.*, XXXVI, Ser. I, Pt. II, p. 957, George Pickett to Samuel Cooper, May 5, 1864.

56. Miller, "Engagements of the Civil War, with Losses on Both Sides, May 1, 1864–June 1865," III, pp. 318–319. Clingman's Brigade was not at the Battle of the Wilderness as stated in Boatner, p. 159. E. K. Bryan, of the 31st Regiment, emphatically denied that his regiment was at the Wilderness, especially after he saw an account in the "Rebellion Records," vol. 125, pp. 815–818, that Company D of the Fifth Michigan had captured the flag of the 31st Regiment at the Battle of the Wilderness, May 6, 1864. Bryan also added that his regiment was at Petersburg and Bermuda Hundred, "several hundred miles" distant from the Wilderness. The distance from the Wilderness battlefield site to Petersburg is, however, only approximately 25 miles. See also, Burgwyn, "Thirty-First Regiment," p. 520.
57. Dupuy and Dupuy, pp. 307–308.
58. Ashe, *History of North Carolina*, p. 907.
59. Dupuy and Dupuy, pp. 306–307.
60. Ashe, *History of North Carolina*, II, p. 907.
61. Burgwyn, "Clingman's Brigade," p. 489.
62. B. R. Johnson, "Report of General B. R. Johnson," *Southern Historical Society Papers*, XII (1884), p. 274.
63. Burgwyn, "Clingman's Brigade," p. 489; and Ashe, *History of North Carolina*, II, p. 907.
64. Burgwyn, "Clingman's Brigade," p. 489.
65. Boatner, p. 248.
66. *Ibid*.
67. Ashe, *History of North Carolina*, II, p. 907.
68. Ashe, *History of North Carolina*, II, pp. 907–908.
69. Boatner, p. 248.
70. *Ibid*.
71. Beauregard, "Swift Creek," *Southern Historical Society Papers*, XXVIII, 321.
72. Report of General Pickett to General B. R. Johnson, May 9, 1864, *Southern Historical Society Papers*, pp. 279–280.
73. *O.R.*, LI, Ser. I, Pt. I, p. 231, "Report of Capt. Joe Norcom, Fourth Company, Battalion Washington Artillery, of operations May 5–21," Swift Creek, May 25, 1864, to Colonel B. F. Eshleman.
74. Dupuy and Dupuy, pp. 306–307.
75. Beauregard, "Swift Creek," *Southern Historical Society Papers*, XXVIII, 322.
76. Miller, III, p. 320.
77. Boatner, pp. 248–249.

78. Brooks, II, p. 121.
79. Hagood, p. 322.
80. Burgwyn, "Clingman's Brigade," pp. 490–491.
81. Ibid.
82. Burgwyn, "Clingman's Brigade," pp. 489–490.
83. Burgwyn, *A Captain's War*, p. 142.
84. Ibid.
85. Burgwyn, *A Captain's War*, p. 143.
86. Robert D. Graham, "Fifty-Sixth Regiment," in Clark, III, pp. 352–353; and Livermore, p. 113.
87. Hagood, p. 323.
88. Graham, pp. 352–353.
89. P. G. T. Beauregard, "The Defense of Drewry's Bluff," in Johnson and Buel, *Battles and Leaders of the Civil War*, IV, p. 202; and O.R., XXXVI, Ser. I, Pt. II, pp. 201–204, General P. G. T. Beauregard to Division Commanders, June 23, 1864.
90. Ludwig, p. 403.
91. Burgwyn, *A Captain's War*, p. 143.
92. Beauregard, "The Defense of Drewry's Bluff," p. 202.
93. O.R., XXXVI, Ser. I, Pt. II, p. 238, "Report of Maj. Gen. Robert F. Hoke," May 25, 1864.
94. Beauregard, "The Defense of Drewry's Bluff," pp. 202–203.
95. O.R., XXXVI, Ser. I, Pt. II, p. 248, May 22, 1864, report of Colonel R. H. Keeble, 23rd Tennessee Infantry, of Operations May 4–16, 1864.
96. Pollard, p. 523.
97. Dupuy and Dupuy, p. 307.
98. Moore, IV, p. 7.
99. O.R., XXXVI, Ser. I, Pt. II, pp. 236–238, "Report of Maj. Gen. Robert F. Hoke, C. S. Army, commanding division, of operations May 16," May 25, 1864.
100. McKethan, "The Fifty-First Regiment," p. 211.
101. Beauregard, "The Defense of Drewry's Bluff," pp. 202–203.
102. Bryan and Meadows, "Thirty-First Regiment," pp. 515–516.
103. O.R., XXXVI, Ser. I, Pt. II, p. 1014, G. T. Beauregard to General Whiting, May 16, 1864.
104. Pollard, p. 523.
105. O.R., XXXVI, Ser. I, Pt. III, p. 140, Quartermaster General M. C. Meigs to Major General Halleck, Chief of Staff, Bermuda Hundred, May 23, 1864.
106. Hans L. Trefousse, *Ben Butler: The South Called Him Beast!* (New York, Octagon Books, 1974), p. 150.
107. O.R., XXXVI, Ser. I, Pt. II, pp. 248–249, "Report of Capt. William N. James, commanding Twenty-fifth and Forty-fourth Tennessee Infantry, of operations May 16," May 22, 1864.
108. Burgwyn, "Clingman's Brigade," pp. 490–491.
109. Miller, III, p. 320.
110. Ibid.; Charles T. Loehr's Address Before George E. Pickett Camp, Confederate Veterans on October 15, 1891, published in Richmond *Times*, 25 Oct. 1891, and reproduced in *Southern Historical Society Papers*, XIX, pp. 109–110.
111. Livermore, p. 113.
112. O.R., XXVI, Ser. I, Pt. II, p. 205, "List of Killed, Wounded and Missing in the Engagement near Drewry's Bluff on Monday, May 16, 1864."
113. Burgwyn, "Clingman's Brigade," p. 492.
114. Boatner, p. 61.
115. William Farrar Smith, "Butler's Attack on Drewry's Bluff," *Battles and Leaders*, IV, p. 211.
116. O.R., XXXVI, Ser. I, Pt. II, p. 166, Brigadier General Edmund W. Hinks, U.S. Army, to Major General B. F. Butler, May 13, 1864.
117. Boatner, pp. 889–890.
118. Miller, III, p. 320.
119. Daniel H. Hill, "Lee's Attacks North of the Chickahominy," in Buel and Johnson, *Battles and Leaders of the Civil War*, II, p. 354.
120. G. Moxley Sorrell, *Recollections of a Confederate Staff Officer* (1905; rpt. Nashville: Mclowat-Mercer Press, 1958) p. 249; and Eaton, p. 280.
121. Dupuy and Dupuy, p. 304.
122. O.R., XXXVI, Ser. I, Pt. III, pp. 527–528, Colonel George H. Sharp to Major General Humphreys, June 3, 1864.
123. O.R., XXXVI, Ser. I, Pt. III, p. 817, "Abstract from field return of troops in Hoke's division, Maj. Gen. Robert F. Hoke commanding, for May 21, 1864."
124. O.R., XXXVI, Ser. I, Pt. III, p. 842, R. F. Hoke to D. H. Hill, May 27, 1864.
125. Miller, "Cold Harbor," *The Decisive Battles*, III, p. 82.
126. Hill, *Confederate Military History: North Carolina*, IV, p. 251.
127. General Robert E. Lee to General Braxton Bragg, telegram, May 31, 1864, cited in Freeman, *Lee's Dispatches*, p. 210.

128. Freeman, p. 817.

129. *O.R.*, XXXVI, Ser. I, Pt. III, p. 858, Assistant Adjutant General W. H. Taylor to Maj. Gen. R. H. Anderson, May 31, 1864.

130. *O.R.*, XXXVI, Ser. I, Pt. III, p. 858, Major General Fitz Lee to General R.E. Lee, Old Cold Harbor, May 31, 1864.

131. Thomas L. Clingman, "Second Cold Harbor," in Clark, *Histories of the Several Regiments,* V, p. 197.

132. Clingman, "Second Cold Harbor," p. 198.

133. Hill, *Confederate Military History: North Carolina,* IV, pp. 251–252.

134. Thomas L. Clingman, "Second Cold Harbor," in Clark, *Histories of the Several Regiments,* V, pp. 197–198.

135. Clingman, "Second Cold Harbor," pp. 198–199.

136. *O.R.*, XXXVI, Ser. I, Pt. I, p. 783, General Phil Sheridan to Major-General Humphreys, May 31, 1864.

137. *O.R.*, XXXVI, Ser. I, Pt. I, p. 783, General Phil Sheridan to Major-General Humphreys, May 31, 1864.

138. *O.R.*, XXXVI, Ser. I, Pt. I, pp. 84–85, C. A. Dana to Edwin M. Stanton, June 1, 1864.

139. *O.R.*, XXXVI, Ser. I, Pt. III, p. 466, Major General Phil Sheridan to Major General Humphreys, June 1, 1864.

140. Clingman, "Second Cold Harbor," p. 199.

141. Clingman, "Second Cold Harbor," p. 200.

142. Clingman, "Second Cold Harbor," pp. 200–201.

143. Clingman, "Second Cold Harbor," p. 201.

144. Clingman, "Second Cold Harbor," pp. 202–203.

145. Clingman, "Second Cold Harbor," p. 203.

146. Clingman, "Second Cold Harbor," pp. 203–204.

147. Clingman, "Second Cold Harbor," p. 204.

148. Clingman, "Second Cold Harbor," pp. 204–205.

149. Clingman, "Second Cold Harbor," p. 205.

150. *Ibid.*

151. Cheshire, p. 149.

152. Ulysses S. Grant, *Ulysses S. Grant: Memoirs and Selected Letters 1839–1865* (New York: The Library of America, 1990), p. 588.

153. W.F. Fox, *Fox's Regimental Losses* (Albany, N.Y.: Albany Publishing Co., 1888), electronic version at http://www.civilwarhome.com/foxspref.htm, unpaginated. Dayton, Oh.; rpt. Morningside Book Shop, 1985, pp. 449–450, 541, 542.

154. Miller, III, p. 322.

155. Long, p. 348.

156. Eaton, *History of the Confederacy,* p. 280.

157. Long, pp. 349–350.

158. Hill, *Confederate Military History: North Carolina,* IV, p. 252.

159. Long, p. 372.

160. Boatner, p. 646.

161. Beauregard, "Petersburg," *Southern Historical Society Papers,* XXVIII, p. 332.

162. Alfred Roman, *The Military Operations of General Beauregard* (New York: Da Capo Press, 1994), II, p. 229, cited in Daniel W. Barefoot, *General Robert F. Hoke: Lee's Modest Warrior* (Winston-Salem, N.C.: John F. Blair, Publisher, 1996), p. 204.

163. *O.R.,* XL, Ser. I, Pt. II, p. 657, Orders by General P. G. T. Beauregard, Petersburg, Va., June 15, 1864.

164. Barefoot, p. 202.

165. Beauregard, "Petersburg," pp. 332–333.

166. Long, p. 272.

167. Long, p. 373.

168. Barefoot, p. 205.

169. Burgwyn, "Clingman's Brigade," pp. 493–495.

170. Long, pp. 373–374.

171. Ludwig, "Eighth Regiment," pp. 405–406; Long, p. 373; and Graham, "Fifty-Sixth Regiment," p. 373.

172. William S. Hoole, *Lawley Covers the Confederacy* (Tuscaloosa, Ala.: Confederate Publishing Co., Inc., 1964), p. 85.

173. Hoole, p. 84.

174. Long, p. 376.

175. Long, p. 375.

176. Long, p. 375.

177. William M. Thomas, "The Slaughter at Petersburg, June 18, 1864," *Southern Historical Society Papers,* XXV (1897), 229. Contrary to the foregoing account, a report in the Sunday *News,* Charleston, South Carolina, July 25, 1897, published in the *Southern Historical Society Papers,* XXV, 222–230, Clingman's Brigade did not come up to the trenches at Petersburg until the 19th of June.

178. Miller, III, p. 322.

179. Boatner, pp. 647–648.

180. Long, p. 380; and Pleasants, p. 48.

181. Hoole, pp. 89–90.
182. Humphreys, p. 251.
183. *O.R.*, XLIII, Ser. I, Pt. II, pp. 551–552, report of Captain J. McEntee cited in report to Major General Birney, August 27, 1864.
184. *O.R.*, XLII, Ser. I, Pt. II, pp. 1158–1159, Capt. Hugh Thos. Douglas to Col. T. M. R. Talcott, August 2, 1864.
185. Pollard, p. 537.
186. Hoole, p. 91.
187. Long, pp. 381–382.
188. Hoole, p. 41.
189. Pleasants, pp. 142–143.
190. Hill, p. 266.
191. Hill, p. 269.
192. Hoole, p. 91.
193. E. P. Alexander, *Military Memoirs of a Confederate* (New York: Charles Scribner's Sons, 1912), p. 569.
194. Livermore, p. 141.
195. Fox, p. 547.
196. Ashe, *History of North Carolina*, II, p. 917; and Burgwyn, "Clingman's Brigade," p. 495.
197. London *Times*, September 9, 1864, cited in Hoole, p. 93.
198. Pleasants, p. 140.
199. Thomas L. Clingman to Col. H. K. Burgwyn, June 25, 1864, W. H. S. Burgwyn Papers, Department of Archives and History, Raleigh, North Carolina.
200. Ludwig, "Eighth Regiment," I, p. 407.
201. Hill, p. 266.
202. Pleasants, p. 46.
203. George M. Rose, "Sixty-Sixth Regiment," in Clark, *Histories of the Several Regiments*, III, pp. 689–670.
204. Ashe, *History of North Carolina*, II, pp. 916–917.
205. Eggleston, p. 176.
206. Long, p. 369.
207. Long, p. 390.
208. *O.R.*, XLII, Ser. I, Pt. II, p. 96, Captain J. McEntee, Army of the Potomac, to Colonel Sharpe, August 9, 1864.
209. *O.R.*, XLII, Ser. I, Pt. II, pp. 296–297, Captain J. McEntee, Army of the Potomac, to Major-General Humphreys, Chief of Staff, August 19, 1864.
210. Long, p. 391.
211. *O.R.*, XLII, Ser. I, pp. 856–858, Report of General P. G. T. Beauregard, August 20, 1864; and Manarin and Jordan, IV, p. 520.
212. Pollard, p. 607.
213. Boatner, pp. 345–346.
214. Humphreys, p. 275.

215. Brevet Major-General Orlando B. Willcox, "Actions on the Weldon Railroad," in Johnson and Buel, *Battles and Leaders of the Civil War*, IV, pp. 568–569.
216. Willcox, p. 570.
217. *Ibid.*
218. *Ibid.*
219. Willcox, pp. 570–571.
220. *O.R.*, XLII, Ser. I., Pt. I, p. 940, "Report of Lieut. Gen. Ambrose P. Hill," to General P. G. T. Beauregard, August 19, 1864.
221. Evans, *Confederate Military History*, IV, p. 269.
222. *O.R.*, XLII, Ser. I, Pt. I, p. 858, Report of General P. G. T. Beauregard, August 20, 1864.
223. *O.R.*, XLII, Ser. I, Pt. II, p. 418, Lieutenant-General U. S. Grant to Major-General Halleck, August 23, 1864.
224. Long, pp. 658–660.
225. Pollard, p. 607.
226. *O.R.*, XLII, Ser. I, Pt. II, p. 329, Union Capt. J. McEntee to Col. G. H. Sharpe, August 20, 1864.
227. Livermore p. 118.
228. Willcox, p. 571.
229. Burgwyn, "Clingman's Brigade," p. 495.
230. Pollard, p. 607.
231. *Ibid.*
232. Bryan and Meadows, p. 518; and Manarin and Jordan, IV, p. 220.
233. Barefoot, p. 222.
234. Pollard, p. 608.
235. *O.R.*, XLII, Ser. I, Pt. II, p. 1224, "Abstract from return of the troops in the Department of North Carolina and southern Virginia, General P. G. T. Beauregard, Commanding, for September 1, 1864."
236. Barefoot, p. 222.
237. *Ibid.*
238. McKethan, "Fifty-first Regiment," Clark, III, p. 213.
239. Barefoot, p. 223.
240. Pollard, p. 608.
241. Burgwyn, *A Captain's War*, pp. 150–153.
242. Hector McKethan to Genl. T. L. Clingman, Chapin's Farm, Oct. 31, 1864, W. H. S. Burgwyn Papers, North Carolina Department of Archives and History, Raleigh, North Carolina.
243. *Ibid.*
244. Richard J. Sommers, *Richmond Redeemed: The Siege of Petersburg* (Garden City, N.Y.: Doubleday & Co., Inc., 1981), p. 148.
245. Hector McKethan to Thomas L.

Clingman, October 31, 1864, Burgwyn Papers, North Carolina Department of Archives and History, Raleigh, North Carolina.

246. *O.R.,* XLII, Ser. I, Pt. II, p. 1166, "Beauregard's Command, Hoke's Division."

247. Hector McKethan to Thomas L. Clingman, December 6, 1864, Clingman Papers, Duke University, Durham, N.C.

248. Burgwyn, *A Captain's War,* p. 153.

Chapter VI

Battles: 1865

> *Let us take our stand here and fight the two armies of Grant and Sherman to the end, and thus show to the world how far we can surpass the Thermopylae of the Greeks.*
> — Thomas L. Clingman to General Joseph E. Johnston, at Smithfield, North Carolina.

Fort Fisher, North Carolina, 2nd battle, January 13–15, 1865[1] (Terry's Expedition)

As of January 1865, Fort Fisher was still in Confederate hands. It was imperative that this remaining fort be held, because it was the key to the defense of the Cape Fear River area, and to the city of Wilmington, the chief center for blockade-running. In fact, Wilmington, while always an important port, became, during the last part of 1864, the only port in the Confederacy that blockade-runners could use.[2]

Fort Fisher, called "the Gibraltar of America," was situated at the mouth of the Cape Fear River.[3] It was a mammoth L-shaped earthworks, constructed in 1861. The land side (north) extended 682 yards across the peninsula. The east side that faced the sea extended 1,898 yards down to the beach. At the southern extremity was Mound Battery, which housed two long-range guns that helped protect the blockade-runners. At the rear of Fort Fisher a line of rifle pits protected the fort from attack from the river.[4] Fort Fisher had withstood Federal attacks in 1862 and 1864. It was under the command of Colonel William Lamb. General Whiting was in command of the Cape Fear defenses, and was thus Lamb's superior.[5]

When rumors began circulating that the Union forces were going to attack Fort Fisher again, President Jefferson Davis appointed his friend General Braxton Bragg to the command of the Department of North Carolina, which included his being in charge of the defense of Fort Fisher.[6] Bragg, a North Carolinian, was the most controversial general in the whole Confederate army. He was respected by neither civilians nor military.[7] Likewise, Major General Butler, the Union general and a laughingstock since he had been "bottled up" at Bermuda Hundred, was to lead the attack on the fort in December of 1864.

The small number of men who were still left in Clingman's Brigade (the 8th, 31st, and 61st regiments, plus the 57th),[8] functioning as a part of Hoke's Division, were moved by rail to Wilmington to help defend Fort Fisher. They reached Wilmington on December 24. Upon their arrival, they found that bombardment of the fort by the Federals had already begun. The men marched to Sugar Loaf Hill, a short distance north of Fort Fisher. The Federals landed the next day, but after a brief skirmish they withdrew to their ships and left the area.[9]

The Federal force was under the command of General Benjamin F. Butler. The naval forces were under the command of Admiral David Dixon Porter. A Federal attempt to destroy the fort by blowing up a ship very near Fort Fisher failed to bring down the fort's walls, so on December 24, 1864, Admiral Porter unleashed 600 guns on his 50 ships at the fort. Up and down the beach for miles the ground was "literally covered with fragments of iron." However, the Federal losses were greater than those within Fort Fisher. Because of faulty construction, two 100-pound Parrott guns exploded on Federal ships. On the *Ticonderoga*, 8 sailors were killed and 12 wounded.[10]

The Federals continued their assault from the sea, and Butler's forces were to launch a land attack. Butler could easily have succeeded, because Fort Fisher had few defenders at the time. However, by December 23, with reinforcements having arrived, the number of Confederate troops in Fort Fisher had increased to about 900; these included some Junior Reserves[11] who later surrendered to Butler's Federal troops. Butler learned from some of the prisoners that part of General Robert F. Hoke's division had arrived in Wilmington. Knowing the importance of keeping

Fig. 19. Fort Fisher, North Carolina. View of the land front, showing destroyed gun carriage in second traverse, January 1865. Timothy H. O'Sullivan (1840–1882), photographer. (Library of Congress)

the port city of Wilmington open, General Robert E. Lee had sent Hoke and 6,000 "veteran troops" to help strengthen the defenses of the Cape Fear area.[12]

The Federal Navy continued its bombardment. Admiral Porter was convinced that it must be "impossible for anything human to stand" such a barrage, and he decreed that it was time for a land assault. Major General Godfrey Weitzel had moved 3,000 troops to within 50 yards of Fort Fisher, but the attack did not take place. Suddenly, the Federal troops turned and marched back up the beach. It seemed General Butler had taken one look at Fort Fisher and lost his courage. Butler tried to cover his actions by saying that darkness was approaching, the weather was threatening, and that the fort had not suffered sufficient damage from the bombardment of the offshore guns. He had decided that it would take a regular "siege" to reduce the fort, and he did not have that authorization. So, instead, he ordered his troops back to Fortress Monroe.[13]

This failure to take Fort Fisher did not sit well with Union lieutenant general U. S. Grant, and he telegraphed President Lincoln on December 28, 1864:

> The Wilmington expedition has proven a gross and culpable failure. Many of the troops are back here. Delays and free talk of the object of the expedition enabled the enemy to move troops to Wilmington to defeat it. After the expedition sailed from Fort Monroe, three days of fine weather were squandered during which the enemy was without a force to protect himself. Who is to blame will, I hope be known.[14]

Grant then ordered Butler replaced by Union general Alfred H. Terry to organize another expedition to take Fort Fisher in any way possible. A force of 8,000 men, known as Terry's Provisional Corps, was put together from the X Corps, J. A. Abbott's Brigade (XXIV Corps), Ames' division, and C. J. Paine's division of colored troops (XXV Corps), together with 4 guns from the 16th N.Y., battery E of the 3rd U.S. Artillery, and 3 companies of siege artillery with 24 guns and 20 small mortars.[15]

The Federal fleet was again threatening Fort Fisher, and the 8th Regiment of Clingman's Brigade was ordered to Sugar Loaf Hill. They arrived on January 12, 1865, and began constructing defensive works between their line at Sugar Loaf and Fort Fisher.[16]

What few men of the 31st Regiment remained were also ordered to Fort Fisher to participate in its defense on January 15, 1865.

The Confederates were kept busy working on the breastworks, avoiding bombardment from the Federal fleet, and repulsing attacks from the Federal troops who had landed at Fort Fisher. From within the fort, General Whiting sent an urgent message to General Braxton Bragg at Sugar Loaf. Whiting told Bragg that the enemy were about to launch an assault, that the Confederates in Fort Fisher were heavily outnumbered, and that the Federal fleet sat offshore only about 700 yards away. No sooner had Whiting sent the message than an all-out land and naval attack was launched against Fort Fisher by the Federals. Hoke's troops were deployed against Paine's colored troops, but "after a few feeble probings" the Confederate attack was halted. Bragg excused himself and his order to halt the attack by saying that he thought the Federal assault had failed.[17]

On January 15, 1865, the fort was surrendered to the Federals by Major James Reilly. General Whiting and Colonel William Lamb had both been wounded in the bombardment.[18] The fall of Fort Fisher allowed the Federals to occupy Wilmington, and to control the Wilmington-Weldon Railroad. These Federal victories "sealed the fate of Lee's Army" in Virginia.[19] The loss of the port of Wilmington closed off the Confederacy to the rest of the world,[20] and as a result the Confederacy was almost destroyed.

Casualties
Federal army
engaged = 8,000   184 killed,
                      749 wounded,
                      22 missing
Federal naval   386[21]

While there was no hope of retaking Fort Fisher from the Yankees, the Confederates hoped to keep the enemy from advancing on Wilmington. The 8th Regiment was charged with covering the retreat of the Confederate forces from Wilmington on February 22, and they did an excellent job.[22] The Confederates retreating from Wilmington crossed the Northeast Branch of the Cape Fear River on a pontoon bridge just minutes ahead of Federal troops: "the advance of the enemy arriving at the south bank just as our last troops had gotten across the river, and our pontoons cut loose."[23]

Kinston, North Carolina (Wise's Forks, Southwest Creek), March 7–10, 1865

Hoke's Division held the line below Wilmington until February 19. They were then pulled back and crossed the Cape Fear River as the Federal troops advanced. Wilmington fell on February 22. Hoke's men were ordered to Kinston to oppose a Federal troop coming from Goldsboro to New Bern. At the Battle of Kinston (also called Wise's Forks and Southwest Creek), from March 7 to 10, the Confederate forces tried desperately to delay a confrontation with the Federal forces of Major General William T. Sherman.

On March 8, Hoke's Division and a small force under Lieutenant General D. H. Hill attacked the Federal left and right, and two isolated Federal regiments were captured by Hoke. However, rather than keeping the initiative, Bragg sent Hill away from the battle. The next day, there was more skirmishing, when Hoke attacked Federal lines. On the 10th of March, Bragg ordered another "double envelopment" using Hoke and Hill forces. After marching through swamps and dense forests to get to the rear of the enemy, Hoke's men did manage an assault that was broken up by cannon fire. The assault was called off by Bragg, and the Confederates retreated to Goldsboro and Smithfield to join with the forces of General Joseph E. Johnston on March 17.[24]

Bentonville, North Carolina, March 19–21, 1865[25]

For more information on this battle, I would recommend a book written in 1996 by Nathaniel Cheairs Hughes, Jr., entitled *Bentonville: The Final Battle of Sherman and Johnston*. Hughes thoroughly explores all aspects of this battle, much more than can possibly be done in this work, in which I will just briefly touch on the part that Clingman's Brigade played in the fight.

At the final battle, Bentonville, although General Braxton Bragg was in "nominal command," Major General Robert F. Hoke, whose forces included Clingman's Brigade, was in charge.[26] Johnston's army was a patchwork of what remained of some previously glorious fighting units. It was composed of "three separate commands that had never fought together." Even though there was a lack of manpower, there was an overabundance of generals, brilliant generals who had led their troops and pooled their expertise in the death struggle for the Confederacy.[27] The list of generals at Bentonville is impressive: Johnston, Bragg, Hampton, Hardee, Stewart, Wheeler, Hoke, D. H. Hill, Loring, Taliaferro, Stevenson, McLaws, and many others.[28]

The scene for the final battle in North Carolina was set. Hoke's Division arrived at Smithfield on March 16, after having crossed the Neuse. His division numbered 4,775 men able to fight, of which "800 were former artillery men," now poised to fight as infantry. The total force was divided into five brigades with Clingman's Brigade, under Colonel William S. Devane, the smallest brigade with only 557 men. The North Carolina Junior Reserve Brigade put forth 35 companies divided into regiments and a battalion numbering about 1,000 men. There was, in addition, William W. Kirkland's Brigade, and Johnson Hagood's South Carolina Brigade. Colquitt's Georgia Brigade, commanded by Colonel Charles Zachary, was also present.[29]

Confederate General Joseph E. Johnston's 20,000 men faced the 30,000-man Federal force of General Henry Warner Slocum. Union general Slocum's XIV and XX Corps advanced to Bentonville, after an encounter with Hardee's troops at Averasboro on March 16. The Union force also included Kilpatrick's cavalry and Sherman's forces moving from Goldsboro to join Schofield and Terry coming from the coast. There was heavy fighting, and Slocum's Federal troops attacked Hoke's Division on the Confederate left. Bragg called for reinforcements, but that deprived Johnston of an "essential division at a critical moment." Hardee's Confederate infantry came crashing out of the thickets in an assault that disorganized the Federal left. The Federals, however, managed to hold until they were reinforced and could drive the Confederates back. Five Confederate assaults were smashed by a "hailstorm of grape and canister."[30]

Johnston had hoped to launch a full attack on the Federals on March 19. However, that was not possible because of Union general Carlin's attack on Hoke. Slocum had time, therefore, to entrench and get in reinforcements. The Confederate attack finally was made in midafternoon, led by Hardee, Stewart, and Hill. Hoke did not take part in the afternoon assault.[31]

The assault was a grand affair — officers on horseback leading a charge against an open field, colors of regiments and brigades waving in the breeze, the rebel yell interspersed with the sharp crack of rifles. Hardee's men routed the Federal XIV Corps. After regrouping, a second Confederate attack was ordered, and Hoke was prepared to enter the fray when he saw a gap in the Union lines that had occurred when Benjamin Fearing's forces had met those of D. H. Hill and retreated. However, he received orders from General Braxton Bragg to launch a "full frontal attack." Hoke reluctantly complied with Bragg's orders, and stormed the enemy through a dense pine thicket. When they emerged, they came face to face with Union General Morgan's entire line.[32] What ensued was some of the fiercest fighting of the war. One of Hoke's men described it as "the hottest infantry fight they had been in except Cold Harbor." A soldier from the 42nd Georgia described Hoke's charge: "it was one of the grandest charges made during the war. I can remember now, how the declining sun shown [sic] through the pine forest in the afternoon as the sun was going down and your gallant division came rushing over us in the last battle of the war. How grandly the officers and men looked like a whirl wind as they made the *last charge*." Another North Carolina officer likened the fighting to that of Gettysburg.[33]

Hoke was in the thick of the fighting, and was even captured at one point, but managed to escape. Even with the addition of McLaw's men, Federal general Morgan's men held their line, and D. H. Hill's Confederates were driven back. When darkness fell, the Union forces were "battered and bloodied but not destroyed."[34]

The next day (March 20), the Federals were joined by the troops of General William T. Sherman and General Oliver Otis Howard. However, there was little fighting on March 20. Sherman got in place to attack on March 21, and Mower's division made an attempt to move through the swamp to get at Johnston's men, and to cut off any retreat by the Confederates. The Federals then launched a frontal attack. Johnston blocked Mower's maneuver with his reserves, and held his main position. Later that night, the Confederates retreated toward Smithfield. Johnston remained at Bentonville to cover the evacuation of his wounded.

The 8th Regiment of Clingman's Brigade traveled from Wilmington to Goldsboro then to Smithfield, and then to the final battle at Bentonville on March 19. The 8th Regiment was held in reserve during the day, and that night was placed on the left of Johnston's forces. The 8th Regiment of Clingman's Brigade was the last to leave the field, and again acted as a rear guard.[35]

Likewise, the 31st Regiment had moved from Wilmington to Goldsboro and then to Smithfield, where they awaited the advance of U.S. General Sherman, from Fayetteville.[36] The 31st North Carolina sustained losses of 50 percent—152 men lost out of 267.[37]

The 51st Regiment, or what was left of it, was in this last battle as well.[38]

Hoke's Division lost a total of 593 men — 45 killed, 370 wounded, and 178 missing (captured).[39]

There were actually relatively few

Overall Casualties

16,127 Federals engaged[40] losses 1,646[41]
16,895 Confederates[42] losses 2,606[43]

casualties in this last battle fought in North Carolina, in which the Union XIV, XV, XVII, and XX Corps, and Kilpatrick's Cavalry, faced the Confederate forces under General Joseph E. Johnston and Wade Hampton's cavalry. Union losses were: killed, 191, wounded 1,168, missing 287; Confederate losses were about the same, with 239 killed, 1694 wounded, and 673 missing.[44]

Although there is no official report, the 51st Regiment sustained heavy casualties in the fighting at Bentonville.[45] Hoke's Division, according to Johnston's report, lost 61 men killed, 471 wounded, and 202 missing.[46]

Clingman's Brigade had the following losses over the 4-day period, March 19–22, 1865,[47] during the battle of Bentonville, North Carolina:

Date	Killed	Wounded	Missing	Total
March 19, 1865	1	18	1	20
March 20, 1865		1	1	2
March 21, 1865	2	16		18
March 22, 1865		1		1
Totals	3	36	2	41

By March 26, 1865, the "aggregate" total present of Clingman's Brigade was 618 men. Of those, only 436 were "effective present," 563 "total present," and 618 "aggregate present."[48] This number is approximately 15 percent of the original brigade strength of about 4,000 men. Hoke estimated the number of men in Clingman's Brigade slightly higher at "769 men present" when he arranged transportation on March 31, 1865.[49]

At Smithfield, the incompetent Bragg

was removed from command, and Hoke's Division was placed under General Hardee. Clingman's Brigade remained a part of Hoke's Division.[50]

The Final Days Until the Surrender, May 1, 1865

Between March 31, 1865,[51] and April 9, 1865, the Confederate Forces[52] were under the command of General Joseph E. Johnston, with General P. G. T. Beauregard second in command. Clingman's Brigade was still a part of Hoke's Division. However, In addition to the four original regiments of Clingman's Brigade, two additional regiments had been added. These regiments were commanded by the following officers:

8th North Carolina	Lt. Col. Rufus A. Barrier
31st North Carolina	Col. Charles W. Knight
36th North Carolina & 40th North Carolina	Maj. William A. Holland
51st North Carolina	Capt. James W. Lippitt
61st North Carolina	Capt. Stephen W. Noble

The 8th Regiment moved to camp at Smithfield for about three weeks, then were ordered to move to Raleigh by way of Chapel Hill. They crossed the waist-deep waters of the Haw River at Ruffin's Mill. From there they proceeded to cross the Alamance River, which was also swollen by recent rains. After the crossing, they marched to Archdale in Randolph County, where they learned of Lee's surrender on April 9, 1865. About 150 men surrendered and were paroled on May 2, 1865.[53]

The 31st Regiment retreated to High Point and the "village of Bush Hill," where the command was surrendered and paroled on May 1, 1865.[54]

Thirty-six members of the 51st Regiment surrendered at Greensboro, N.C., with what remained of the other regiments of Clingman's Brigade.[55]

The 14 remaining members of the 61st Regiment, including officers Captain Augustus D. Lippitt of Company G and Lt. William H. Patrick of Company B, surrendered and received their paroles on May 1, 1865, at Greensboro.[56]

Thus ended the role of Clingman's Brigade as a fighting unit of the Confederate Army in the War Between the States.

Notes

1. Boatner, pp. 293–294.
2. Lefler and Newsome, p. 459.
3. *Ibid.*
4. Barrett, p. 265.
5. Hoke, p. 240.
6. Hoke, p. 241.
7. *Ibid.*
8. *Battles and Leaders*, "The Opposing Forces at Fort Fisher, N.C.," IV, 661.
9. Manarin and Jordan, XII, p. 273.
10. Barrett, pp. 267–268.
11. Barrett, p. 269, footnote.
12. Barrett, p. 269.
13. Barrett, pp. 269–270.
14. Grant, *Memoirs and Selected Letters*, p. 668.
15. Boatner, p. 293.
16. Manarin and Jordan, IV, p. 520.
17. Barrett, p. 270; *O.R.*, XLVI, Ser. I, Pt. I, pp. 424, 433–434, cited in Barrett, p. 270.
18. Barrett, pp. 277–279.
19. Lefler and Newsome, p. 459.
20. Barrett, p. 279.
21. *Battles and Leaders*, "The Opposing Forces at Fort Fisher," IV, pp. 661–662.
22. Ludwig, p. 410.
23. Bryan and Meadows, p. 518.
24. Manarin and Jordan, XII, p. 273.
25. Boatner, p. 62.
26. Barefoot, p. 296.
27. Barefoot, pp. 296–297.
28. Barefoot, p. 297.
29. Nathaniel Cheairs Hughes, Jr., *Bentonville: The Final Battle of Sherman and Johnston* (Chapel Hill, N.C.: The University of North Carolina Press, 1996), p. 40. See also *O.R.*, XLVII, Ser. I, Pt. II, p. 1424, "Abstract

from field return of Hoke's Division for March 17, 1865."
    30. Manarin and Jordan, XII, p. 274.
    31. Barefoot, p. 297.
    32. *Ibid.*, p. 298.
    33. *Ibid.*
    34. *Ibid.*, p. 299.
    35. Ludwig, p. 412.
    36. Bryan and Meadows, p. 519.
    37. Barefoot, p. 299.
    38. Manarin and Jordan, pp. 273–275.
    39. Barefoot, p. 299.
    40. Livermore, p. 141.
    41. Fox.
    42. Livermore, p. 141.
    43. Fox, p. 551.
    44. Miller, III, p. 344.
    45. Manarin and Jordan, XII, p. 274.
    46. *O.R.*, XLVII, Ser. I, Pt. 1, p. 1056, cited in Manarin and Jordan, XII, p. 275.
    47. *O.R.*, XLII, Ser. I, Pt. I, p. 1080, "Return of casualties in Hoke's Division, Department of North Carolina, March 19–22, 1865."
    48. *O.R.*, XLVII, Ser. I, Pt. III, p. 697, "Organization of Hardee's Corps, March 26, 1865."
    49. *O.R.*, XLVII, Ser. I, Pt. III, p. 745, Major General R. F. Hoke to Maj. John Hughes, quartermaster, Hoke's Division, March 31, 1865.
    50. Manarin and Jordan, XII, p. 275.
    51. *O.R.*, XLVII, Ser. I, Pt. III, p. 732, "Organization of the Army near Smithfield, N.C., commanded by General Joseph E. Johnston, March 31, 1865, Hardee's Army Corps, Hoke's Division, Clingman's Brigade."
    52. *O.R.*, XLVII, Ser. I, Pt. I, pp. 1061–1062, "No. 285, Organization of the Confederate Forces, commanded by General Joseph E. Johnston."
    53. Manarin and Jordan, IV, p. 521.
    54. Bryan and Meadows, p. 519.
    55. Manarin and Jordan, XII, p. 275.
    56. Manarin and Jordan, XIV, p. 646.

Chapter VII

A History of the 8th Regiment

Be my Brother or I will Kill You.
—Sebastien Roch Nicholas Chamfort (1741–1794)
From Carlyle, *French Revolution*, 1837, vol. II, pt. 1, ch.12

Major and Minor Battles

Roanoke Island, North Carolina, February 8, 1862

Neuse River Bridge, Goldsboro, North Carolina, December 17, 1862

Battery Wagner, South Carolina, July-August, 1863

New Bern Expedition, January 28-February 10, 1864

Bachelder's Creek, North Carolina, February 1, 1864

Bernard's Mill, Black Water River, Suffolk, Virginia, March 29, 1864

Plymouth, North Carolina, April 17–20, 1864

Washington, North Carolina, April 27, 1864

Drewry's Bluff, Virginia, May 16–20, 1864

Cold Harbor, Virginia, May 31, June 1–3, 1864

Siege of Petersburg, Virginia, June 1864-April 1865

Globe Tavern, Virginia, August 18–21, 1864

Fort Harrison, Virginia, September 29–30, 1864

Fort Fisher, North Carolina, 2nd battle, January 13–15, 1865

Bentonville, North Carolina, March 19, 21, 1865[1]

A history of this regiment was written in 1900 by H. T. J. Ludwig of Mount Pleasant, North Carolina, formerly a drummer with Company H. His history has been published in Walter Clark's' multivolume work entitled *Histories of the Several Regiments and Battalions from North Carolina in the Great War, 1861–1865, Written by Members of the Respective Commands*, published in 1901.

The 8th Regiment was organized on September 14, 1861, at Camp Macon, near Warrenton, North Carolina. Eventually to be composed of ten companies, seven companies were formed originally, with the eighth company organized two days later under the leadership of Colonel Robert Ransom.[2] By September 20, this regiment had been transferred to service with the Confederate States of America. Two additional companies were mustered in on September 28, 1861. By the end of September, the 8th Regiment was composed of the standard 10 companies.[3] These companies were designated Company A through Company K, and were filled with men from counties in eastern North Carolina: Currituck, New Hanover, Caswell, Bertie, Hertford, and Pasquotank. However, Company I was from Alamance County, and Company K was from Rowan County.[4]

Initial training began at Camp Macon, before the regiment transferred to Roanoke Island. There, the regiment began setting up camp and working on the fortifications. By the first of October, the regiment consisted of approximately 650 men. They, together with the Third Georgia Regiment and others, attacked the enemy at Chicamacomico on October 4. The raid was successful and resulted in the capture of the enemy's camp and 55 prisoners. The regiment was then ordered to go to Hatteras. They moved to Pamlico Sound but returned to Roanoke Island on October 6. They were occupied with regular drills and work on the fortifications.[5]

The 8th Regiment, along with other units, spent the Christmas of 1861 and the winter months on Roanoke Island. Company H was ordered to Battery Huger on the northern part of the island. The rest of the regiment established camp near Fort Bartow. The troops expected an attack by the Yankee fleet at any time. That attack came on February 7, 1862, with the shelling of Fort Bartow. The Federals of the Burnside Expedition landed a large force of about 15,000, and a battle ensued on February 8. The Federals overwhelmed the 1400 Confederates, of which the 8th Regiment made up about a third of that number (586). The enemy crossed an "impassable marsh and flanked our little army." The fight was continued by the Confederates until it was determined that "further slaughter would have been useless and inhuman."[6]

Casualties in the 8th Regiment were five men killed, and seven wounded. Over the course of the time the regiment was stationed on Roanoke Island, 14 men died of sickness.[7]

After the battle of Roanoke Island, the captured Confederates were held for two weeks before being transferred to Elizabeth City, where they were paroled and allowed to return home. By the fall of 1862, the regiment was "re-assembled" at Camp Mangum near Raleigh. It was then assigned to Clingman's Brigade.[8]

Ludwig noted in his history of the 8th Regiment that the men participated in the funeral of Colonel Lawrence O'B. Branch, who had been killed at the battle of Sharpsburg (Antietam) on September 14, 1862.[9] Branch was, of course, buried with full military honors.

In October, the regiment was ordered from Camp Mangum to move to Camp Campbell, then to Kinston, and finally to Wilmington. The 8th Regiment took part in the fighting for the Neuse River Bridge near Goldsboro on December 17, 1862. They suffered the loss of 3 killed and 6 wounded. The winter of 1862-1863 was spent at Camp Whiting near Wilmington.[10]

Early in 1863, the 8th was part of the group of soldiers ordered to James Island near Charleston, South Carolina. They were sent to Savannah, Georgia, but after only 10 days were moved back to James Island, which bordered Charleston's harbor. A number of men died there from malaria.[11]

As the Federal pressure on the coast of North Carolina increased, Clingman's Brigade, including the 8th Regiment, were ordered to return to North Carolina. The regiment set up at Camp Ashe on Old Topsail Sound. Ludwig fondly noted how the men enjoyed fishing when they were not on duty. The "fishing holiday" was to last only a couple of months before the men were ordered back to Charleston where they faced the horrors of the Federal assault on Morris Island and Battery Wagner.[12]

The Federal siege of Battery Wagner on Morris Island on the south side of Charleston Harbor began July 10 and lasted 58 days, until September 6. During that time, the 8th Regiment of Clingman's Brigade were on duty on Morris Island for about 21 days: "from July 22d to August the 1st, from August the 8th to the 15th, and from August 22d to the 29th, the dates being given as approximately correct," according to Ludwig.[13] The almost unbearable conditions on Morris Island and in Battery Wagner necessitated the frequent rotation of the men defending Battery Wagner.

> While on the island the men were exposed at all times to the enemy's fire, both from land and sea. An attack had to be prepared for at any instant, either day or night. The men had to be ready for action at any moment. It was no place for rest. The battery, frequently shelled by the enemy's ironclads, had to be repaired. To expose one's self to view meant being shot at with the attending consequences. The men had to keep under cover of the battery or in pits near by, dug in the sand-hills along the beach. Under such circumstances it was necessary to relieve the men once about every seven or eight days.[14]

The newspapers in North Carolina reported news of battle casualties from other papers. Reprinted from the Charleston *Mercury* were reports of casualties, both from friend and foe, in the 8th Regiment at Battery Wagner on August 30, 1863.

"Captain Colt, company I, 8th regiment, slight injury to eyes; private William Barber, company A, 8th regiment, amputated finger; Capt. J. B. Cally, 8th regiment, slight shell wound in chest; private Thomas Harrell, company E, 8th regiment, killed by comrade, accidentally."[15]

The Union forces were determined to take Charleston, which they considered "the cradle of the rebellion." Their assault was slow and relentless, but the Confederates defending Morris Island and Battery Wagner were just as determined not to surrender. The conditions on Morris Island were horrible beyond belief. There was no place for cooking — food had to be carried from Charleston. The water was bad. The constant bombardment was nerve-racking. However, "the men were veterans," and "understood the value of strictly obeying orders." According to historian Ludwig, "The gallantry of the men who composed the regiment was never displayed more conspicuously than when defending Battery Wagner." He stated authoritatively: "The duties performed on Morris Island constitute one chapter in the history of the regiment of which every member may be justly proud."[16]

One of the worst days occurred on July 24 when the enemy kept up a steady bombardment for several hours. On that day, the 8th Regiment was stationed at Battery Wagner on Morris Island. Some of the men of the 8th were in the bombproof shelter, some on the sally port, and some guarding the parapet. The artillery shells were of a large caliber, "some of them measuring fifteen inches in diameter." If one exploded near a soldier, bleeding from his nose and ears would result simply from the force of the explosion.[17]

The Federal troops continued to inch closer day by day to Battery Wagner. The defending Confederates had to work day and night in shifts. A corps of about 20 handpicked sharp-shooters from the 8th Regiment were organized. Their efforts were described by Colonel Harrison in his report on August 12, 1863: "My sharp-shooters under Lieutenant Dugger, Eighth North Carolina Regiment do good work, though the Yankees are very shy and seldom show their heads."[18]

Eventually, after a long and bitter siege in the heat of a Charleston summer, Morris Island was abandoned, and the 8th Regiment was assigned to duty on Sullivan's Island on the north side of Charleston Harbor. They remained there until the end of November when they were moved to Wilmington, North Carolina, and eventually were sent to Petersburg, Virginia. They arrived in Petersburg on December 14, 1863. "It being evening when we arrived, the regiment was ordered to bivouack in the streets. Accordingly small fires were built in the street near the edge of the sidewalk, whilst the rock pavement served as our sleeping-place."[19]

After only a few weeks in Petersburg, on January 29, 1864, the 8th Regiment was ordered to move to Kinston, North Carolina, where they were engaged in a fight with Union troops at Batchelder's Creek. In this encounter with the enemy, Colonel H. M. Shaw was "struck in the head by a bullet" and killed while "sitting on his horse in the middle of the road, General Clingman being close to him."[20]

On February 4, 1864, after the death of Colonel Henry M. Shaw near New Bern, General Clingman wrote from a camp near Kinston, North Carolina, to Mrs. Henry M. Shaw, the widow of the fallen officer. The letter was published in the Raleigh *Semi-Weekly Register*[21] on February 12, 1864. Shaw had been a colonel in Clingman's Brigade for almost 18 months.

Clingman described Shaw's death:

> As we were riding together at the head of the Brigade, on the morning of the first instant, about 3 o'clock, he received the wound, and his death was immediate, and seemingly without pain, while the placid smile that rested on his countenance after death, struck the beholder as implying a satisfaction that he had fallen in the discharge of his duty.

In praise of the officer, Clingman wrote: "No more exemplary officer, no truer and more patriotic man has fallen in this bloody contest, and no one more sincerely lamented by all to whom he was well known." He noted that colonel Shaw was "more attentive to all the duties of his position than any officer that I have ever been in contact with, and the drill and discipline of his Regiment made it the object of the highest commendation wherever it was seen."

Colonel Shaw's death was a great loss to the regiment, and he was honored in the regimental history:

> His coolness under fire, and his calmness at all times in the presence of danger had an inspiring effect on the regiment, and doubtless much of the deliberation with which the men performed their duties on the field or in camp was due to the example set by their Colonel.[22]

The brigade commander, General Thomas L. Clingman, noted in his report: "the troops under my command performed the movements ordered with as much coolness and precision as I ever saw them on drill." He also praised Colonel Shaw, and noted that "there was not a single instance of desertion or straggling from his command during the expedition."[23]

After this engagement, the 8th Regiment was returned to Petersburg, Virginia. The 8th Regiment was then temporarily attached to General Matt W. Ransom's Brigade and sent on an expedition, commanded by General Robert F. Hoke, to recapture Plymouth, North Carolina. They traveled by railroad from Petersburg to Tarboro, then marched on foot to Plymouth, where they arrived on April 17. The 8th Regiment was positioned near the enemy's main line of fortifications. In addition to gunfire from the fortifications, the regiment was bombarded from the river by the Federal gunboats. One shell from a gunboat exploded in front of the regiment and killed and wounded "fifteen men of Company H."[24] Fighting continued over the next day, and the 8th Regiment was positioned in front of one of the enemy forts. When ordered to advance from its position toward the fort, the Rebel "yell" was given and the regiment moved forward under heavy fire from the fort.[25] The men performed admirably under heavy fire.

> Just at the moment the "yell" was raised the enemy's infantry poured a destructive

fire into the ranks of the [8th] regiment. Our artillery ceased firing as the regiment approached near the fort. The men rushed on, leaped into the ditch and attempted to scale the fort. While the men were attempting to climb over the outside of the fort the enemy threw hand-grenades into the ditch. Those who were in the ditch had to get out of it. The regiment then swung around to the right and attempted to break through the palisades on the side of the fort. The palisades had loop-holes, through which the enemy fired on our line. At this point many of the men were shot though the head. The regiment rushed up to the palisades, and as the enemy pulled their guns out of the loopholes our men put theirs in and fired at those on the inside. Such deadly work could not last long. The Eighteenth Regiment swung a little further around to the gate leading to the rear of the fort. The gate was burst open. The regiment rushed in and the fort surrendered. "Three cheers for North Carolina" were given by the regiment, thus announcing that the assault had been successful.[26]

Following this successful capture, the men of the 8th North Carolina Regiment attempted to take Fort William. The assault met with heavy fire, and they were forced to retreat, and the regiment lost many of its men in doing so. Totally surrounded, Fort William surrendered and the capture of Plymouth was secured. That success was not won without heavy casualties. The 8th Regiment lost 154 men killed and wounded, about a third of the total number. Individual casualties were Lieutenant Langley of Company G, killed; Captain Cook, Company H, and Lieutenant Thompson, Company F, wounded. The color-bearer of the regiment, Francis J. Perkins, was mortally wounded.[27]

After retaking Plymouth, the Confederate forces moved to Washington, North Carolina. They engaged in a skirmish with the rearguard of the enemy, and Lieutenant Caffey, of Company I, was wounded.[28] The Federal troops fled Washington, but not before looting and setting fire to the town. When the Confederates arrived, they found a "ruined City ... chimneys and Heaps of ashes to mark the place where Fine Houses once stood, and the Beautiful trees, which shaded the side walks, Burnt, some all most to coal."[29]

Leaving Washington, the 8th North Carolina Regiment was moved to New Bern before being transferred back to Petersburg, Virginia, on May 6, 1864. The Federal forces had destroyed the railroad bridge over the Nottoway River, and the Confederates had to march part of the way on the return to Petersburg.[30]

This move signaled participation by the 8th North Carolina Regiment in some of the major battles which took place in the state of Virginia. Once in Petersburg, the 8th Regiment returned to being part of Clingman's Brigade, and were, therefore, part of the fighting at Drewry's Bluff which began May 16, 1864. A line of battle was established beginning on the left with Ransom's Division, Hoke's Division on the right, and Clingman's and Corse's Brigades being held in reserve. After Ransom's and Hoke's men were "hotly engaged," and Johnson's Brigade was "hard pressed," the reserves were ordered in. The 8th Regiment of Clingman's Brigade moved forward "to charge with the steadiness characteristic of Carolina's soldiers." The enemy was driven back that day, but the fighting continued on May 17, 18, and 19th.[31] When the Union forces fell back and established a line across Bermuda Hundred Neck, Confederate General Beauregard ordered an advance, and the 8th Regiment was part of the charge. General Beauregard stated in his report: "Too much praise cannot be given to the officers and men who fought the battle of Drewry's Bluff."[32]

The five days that included the battles of Drewry's Bluff and Bermuda Hundred resulted in the loss by death or injury of between 80 and 100 men from the 8th

Regiment. Wounded officers included Captain Cook, of Company H, and Captain Hines, of Company G.[33]

As part of Hoke's Division, Clingman's Brigade, including the 8th Regiment, took part in supporting the Army of Northern Virginia under the command of General Robert E. Lee. Lee's tactics were geared to defend Richmond at all costs. Some of the hardest battles of the war took place near Richmond as Lee faced Union General Ulysses S. Grant.

Having just missed the engagement of the enemy at the Wilderness and Spotsylvania Court House, Clingman's Brigade joined other Confederate units at Cold Harbor.

On May 31, 1864, the battle of Cold Harbor began, and the 8th Regiment "was attacked by the enemy's cavalry in flank and rear," and sustained heavy casualties, which forced them to fall back. A major assault by the Federal forces took place the next day (June 1) against the Confederate line. The 8th Regiment of Clingman's Brigade was on the left of Hoke's Division. Against the enemy charges, the men of the 8th gave way, then advanced several times, until they succeeded in holding the line.[34] A. A. McKethan described the heroic actions of Clingman's 8th Regiment:

> Having driven the enemy from our front, the order to retire was not understood by part of our men and they were cut off, but not willing to give up, they, together with Lieut.-Col. Jno. R. Murchison and part of his, the Eighth North Carolina Regiment, continued the fight till entirely surrounded, not only with live, but also dead yankees.[35]

The fight continued as light skirmishing on June 2, and again an assault was launched by the enemy on June 3.[36] Casualties suffered by the 8th Regiment over the four-day battle at Cold Harbor were heavy. A total of 275 officers and men were either killed, wounded or captured in the 8th alone.[37]

Clingman's Brigade, including the 8th Regiment, were ordered to move from Cold Harbor to help defend the fortifications around Petersburg, Virginia. They arrived there on June 16 for an extended tour of duty in the trenches. The men "walked in ditches, ate in ditches, and slept in pits." The Yankees were positioned only about 300 yards away. The days were spent in repulsing assaults launched by the Federal forces. The duties of Clingman's men also included holding the defensive line after the Federals attempted to break through by means of a tunnel stacked with explosives which they detonated,[38] creating an enormous crater.

The next major action in which the 8th Regiment was involved occurred south of Petersburg on the Petersburg & Weldon Railroad. On August 19, 1864, the regiment was moved out of the Petersburg trenches to attack a strong force of the enemy which threatened the railroad. Along with the rest of Clingman's Brigade, which had been attached to Mahone's Division for this action, the 8th Regiment was ordered to advance through a "dense thicket." The men became scattered and some were captured. The fighting was disorderly, making it difficult to determine friend from foe. Bullets seemed to come from all directions. In the end, however, the Confederates were victorious, and about 3,000 of the enemy were captured.[39] This action, often referred to as Globe Tavern, was the battle in which Brigadier General Thomas Lanier Clingman was wounded in the leg. After this, Clingman was no longer able to lead his Brigade.

The next military action was directed at reclaiming Fort Harrison, which had been captured by the enemy on September 28, 1864. Clingman's Brigade was directed to make a frontal assault, with Colquitt's Brigade to follow. The charge was to take place in the daytime, "over open ground, about two hundred yards to the fort." It was clearly a *suicide* mission, comparable almost to the assault of the third day's fighting at Gettysburg on July 3, 1863, known forevermore as "Pickett's Charge."

> When the order to advance was given the men moved forward with a rapid run. The order was not to fire until the fort was reached. As soon as the forward movement began, and the regiment had got to the top of the hill, the enemy opened a terrific fire on the advancing line. Before it got to the fort the regiment was almost annihilated.[40]

The 8th Regiment entered the attack on Fort Harrison with approximately 175 men and officers. At the end of the battle, only 25 were left, commanded by Lieutenant Dugger of Company F. All the rest had either been killed, wounded, or captured. Colorbearer J. R. Barnhardt, "finding that he could not escape capture, tore the old flag that had seen so much service to pieces," to prevent it from being taken by the enemy.[41]

After the fall of Fort Harrison, the 8th Regiment was assigned to construct breastworks on the Darbytown Road, where they repulsed several enemy assaults. They continued there until the latter part of December, when Hoke's Division, including what was left of Clingman's Brigade, were ordered to move to Wilmington, North Carolina. The troops left on December 22 and traveled on boxcars from Richmond to Danville in "bitter cold." From Danville, they had to march on foot to Greensboro, North Carolina, where they again took the train to Wilmington.[42] The men of the 8th Regiment of North Carolina spent a lonely Christmas in transit from one battlefield to another.

Because the Federal fleet was again threatening Fort Fisher, the 8th Regiment was ordered to Sugar Loaf Hill about four miles north of the little fort. Arriving there on January 13, 1865, they set to work on throwing up defensive works between their line at Sugar Loaf and Fort Fisher. After the defenders of Fort Fisher surrendered, the Confederates were kept busy working on the breastworks, avoiding bombardment from the Federal fleet, and repulsing attacks from the Federal troops who had landed at Fort Fisher. While there was no hope of retaking Fort Fisher from the Yankees, the main objective of the Confederate forces was to keep the Federals from advancing on Wilmington. With defensive works and occasional skirmishing, this tactic was successful in stalling the advance until the Confederates were ordered to fall back toward Wilmington on February 18. The 8th Regiment was charged with covering the retreat of the Confederate forces from Wilmington on February 22, and they did an excellent job.[43]

From Wilmington, the 8th Regiment moved to Kinston, then to Wise's Fork near New Bern. An engagement occurred March 8–10. From there, the regiment traveled to Goldsboro then to Smithfield, and to the final battle at Bentonville on March 19. The 8th Regiment was held in reserve during the day, and that night placed on the left of Johnston's forces. After light fighting on the 20th of March, a heavy assault was made by the Federals on the 21st, and the Confederate forces withdrew to Smithfield. The 8th Regiment of Clingman's Brigade was the last to leave the field, and again acted as a rear guard.[44]

They 8th Regiment moved to camp at Smithfield for about three weeks, then were ordered to move to Raleigh by way of Chapel Hill. They crossed the waist-deep waters of the Haw River at Ruffin's Mill. From there they proceeded to cross the Alamance River, which was also swollen by recent rains. After the crossing, they marched to Archdale in Randolph County, where they learned of Lee's surrender on

April 9, 1865. Along with other Confederate troops in North Carolina, the 8th Regiment surrendered on April 26, and were paroled on May 2.[45]

Thus ended nearly four years of hard service. Of over 1,300 men who were members of the 8th North Carolina Regiment at some point during the war, only about 150 men (roughly 8.66 percent) were present at the final surrender.[46]

The men and boys of the 8th Regiment of Clingman's Brigade served bravely and honorably. According to the company's historian, H. T. J. Ludwig, the men of the 8th Regiment

> ...never refused to move forward when ordered, or to rally when pressed back by the enemy. They went where duty called them. The best of soldiers can do no more. The history they made belongs to North Carolina.[47]

Notes

1. Sifakis, p. 97.
2. Ludwig, "Eighth Regiment," I, p. 388. Hereinafter cited as Ludwig.
3. Manarin and Jordan, IV, p. 515.
4. Ludwig, pp. 387–389.
5. *Ibid.*
6. Ludwig, pp. 389–390.
7. Ludwig, p. 390.
8. *Ibid.*
9. Boatner, p. 80.
10. Ludwig, p. 391.
11. Ludwig, p. 391.
12. Ludwig, p. 392.
13. Ludwig, p. 393.
14. *Ibid.*
15. [Raleigh] *The Semi-Weekly Standard*, 4 September 1863.
16. Ludwig, pp. 394–395.
17. Ludwig, p. 393.
18. Ludwig, p. 394.
19. Ludwig, p. 395.
20. 25. Ludwig, p. 397.
21. [Raleigh] *The Semi-Weekly Register*, 12 February 1864.
22. Ludwig, p. 397.
23. Ludwig, pp. 397–398.
24. Ludwig, p. 399.
25. Ludwig, p. 400.
26. *Ibid.*
27. Ludwig, p. 401.
28. Ludwig, p. 402.
29. Barrett, *The Civil War in North Carolina*, p. 221.
30. Ludwig, p. 402.
31. Ludwig, p. 403.
32. Ludwig, pp. 403–404.
33. Ludwig, p. 404.
34. Ludwig, pp. 404–405.
35. McKethan, p. 212.
36. Ludwig, pp. 404–405.
37. Ludwig, p. 405.
38. Ludwig, pp. 406–407.
39. Ludwig, p. 407.
40. Ludwig, p. 408.
41. *Ibid.*
42. Ludwig, p. 409.
43. Ludwig, p. 410.
44. Ludwig, p. 412.
45. Ludwig, p. 413.
46. *Ibid.*
47. Ludwig, pp. 413–414.

Chapter VIII

A History of the 31st Regiment

The man who flees will fight again.
— Tertullian (c. 155–225)

Major and Minor Battles

Roanoke Island, North Carolina, February 8, 1862

White Hall [Whitehall], near Goldsboro, North Carolina, December 16, 1862

Battery Wagner, South Carolina, July–August, 1863

Batchelder's Creek, North Carolina, February 1, 1864

Plymouth, North Carolina, April 17–20, 1864

Drewry's Bluff, Virginia, May 16–20, 1864

Cold Harbor, Virginia, June 1–3, 1864

Petersburg, Virginia, siege, June 1864–April 1865

Globe Tavern, Virginia, August 18–21, 1864

Fort Harrison, Virginia, September 29–30, 1864

Fort Fisher, North Carolina, 2nd battle, January 13–15, 1865

Bentonville, North Carolina, March 19, 21, 1865[1]

The 31st Regiment was organized on September 19, 1861. The regiment was organized at Hill's Point, Beaufort County. Term of service was to be for only 12 months. John V. Jordan, of Craven County, was elected the first colonel, with Daniel G. Fowle, of Wake County, lieutenant colonel, and Jesse J. Yates, of Hertford County, major. At the time of organization, the regiment was made up of 950 men.[2]

The regiment's first assignment was on Roanoke Island, North Carolina. There were several small sand-covered forts on the island—Fort Bartow, Fort Blanchard, Fort Huger. The defensive force consisted of the 8th Regiment under Colonel H. M. Shaw; 31st Regiment, commanded by Colonel J. V. Jordan, and part of the 17th Regiment under Major Gabriel H. Hill. The entire force was under the command of Brigadier General Wise.[3]

The enemy landed a large force of about 15,000 men with artillery, and soon overran the Confederate forces. Colonel Shaw ordered the guns "spiked," to prevent use by the Federals, and ordered the men to move to the northern part of the island. However, they were soon surrounded and forced to surrender. Losses were heavy: 285 men either killed, wounded or missing. They were held until exchanged in September 1862. The regiment was reorganized at Camp Mangum on September 18, 1862.[4]

In December, the 31st Regiment was ordered to Kinston, North Carolina. Along with the 8th Regiment, Colonel Poole's Regiment, and Colonel Nethercut's Regiment, as well as Starr's and Badham's Artillery, they moved toward New Bern in order to draw the enemy from Tarboro. Colonel H. M. Shaw was in charge of the expedition, and they proceeded to Deep Gully. The enemy retreated, but in the process destroyed the bridge at Deep Gully near New Bern.[5]

The regiment was then ordered to White Hall on the Neuse River, where they took part in a battle there on December 16, 1862. The 31st Regiment was ordered to "picket the north bank of the river, but those orders were canceled on the morning of December 17, and the regiment, minus a 200-man detail, was sent to Best Station." From Best Station, most of the regiment moved to Spring Bank, near Goldsboro on December 18.[6]

"In that engagement a portion of the regiment was withdrawn under fire by Lieutenant-Colonel Liles without orders. But at that time we were not yet well under discipline, and officers sometimes acted independently."[7]

Losses in this encounter were two killed and 22 wounded. The men and officers were praised for their "great coolness under fire on this occasion."[8]

The 31st Regiment actually did not join Clingman's Brigade until after the battle at the Neuse River bridge on December 16, 1862,[9] but having become part of the brigade,[10] the 31st was ordered to Wilmington, and then to Charleston, South Carolina. Duties in South Carolina included defending James Island from attack, doing picket duty, and skirmishing. They were sent to Savannah and were there when the attack was launched on Fort McAllister. The 31st Regiment of Clingman's Brigade "was held in reserve, in rear of the fort," but were not needed because the enemy withdrew.[11]

On their first tour of duty in and around Charleston, the North Carolina troops met with less than standard Southern hospitality. An article appeared in a North Carolina newspaper concerning the 31st North Carolina Regiment which was, at that time, stationed on James Island, about eight miles from Charleston, South Carolina. The writer of the article stated that he had talked with a "friend yesterday who was just from Charleston," who described the condition of the North Carolina boys defending Charleston. Reportedly, there was much sickness in the regiment, "mainly typhoid fever," and that two of the Wake company, George W. Barber and Willis Wilson, had died, and about 20 others were sick.

The inhospitable conduct of the South Carolina residents was shown by their refusal to take "our State Treasury notes." The writer was of the opinion that if the Charleston residents did not want our "Treasury notes," then we "do not want them to have our troops." The writer noted the "ill feeling which exists between this State [North Carolina] and South Carolina," but denied that the people of North Carolina were "responsible for this feeling." The writer thought it ironic that North Carolinians had hastened to the relief of South Carolina, and that many of our troops were now in that state, "prepared to die in her defense; and the return we get for this is a refusal of our currency, and the bitterest denunciations of a large majority of our people as "Conservative traitors.'"

In retaliation, the writer of the newspaper article urged he people of North Carolina to refuse "South Carolina Treasury notes and shin-plasters...."[12]

Back on James Island, the men battled sickness and fever. They were moved to Mount Pleasant where they were charged with patrolling Sullivan's Island and alternatively, with sharing duty on Battery Wagner.[13]

Ordered to move to Virginia, the regiment got only as far as Wilmington, North Carolina, before they were ordered to return to Charleston, South Carolina. They arrived in Charleston in time to be part of the heavy assault on Battery Wagner launched on July 18 by the Federal forces. This was one of the most sanguinary battles of the war, taking into account the disparity of numbers [9,000 Federals versus 1,600 Confederates], and the advantage of the enemy with their fleet, consisting of iron-clad vessels, monitors and mortar fleet, as well as land batteries of heavy rifled guns, which opened bombardment on the fort at early morning and kept it up continuously until after dark, at which time, by a signal of a rocket thrown up from the shipping, the cannonading ceased, and the infantry front line consisting of 3,000 men, made the assault. The reserve of 6,000 did not sustain it, seeing their comrades thickly strewn over the plains dead and dying, they faltered and could not be gotten to the front. The number killed and wounded on our side was small, as we were protected by breastworks, the enemy's loss was very heavy....[14]

Some of the casualties suffered by the 31st Regiment after the massive Federal assault of July 18, 1863, on Morris Island were reported in the newspapers in North Carolina. Listed as casualties in the 31st were: Willis Kinlock, Company A, 31st Regiment, abdomen; and J. D. Johnson of Company B.[15]

During the attack on Battery Wagner on July 18 alone, the 31st Regiment had 7 men killed, 31 wounded and 1 was missing.[16]

From the horror of Morris Island and Battery Wagner, the 31st Regiment moved, as part of General Robert F. Hoke's Division, to Virginia where the major battles were to occur in 1864. They camped at the "Jordan Farm" near Petersburg. They were then stationed at Ivor Station near the Blackwater River. It was at this position that the 31st Regiment of Clingman's Brigade encountered an enemy force of "150 infantry, 25 cavalry and two mountain howitzers." Four companies of the 31st and a part of Sturtevant's Battery plus some cavalry pursued the enemy and prevented them from boarding the steamer *Smith Briggs* which awaited them in the Blackwater River. The steamer was fired upon by the Confederates, and the enemy surrendered. The ship, which was Union General Benjamin F. Butler's flagship, was burned.[17]

After a short stay doing picket duty at City Point, the 31st Regiment was ordered to Drewry's Bluff, where they were situated to the right of the center with Hoke's Division. The 31st preformed admirably. President Jefferson Davis remarked that the charge of the 31st and 51st regiments at Drewry's Bluff "was the most gallant charge he ever witnessed."[18] A report in a Richmond newspaper read: "The charge made by the Thirty-first and Fifty-first Regiments on the enemy's lines, was most gallantly made, eliciting high compliments from both Generals Hoke and Clingman."[19]

The success at Drewry's Bluff culminated in Union general B. F. Butler retreating to Bermuda Hundred. The Confederates left him there, while troops were moved by train to Cold Harbor on May 31, 1864. The 31st Regiment arrived in the afternoon and were put in reserve for a dismounted cavalry skirmish. Being greatly outnumbered, the 31st was "soon flanked on our right, the enemy's skirmishers lapping entirely across our rear." They were thus forced to move back about a mile to the rear, where they threw up breastworks during the night "with the aid of bayonets, tin plates, etc." This site was to be "the attacking point of the memorable and bloody battle of the second Cold Harbor," one of the bloodiest battles of the entire war.[20]

The attack on June 1, 1864, by the Federal forces under General U. S. Grant was directed at Clingman's Brigade of Hoke's Division. It began about 3 o'clock P.M.

> The enemy advanced not only in line of battle, but on our left wing in heavy column, masked by the line of battle in front. This attack was signally and repeatedly repulsed with great loss to the enemy, in the entire front of our [Clingman's] Brigade. On the left flank of the brigade was the Eighth, then Fifty-first Regiment, then Thirty-first Regiment and Sixty-first from left to right, as designated. There was an interval between our brigade and a brigade on our left, in consequence of a swamp intervening between the two, which was considered impassable, therefore not protected by breastworks or troops; in this interval the enemy's heavy columns pressed forward and effected a lodgment, which then enfilading our line, compelled the Eighth and Fifty-first Regiments to fall back.[21]

The entire brigade was under continuous fire as they attempted to form a new line "across the open field, parallel to the original line." As they attempted to regroup, the 27th Georgia Regiment of Colquitt's Brigade advanced and helped Clingman's Brigade drive the enemy back, and the "whole of our original line was re-occupied, but the position on our left [the interval] remained in possession of the enemy without any attempt to retake it."[22]

The losses on both sides were heavy. In the three-week period which included Drewry's Bluff and Cold Harbor, Clingman's Brigade lost 1,172 men, as Brigadier General T. L. Clingman stated in a report dated June 5, 1864.[23] Clingman's entire staff were either "killed or wounded during one afternoon at Cold Harbor. "The writers of the regimental history, Adjutant E. K. Bryan and Sergeant E. H. Meadows, were both wounded at Cold Harbor. Bryan was unfit for duty for several months and Meadows was unfit for any additional military duty.[24]

Following the cessation of fighting at Cold Harbor, the focus shifted to Petersburg. Clingman's Brigade spent several months in the trenches during the hottest months of summer. "Subsequently, during the battle of Fort Harrison [September 29–30, 1864], the 31st Regiment of Clingman's Brigade suffered such heavy losses that only about 60 men out of the entire regiment remained," commanded by First Lieutenant Williams, the highest-ranking officer present.[25]

What few men remained were then ordered after the first of the year to Fort Fisher to participate in its defense on January 15, 1865. Since the enemy had already landed, the 31st and others fell back to Wilmington. The retreating Confederates crossed the Northeast Branch of the Cape Fear River on a pontoon bridge just minutes ahead of Federal troops: "the advance of the enemy arriving at the south bank just as our last troops had gotten across the river, and our pontoons cut loose."[26]

From Wilmington, the 31st Regiment moved to Goldsboro and then to Smithfield, where they awaited the advance of U.S. general Sherman from Fayetteville. The final battle at Bentonville, North Carolina, on March 19, 1865, pitted Confederate General Johnston against an overwhelming force under Sherman. Johnston retreated to Raleigh. The 31st Regiment retreated to High Point and the "village of Bush Hill," where the command was surrendered and paroled on May 1, 1865.[27]

Notes

1. Sifakis, p. 130.
2. James C. Birdsong, "Sketch of the Thirty-First Regiment," *Brief Sketches of the North Carolina State Troops in the War Between the States* (Raleigh, N.C.: Josephus Daniels, State Printer and Binder, 1894), p. 121.
3. Bryan and Meadows, "Thirty-First Regiment," II, p. 509. Hereinafter cited as Bryan and Meadows.

4. Bryan and Meadows, pp. 510–511.
5. Bryan and Meadows, p. 513.
6. Manarin and Jordan, "31st Regiment N.C. Troops," VIII, p. 426.
7. Bryan and Meadows, p. 513.
8. Birdsong, p. 9.
9. Bryan and Meadows, p. 513.
10. Bryan and Meadows, p. 513, note in their regimental history that Clingman's Brigade was "commanded by General Thomas L. Clingman, Statesman and soldier, ... a more fearless and gallant soldier never drew sword."
11. Bryan and Meadows, p. 513.
12. [Raleigh] *The North Carolina Standard*, 17 March 1863.
13. Bryan and Meadows, p. 514.
14. *Ibid.*
15. [Raleigh] *The North Carolina Standard*, 21 July 1863.
16. Manarin and Jordan, VIII, p. 427.
17. Bryan and Meadows, p. 515.
18. *Ibid.*
19. Bryan and Meadows, pp. 515–516.
20. Bryan and Meadows, p. 516.
21. Bryan and Meadows, pp. 516–517.
22. Bryan and Meadows, p. 517.
23. *Ibid.*
24. Bryan and Meadows, p. 518.
25. *Ibid.*
26. *Ibid.*
27. Bryan and Meadows, p. 519.

Chapter IX

A History of the 51st Regiment

The good die early and the bad die late.
— Daniel Defoe (c. 1660–1731)

Major and Minor Battles[1,2]

Neuse River Bridge, Goldsboro, North Carolina, December 17, 1862
Battery Wagner, Charleston, South Carolina, July 18, 1863–September 1863
New Bern, North Carolina, January 28–February 10, 1864
Batchelder's Creek, February 1, 1864
Plymouth, North Carolina, April 17–20, 1864
Drewry's Bluff, Virginia, May 16, 1864
Cold Harbor, Virginia, June 1–3, 1864
Petersburg, Virginia, June 1864–April 1865
Globe Tavern, Virginia, August 18–21, 1864
Fort Harrison, Virginia, September 29–30, 1864
Fort Fisher, 2nd battle, January 13–15, 1865
Bentonville, North Carolina, March 19–21, 1865

The 51st North Carolina Regiment was made up of companies from the Cape Fear region, the counties of Cumberland, Sampson, Duplin, Columbus, Robeson, and New Hanover. It was organized on April 13, 1862, with John L. Cantwell as colonel, William A. Allen, lieutenant colonel, and Hector McKethan, major. The regiment spent the summer months training at a camps near Wilmington and Southport. Companies D and K were employed building an "iron-clad fort" south of Wilmington. In August, the regiment was ordered to move to Kinston, North Carolina, where they were given picket duty at Core Creek.[3]

On October 1, 1861, the 51st Regiment, along with the 8th and the 61st regiments of North Carolina Troops, were assigned to become part of Clingman's Brigade. The exact dates on which the units of Clingman's Brigade were assigned are uncertain. It is probable that the 51st and 61st regiments were placed under Clingman's command on or about October 1, 1861, and that the 8th and 31st were assigned to him in late November.[4] At that time, Colonel John L. Cantwell resigned, and Colonel William A. Allen "assumed command." As part of Clingman's Brigade, the regiment continued doing picket duty and were sent on various scouting expeditions on the coast of North Carolina near New Bern.[5]

The 51st Regiment took an active part in the fighting against the Federal forces under Union brigadier general John G. Foster near the road and railroad bridges over the Neuse River on December 17, 1862. A. A. McKethan remarked: "Our men behaved with conspicuous gallantry and forced the enemy to retire before them." In this engagement, the regiment lost about 50 men killed and wounded. After the battle, the regiment returned to Wilmington for "winter quarters."[6]

Lieutenant Colonel William A. Allen and Vice Chaplain James B. Alford resigned. Allen, who had previously served as captain of Company C, 51st Regiment, had been appointed lieutenant colonel on April 30, 1862. He had then transferred to the field and staff of Clingman's Brigade. He resigned on January 5, 1863, because of "imputation[s] against my character" and also because of "rheumatism." At the time of his resignation, Allen was "being court-martialed" for arriving intoxicated at his camp on the night of December 30, 1862, at Rockfish Church and for using "the most abusive and insulting language" to Major Hector McKethan that night. He also challenged McKethan to a duel with "pistols." Allen's resignation was accepted on January 19, 1863.[7]

Vice Chaplain Alford, a Methodist Episcopalian, undoubtedly remained with the brigade. On August 20, 1864, he was appointed chaplain and was present or accounted for through January 2, 1865. He survived the war to be paroled at Greensboro on May 1, 1865.[8]

During their stay in the vicinity of Wilmington, North Carolina, Company D of the 51st Regiment was sent to Robeson to capture deserters. Attention was also focused on the activity of Federal ships. One Federal ship ran aground and its crew captured and jailed.[9]

Food shortages became acute, and Private William J. Burney complained to his father that he had "not had any meat since last Wednesday dinner [February 5, 1863] And I can not tell you when we will get any."[10]

The 51st Regiment was ordered to Charleston, South Carolina, in February 1863. They were sent from there to Savannah, Georgia, then returned to James Island which bordered Charleston Harbor. The climate was unhealthy there on the marshy island and the men "suffered greatly from sickness and scanty and unwholesome rations." They were glad to be returned to Wilmington the first of May to camp on Topsail Sound. Shortly after their arrival, Companies B, D, E, and H were detached and sent to the Wilmington and Weldon Railroad at Magnolia, in Duplin County, under the command of Major McDonald. On July 1, a detachment intercepted a Federal raiding party near Warsaw, and forced the Federal troops back toward New Bern. The four companies then rejoined the rest of the regiment at Wilmington. On July 11, 1863, Clingman's Brigade was ordered to return to Charleston, where a Federal assault on Morris Island by both land and sea had begun on July 10.[11]

On July 12, 1863, the 51st Regiment was sent to Morris Island to garrison Battery Wagner, a small work of sand, turf and palmetto logs on the tip of the island, next to the harbor and only a few hundred yards south of Fort Sumter. The fortifications at Battery Wagner extended "from the beach east to Vincent Creek and on the west about 200 yards." On the west were "wooden quarters for officers and men, and bomb-proof capable of holding from 800 to 1,000 men."[12]

While stationed at Battery Wagner, the men were:

> ...almost continuously exposed to the sharpshooting and cannonading of the enemy until the 18th [of July, 1863], suffering almost beyond endurance from heat and great scarcity of water and rations, to say nothing of the inferior quality of the same, and from the terrible shelling which was only equaled during the war at Fort Fisher, the average being twenty-eight shells per minute by actual count from sunrise to 7 p.m.[13]

When the massive Federal assault on Battery Wagner began on July 18, the men on Battery Wagner had 13 pieces of heavy artillery at their command: a 10-inch Columbiad, a 32-pound rifle, a 42-pounder, two 32-pound Carronades, two Naval Shell guns, one 8-inch sea-coast Howitzer, four smooth-bore 32-pound guns, and one 10-inch sea-coast mortar.[14]

However, according to A. A. McKethan, "only one" was of much use against the monitors, and the Federal land batteries "were beyond the reach of the other guns, so that we had little to do but submit to the hail of iron sent upon us by the superior and longer range guns of the enemy from sunrise until sunset."[15]

The 31st North Carolina had been sent to Battery Wagner on the night of July 17. Also there were the 51st Regiment under Colonel Hector McKethan, as well as a Charleston battalion commanded by Lieutenant Colonel Gailard, two companies of the First South Carolina Regulars, "acting as artillery." In addition, the 63rd Georgia Heavy Artillery and DePass' Battery were on hand — a total of about 1,700 men.[16]

The 51st and the Charleston Battalion were ordered to defend the parapets along the south front. Four companies of the 31st Regiment were to guard the area along the sea face adjacent to the 51st Regiment. The remainder of the 31st were held in reserve at Battery Gregg, on the tip of Morris Island. On the morning of July 18, the Federal forces launched a massive land and sea bombardment of Battery Wagner.

> During the bombardment we had concentrated upon our little band forty-four guns and mortars from the land batteries of the enemy, distant from 1,200 to 2,000 yards, and the heavy guns from the ironsides, five monitors and five gunboats, say about fifty guns, making a total of ninety-four guns. The sand being our only protection, fortunately one shell would fill up the hole made by the last, or we would have been annihilated.[17]

A barrage of over 9,000 shells, as reported by General Taliaferro,[18] rained down on the little sand fort for eleven hours. An eyewitness wrote:

> Huge clouds of sand were blown into the air from the craters formed by the bursting shells [another Confederate officer wrote]; the water of the bay was lashed into foam and thrown high in jets of spray by the ricocheting shots from the ironclads bounding from the water over the parapets and bursting within the work, while a dense cloud of sulphurous smoke hung like a pall over the scene.[19]

To minimize losses as much as possible, only those necessary "to guard and work the guns" were required to remain exposed. The remainder of the men stayed, as much as possible, in the bombproofs. However, "at a given signal each man was expected to report at his station in the works." At dusk on July 18, the signal was given and the men of the 51st Regiment, "encouraged and led by the officers," took their posts.[20]

The enemy's advance carried out between sunset and dusk was led by Colonel Robert Gould Shaw's 54th Massachusetts of black soldiers.[21] The men of the 51st Regiment defending the battery had not had time to mount the guns, so the "assault was met solely by our infantry, not a cannon being fired; but so murderous was our fire that the advancing columns broke and rushed to the rear through the ranks of their own support, causing confusion and delay." As Colonel Shaw was hit by gunfire, and fell dead on the top of the breastworks, his men "fled in wild terror."[22] Those men of the 54th Massachusetts who had reached the ramparts of Battery Wagner were "pull[ed] ... over" and "knock[ed] ... in the head" by the Confederates defending the fort. The Confederates were "infuriated at the sight of negro troops."[23]

By the time of the second Federal assault, the men of the 51st Regiment had had time to mount their heavy artillery guns, and opened fire on the enemy. Deadly fire was poured into the Federal troops, and they broke ranks again. A third and final assault was launched at about 10 o'clock that night. A Federal force which had made a "lodgment" behind the bombproof and the magazine was soon attacked in their rear by the 32nd Georgia Regiment and, with the Federal commanding officer dead, the Yankees surrendered.[24]

The next day (July 19), dead bodies littered the ground, and "at the bottom of the moat they lay in a pile like a swarm of insects struck by pestilence. Negroes and white were strewn together along the white sands for three quarters of a mile...."[25]

More than 1,500 Federal troops were dead, wounded, or prisoner. The 51st Regiment of Clingman's had borne the brunt of the Federal assault. Out of a total of 175 Confederate losses on July 18, the 51st Regiment lost 34 men killed and 40 wounded. (Officially, casualties in the 51st Regiment were reported as 16 men killed, 52 wounded and 6 missing — about a third of the total Confederate force on Morris Island on July 18.[26]) McKethan cites the enemy losses at "2,000, 800 of whom were buried in front of the fort next morning."[27]

The 51st Regiment of Clingman's Brigade suffered heavy casualties while defending Battery Wagner from the Federal assault of July 18. In Raleigh, the *North Carolina Standard* reported the casualties suffered by the 51st: A. Branch, Company K; L. M. White, Company D; T. J. Thornton, Company B, in the side; Captain E. Sutherland, Company A, "shot through the thigh at Fort Wagner, July 18"; Private N. Barber, Company F, "wounded by a shell" at Fort Wagner, July 18; Lt. J. D. Meloy, Company D, 51st Regiment, in the neck; Arch Graham, Company D; H. Hunter, Company C; Sergt. McArthur, Company C; Lt. G. W. Thompson, Company F, wounded in the leg, "since dead"; Sergt. W. B. Bowden, Company C, a head wound; U. Bass, Company I, scalp wound; S. Granthem, Company F, scalp wound; B. Porter, Company I, scalp wound; J. Abner, Company C; and J. Henderson, Company F, bayonet wound.[28]

The 51st Regiment was relieved and left Morris Island for Sullivan's Island. The men and officers were "complimented by General Beauregard for the manner in which they had behaved." In addition, a newspaper account praised the men: "The Fifty-first North Carolina brilliantly sustained the honor of their State and were highly commended, especially the field officers, Colonel Hector McKethan, Lieutenant-Colonel C. B. Hobson, and Major J. R. McDonald."[29]

One of the participants in repulsing the Federal assault of Battery Wagner on July 18, 1863, Lieutenant J. A. McArthur, Company I, 51st Regiment, was the "officer of the day" and had a guard of 65 men "detailed from the different commands" stationed on the island.

> In the third and last assault when the enemy secured a lodgment near the bombproof, he was ordered by General Taliaferro, in command of the post, to go with his guard to relief of that part of the line. As Lieutenant McArthur, led by one of the

Opposite, right: Fig. 20. Officers of the 51st Regiment, North Carolina Troops, one of the regiments of Clingman's Brigade. (From top, clockwise) Col. John L. Cantwell; Capt. Robert J. McEachern, Co. D; Capt. W. F. Murphy, Co. K; Capt. H. C. Rockwell, assistant quartermaster; Capt. George Sloan, Co. I; and Col. Hector McKethan. (Courtesy of the North Carolina Division of Archives and History, Raleigh, North Carolina. From *Histories of the Several Regiments and Battalions from North Carolina in the Great War, 1861–1865. Written by Members of the Respective Commands,* ed. Walter Clark [Goldsboro, N.C.: Nash Brothers, 1901], III, p. 203.)

men with a torch ascended the bombproof, the enemy began to fire upon them, and the fire was promptly returned as they advanced, but as they neared the enemy an Irishman from one of the Charleston companies in McArthur's detail, appealed to him to have the firing cease, as he had recognized the voice of his brother in the ranks of the enemy, which turned out to be true, for when they surrendered a few minutes afterwards the brother was found among the prisoners. Next morning the prisoners were formed to be sent to Charleston, when our Irishman appeared the second time begging that his brother should not be sent to prison, and when told that it could not be helped, as he had been captured with the others, he then proposed that his brother be permitted to enter the ranks by his side, and in this way the prisoner was transformed to a Confederate soldier.[30]

The 51st Regiment did their share of duty on Morris Island as the Federal forces, under Union general Gillmore, continued their siege over the next two months. The 51st returned again to Morris Island on July 29 to be relieved on August 3, during which time they lost 2 men killed and 7 wounded.[31] The battle flag of the 51st North Carolina Troops was "sadly torn by a shell while mounted on top of the Battery on the night of 18 July" and Colonel Hector McKethan requested a new one.[32]

Having reached the ditch in front of Battery Wagner, the Federals planned a final assault for September 7, but the little fort was abandoned by the Confederates the night of September 6. The 51st Regiment remained on Sullivan's Island and other sites in the Charleston vicinity until early in November when they were ordered to return to North Carolina. On November 24, the 51st Regiment arrived by rail at Tarboro, then marched to Williamston, where they were given to duty at Foster's Mill, in Martin County. Stationed at Tarboro from December 13, 1863, until January 5, 1864, the men were ordered to Petersburg, Virginia, to be stationed at Camp Hill. They did not remain long at Petersburg but returned to North Carolina to engage in the skirmish at Batchelder's Creek, and assisted in "driving the enemy from their positions and pushing them into New Bern."[33]

Returning to Petersburg, Virginia, the 51st Regiment remained there until ordered to Ivor Station on April 1. They marched to Suffolk, Virginia, and drove the Federal pickets to outside the town. The next month, about May 1, Union general Butler landed a large force at City Point, Virginia, and the 51st Regiment was recalled to Petersburg. They moved to Dunlop's Farm, and skirmished with the enemy for several days.[34]

The fighting in Virginia intensified. The 51st marched to Drewry's Bluff, a key fortification point on the James River between Richmond and Petersburg, and occupied the works there on May 12, 1864. On May 16, a charge against the enemy was ordered by General Beauregard. According to McKethan:

> This we did over ground strewn with fallen trees, the limbs of which had been sharpened as an additional protection for the works, but we pressed forward carrying line after line of the enemy until we had them in full retreat, and had the forces from Petersburg cooperated in the same manner we would have captured Butler's entire command.[35]

The 51st Regiment sustained heavy losses at Drewry's Bluff. Ten officers and 150 men were killed, wounded, or captured. Among the officers, Captain William H. Pope, Company E, and Lieutenant J. B. McCallum of Company D were killed.[36]

After skirmishes with the enemy on May 18 and 19, even greater casualties on both sides were to be sustained in the engagement at Cold Harbor (the second battle at that site). The regiment marched to Cold Harbor and were embroiled in a skirmish on May 31. The actual battle of Cold Harbor began June 1.

Here we were charged by line after line of the enemy, each line coming within a few yards of us, but our fire was so murderous they could not live under it; but notwithstanding we killed thousands of them, fresh lines were thrown at us until finally a lodgment was secured in a branch supposed to be impassable, and we were flanked and compelled to retire.[37]

Over June 1–2, the 51st Regiment lost 11 officers and 183 men, a total of 194.[38]

They remained at Cold Harbor for several days. They then moved to Malvern Hill and reached Petersburg in time to "prevent Butler from occupying the city."[39]

The regiments of Clingman's Brigade were spread across the defensive works at Petersburg. The 51st was engaged in repulsing the enemy on both June 16 and 17, 1864. At one point, the Federals broke through the line at a point "held by Wise's Virginia Brigade," and began a deadly fire upon the Confederate forces at a point held by the 51st and the 35th regiments. Five companies of the 51st, led by Colonel Hector McKethan, moved to the rear, and with the assistance of the 24th North Carolina charged and rushed with "fixed bayonet" and used both bayonet and rifle butt to regain the ground lost. One of the wounded, however, was Colonel McKethan.[40]

The siege of Petersburg, which began in June 1864, continued unabated until April 2, 1865. The city was defended by a network of trenches. Clingman's Brigade, including the 51st Regiment, helped man the fortifications from June 16 to August 19, when they were ordered to stop a Federal raiding party south of Petersburg on the Wilmington & Weldon Railroad. Although the action at the railroad was a Confederate victory, and a number of Yankees were captured, the Confederates suffered a number of casualties. Brigadier General Thomas Lanier Clingman was wounded and the brigade "lost the services of this gallant soldier till near the close of the war, the command of the brigade devolving on Colonel McKethan of the Fifty-first."[41]

Without Clingman, the men of Clingman's Brigade continued to function as a unit, and were ordered to the north side of the James River to retake Fort Harrison. The battle over September 29–30, 1864, was a grave mistake, and "a terrible blunder on the part of some one," the assaulting parties going in and being cut down by deadly enemy fire.[42] Colonel Hector McKethan (experienced soldier that he was) saw the futility of the action, and "protested against making the assault," but he and his fellow regimental leaders were "ordered by [their] superior officers to go forward, nobly offer[ing] themselves and their commands as sacrifices for their country."

As ordered the 51st Regiment of Clingman's Brigade moved quickly forward with the rest of the brigade, and "preserved their alignment until the stockade was reached, which they found impossible to pass." To go forward was impossible and "to retreat was death." The charge on Fort Harrison has been judged to be equal to or in excess of the Charge of the Light Brigade at Balaklava. It was agreed that "some one had blundered" but it was the duty of the common soldier to obey, no matter what he thought. Out of an estimated 200 men, the 51st Regiment lost seven officers and 97 men. What was left of Clingman's Brigade, under McKethan's command, was moved to occupy a line of works around Richmond near the Darbytown Road.[43,44]

During the 4½ months from May 15 to October 1, 1864, the fighting force available to the 51st Regiment, North Carolina Troops of Clingman's Brigade, was reduced from a total of 1,100 officers and men to 145 men.[45]

Along with others left from Clingman's Brigade that were now part of Hoke's Division, the regiment was ordered to move by rail to Wilmington to help defend Fort Fisher. When they reached

Wilmington on December 24, they found that bombardment had already begun. The men marched to Sugar Loaf Hill. The Federals landed the next day, but after a brief skirmish they withdrew to their ships and left the area. U.S. general Butler then was replaced by Brigadier General Alfred H. Terry, who returned with the Federal fleet on January 12.[46]

The 51st Regiment had returned to Wilmington about December 23, but was sent back to Fort Fisher with the rest of Hoke's Division. The Federal gunboats were shelling Fort Fisher, with "an even more awesome barrage than the one delivered against Fort Wagner," and General Braxton Bragg, who was Hoke's superior officer, ignored the pleas for help and reinforcements, so the fort had to be abandoned. Fort Fisher was stormed and captured on January 15.[47]

Hoke's Division held the line below Wilmington until February 19; three days later the city fell to the Federals, on February 22. Hoke's men were ordered to Kinston to oppose Federal troops coming from Goldsboro to New Bern. A battle occurred at Kinston (also called Wise's Forks and Southwest Creek), March 7–10.

On March 8, 1865, Hoke's Division and a small force under Lieutenant General D. H. Hill attacked the Federal left and right, and two isolated Federal regiments were captured by Hoke. The next day, there was more skirmishing when Hoke's Division attacked Federal lines. On the 10th of March, Bragg ordered another "double envelopment" using Hoke and Hill forces. After marching through swamps and dense forests to get to the rear of the enemy, Hoke's men did manage an assault, but it was broken up by cannon fire. The assault was called off by Bragg, and the Confederates retreated to Goldsboro and Smithfield to join with the forces of General Joseph E. Johnston on March 17.[48]

At Bentonville on March 19, 1865, there was heavy fighting when General Henry W. Slocum's Federal troops attacked Hoke's Division on the Confederate left. Hardee's Confederate infantry came crashing out of the brush and thickets in an assault that disorganized the Federal left. The Federals, however, managed to hold until they were reinforced and then they drove the Confederates back. Five Confederate assaults were smashed by a "hailstorm of grape and canister."[49]

The next day, the Federals were joined by the troops of Sherman and Howard. Johnston remained at Bentonville to cover the evacuation of his wounded. There was skirmishing all along his line, and Johnston fell back to Smithfield. Although there is no official report, the 51st Regiment sustained heavy casualties in the fighting at Bentonville.[50]

There were 36 members of the 51st Regiment at the surrender — they were all paroled.[51]

Some of the survivors of the 51st Regiment, North Carolina Troops, held a reunion at Syke Mill near Trefall, North Carolina, on September 5, 1903. A photograph was published in the Fayetteville *Observer-Times* of one of the veterans, John W. Atkinson, holding the battle flag of the 51st Regiment. This picture, submitted by Howard Muse, can be seen at Tim Bradshaw's website.[52]

Notes

1. Sifakis, pp. 151–152.
2. A. A. McKethan, "Fifty-First Regiment," in Clark, *Histories of the Several Regiments and Battalions from North Carolina in the Great War, 1861–1865, Written by Members of the Respective Commands,* III, pp. 204–221.
3. McKethan, p. 205.
4. Manarin and Jordan, XII, p. 259, footnote 6.
5. McKethan, p. 206.
6. *Ibid.*

7. Manarin and Jordan, XII, p. 276.
8. Manarin and Jordan, XII, p. 277.
9. Manarin and Jordan, XII, p. 260.
10. Manarin and Jordan, XII, p. 260. Letter from William J. Burney to his father, February 13, 1863, Burney Letters, Civil War Roster Project, Division of Archives and History, Raleigh, North Carolina.
11. Manarin and Jordan, XII, p. 261; McKethan, p. 206.
12. McKethan, p. 207.
13. McKethan, pp. 206–207.
14. McKethan, p. 207.
15. *Ibid.*
16. *Ibid.*
17. McKethan, p. 208.
18. *Wilmington Journal* [weekly], July 23, 1863. "The average per-minute volume of the Federal fire on July 18 is not entirely certain. Most historians accept General Taliaferro's report that the bombardment lasted for eleven hours 'without cessation or intermission' and consisted of '9,000 solid shot and shell of all sizes, from 15-inch downward.'" *O.R.*, Ser. I, XXVIII, Pt. I, p. 417, cited in Manarin and Jordan, XII, p. 263, footnote 27.
19. Samuel Jones, *The Siege of Charleston* (New York: The Neale Publishing Company, 199), p. 233, cited in Manarin and Jordan, XII, 263.
20. McKethan, p. 208.
21. The attack on Battery Wagner by the 54th Massachusetts Regiment has been memorialized in the motion picture *Glory* (1989).
22. McKethan, pp. 208–209.
23. Unpublished "Personal Reminiscences of the Civil War," Private A. T. Jackson (Company I, 51st Regiment N.C. Troops), Civil War Collection, Box 71 Folder 1, page 2, Division of Archives and History, Raleigh, North Carolina, cited in Manarin and Jordan, XII, p. 263.
24. McKethan, p. 209.
25. Peter Buchard, *One Gallant Rush: Robert Gould Shaw and his Brave Black Regiment* (New York: St. Martin's Press, 1965), 142, cited in Manarin and Jordan, XII, p. 264.
26. *Wilmington Journal* [weekly], July 23, 1863; *O.R.*, Ser. I, XXVIII, Pt. I, p. 77, cited in Manarin and Jordan, XII, p. 264, footnote 35. "Service records indicate the regiment lost 23 men killed or mortally wounded, and 50 wounded, none captured. See also *O.R.*, Ser. I, XXVIII, pp. 524–526; National Archives, Confederate States Army Casualties: Lists and Narrative Reports, 1861–1865 (M*36), Roll 3."
27. McKethan, p. 209.
28. [Raleigh] *The North Carolina Standard*, 21 July 1863.
29. McKethan, pp. 209–210.
30. McKethan, p. 210.
31. Manarin and Jordan, XII, p. 265.
32. Letter from Colonel Hector McKethan, dated September 29, 1863, from Headquarters 51st Rgt. N.C. Troops, Long Island, S.C. to Capt. White, A. A. Genl., in Thomas Lanier Clingman Papers, Southern Historical collection, Wilson Library, University of North Carolina at Chapel Hill, North Carolina.
33. McKethan, p. 210.
34. McKethan, p. 211.
35. *Ibid.*
36. *Ibid.*
37. McKethan, p. 212.
38. *Ibid.*
39. *Ibid.*
40. *Ibid.*
41. McKethan, p. 213.
42. *Ibid.*
43. McKethan, pp. 214–215.
44. The assault on Fort Harrison was launched on General Robert E. Lee's orders over General Robert F. Hoke's protest. Manarin and Jordan, XII, p. 271.
45. McKethan, p. 214.
46. Manarin and Jordan, XII, p. 273.
47. *Ibid.*
48. *Ibid.*
49. Manarin and Jordan, XII, p. 274.
50. *Ibid.*
51. Manarin and Jordan, XII, p. 275.
52. Tim Bradshaw, "Battle Flag of the 51st North Carolina Troops, http://www.geocities.com/Pentagon/Bunker/5870/flag.html.

Chapter X

A History of the 61st Regiment

All men think all men mortal but themselves.
— Edward Young (1683–1765)

Major and Minor Battles

Kinston, North Carolina, December 14, 1862
Neuse River Bridge, Goldsboro, North Carolina, December 17, 1862
Battery Wagner, Charleston, South Carolina, July 18, 1863, August 6, August 21, 1863
Drewry's Bluff, Virginia, May 16, 1864
Cold Harbor, Virginia, June 1–3, 1864
Petersburg, Virginia, June 1864–April 1865
Globe Tavern, Virginia, August 18–21, 1864
Fort Harrison, Virginia, September 29–30, 1864
Fort Fisher, 2nd battle, January 13–15, 1865
Bentonville, North Carolina, March 19–21, 1865

The regimental history of the 61st Regiment was written by Nathan A. Ramsey, Captain of Company D.[1] The regiment was organized in August 1862 and was made up of 10 companies. Each company was made up of approximately 100 men, with a range of 63 in Company F to 133 in Company H. The men making up the 10 companies came from Beaufort, New Hanover, Sampson, Craven, Lenoir, Jones, Martin, and Wilson counties on the coast, from Chatham County in the sandhills, and from Alleghany County in the Blue Ridge Mountains.

Because this regiment was not organized at the beginning of the war, these men were not involved in the Confederate defeat on Roanoke Island and the subsequent imprisonment of many Confederate soldiers. After this regiment was organized, it was assigned to become part of Clingman's brigade, commanded by Brigadier General Thomas Lanier Clingman. Initially stationed at Camp Lamb near Wilmington, the regiment moved on September 16, 1862, to Smithfield. Nine days later, after an outbreak of "yellow fever," it moved to Camp Radcliff.

During the fall months of 1862, the regiment marched to and from one coastal city to the next. They were marched to Goldsboro, Tarboro, and Plymouth. They were ordered on a forced march of 39 miles to arrive at Spring Green on November 4. A deep snow fell on November 6, and because of all the previous marches, 100 men in the regiment were barefooted. Thirteen members of Company D from Chatham County, North Carolina, died as a result of the cold, lack of proper clothing and shoes, and diseases brought on by exposure to the elements.² (See Chapter XI for more about the barefoot soldiers.)

The first battle in which the 61st was involved was near Kinston at the railroad bridge over the Neuse River. When they arrived at Southwest Creek on December 12, 1862, they found the bridge over the creek had been destroyed by "our troops." The 61st Regiment was posted on the west side of the creek to delay the advance of General Foster and his Union troops. Foster was known to be marching from New Bern with 10,000 infantry, six batteries and 40 pieces of artillery, with support of 640 cavalry. General Nathan G. Evans, of South Carolina, commanded the Confederate forces, which numbered 2,014.³

Foster reached the location the morning of December 13. One company of the 61st Regiment was involved in a skirmish at the bridge crossing, with a few casualties. Lieutenant Colonel Devane, with seven companies, removed to Hines' mills, about four miles away, and deployed the entire force "as skirmishers." Soon the fighting began. "Minie balls whistled through the air," as the men found themselves in a cross fire. They held their ground for a while, but eventually were forced to fall back because of the superior numbers of the Federal forces. The regiment retreated toward Kinston, but halted after retreating only about a mile to the rear. They formed a line of battle and a group of skirmishers advanced forward toward the enemy and fired off one round. They quickly retired, having determined that the "woods were full of blue coats," and that several Union regiments were flanking them on the left. They then received orders from General Evans to fall back, firing several rounds as they did so.⁴ Another stand was made in a field nearby, where an artillery "duel" continued for about an hour. There was also small-arms fire from the enemy, which was not returned by the 61st, because their guns were "inferior and we could not reach them."⁵ Casualties were slight during their initial battle as a part of Clingman's Brigade.

The Confederates left in the night through a swamp and arrived at Harriet's Chapel. It was bitterly cold, and the men were "wet, half-frozen, hungry and worn out," yet they did not complain.⁶

On December 14, 1862, the 61st Regiment, along with Evans' South Carolina brigade, awaited Foster's attack. The Confederates faced the Federal brigades of Wessell, Amory, and Stevenson. At one point during the battle, the 61st Regiment had to fall back because they were entirely out of ammunition. In spite of this, they were ordered back to the line by General Evans, and "all hands without a murmur promptly obeyed and returned to within 150 yards of the enemy without a solitary cartridge and half the men without bayonets." The Confederate forces were vastly outnumbered, and after 2½ hours of fighting, the Confederate forces were forced to fall back across the Neuse River. The Federals followed behind them so closely that they were able to take 400 Confederates prisoner.⁷

The final peril was having to pass over a burning bridge while under a heavy crossfire from the enemy only 250 yards away. Several of the men of the regiment were lost.⁸ In this event, the 61st Regiment lost 3 men killed, 13 wounded, and 69 captured.⁹

After the fight at Kinston, the 61st Regiment, under command of General Evans, marched to Goldsboro and arrived there on December 17, 1862. From Goldsboro they "tramped every step of the way right down the railroad track to Wilmington," and remained there from January 2, 1863, to February 8. The trek to Camp Lamb at Wilmington took 5½ days, through "continuous mud & water," and through the "most severe weather."¹⁰ A short interval was spent at Camp Davis on Masonboro Sound. The men pitched their tents within hearing distance of the waves crashing from the Atlantic Ocean on the shore.[11]

The men of the 61st Regiment spent their time on the North Carolina coast in drill, guard duty, and constructing breastworks. There were outbreaks of smallpox, measles, and mumps. Not all of the men had received the required smallpox vaccinations, and there were a few deaths.[12]

The regiment was ordered to move to Charleston, South Carolina, and they arrived there on February 18, 1863, for the first of two stints in South Carolina. On March 3, they moved to Savannah, Georgia, but, after only a week, returned to Charleston. The men of the 61st Regiment enjoyed their stay in Savannah and described it as a city of "most pleasant and delightful character." In Savannah, they were made welcome and were "royally entertained."[13]

The 61st Regiment was returned to Charleston and stationed on James Island, which was situated on the south side of the harbor between the Ashley River and Wappoo Creek. The 61st were not very fond of Charleston, South Carolina, and contrasted Charleston unfavorably with Savannah. They compared their return to Charleston to "dropping out of Paradise into Hell!" Stationed initially on James Island, the site was a "little Sahara" made worse by gnats and mosquitoes, and clouds of wind-driven sand. The men complained that the prices charged for food were double those in Savannah, and that North Carolina money was not accepted in payment. Knowing of the plight of Cumberland County soldiers serving in the 61st Regiment on James Island in the spring of 1863, the people back home in Fayetteville donated $3,408.55 in money and bacon to help out.[14]

Undoubtedly the food problem made a lasting impression on some of the men of the 61st Regiment. A sample of the prices the soldiers were forced to pay was mentioned in the regimental history: a small turnip was 15 cents, a baked sweet potato, 25 cents, and ground peas were 40 per quart.[15] The men endured the situation on James Island for eight weeks with bad water, poor and scanty rations, insects, and sand storms, all of which added to the decline in both health and morale.

The 61st and other regiments of Clingman's Brigade were moved from James Island to Sullivan's Island, where they fared somewhat better, until they had to serve a tour of duty on Morris Island.

Not all the activity was centered on Morris Island. On July 16, the 61st and four other regiments, with artillery and cavalry support, attacked Federal forces and naval vessels near Grimball's Landing on the Stono River. The Confederates fired on the Federal transport ships *Mayflower* and *John Adams*, as well as on the other naval vessels, *Pawnee* and *Marblehead*.[16]

During this attack, the 61st North Carolina was stationed on the right in support of the battery shelling the gunboats. Led by Colonel Radcliffe, artillery and infantry moved to attack, and with speed and silence, were able to surprise the enemy, and get off six rounds of shot aimed at the *Pawnee* before the boat could prepare to return the fire. "The rapidity and accuracy with which our batteries fired on this occasion has scarcely been equaled in artillery practice, more than one-third of the missiles discharged from our guns taking effect on the *Pawnee*...." After a two-hour battle, the damaged Federal boats withdrew.[17] One member of the 61st Regiment described Radcliffe's attack as "a perfect success. The 61st drove the enemy's pickets and reserves, and many of whom took refuge on board the *Pawnee*." He noted that when the gunboats retreated down the river,[18] "they shelled our artillerists and the 61st Regiment, all of whom were much exposed in an open field...."[19] Colonel Radcliffe was proud of the courage his men exhibited, and stated that during this encounter, his regiment, both officers and men, "showed ... by their proximity to danger, that they would never desert the batteries."[20]

On July 18, three of the regiments of Clingman's brigade were ordered to Sullivan's Island (8th, 51st, and 61st), followed the next day by the 31st Regiment. Over the course of the next seven weeks, these four regiments alternated tours of duty on the hellish Morris Island. The 61st Regiment defended Battery Wagner on July 25–31, August 6–11, and August 21–28.

Because of their determination to take the little fort the Federal bombardment was continuous, and seemed to even intensify as time passed. When the 61st Regiment was in Battery Wagner July 25–31, one soldier described it as:

> ...the most awful disquietude ... I ever witnessed, all of which was caused by the attack upon Wagner by five or six gunboats, three or four Monitors, the Aironsides [ironclads] & two Morter [mortar] Boats, in addition to their land Batteries.... Upon this narrow strip of land, exposed as it is to a cross fire almost, it would seem to one unacquainted with the changes of war that none but [those] who occupy the boom-proof [bombproof], of Wagner, could live, & hardly here; but it is true that [during] the five days we remained, the casualties were but few.... Those who cannot get in the Bomb proof are strung along the beach upon the sand Hills [dunes] from Wagner to Battery greg a distance of about a half mile & in full range of their [the enemy's] Gunboats & land Batteries. During the time of my stay, two Regts. occupied these Sand-Hills. Ours was one of the Regits, for I dont think a N. C. Regt. Ever got the safety of the Boom-proof & in fact I prefer being killed in the open air to dying with sufication.[21]

Captain N. A. Ramsey stated emphatically in his regimental history:

> During the four years of my experience in the army I found no place so uninviting as Battery Wagner on Morris Island. The bomb-proof, the only place of safety, cannot be well described, for all its dreary loathsomeness and horrors, and I will not attempt it.[22]

An account of what the men of the 61st had to endure on Morris Island was published in the *Wilmington Journal:*

> During the bombardment of Battery Wagner many little incidents have occurred which deserve a name in history. Among these is the following: On 29 July, 1863, the enemy got the range of a ten-inch Columbiad so completely as to render the place of extreme danger, and the South Carolina troops that manned the gun left it and ran into the bombproof for shelter. Their Captain ordered them back to their post, but they refused for a time to obey. While the men were wrangling with their officer, a soldier named Stedman from Company B, Sixty-First North Carolina Troops, *by himself, loaded, sighted and fired* the abandoned gun, hitting the Yankee boat at which he shot, while a hundred balls were whistling around him. Remember that this was a North Carolina soldier. Let us be proud of him. I thank God it was my happy privilege and good fortune to witness the abandonment of this gun, and the magnificent heroic conduct of Robert Winship Stedman. There was no braver soldier among the hosts of the Confederate army than Winship Stedman. God bless his memory![23]

(For more information on Robert Winship Stedman, see Chapter XI.)

The last tour of duty on Morris Island to be endured by the men of the 61st Regiment began on August 21. By this time, the Federal forces had advanced to within about 250 yards of Battery Wagner, and within 75 yards of the Confederate rifle pits. An attack was launched by the 24th Massachusetts on August 26, supported by the 3rd New Hampshire Infantry, toward a position held by Companies D, E, and G, of the 61st Regiment. Casualties on August 26 sustained by the 61st Regiment were 8 men killed (or mortally wounded), 22 wounded, and 67 captured. All but one of the men captured were from Companies D, E, or G.[24] Union general Quincy Gillmore reported that his Federals troops had captured 68 men, including 2 officers on August 26. General Beauregard stated that the Federals had captured "76 out of 89 men of the Sixty-first North Carolina Volunteers, who formed the picket."[25]

The 61st Regiment suffered casualties even while being transported by water from Morris Island on the night of September 2, 1863.

> ...the steamer *Sumter* was engaged in transporting detachments of the 61st North Carolina, 23rd Georgia and 20th South Carolina, from Morris Island to another part of the harbor. It had reached a position, coming in outside of fort Sumter, when, by some unfortunate blunder, it was fired upon by [Fort] Moultrie. A shot passed through its hull, causing it partially to sink, killing at the same time five men and wounding several others. Many of the men endeavored to escape by swimming, and of these twenty, it is said, were drowned. Barges were sent to the rescue and six hundred were saved from the wreck.[26]

The 61st Regiment spent the summer and fall of 1863 in the Charleston Harbor area, stationed on James, Morris, and Sullivan's Islands. They endured great hardships week after week and month after month. They spent their days on Sullivan's Island mostly doing picket duty. The sandbanks were their only protection from the "wind, the rain and the shells of the enemy." As the hot summer days gave way to the cooler night temperatures of fall, the hardships increased because as one soldier noted:

> Our tents and a good many of our blankets, cooking utensils, etc. are yet in Wilmington. The wind blows cold and just before day in the morning we suffer much for want of bedding. We have been in this condition for some time, and have no hopes of being relieved as long as the siege of Charleston continues. Our men, however, are much more cheerful than you would suppose under such circumstances. It would do your heart good to attend one of our moonlight prayer-meetings on the bald pate of some of these white sand hills.[27]

Finally, in December 1863, just before Christmas, this regiment and the rest of what was left of Clingman's Brigade were allowed to return to Wilmington, North Carolina.[28]

The next major action involving the 61st Regiment was against Union General Benjamin F. "Beast" Butler near Petersburg, Virginia. They participated in the battles at Drewry's Bluff, Chaffin's Farm, Bermuda Hundred, Cold Harbor and Fort Harrison, and suffered many casualties.

Drewry's Bluff

At Drewry's Bluff, on May 16, during a heavy Federal Attack, the 61st Regiment, along with the 8th, were sent to support General Bushrod Johnson. Hoke also sent two of Clingman's Regiments to protect Johnson's flank. However, they were placed in a position where their effectiveness was not as great as it should have been and "the moral and material effect of their presence was lost."[29]

The 61st Regiment lost 16 men killed or mortally wounded and 58 wounded during the period May 13–16, 1864.[30]

Cold Harbor

On June 3, 1864, at Cold Harbor, a shell fired by the enemy landed in the trenches occupied by the men of the 61st Regiment. Sergeant Thomas L. Graves, of

Company A, picked up the smoking shell and threw it out of the works, "saving many lives at the risk of his own." During the battle at Cold Harbor, another brigade gave way, and the enemy rushed through the break in the lines to attack Clingman's Brigade on the left flank. However, Clingman was in the trenches with the 61st Regiment, and when he saw the enemy in the rear, he "rushed forward and was gallantly followed by the regiment." The enemy was driven back. Clingman had no weapon, only a piece of fence rail.[31]

Private John M. Lewis, Company D, 61st Regiment, wrote his wife on June 10, 1864, that they had lost 1,100 men, either killed or wounded, since the fighting began back on May 7. But Lewis believed that the Yankees had lost more men than the Confederates.[32]

On June 16, the Federals attacked the Petersburg line south of the Hare farm. The Federal forces consisted of Winfield S. Hancock's II Corps, and brigades from the XVIII and IX corps. Hancock's attack hit hard at the Confederate forces under Bushrod Johnson and Hoke's Division, which was composed of Brigadier General James G. Martin's and Clingman's brigades. Hancock's men captured redans and some trenches, but with heavy casualties. Clingman's troops "took the brunt" of the Federal assault, but "repelled the attack with little difficulty." The activity in this action is unclear, because of a paucity of reports from both Federal and Confederate commanders, which makes it almost impossible to actually determine what happened to Clingman's men. A battlefield map drawn June 16 shows Clingman's left but not his right, and indicates that it was struck "head-on by one of Hancock's assault columns."[33] However, it is known that casualties were light. The 61st Regiment lost only one man mortally wounded and 17 captured.[34]

The next day at dawn, the Federals charged again, and captured 600 Tennessee soldiers who were asleep. The Federals did not succeed in breaking through the lines, however, and an attack in the afternoon was stopped by fire from the brigades of Clingman and Wise when one of the Federal units "became disoriented and began advancing almost parallel to Clingman's line." Clingman did not know this, and thought that the attack was a "feeble demonstration" that had been repulsed. However, at 6 P.M., Union brigadier general James H. Ledlie's IX Corps attacked the Confederates of Wise's Brigade and the 23rd South Carolina, which was positioned between Wise and Clingman. Wise's men "ran like sheep."[35] Clingman had to move his brigade to the right along the trenches to close up the gap. Four companies of the 61st North Carolina, led by Lieutenant Colonel Devane, set up a position at a right angle to the rest of the brigade to protect the rear.[36] They were soon joined by the 51st Regiment, to extend the line over to the 61st from Clingman's position.[37] The 51st entered the trenches with the 61st, and together with the help of the 34th Virginia Regiment of Wise's Brigade, kept the enemy at bay. The firing and advances against the lines continued unsuccessfully along the front manned by Clingman and other Confederates until nearly 10 o'clock. Around midnight, with only the light of the moon to guide them, a charge was made by Archibald Gracie's and Matt Ransom's brigades which drove the Federals back and "reestablished" the lines that had been broken around Petersburg. During this fight, the 61st Regiment lost 9 men killed and 10 wounded.[38]

On June 18, 1864, the 61st Regiment had "at least 2 men killed or mortally wounded, 4 wounded, and 1 captured." During the three-day period June 16–19, this regiment lost "16 men killed or mortally wounded, 31 wounded, and 18 captured."[39]

The men of Clingman's Brigade, including the 61st Regiment, remained at

Petersburg, living in the trenches. Ludwig, of the 8th Regiment, described the conditions which the men endured. They had to walk in the trenches and eat in the trenches, and at night they had to sleep in open pits. The picket lines of the opposing forces were very close together:

> No picket could be kept out in day-time. Hardly a day passed that the enemy did not fire on us from the battery immediately in our front, or from mortar batteries to our right.[40]

The weather at Petersburg did not help the situation. It was very hot and very dry, and had not rained in 50 days, one soldier wrote on July 18.[41] However, if it had rained, life in the trenches would have been far worse.

Throughout the month of July, Clingman's men worked on improving the fortifications around Petersburg, and tried to adjust to siege warfare. To break the stalemate, the Union forces had employed miners from some of the Pennsylvania regiments to dig a tunnel under the lines. On July 30, the 510-foot tunnel, packed with tons of gunpowder, was detonated. It exploded like a "volcano," and blew up 9 companies of Elliott's South Carolina troops. A crater was opened that was approximately 170 feet long, 60–80 feet wide, and 30 feet deep.[42] The crater was a horrifying pit, filled with wounded and dying Confederates and Federal troops trying to climb over them and the debris to reach the Confederate lines. The Confederate regiments in the trenches were bombarded by mortar shells, and Federal troops rushed to attack. Two brigades of Brigadier General William Mahone's Division were preparing to attack when assaulted by a weak Federal line, composed mainly of African-American troops. Though outnumbered, Mahone's men drove the Federals back into the trenches around the crater. Captain Edward Mallett of Company C, 61st Regiment, was sent in to reinforce Mahone's men.

> We had to march about two miles hurriedly, which, owing to the fact of the men being so long cramped up in the trenches, greatly exhausted many of them. On reaching the ground, having gone through a heavy shelling to do so, we were held for a while in reserve in a ravine, exposed to the hot sun but with only a limited supply of water. Several of the men fainted."[43]

Another attack, launched by Mahone, supported by the 61st, "carried the lip of the crater." According to Captain Mallett, the 61st Regiment was the only one of Clingman's regiments sent to the crater "as reinforcements."[44] This involved actually jumping into the crater, where the enemy forces were slaughtered through the use of rifle butts and bayonets. Some of the Black Federal soldiers were "shot, bayoneted, or bludgeoned while trying to surrender."[45]

Captain Mallett was put in command of the regiment after Colonel Radcliffe suffered a concussion from an exploding shell, and Lieutenant Colonel Devane was also absent due to a wound. Major Henry Harding was there, but did not lead the 61st in the attack. Harding resigned three days later.[46]

The fighting at the crater and the charge he led was described in detail by Captain Mallett:

> It was only intended at first that we should remain in reserve, as support; but the troops of Mahone's brigade failing to do all that was expected of them, we were ordered in with Wilcox's brigade [actually, Brig. Gen. John C. C. Sander's Brigade], and the 7th N. C. [17th South Carolina], to charge and retake the remaining portion of works.... I have heretofore felt that I would not be hurt, but in making this charge over about three hundred yards of open field, exposed to a hail storm of bullets, and about twenty pieces of artillery, and seeing the men cut down

all around me, I must say I never expected to reach the works; but a kind Providence protected me. After reaching the works we had a stubborn fight with the enemy for about a half hour, ... The enemy finally surrendered by hoisting a dirty Confederate shirt on a ramrod as a white flag. About one hundred surrendered at this time. I took a fine sword from an officer.... The fight ended about 3 o'clock (having commenced at daylight).... The hole made by the explosion from the enemy's mine is about twenty feet deep and some thirty or forty yards across, the sides and bottom of which were completely covered with dead yankees and negroes. It was the most awful sight I ever saw. We killed all of 500, and took over 1,000 prisoners.[47]

The losses as compiled from the rosters in volume XIV, *North Carolina Troops, 1861–1865: A Roster*, indicate that in the battle for the crater on July 30, 1864, 13 men of the 61st Regiment were killed and 31 wounded.[48]

In addition to combat duties, the 61st Regiment were sometimes used to round up deserters and once were sent to protect the citizens of North Carolina from "lawless deserters and conscripts." The citizens of Chatham and Moore counties got up a petition and Company D, 61st Regiment, was sent to round up deserters. Most of the men of Company D were from Chatham County and knew the territory. In a skirmish between the lawless men and Company D, the leaders of the gang were killed, over a hundred captives were taken, and order was restored to the community.[49]

Globe Tavern

The 61st Regiment was involved in the fighting for control of the Petersburg and Weldon Railroad. Union general U. S. Grant sent General Warren's V Corps south of Petersburg on August 18, where they captured the Globe Tavern, and tore up railroad track. A counterattack was launched by Confederate General Heth's Division which halted the Federal advance. While Heth attacked the Federal front, Mahone's, Colquitt's, and Clingman's brigades attacked the rear and captured more than 1,700 prisoners. The fighting in the dense woods was so intense it was impossible to preserve a "line of battle." The Confederate forces became scattered, and some were captured. Private J. M. Lewis of the 61st Regiment wrote that his regiment had attacked the Yankees from the rear and taken about 3,500 prisoners, but that they had not retaken the railroad from the Federal forces. Losses in the 61st Regiment on August 19 were one man wounded and 12 captured.[50]

Disaster at Fort Harrison

The 61st Regiment took part in the disastrous attempt to retake Fort Harrison on September 30, 1864. The regiment was led by recently promoted Major Mallett. Mallett was severely traumatized by the battle. He wrote of it afterwards:

> We indeed had a terrible time at Fort Harrison, I trust I shall never see the like again.... [I was] within 50 yds of the enemys works and [it was still] three hours before dark, and encouraged the men around me to have patience[,] that we would certainly escape, which all the others would have been able to do if our wounded ... had not called so loudly on the yankees for assistance and they consequently came over to them. I remained [behind] urging the men off until the Yankees were about ten steps from me ordering me to surrender which I politely declined doing, making it convenient at same time to "change my face" [about-face].[51]

McKethan's troops (Clingman's Brigade) performed admirably at Fort

Harrison. They alone "had attempted to carry out their orders. The result was very heavy casualties for the 61st Regiment: 22 men killed or mortally wounded, 53 wounded, and 62 captured, 11 of whom were wounded."[52]

Fall of Fort Fisher

Because of Union general Benjamin F. Butler's failure to capture Fort Fisher, he was replaced by Union brigadier general Alfred H. Terry. Terry launched an assault on Fort Fisher with a force of 9,600 men who landed "north of the fort under cover of naval gunfire." The 61st Regiment was sent from Petersburg back to Wilmington, and attached to Hoke's Division of 6,400 men.[53]

Southwest Creek

The 61st remained at Wilmington until after the fall of Fort Fisher. They were part of Hoke's Division that met Federal general Schofield's army at Southwest Creek for a battle March 8–10, 1865.[54]

Bentonville, North Carolina

The last battle in which the 61st Regiment participated was at Bentonville on March 19, 1865. Ramsey was put in charge of the skirmish line, and instructed to "go forward." The battle was described by Benson J. Lossing:

> Soldiers in that command who have passed through this score of battles will tell you they never saw anything like the fighting at Bentonville. Sherman and the National forces received six distinct assaults by the combined forces of Hoke, Hardee, and Cheatham, under the immediate supervision of General Johnston himself without giving one inch of ground, and doing good execution on the enemy's ranks, especially with our artillery, the enemy having little or none.[55]

Two major casualties occurred at Bentonville on March 19, 1865: Major Edward Mallett was killed, and Lieutenant Colonel William S. Devane was wounded.

Casualties in the 61st Regiment, Clingman's Brigade

Compiled from Information Supplied by Captain Nathan A. Ramsey, Company D, 61st Regiment in Walter Clark, *Histories of the Several Regiments....* vol. III, pp. 503–505.

Company (Number enlisted)	Died	Discharged	Killed	Missing	Prisoners	Wounded	Total
A (104)	14	9	3	2	6	21	55
B (82)	6	12	4		11	5	39
C (122)	13	5	19	6		14	57
D (184)	26	10	17		44	14	111
E (119)	6	8	3		19		36
F (63)	?	?	?	?	4	7	12
G (94)	18	4	9		18	10	59
H (133)	11	17	2		11	1	42
I (127)	18	7	9	1	8	26	69
K (106)	24	6	1		18	15	64
Total (1134)	136	78	67	9	139	115	544

After Bentonville, the 61st Regiment began their last retreat. After the official surrender on April 26, the 61st Regiment was paroled near High Point on May 2, 1865, and the weary soldiers headed for home.

Notes

1. N. A. Ramsey, "Sixty-first Regiment," in Clark, III, pp. 502–514.
2. Ramsey, pp. 506–507.
3. Ramsey, p. 507.
4. Ramsey, pp. 507–508.
5. Ramsey, p. 508.
6. *Ibid.*
7. Ramsey, pp. 508–409.
8. Ramsey, p. 509.
9. Manarin and Jordan, XIV, p. 599.
10. S. S. Biddle, Jr. to Rosa Biddle, January 5, 1863, Biddle Letters, New Hanover County Museum of the Lower Cape Fear, Wilmington, North Carolina, cited in Manarin and Jordan, XIV, p. 602.
11. Parrott F. M. Daniel to his mother, February 11, 1863, Asa J. Daniels Papers, private Collections, North Carolina Department of Archives and History, Raleigh, North Carolina, cited in Manarin and Jordan, XIV, 602.
12. Manarin and Jordan, XIV, p. 602.
13. Ramsey, p. 509.
14. Ramsey, p. 510.
15. *Ibid.*
16. *O.R.*, XXVIII, Ser. I, Pt. l, p. 755, cited in Manarin and Jordan, XIV, p. 608.
17. *O.R.*, XXVIII, Ser. I, Pt. 1, p. 590, cited in Manarin and Jordan, XIV, p. 608.
18. *O.R.*, XXVIII, Ser. I, Pt. l, pp. 375, 385, 393, 397, 407–410, 434, 443–444, 492, 499–500, cited in Manarin and Jordan, XIV, p. 610.
19. Letter from a member of the 61st Regiment, published in the *Wilmington* [Weekly] *Journal*, July 23, 1863, cited in Manarin and Jordan, XIV, p. 608, footnote 44.
20. *O.R.*, XXVIII, Ser. I, Pt. 1, p. 590.
21. A. J. Moore to Bettie Farmer, August 2, 1863, Moore Letters, cited in Manarin and Jordan, XIV, pp. 610, 610.
22. Ramsey, p. 511.
23. *Wilmington Journal*, article written in early August 1863, cited in Ramsey, p. 511.
24. Manarin and Jordan, XIV, p. 612.
25. *O.R.*, XXVIII, Ser. I, Pt. 2, p. 66; *O.R.*, XXVIII, Ser. I, Pt. 2, p. 85, cited in Manarin and Jordan, XIV, p. 612.
26. [Raleigh] *The Semi-Weekly Standard*, 4 September 1963.
27. A soldier of the Sixty-first to a Raleigh newspaper, September 23, 1863, cited in Manarin and Jordan, XIV, p. 613.
28. Ramsey, pp. 511–512.
29. Manarin and Jordan, XIV, p. 618; *O.R.*, XXXVI, Ser. I, Pt. II, p. 203.
30. Manarin and Jordan, XIV, p. 619.
31. Ramsey, p. 512.
32. James Manley Lewis to wife, Susannah Camelia Lewis, June 10, 1864, in John Manly Lewis Confederate pension application file, North Carolina Department of Archives and History, Raleigh, North Carolina, cited in Manarin and Jordan, XIV, p. 623, footnote 83.
33. Thomas J. Howe, *The Petersburg Campaign: Wasted Valor, June 15–18, 1864*, 2nd ed. (Lynchburg, Va.: H. E. Howard, 1988), p. 47, cited in Manarin and Jordan, XIV, p. 624, footnotes 84 and 85.
34. Manarin and Jordan, XIV, p. 624.
35. *Daily Confederate* (Raleigh), July 18, 1864; diary (typescript) of William Russell, 26th Virginia, June 17, 1864, Petersburg National Military Park, Petersburg, Virginia, cited in Manarin and Jordan, XIV, p. 624.
36. *Daily Confederate* (Raleigh), July 18, 1864, cited in Manarin and Jordan, XIV, p. 624.
37. Manarin and Jordan, XIV, p. 624.
38. Manarin and Jordan, XIV, p. 625.
39. Manarin and Jordan, XIV, p. 626.
40. Ludwig, "Eighth Regiment," I, p. 407.
41. Edward Smithwick to his mother, July 18, 1864, Smithwick Papers, cited in Manarin and Jordan, XIV, 627.
42. Manarin and Jordan, XIV, p. 627.
43. *Daily Confederate* (Raleigh), August 6, 1864. See also, *O. R.*, XL, Ser. I, Pt. I, p. 791, cited in Manarin and Jordan, XIV, p. 628.
44. Manarin and Jordan, XIV, p. 628, footnote 96.
45. Manarin and Jordan, XIV, p. 628.
46. William Lucius Faison, Adjutant, 61st Regiment, to Edward White, August 2, 1864, William Lucius Faison Papers, Southern Historical Collection, University of North Carolina Library, Chapel Hill, cited in Manarin and Jordan, XIV, p. 629, footnote 98.
47. *Daily Confederate* (Raleigh), August 6, 1864. See also *O.R.*, XL, Ser. I, Pt. I, pp. 791–792, cited in Manarin and Jordan, XIV, pp. 628–629.

48. Manarin and Jordan, XIV, 629.

49. Ramsey, pp. 512–513.

50. J. M. Lewis to S. C. Lewis, August 22, 1864, in John Manley Lewis's Confederate pension application file, quoted in Manarin and Jordan, XIV, p. 630.

51. Edward Mallett to S. S. Biddle, Sr., October 24, 1864, Simpson and Biddle Papers, quoted in Manarin and Jordan, XIV, p. 634.

52. Manarin and Jordan, XIV, p. 634; and footnote 110, p. 634.

53. Manarin and Jordan, XIV, p. 623.

54. Ramsey, p. 513.

55. *Ibid.*

Chapter XI

Heroes, Cowards or Fools

Show me a hero and I'll write you a tragedy.
F. Scott Fitzgerald (1896–1940)

The soldiers who made up Clingman's Brigade were only human, and as such they were not invincible, immortal, or infallible. The individual soldiers of the brigade normally obeyed orders and acted as they had been trained to perform under fire. In fact, on many occasions, individual soldiers and specific regiments of Clingman's Brigade received compliments from those in authority for their bravery and daring. However, over the course of the war, the actions of these men, both as a group and individually, ran the gamut from heroic to cowardly, and all the various degrees in between. Although we like to think of the Confederate soldier as being the hero in a great tragedy and always rising to the occasion with whatever action was needed to save the day, this was not always the case. There were incidents in which soldiers of Clingman's Brigade disregarded their orders and, therefore, endangered the Confederate position and the lives of many. This was the case with the men of the 31st Regiment stationed at Battery Wagner on July 18, 1863.

Yet, at the same time, there were individuals who consistently performed above and beyond the call of duty. Men such as Robert Stedman, Hector McKethan, and William H. S. Burgwyn stand out for their unselfish actions. The following will show several instances of heroic, cowardly, as well as foolish behavior of the soldiers of Clingman's Brigade.

The Shame of the 31st Regiment

One incident has forever stained the record of Clingman's Brigade, and no matter what the brigade did during the remainder of the war, this one act stood out — the refusal of the men of the 31st Regiment to obey orders to man the parapets at Battery Wagner during a heavy Federal assault. This failure almost lost the fort to the Union forces, and could possibly have resulted in the loss of Charleston in the summer of 1863.

It was at Charleston during the siege of Battery Wagner on Morris Island on July 18, 1863, that some of the men of the 31st Regiment of Clingman's Brigade refused to occupy their position on the parapets. For whatever reason, they "ingloriously deserted the ramparts, when, no resistance being offered at this point, the advance of the enemy, pushing forward, entered the ditch and ascended the work at the extreme left salient of the land face, and occupied it."[1] Lieutenant Colonel Charles W. Knight reported as follows:

> The line occupied by my regiment extended from the second gun from the bomb-proof to where the gun was dismounted, part of the line from the sally-port on the right to the right of Colonel McKethan's command [51st Regiment, N.C. Troops]. The working parties from Cumming's Point were engaged outside the sally-port main entrance.
> Owing to not being able to get my men in position where the bursted gun was, we were repulsed; afterwards made a charge upon them and were again repulsed. The number of men that made the charge was 20. The working party from Cumming's Point got in position in time to repulse the enemy at the main entrance.[2]

The 31st North Carolina Regiment of Clingman's Brigade not only brought shame and disgrace to the brigade when that regiment refused to man the parapets on July 18, but its refusal almost allowed the enemy to "enter the ditch" in front of Battery Wagner and capture the little fort.[3] However, Brigadier General William Booth Taliaferro called for volunteers to dislodge the enemy, and the men of the 51st Regiment of Clingman's Brigade "promptly stepped forward."[4] Thus, the fort was saved that day.

Colonel Hector McAllister McKethan

One of the tragic heroes of the war, Hector McKethan, of Scots ancestry, was born on September 15, 1834, at Fayetteville, Cumberland County, North Carolina. Named for his maternal grandfather, Hector was the oldest son of Alfred Augustus and Loveday Campbell McAllister McKethan. His brothers were Edwin Turner McKethan and Alfred Augustus McKethan, Jr.[5] He and his father, Alfred A. McKethan, ran a carriage works (a letter in Appendix D to brother Edwin Turner McKethan, dated February 5, 1863, mentions finishing some of the buggies).

Hector had been a member of the Fayetteville Independent Light Infantry since July 27, 1854. In the rifle competition held at the 62nd Annual Muster of the FILI, Hector's shot was deemed the "best single shot."[6]

On April 17, 1861, at age 26, Hector was enrolled in state military service when the Fayetteville Independent Light Infantry, also known as the "Old Independent Company," became Company H, 1st Regiment, North Carolina Infantry. This was a free-standing militia unit originally organized in August 23, 1793, and is the oldest still-active military command in the Southern states. As a member of the Fayetteville Independent Light Infantry, McKethan participated in the capture of the Federal arsenal on Haymount Hill in Fayetteville. The seizure of the arsenal for the Confederate government resulted in the capture of a large number of arms and much ammunition, and the equipment for manufacturing more. The men of this company occupied the arsenal until May 9, 1861, when they were ordered to Raleigh.[7]

Hector McKethan enlisted for a term of duty of 6 months. He was appointed 3rd lieutenant with his promotion to date from May 21, 1861.[8] This rank is also known as junior second lieutenant."[9] Hector's company, Company H, 1st Regiment, was among the very first units to leave North Carolina for Virginia. Companies F, H, and K left Raleigh on May 18 and arrived in Richmond that night. The entire regiment moved toward Bethel Church where, on June 10, 1861, the first actual battle on land between Union and Confederate forces occurred. A Federal force of about 2,500 from Fort Monroe were routed by a Confederate six-month tour of duty was over, McKethan mustered out on November 12–13, 1861.[13] He was appointed captain of Company I, 51st Regiment, on March 19, 1862. On April 20, 1862, McKethan was elected major and transferred to the field and staff of the regiment.[14] Company I was composed of men from Cumberland and Sampson counties and was mustered into service on April 23, 1862, when it was assigned to become a part of the 51st Regiment.

Hector's brother 3rd Lieutenant Alfred Augustus ("Gus") McKethan, Jr., of Company K (also transferred to Company B) of the 51st Regiment, North Carolina Troops, wrote the regimental history of the 51st Regiment, published in Walter Clark's multi-volume work.[15] Brother Edwin Turner McKethan also served as a 1st lieutenant in Company K, 51st Regiment. Company K was known as the "Confederate Stars."[16]

McKethan and other field officers were praised by General Taliaferro for their heroic action in saving Battery Wagner on July 18, 1863.[17]

Fig. 21. Colonel Hector McKethan, 51st Regiment, North Carolina Troops. (Courtesy of the North Carolina Division of Archives and History, Raleigh, North Carolina. From *Histories of the Several Regiments and Battalions from North Carolina in the Great War, 1861–1865, Written by Members of the Respective Commands*, ed. Walter Clark [Goldsboro, N.C.: Nash Brothers, 1901], III, p. 203.)

force of about half that number, approximately 1,200 men. Eighteen Federal soldiers were killed and only one Confederate died.[10] Because of the part the 1st Regiment played in the battle at Bethel Church, the state authorized the word "Bethel" to be inscribed on the regimental flag, and this regiment was henceforth known as the "Bethel Regiment."[11]

McKethan served with distinction in Company H (the Enfield Blues), 1st Regiment, at First Manassas, when he "crossed over under a heavy fire to the assistance of troops attached on the left...."[12] After his

... while I feel it is my duty to mention the disgraceful conduct of the Thirty-First North Carolina Troops, I am proud to bear testimony to the efficiency and gallantry of the other troops. Colonel McKethan's regiment, Fifty-first North Carolina troops, redeemed the reputation of the Thirty-first regiment. They gallantly sought their position under a heavy shelling, and maintained it during the action. Col. McKethan, Lieutenant-colonel [C. R.] Hobson and major McDonald are the field officers of this regiment and deserve special mention.[18]

At Cold Harbor on June 1, 1864, McKethan was in the midst of the fighting.

Captain W. H. S. Burgwyn, on the staff of Clingman's Brigade, had moved in front of the 51st Regiment, when he was wounded. He described McKethan's actions at a time when he, Burwgyn, was in front of the lines of McKethan's 51st:

> ...I [Burgwyn] received a tremendous blow which struck me I thought about the knee making me fall like an ox and suffering intense pain; I knew I [was] very painfully wounded and I thought my knee joint was shattered. Colonel McKethan grasped my hand and asked me how I was wounded and I told him I thought it might be mortally. He expressed great concern at my being wounded and ordered four of his men to carry me off.[19]

McKethan continued to provide admirable leadership until he was wounded near Petersburg, Virginia, on June 17, 1864. He recovered and returned to duty prior to September 1, 1864.[20] Hector returned to command the brigade just in time to witness the disaster at Fort Harrison on September 30.

This was his first fight after assuming command of Clingman's Brigade. Colonel McKethan saw that it would be impossible to take Fort Harrison, and he protested against making the assault. His superior officers disregarded his protest and ordered him and his troops to move forward. "Never was an assault made more gallantly or against greater odds."[21]

Described as a "young, chivalrous and daring colonel of the Fifty-First," Colonel McKethan never got over the disaster at Fort Harrison. As long as he lived, he could not speak of the events of September 30, 1864, "without quivering lips and moistened eyes" when he described the "fearful slaughter" of his men in what was deemed by many a "hopeless" assault. Yet, McKethan never failed to praise the efforts of his men and officers on that fateful day, when reinforcements "failed to come to his assistance."[22]

After the disaster at Fort Harrison, McKethan and his command were assigned to protect the lines around Richmond, where they remained until December.[23] Late in December they were ordered to Wilmington, North Carolina. Hector was hospitalized at Wilmington on January 15, 1865, with "melancholia." He transferred to another hospital on February 1, 1865.[24]

McKethan's "melancholia" may have been the result of the guilt he felt for the disaster at Fort Harrison, or simply from the strain of the past four years of service in the Confederate army. Fort Harrison may, simply, have been "the straw that broke the camel's back."

Colonel Hector McKethan was one of those rare men who did not know the meaning of the word *fear*. He was loved and respected by his men, who fondly called him "Old Hec."[25] He was a good man, who loved his family, and tried his best to do his duty to his state and country.

Although Hector McKethan survived the war, his health was ruined. He never married, and lived with his father in Fayetteville where he died at "10 minutes to 4 P.M.,"[26] Sunday, November 6, 1881. He was 47 years old. He was buried with full Masonic and military honors in the Cross Creek Cemetery, Fayetteville, North Carolina.

The obituary[27] of Hector McAllister McKethan was a grim final tribute:

> Col Hector McKethan, the brave commander of the 51st N.C. Regiment, during the rebellion, died at the residence of his father in Fayetteville last Sunday afternoon. Col McKethan, at the beginning of the war, entered the service of his country as first-lieutenant of Co. H, Fayetteville volunteers, and at the expiration of the first six months, the term for which his company enlisted, he returned home with the remnant of the Fayetteville battalion who had not yet re-enlisted, but not to remain. Shortly after his return,

cooperating with others, Col McKethan succeeded in organizing the 51st regiment and again entered the army. He was soon thereafter elected Colonel, and from that date to the close of the struggle proved himself worthy of the distinguished honor he enjoyed. He was a brave soldier, a discreet and valiant commander, and distinguished himself on many a bloody battle field. Having the esteem of his soldiers, they followed his lead and obeyed his command with a readiness which fully attested their devotion to him as a comrade and their confidence in his skill as their leader. More than once did he return from bloody contests with but a small number of those courageous fellows who entered with him. Just before the close of the war Col McKethan was called to act as Brigadier-General [sic] during the temporary absence of that officer, and was wearing the epaulettes of that office when the conflict ended. Brave and generous as he was, he's gone. Peace to his ashes; and may his surviving comrades, who laid him to rest at the tomb with military honors, see that his grave's kept green!

Perhaps Colonel Hector McKethan would rest easier if he knew that the battle flag issued to the 51st Regiment after the battle for Fort Harrison is on display at the Bennett House in Durham, North Carolina, the site of the surrender of General Joseph Johnston to General William T. Sherman. The flag is inscribed with the names of the principal battles the regiment participated in: *Goldsboro, Battery Wagner, Drewry's Bluff, Cold Harbor, Petersburg,* and *Fort Harrison*.[28]

Lieutenant Robert Winship Stedman

Robert Winship Stedman was perhaps the most courageous man in Clingman's Brigade. On more than one occasion, Stedman took charge of the situation and saved the day. He was not even defeated by the horror of Morris Island, which brought out the worst in men.

The most difficult situations tend to bring out the best characteristics in some individuals, and one such individual was Robert Winship Stedman, who found himself in the summer of 1863 in a living "Hell" created by the Federal bombardment of Battery Wagner on Morris Island in Charleston Harbor. Although the conflict there is overshadowed in history by the losses of Gettysburg and Vicksburg, nowhere along the Confederate lines were conditions worse or the fighting heavier than on Morris Island during that long, hot summer of 1863. Newspaper accounts during the siege described the fighting, the casualties, the carnage, and sometimes the courage.

Private Robert Winship Stedman, an artillerist of Company D, 61st North Carolina Regiment of Clingman's Brigade, helped to *untarnish* the image of Clingman's Brigade, and in doing so, he qualified as a genuine "hero." That he should act heroically is not surprising, considering Stedman's remarkable ancestry punctuated by generations of public service.

Robert Winship Stedman was an exceptionally handsome young man, with a John Barrymore–like profile (see Fig. 22).[29] His ancestry is quite remarkable, beginning with the migration after the Revolutionary War of three Stedman brothers (Winship, Nathan, and Elisha) from Connecticut to North Carolina. Winship Stedman, the grandfather of our hero, settled in Pittsboro, in Chatham County, where he was a prosperous store keeper. He willed his store to his son, Nathan A.[30] Nathan A. Stedman served his county and state in the North Carolina House of Representatives in 1827, and the North Carolina Senate in 1832–1833. He was comptroller of the state in 1834.[31]

The third generation was represented by our hero, Robert Winship Stedman,

Fig. 22. Robert Winship Stedman, Co. C, 61st Regiment, North Carolina Troops. (Courtesy of Division of Cultural Resources, Raleigh, North Carolina. From *Histories of the Several Regiments and Battalions from North Carolina in the Great War, 1861–1865, Written by Members of the Respective Commands,* ed. Walter Clark [Goldsboro, N.C.: Nash Brothers, 1901] III. p. 502.)

born May 8, 1837,[32] grandson of Winship Stedman, and son of Nathan A. and Euphania White Stedman of Fayetteville. Robert Winship Stedman had previously served as a private in the 2nd Company B, 36th Regiment, N.C. Troops (2nd Regiment, N.C. Artillery). He enlisted in Cumberland County on March 1, 1862, and transferred to Company D, 61st Regiment on November 29, 1862.[33] He performed his duties with courage in some very difficult situations, especially during his term of duty on Morris Island and in Battery Wagner.

On July 29, 1863, the Confederate soldiers in Battery Wagner on the northern tip of Morris Island were under heavy fire from the Federal forces, and some of the Confederate artillerists abandoned their guns. However, the very quick action of Private Robert Winship Stedman, an artillerist of Company D, 61st North Carolina Regiment, saved the day. The *Western Democrat* reported:

> ...the enemy got the range of a ten-inch columbiad so complete as to render the place [one] of extreme danger, and the South Carolina troops that manned the gun left it and ran into the bomb proof for shelter. Their captain ordered them back to their posts, but they refused for a time, to obey. While the men were wrangling with their officer, a soldier named Steadman [sic] ... by himself, loaded sighted, and fired the abandoned gun, hitting the Yankee boat at which he shot, while hundreds of balls whistled around him."[34]

Private Robert Stedman did not lose his courage when Morris Island was lost. Later that year, Stedman was elected 3rd lieutenant, Company A, 44th Regiment, North Carolina Troops, on December 1, 1863, and transferred to that regiment,[35] which was subsequently sent to Virginia. During the Battle of the Wilderness, May 5–7, 1864, there were several pieces of Confederate artillery in danger of being captured. The horses that pulled the heavy guns were all either dead or disabled. Lieutenant Stedman volunteered to "drag the guns back down the road out of danger," if 40 men would help.

Forty men immediately stepped forward and said they would assist, "although they all knew the effort was full of peril." The job was done, but only three of those volunteers escaped injury, and Stedman himself was wounded by grape shot.[36] Again, at Burgess' Mill in October 1864, Lieutenant Stedman "with less than fifty men charged and captured a battery of artillery which was supported by considerable force of infantry."[37] On October 27, 1864, Stedman was captured and confined at Old Capitol Prison, Washington, D.C. He was transferred to Fort Delaware on December 16, 1864, and held there until finally released on June 7, 1865, after taking the Oath of Allegiance.[38]

Stedman survived the four years of war and a Yankee prison only to be gunned down in a shootout on the streets of Fayetteville. The dispute that ended in gunshots apparently arose over politics. Stedman and Dr. William H. Morrow had attended a political meeting in Jonesboro. Morrow, an ex-surgeon of the Confederate States Army, had taken the Oath of Allegiance, and obtained a job as United States deputy marshal. In politics, he had since sided with the "Radical party." As the men were returning to Fayetteville on the train, they quarreled and Morrow drew a pistol on Stedman, who was unarmed at the time. When they reached Fayetteville, Stedman obtained a pistol from a local gunsmith. Later, he walked down the street opposite the Fayetteville Hotel where Morrow was staying. Morrow "appeared in the door way [of the hotel] and leveled his pistol" at Stedman. However, Stedman fired first, and the shot struck Morrow below the left nipple. Morrow fell to the ground. Several more shots were fired by each, until Stedman was hit in the lung and Morrow in the hip. Stedman turned, walked away, and then collapsed. He was taken into the hotel and died 20 minutes later. His last words were: "Boys, I am killed by a scalawag." Morrow lived until the following morning.[39]

Stedman's death was reported in newspapers across the state and his activities during the war were noted. The newspaper account of his death stated that Stedman "was one of the first soldiers who went into the war from this State, he having been an original member of the First North Carolina regiment," and "participated in the fight at Big Bethel." He is credited with having "killed the first Federal soldier known to have fallen in the war, and was personally complimented by General Magruder."[40]

Stedman was praised by Generals Kirkland and A. P. Hill for his rescue of the field artillery pieces at the Wilderness. One newspaper account described Stedman as one who had "passed thro dangers and difficulties unnumbered to meet his death at the hands of a renegade traitor to his native State."[41] Stedman died September 18, 1868, and was buried in Cross Creek Cemetery, Fayetteville. Subsequent replacement of his original tombstone has resulted in the year of death being given incorrectly as "1869."[42] So ended the life of a true Confederate hero.

The sites of Battery Wagner and Battery Gregg on Morris Island, the scene of a such a bloody struggle between the Federal and Confederates troops, can no longer be visited. Those little forts, the scene of such suffering, hardship, and heroism, were washed into the Atlantic Ocean many years ago. Out of such grief and tragedy, acts of heroism performed by men such as Robert Winship Stedman and others who endured the "Hell" provide us with glimpses of courage and valor that are truly worthy of being remembered.

Captain W. H. S. Burgwyn — A Gallant Hero at Drewry's Bluff

William H. S Burgwyn and his twin brother were born July 23, 1845, in Boston, Massachusetts, at the home of his maternal grandmother. William was the son of Anna Grenenough and Henry King Burgwyn. The Burgwyns were descended from the Welsch clan of Gwynn. The immigrant ancestor of the Burgwyn family arrived in Wilmington, North Carolina, in 1750. William's father, Henry King Burgwyn, attended the West Point Military Academy. The family was one of wealth and prestige, both in the North and South.[43]

Young William received an excellent education. After being tutored privately as a young child, at age 9 he was sent to the Episcopal School for Boys at Burlington, New Jersey, and at age 11 to Reverend Frederick Gibson's school near Baltimore, Maryland. He studied at Horner's School in Oxford, North Carolina, from 1857 to 1858, then attended Georgetown College near Washington, D.C. In 1860, William returned to North Carolina to enter the University at Chapel Hill. He was forced to withdraw because of a bout of typhoid fever. After his recovery, he studied briefly at the military academy in Hillsborough, North Carolina. The school closed when the war began.[44]

In 1861, at age 15, William enlisted in the North Carolina troops, and because of his brief military training, was appointed 2nd lieutenant. He was attached to Colonel Johnston Pettigrew's 22nd North Carolina Troops. After a brief time spent on the Potomac River in Virginia where batteries were being constructed, William Burgwyn was sent to Camp Mangum in North Carolina as an adjutant. He was promoted to 1st Lieutenant on July 4, 1862.[45]

In July 1862, Burgwyn joined the 35th North Carolina Regiment, commanded by Matt Ransom. He just missed the Seven Days' Battles. It was after this that Burgwyn began keeping a diary. He saw action at Sharpsburg (Antietam) and Fredericksburg in 1862. He was in North Carolina in 1863, and then in Virginia in 1864.[46] He joined Brigadier General Thomas L. Clingman at Petersburg on January 12, 1864, to become an aide-de-camp on the staff of Clingman's Brigade.[47]

On May 10, 1864, the 51st Regiment of Clingman's Brigade were ordered to assist in the defense of Drewry's Bluff, on the James River, just south of Richmond. Skirmishes continued over the next few days. On May 16, the men of Clingman's 51st Regiment were part of an assault that saw 4,000 casualties among the Federal forces. Union general Butler was driven back to Bermuda Hundred, a small neck of land lying between the James and Appomattox Rivers. With General Robert Ransom's men on Clingman's left, an attack was launched by the forces of General Hoke— General Corse's brigade and Brigadier General Clingman's men of the 31st and 51st. Although an aide on Clingman's staff, Burgwyn took the initiative, picked up the colors for the men to follow, and led them into battle. When the colors fell a second time, it was Burgwyn who rescued them.

Captain W. H. S. Burgwyn recalled the incident:

> I sprang upon the parapet, waved my hat and yelled with all my might. As soon as I could cross the ditch in front I ran ahead of the [Fifty-first] regiment, waved my hat and called on the men to follow, and nobly did they come on, though the enemy's sharpshooters fired as fast as they could pull trigger from the rifles that shot seven times in succession [Spencer rifles]. Though the line was considerably disorganized in crossing the ditch and in going

through the thick underbrush, not a man faltered. About three hundred yards from our works, fearing the enemy's fire and the bad ground before us might throw the men into confusion, there appearing some hesitation in the advance, I seized the colors of the Fifty-first Regiment and called on the men to follow. Running in advance about 200 yards, we came to the enemy's first line posted by squads in pits. As we rushed upon one of these pits, occupied by four men and an officer, I fell exhausted, which probably saved my life as the men fired as I fell, one ball passing through the brim of my hat. Rising with a shout, I rushed past the pits, and the Yankees surrendered in crowds. I had then just time to hand the colors to the color-bearer, when I fell down almost fainting, and a severe fit of vomiting seized me; but by the time the regiment had gotten somewhat into line, this passed off and seeing a piece of artillery about 250 yards distant firing at us, I again seized the colors and called on the men to charge the battery. With a yell that must have caused the Yankees to quake, we started, passed by the gun and kept on at full speed to charge the enemy's main line of battle about 450 yards off, posted behind rifle pits. Giving the colors to the color-bearer, I ran in advance, took off my hat, waved it over my head, cheering as loud as I could, which was not very loud, as I was now as hoarse as a raven. The first to reach the works I fell down again exhausted, but rising up as the men commenced to mount the works, I climbed over and we started after the flying enemy.[48]

This heroic action was not without repercussions, however. After leading the men to an advanced position, Burgwyn and the men who followed him found that they were being fired upon from the front and both flanks. They had to fall back to the "last works we charged, and then to the next, and finally to the line of the enemy we first struck in the charge," where they regrouped.

Clingman was very proud of Captain W. H. S. Burgwyn. When Colonel Henry King Burgwyn inquired of Clingman as to his son's conduct, Clingman answered with praise for the young Burgwyn for his actions on several occasions (see Appendix D). He described the young Captain as having "always shown himself intelligent, energetic and efficient." He noted that at New Bern, W. H. S. Burgwyn had "carried out orders with the same alacrity in danger that he did out of it." Clingman highly praised Burgwyn's actions at Drewry's Bluff where the young captain had been "in the front rank of the attack." He noted that he had also "rendered good service" at Bermuda Hundred. At Bermuda Hundred, Burgwyn had become ill, and Clingman had ordered him to the rear. However, just a few days later, on May 31, the young man joined Clingman and insisted on remaining with him, camping alongside the General on the ground that night.[49]

According to Clingman, Captain Burgwyn was "active in assisting to form the new line of battle and while advancing with it to the attack" at Cold Harbor, was wounded, but not seriously. Clingman was in hopes that Burgwyn would be able to return, which he did, only to be captured at Fort Harrison later in the year. Clingman promised Burgwyn's father that if the younger man wanted to return to his staff and could, there would be a position available as adjutant general.[50]

Captain William H. S. Burgwyn was captured at Fort Harrison on September 30, 1864. Shortly after the battle, on October 3, Colonel Hector McKethan wrote to inform General Clingman:

> ...Capt. Burgwyn who had recently reported and been assigned to duty as Inspector for the Brigade was, I regret to say, captured. He was unhurt when Maj. Mallett left him & I hope he is safe, with great gallantry he went in with the front line of the Brigade and found himself too near the enemies works to escape. He had

worked with great energy since his return and with marked benefit to the Brigade and I shall miss him sadly."[51]

Clingman worked to gain a promotion for Burgwyn, even while the young man was still a prisoner. In a letter to James A. Seddon, he remarked that Captain Burgwyn had been with his staff at New Bern, Drewry's Bluff, Bermuda Hundred, and Cold Harbor. He commented that Burgwyn "was always efficient and prompt and too careless sometimes in exposing himself to danger." He remembered that Burgwyn had been wounded at Cold Harbor and had only just recovered from that wound when he was captured at Fort Harrison. Clingman believed that Burgwyn's capture had been, in part, the result of his "inability to use fully his impaired limb, which was still weak."[52]

Captain Burgwyn was imprisoned at Fort Delaware and not paroled until March 1865. He surrendered with General Joseph E. Johnston in May. After the war's end, he returned to the University of North Carolina where he graduated three years later "with first honors." He continued studies in law at Harvard, and moved to Baltimore, Maryland, in 1869. Although he studied medicine at Washington Medical University and received his M.D. in 1874, he never practiced medicine. He returned to North Carolina and established the Banking House of W. H. S. Burgwyn and Company. This became the state bank known as the Bank of Henderson. He also established a plug and chewing tobacco manufacturing company, which marketed such brands as "Old Dinah," "Lost Cord," "Johnny Reb," and "Prairie Bull." A progressive individual, Burgwyn was instrumental in starting an electric light and water works system in Henderson. He also helped start an educational organization that would become North Carolina State University.

In addition to his business enterprises, William H. S. Burgwyn left a heritage that included regimental histories of the 35th Regiment, North Carolina Troops, and Clingman's Brigade, which were published in Walter Clark's *Histories of the Several Regiments and Battalions from North Carolina in the Great War, 1861–1865*. He also left six volumes of diaries, which were donated to the North Carolina Department of Archives and History. He married in 1876 at Baltimore, Maryland, Miss Margaret Carlisle Dunlop, a native of Richmond, Virginia. They had no children. Captain Burgwyn died January 3, 1913, and was buried in Raleigh.[53]

Brigadier General Thomas Lanier Clingman

Brigadier General Thomas Lanier Clingman was not above performing heroic deeds or placing himself in mortal danger. All of his life, he acted with dash and daring. He was described by James C. Johnston as "gregarious, pompous, and full to overflowing with himself."[54] An adversary and fellow Whig congressman, David Outlaw, described Clingman in 1849 as "not exactly crazy," but said that his "mental balance wheels, necessary to regulate properly the machine, either are absent or out of order."[55] Everyone agreed that Clingman was ambitious, and that he aspired to become the "first President of the Southern Confederacy."[56]

Because Clingman was outspoken, this trait brought him to a deadly situation—a duel "on the field of honor."[57] The two most famous "fire-eaters" before the war were Clingman and William L. Yancy, both members of Congress. On January 7, 1845, Clingman and Yancy were engaged in a heated debate in the House of Representatives. Clingman was insulted at some of Yancy's remarks, and notes passed between them, but the conflict could only be resolved by a duel. Clingman issued a challenge and it was accepted by Yancey.

Articles of Dueling

Art. 1. Weapons to be used, *smooth bore pistols*, of the usual duelling length,
Art. 2. Distance ten paces, (or thirty feet),
Art. 3. Pistols to be held *perpendicular*, the muzzles *up or down*, at their election,
Art. 4. The word to be given in a *clear, distinct,* and *loud* tone, as follows "*Gentlemen; are you ready: Fire — one — two — three-halt*"— at intervals of one second each.
Art. 5. The wind and sun to be equally divided.
Art. 6. The giving of the *word*, and the choice of *position*, to be decided by the toss of a dollar,
The one winning may elect *either*, but *not both*,
Art. 7. The pistols to be loaded by the seconds with powder and single ball, in the presence of all parties,
Art. 8. Each party will be permitted to have on the ground a surgeon and three friends, all of whom must be unarmed,
Art. 9. The seconds to be armed with pistols, loaded with powder and single ball,
Art. 10. The seconds to be permitted to examine the person and dress of each principal.
Art. 11. Neither principal to commence lowering or raising his pistol before the word "fire," nor after the word "halt."[58]

The duel was to take place on Monday, January 13, at 7 o'clock between Beltsville and the District of Columbia line, near the Washington turnpike. Both men fired and missed.

One of those present, Charles Lee Jones, declared that Clingman had "remained perfectly cool, fired, missed his adversary, but drawing his fire, in the ground, considerably out of line, the bullet scattering dust and gravel upon the person of Mr. Clingman."[59] At the urging of the friends present, both men resolved their differences amicably, without further gunfire.

That wild disregard for his personal safety was evident over the course of three days of fighting at Drewry's Bluff. Against heavy odds, the men of both Clingman's and Course's brigades performed well. General Robert F. Hoke, in his report to General Beauregard, stated that "great credit" should be given those commanders and their men for "their action." Even though both Confederate brigades were small, they performed their duty well. Hoke noted that his brigade commanders, including Clingman, "entered into the move with spirit, and rendered every co-operation."[60]

Many of Clingman's actions brought success in battle and praise for him and his men. At Cold Harbor, on May 31, 1864, the Confederate cavalry on Clingman's left "gave way," and through this break the enemy passed and attacked Clingman's Brigade on the left flank. Clingman noticed that "owing to the misconduct" of the commander of a detachment of his 51st Regiment, "they failed to drive the enemy there." The commander had been ordered to fire three times, but failed to do so, and "kept his men lying down in the road...." Clingman guessed that the enemy would soon surround them, and he ordered Colonel Hector McKethan to fall back, along with two other regiments. Just as Clingman himself was attempting to fall back, a shell took away the front part of his hat, and wounded him slightly on the forehead. Although stunned, he managed to get his regiments to safety. A few soldiers were captured but losses were fewer than 100.[61]

Not one to view the action from afar, Clingman was in the trenches at Cold Harbor on June 1 with the 61st Regiment when he saw that the enemy had gotten in the rear of the regiment. Clingman "rushed forward and was gallantly followed by the regiment," and the enemy was driven back. The only weapon Clingman had was "a piece of fence rail."[62]

Clingman and his men endured under the most adverse conditions in the trenches around Petersburg during the summer of 1864. The troops had to be rotated every three days. The heat, added to poor sanitary conditions, made everyone miserable.[63] There was no shelter from either rain or sun, and they were under constant bombardment from the nearby Federal guns. To expose one's head above the trenches was to invite death from a Yankee bullet. Malaria, diarrhea, and scurvy debilitated men and officers alike. There was no coffee, sugar or vegetables, and any food the men received had to be carried for a considerable distance from behind the lines. Clingman stated in a letter to his friend Col. H. K. Burgwyn, that he, Clingman, had been in the "trenches" for "more than fifty days." This period included time he had spent at Drewry's Bluff, Cold Harbor, and also Bermuda Hundred. Clingman inspired his men as he served alongside them in the trenches during June, July, and August 1864. The North Carolinians have been described as behaving "admirably" at Petersburg, Virginia.[64]

In another incident, Clingman's wild bravery and foolish disregard for personal danger resulted in an injury that effectively kept him from commanding his troops for the remainder of the war. The incident began when the Federal forces, directed by General Grant, began a move to extend their line to gain control of the railroad from Petersburg to Weldon, North Carolina, a vital supply line from the south which Lee needed to feed his troops. As Grant extended his lines south from Petersburg, Lee had no choice but to do likewise to protect the railroad from North Carolina to Petersburg.[65] The Federal V Corps launched several assaults along the railroad south of Petersburg, including one on August 19, 1864, where they were met by the Confederates forces.[66] Clingman's Brigade was among those dispatched to defend the railroad. His troops managed to penetrate some 600 yards through the Federal lines, and emerged from some woods within sight of the Globe Tavern. The Federal troops advanced and drove the Confederates back a short distance, but the boys in Gray soon regrouped and advanced again, only to be driven back a second time.[67] In one of those advances through the woods, Colquitt's and Clingman's men became disorganized and were ordered to their camps to regroup, an action which was reported by General Beauregard to General Lee. In a subsequent Federal attack, the Confederate forces held their line, and made a final "desperate attack," but were again repulsed. In the fighting, Clingman was wounded badly in the leg.[68]

Clingman had ordered some of his aides to ascertain the enemy's position, and had been assured that the enemy were located "behind some timber." The general was not satisfied with the reports and had to see for himself. Therefore, he rode out to make his own reconnaissance. As he rode near the spot where the enemy was reported to have been, he discovered that the reports had been correct. However, this knowledge came too late, and he found that he had ridden past the enemy and had gone too far to retreat without being seen. Believing that he was out of the range of the enemy guns, he spurred his horse, and "made a dash for life," but a ball fired from an enemy rifle struck him in the leg.[69] Some of Clingman's officers remarked that the accident could have been avoided.[70] Clingman was taken to a field hospital, and just before being given chloroform, "he put his pistol under his pillow," and told the surgeon, "If I wake up and find my leg cut off I'll be damned if I don't shoot the man who did it." Luckily, the surgeon did not find it necessary to amputate Clingman's leg.[71]

Clingman's actions were not without repercussions. Rumors were rampant. Confederate deserters reported to the Federal forces that General Clingman had lost a leg[72] and was mortally wounded.[73] The Richmond, Virginia, newspapers fueled the rumors, and reported that there were two known generals dead, and noted the "great despondency over the affair on the Weldon road."[74] Five days later, both deserters and Confederate soldiers taken prisoner by the Yankees still erroneously believed that Generals W. H. F. Lee, Clingman, Sanders, and Harris had been killed.[75] Undoubtedly, the rumors regarding the death of Clingman and other generals added to the demoralization of the troops. Clingman kept his leg, but he was unable to perform his duties as brigade commander.[76] He went to back to North Carolina to recuperate. Believing in the restorative powers of tobacco, Clingman applied a poultice of tobacco leaves to his leg wound, but was on crutches for several months.[77]

After the war, Clingman was, like many other veterans, "desolate and depressed in mind, wounded and exhausted in body, and utterly impoverished; yet he was ever ready to aid in building up the waste places of his country, and to repair ... the desolations of internecine strife."[78] He eventually traveled to Washington and later New York, and continued to be thwarted in his attempt to regain his seat in the United States Senate.[79] His role in the war ended any further national political aspirations.

The people of Buncombe County had faith in him, however. They elected him to the constitutional conventions of 1868 and 1875.[80] He was also a delegate to the national Democratic conventions of 1868 and 1876, and the state Democratic convention of 1876.[81]

He tried various means by which to recoup his fortunes. Intrigued by electricity, he was confident that it would soon illuminate the world. He worked on various processes for electric lighting and secured patents in the United States and several European countries. But these efforts failed because of his lack of "proper business direction and control."[82]

He turned his attention to other prewar activities. Together with William O. Walton he acquired three tracts of land totaling 1,920 acres in McDowell County, on which there were iron deposits.[83] He became a "one-man chamber of commerce for Western Carolina," and publicized the mineral resources of the area.[84]

He published two editions of his speeches and other writings, entitled *Selections from the Speeches and Writings of Honorable Thomas L. Clingman of North Carolina with Additions and Explanatory Notes*.[85] The first edition was published in 1877, and the second in 1878.

Although Clingman neither smoked nor chewed tobacco, he believed strongly in its curative powers. He had used it to heal an ankle sprain in 1847 after being thrown from a horse, and again in 1864 when he was shot in the leg. In 1885, he published a pamphlet entitled "The Tobacco Remedies—The Greatest Medical Discovery."[86] He went on to establish the Clingman Tobacco Cure Company at Durham, at which he processed tobacco that could be used as a cake, ointment, or plaster "to cure everything from gout to pleurisy, as well as insect bites, cuts, and bruises." He advertised extensively, but eventually even his home-town newspaper, the *Asheville Citizen*, became skeptical.[87] He reportedly spent the remnant of his "fortune" on publishing a pamphlet about his tobacco cure.[86] His family saw his inability to manage his financial affairs as his one deficiency.[89]

Clingman often spoke throughout the South at all kinds of gatherings and at various colleges and universities.[90] He was invited to lecture before the Philosophical Society of Washington, D.C. in May 1874 on volcanic action[91] in North Carolina, and again in January 1877 on water spouts.[92] He used these speaking engagements to heal the wounds caused by the war and to unite the country again. Yet, while complimenting the efforts of the soldiers furnished by North Carolina, he seldom mentioned his own role. He, like North Carolina Governor Zebulon B. Vance, was more concerned with the lack of recognition accorded North Carolina's Confederate troops, and Clingman repeatedly complimented them on their courage and abilities.

As to his own role, Clingman admitted that he was one of those Confederates "who did not abandon the contest til its close."[93] He firmly believed that he had rather be remembered as an "individual who lost most in the great struggle, than to have come out of it unscathed and prosperous." Yet, politician that he was, it is difficult to determine his true feelings about the war from his published speeches. He did write that he felt "a regret that I had not fallen in battle."[94] Perhaps this statement was made to an audience who saw Reconstruction as worse than death, or to comfort those of his audience who had lost loved ones in the war, or perhaps because he liked to think of himself as a Greek or Viking warrior, who believed it was more glorious to be carried home on his shield than carrying it.

Clingman continued to live in Asheville at the Swannanoa Hotel, where he spent his time talking to anyone who would listen.[95]

Mrs. J. E. Malone rode in a coach with Clingman on the way to Salisbury, and she described him as a "very noticeable figure; not so handsome, but of very striking appearance" (see Fig. 2 Chapter II). She noted that during the trip Clingman seemed "wholly engrossed in his own thoughts." When the stagecoach stopped, Clingman asked for a drink of water. Upon hearing the general's voice, a man emerged from behind the station and exclaimed, "I have followed that voice too often in the dark not to know it now." The man had been one of General Clingman's soldiers, and when Clingman reached out to shake the man's hand, he exhibited a real warmth. From that moment on, Mrs. Malone saw Clingman in a different light, as a "gallant soldier, who still after the lapse of twelve years, lived in the very hearts of the brave men he had commanded."[96]

Clingman's last days were indeed sad. As his health deteriorated and his mind began to fail, his nieces and nephews attempted to care for him.[97] In 1896, he was taken to the Confederate Soldiers' Home, but "this was too much for the pride of his state," and he was brought back to Asheville. There he lived upon funds which were "delicately placed at his disposal by friends," who would not permit such an "exalted citizen" to end his life in a "charitable institution."[98] Yet, his mental condition continued to deteriorate, and he was taken to the State Hospital for the Insane at Morganton, where he died on November 3, 1897. He requested that he be buried in his Confederate uniform. That request was honored, and he was buried in Concord on November 5, escorted to the cemetery by a group of Confederate veterans. The funeral was attended by a large number of people.[99]

Clingman was not allowed to rest in peace in Concord. At the request of his "old soldiers" and the people of Asheville and Buncombe County, his body was reinterred in Asheville's Riverside Cemetery.[100]

The Barefoot Soldiers of Company D, 61st Regiment

The death of 13 brave soldiers is one of the tragic stories of the war. In the winter of 1862, the 61st Regiment had been marching around the eastern part of the state of North Carolina since the first of October. They had marched to Goldsboro, then to Tarboro, then to Plymouth. On November 2, 1862, they marched from Plymouth over 39 miles to Spring Green. They then marched to Cross Roads. On November 6, a deep snow fell, and there were 100 men in the regiment who were "barefooted." It was a very cold, bleak day, and Captain Ramsey was concerned about 13 of his men who had no shoes. He would rather have had them stay behind and chance being taken prisoner than continue marching without shoes. However, the 13 barefoot men would not abandon their regiment. Only four days later, on the November 10, the first one of "these noble heroes who gave up his splendid life was Thomas Cotten, dying of pneumonia ... in ... Tarboro." Seven others died shortly thereafter, and two more died in Greenville. Ramsey bemoans their loss: "These thirteen men, barefooted and poorly clad, rather than remain behind, preferred to go forward, and ten of them paid the penalty in but a few days." The 13[101] men of Company D, 61st Regiment from Chatham County, North Carolina, who died were[102,103] (see below):

Name	Date of Death	Place of Death	Cause of Death/Age
Thomas Cotten	November 10, 1862	Tarboro, N.C.	pneumonia, age 25
J[ames] Carpenter	November 22, 1862	"	consumption, age 31
Monroe Thompson	November 22, 1862	"	not reported, age 26
Terry Poe	November 22, 1862	"	not reported, age 26
Wyatt Carpenter	November 26, 1862	"	not reported, age 20
J. A. Pilkinton	November 22, 1862[104]	"	not reported, age 35
William Gunter	December 2, 1862	"	not reported, age 20
Jefferson Womack	January 29, 1863	"	pneumonia, age 25
Nicholas L. Covert	December 9, 1862	Greenville, N.C.	measles, age 28
Elias Fields	December 25, 1862	"	not reported, age 25
Nathan Webster[105]	December 24/26, 1862	?	not reported, age 27

Notes

1. Manarin and Jordan, *North Carolina Troops,* VIII, p. 427.
2. *O.R.,* Ser. I, XXVIII, Pt. 1, p. 524, quoted in Manarin and Jordan, VIII, p. 427.
3. *O.R.* , XXVIII, Ser. I, Pt. I, p. 524, report of Colonel Charles W. Knight.
4. *O.R.,* XXVIII, Ser. I, Pt. I, pp. 417–418, General William B. Taliaferro to W. T. Nance.
5. Fayetteville Independent Light Infantry, Confederate Memorial Program, Cross Creek Cemetery, Fayetteville, North Carolina, May 10, 1991, held in honor of Hector McAllister McKethan, Captain, Fayetteville Independent Light Infantry, Colonel, 51st North Carolina Regiment. Hereinafter cited as McKethan Memorial Program.
6. *Ibid.*
7. *Ibid.*
8. Manarin and Jordan, III, p. 41.
9. Letter dated September 21, 1861, from Major James H. Lane to Adj. General, North Carolina State Troops, RG 501, James H. Lane Papers, Auburn University, Auburn, Alabama.
10. Robert E. Denny, *The Civil War Years:*

A Day-By-Day Chronicle (New York: Random House, 1991), p. 50.

11. Manarin and Jordan, III, p. 2.

12. Letter from Daniel H. Hill to Governor J. W. Ellis, dated June 21, 1861, cited in John W. Ellis, *Papers of J. W. Ellis*, Nobel J. Tolbert, ed. (Raleigh: Department of Archives and History, 1964), II, pp. 856-865.

13. Manarin and Jordan, III, p. 41.

14. Manarin and Jordan, XII, p. 277.

15. See "Alice Mason's Genealogy Page," at web site: http://mason.math.tntch.edu/alice.htm, and the "Descendancy Chart for James McKethan," at http://mason.math.tntech.edu/jasmck3.htm.

16. Manarin and Jordan, XII, pp. 289, 382, 387.

17. McKethan, "Fifty-first Regiment," p. 209.

18. *O.R.*, XXVIII, Ser. I, Pt. I, pp. 418–419, report of General William Booth Taliaferro.

19. Burgwyn, *A Captain's War*, p. 148.

20. Manarin and Jordan, XII, p. 276.

21. McKethan, "Fifty-first Regiment," p. 213.

22. Burgwyn, "Clingman's Brigade," IV, p. 497.

23. McKethan Memorial Program.

24. Manarin and Jordan, XII, p. 276.

25. Rev. D. S. McAllister, *Genealogical Record of the Descendants of Col. Alexander McAllister of Cumberland County, N.C.; Also of Mary and Isabella McAllister* (Richmond, Va.: Whitney and Shepperson, Printers, 1900), p. 140, cited in notes at http://mason.math.tntech.edu/mason/d0003/g0000014.htm.

26. A. A. McKethan family Bible, quoted at http:///mason.math.tntech.edu/mason/d0003/g0000014.htm.

27. Obituary, "Death of Co. McKethan," in Laurinburg, North Carolina, *Enterprise*, Wednesday, 9 Nov. 1881, cited at http:///mason.math.tntech.edu/mason/d0003/g0000014.htm.

28. Tim Bradshaw, "Battle Flag of the 51st North Carolina Troops," page 1, http://www.geocities.com/Pentagon/Bunker/5870/flag.html.

29. Photograph of Robert W. Stedman, Private, Co. B, 61st North Carolina Regiment, originally published in Clark, *Histories of the Several Regiments*, vol. III, page facing 503, courtesy of the North Carolina Department of Archives and History, Raleigh, North Carolina.

30. Will of Winship Stedman, Chatham County, North Carolina, Will Book B, p. 147, dated February 13, 1828.

31. John H. Wheeler, *Historical Sketches of North Carolina from 1584 to 1851* (1851; rpt. Baltimore: Regional Publishing Co., 1964), 87, 108.

32. Tombstone, Cross Creek Cemetery, Fayetteville, North Carolina, photograph courtesy of Carolyn Knott.

33. Manarin and Jordan, vol. I, p. 206.

34. Charlotte, North Carolina, *Western Democrat*, August 18, 1863, cited in Manarin and Jordan, XIV, pp. 689–690.

35. Manarin and Jordan, XIV, pp. 689–690.

36. Charles M. Stedman, "Forty-fourth Regiment," in Clark, III, p. 28.

37. *Ibid.*, p. 32.

38. Manarin and Jordan, X, p. 399.

39. "Tragedy in Fayetteville — Violent Death of Two Men," *Watchman & Old North State* (Salisbury), September 25, 1868, p. 3.

40. *Ibid.*, 3.

41. *Ibid.*, 4.

42. Photograph of tombstone, courtesy of Carolyn Knott.

43. Burgwyn, *A Captain's War*, p. xiii.

44. Burgwyn, *A Captain's War*, p xiv.

45. Burgwyn, *A Captain's War*, p xiv.

46. *Ibid*.

47. Burgwyn, *A Captain's War*, p. 114.

48. Burgwyn, "Clingman's Brigade," IV, pp. 491–492.

49. Letter from Brig. Gen. Thomas L. Clingman to Col. H. K. Burgwyn, father of Capt. W. H. S. Burgwyn, written from the trenches at Petersburg, Virginia, on June 25, 1864, W. H. S. Burgwyn Papers, Department of Archives and History, Raleigh, North Carolina.

50. *Ibid*.

51. Hector McKethan to Genl. T. L. Clingman, Chapin's Farm, October 3, 1864, William H. S. Burgwyn Papers, North Carolina Department of Archives and History, Raleigh, North Carolina.

52. T. L. Clingman to Hon. James A. Seddon, Raleigh, North Carolina, October 15, 1864, W. H. S. Burgwyn Papers, Department of Archives and History, Raleigh, North Carolina.

53. Burgwyn, *A Captain's War*, pp. xv-xvi.

54. James C. Johnston to William S. Pettigrew, March 6, 1850, cited in Siegmann, p. 79.

55. David Outlaw to wife, December 17, 1849, cited in Siegmann, p. 75.

56. *Congressional Globe*, XXIV 2, 1st Ses-

sion, 32nd Congress, p. 1156, cited in Siegmann, p. 105.

57. William L. Yancey, *Memoranda of the Late Affair of Honor Between Honorable T. L. Clingman, of North Carolina, and Honorable W. L. Yancey, of Alabama* (Washington, D.C.: by the author, 1845); Don C. Seitz, *Famous American Duels* (New York: Thomas Y. Crowell, 1929), p. 316; "Career of T. L. Clingman," p. 304; Burton J. Hendrick, *Statesman of the Lost Cause* (Boston: Little, Brown & Co., 1939), p. 142; Robert H. Bartholomew, "Tar Heel Fought Duel with Foe in Congress: Clingman Met Yancey in 1845," Winston-Salem, North Carolina *Journal & Sentinel*, 29 June 1952; and Sarah Biggs, "Clingman's Dome Named After Dueling Dentist," Winston-Salem, North Carolina, *Journal & Sentinel*, 10 July 1955.

58. Yancey, *Memoranda of the Late Affair of Honor between Hon. T. L. Clingman of North Carolina and Hon. William L. Yancey of Alabama*; Don C. Seitz, *Famous American Duels* (New York: Thomas Y. Crowell, 1929), p. 316.

59. John P. Arthur, *Western North Carolina: A History 1730–1913* (1914), (rpt. Spartanburg, S.C.: The Reprint Company, 1973), p. 367.

60. *O.R.*, XXXVI, Ser. I, Pt. II, p. 238, "Report of Major General Robert F. Hoke, May 25, 1864; and *O.R.*, XXXVI, Ser. I, Pt. II, pp. 236–238.

61. Clingman, "Second Cold Harbor," in Clark, V, pp. 197–199.

62. Ramsey, p. 512.

63. Henry Pleasants, Jr., and George H. Straley, *Inferno at Petersburg* (Philadelphia: Chilton Company, 1961), p. 46.

64. Ashe, *History of North Carolina*, II, pp. 916–917.

65. A. L. Long, *Memoirs of Robert E. Lee: His Military and Personal History Embracing a Large Amount of Information Hitherto Unpublished* (New York: J. M Stoddart & Co., 1886), p. 391.

66. *O.R.*, XLII, Ser. I, p. 858, report of General P. G. T. Beauregard, August 20, 1864; and Manarin and Jordan, IV, p. 520.

67. Orlando B. Wilcox, "Action on the Weldon Railroad," in Johnson and Buel, *Battles and Leaders of the Civil War*, IV, p. 569.

68. Burgwyn, "Clingman's Brigade," p. 495; and *O.R.*, XLII, Ser. I, p. 858, August 20, 1864.

69. J[arratt], "General Thomas L. Clingman," p. 169.

70. Kerr, p. 393.

71. J[arratt], "General Thomas L. Clingman," p. 169.

72. *O.R.*, XLIII, Ser. I, p. 858; and *O.R.*, XL, Ser. I., Pt. I, p. 19, U. S. Grant to H. W. Halleck, August 23, 1864.

73. *O.R.*, XL, Ser. I, Pt. II, p. 447, U.S. colonel Sharp to Lieutenant Davenport of Butler's Staff.

74. *O.R.*, XL, Ser. I, Pt. II, p. 442.

75. *O.R.*, XL, Ser. I, Pt. II, p. 442, General George G. Meade to General U. S. Grant, August 24, 1864.

76. Hill, p. 269.

77. Billy Arthur, "The Cure-All of General Clingman," *State*, L (July 1982), p. 9.

78. John H. Wheeler, *Reminiscences and Memoirs* (1884; rpt. Baltimore: Genealogical Publishing Co., 1966), p. 74.

79. Rutledge, p. 28.

80. J[arratt], "General Thomas L. Clingman," p. 170; Clark, II, p. 723; and Clingman, "Speech Delivered at Hendersonville, North Carolina," September 12, 1876, in Clingman, *Speeches and Writings*, p. 593.

81. *Who Was Who in America*, p. 180; and Frontis W. Johnson, ed., *The Papers of Zebulon B. Vance*, I (Raleigh, N.C.: North Carolina Department of Archives and History, 1963), p. 55n; Rosenberg, p. 243; and Wills, p. 24.

82. Kerr, pp. 394–395.

83. Mr. and Mrs. Judson O. Crow, *Land Entry Abstracts*, I (Spartanburg, S.C.: The Reprint co., 1982), p. 343—Entry Nos. 1988, 1898, and 1990, dated April 4, 1866, McDowell County, North Carolina.

84. Arthur, "The Tobacco Cure," *State*, L (July 1982), p. 9.

85. Thomas L. Clingman, *Selections from the Speeches and Writings of Honorable Thomas L. Clingman of North Carolina with Additions and Explanatory Notes,* 2nd ed. (Raleigh: John Nichols, Book and Job Printer, 1878).

86. Thomas L. Clingman, "The Tobacco Remedies—The Greatest Medical Discovery," in North Carolina Collection, Wilson Library, University of North Carolina, Chapel Hill, North Carolina.

87. Arthur, "The Tobacco Cure," 9–10.

88. R. A. Brock, ed., "The Career of T. L. Clingman," reprinted from the Philadelphia *Times,* October 10, 1896, in the *Southern Historical Society Papers*, XXIV (1896), p. 307.

89. Kerr, p. 395.

90. Clingman, "Davidson Speech," in Clingman, *Speeches and Writings*, pp. 39–53;

and Clingman, "Religious and Popular Orators: An Address Delivered at the Commencement of the University of the South, August 5, 1875, at Sewanee, Tenn.," in Clingman, *Speeches and Writings*, pp. 23–39.

91. Clingman, "Volcanic Action: Lecture Delivered before the Washington Philosophical Society, May, 1874," in Clingman, *Speeches and Writings*, pp. 78–83.

92. Clingman, "Water Spouts: Lecture before the Philosophical Society of Washington, January, 1877," in Clingman, *Speeches and Writings*, pp. 68–77.

93. Clingman, "Charlotte speech," in Clingman, *Speeches and Writings*, p. 112.

94. Clingman, "Davidson speech," in Clingman, *Speeches and Writings*, pp. 45, 48.

95. Frontis N. Johnston, ed., *Papers of Zebulon B. Vance* (Raleigh, N.C.: North Carolina State Department of Archives and History, 1963), I, p. 55n.

96. Mrs. C. E. Malone Ms., North Carolina Department of Archives and History, Raleigh, North Carolina.

97. Frances H. Casstevens, "The Puryear Family," in *Heritage of Yadkin County, North Carolina*, p. 561; J[arratt], "General Thomas L. Clingman," p. 170; and Bassett, p. 396.

98. Brock, p. 306.

99. "Gen. Clingman Dead, The Noble Former Senator and General Passed Away in the State Hospital of the Insane — Sketch of His Eventful Life," *The Union Republican*, 11 Nov. 1897.

100. Alice D. Grimes, "I'm Going to Be President," *State*, II (1934), 23.

101. Ramsey, pp. 506–507, only lists the names of 10 men.

102. *Ibid.*

103. Manarin and Jordan, XIV, p. 680.

104. Manarin and Jordan, XIV, p. 688. Information given here differs with Ramsey's report, citing date of death as December 29, 1862, at Raleigh, North Carolina.

105. Manarin and Jordan, XIV, p. 691. Webster is not listed individually in Ramsey's report, but he is probably one of three who died who are not named.

Chapter XII

Problems of a Brigade Commander

Discipline is the soul of an army. It makes small numbers formidable, procures success to the weak, and esteem to all.
— George Washington (1732–1799)
Letter of Instruction to the Captains of Virginia Regiment
July 29, 1759

A myriad of problems faced a brigade commander. It was the responsibility of the brigade commander to see to the health and welfare of a large group of men. He was responsible for the training of the men in the brigade in the art of war. He had not only to follow orders from his superiors, but he had to issue orders to his troops, to settle disputes, to solve problems, and see that discipline was enforced among a sometimes rowdy, sometimes unruly group of men brought together by a common cause.

Military organization in both the Union and Confederate armies was basically the same. The individual soldiers were placed in companies. Each company had approximately 100 men. The company was then assigned to a regiment. The companies were designed by letters of the alphabet (except for "J," which was always omitted). The average regiment had 10 companies, although sometimes artillery and cavalry regiments had 12 companies. Regiments were then assigned to brigades. Usually, a brigade was composed of four regiments (such as Clingman's Brigade), but could have as few as two. A brigade generally became part of a division, such as Hoke's Division. The division was part of a corps, such as Jackson's Corps, and the corps was part of an army. For the Confederates, this army might be either Lee's Army of Northern Virginia or one of 23 others. The Union forces had at least 16 armies.

Most regiments were made up of about 10 companies. According to Thomas L. Livermore, in the Department of North Carolina, the average number of men per company was 93.[1] A brigade composed of four regiments, each with about a thousand men, would equal a force at full strength of approximately 4,000 men. A division would, theoretically, have 12,000 men.[2]

To keep the brigade running smoothly took the cooperation of many men. The responsibility of food, clothing, arms, ammunition, promotions, detention for various infractions, and troop movements were all a part of carrying out orders from division, corps or district commanders. Clingman was fortunate to have Assistant Adjutant General Edward White[3] (see Figs.

25 and 26), Hal Puryear, William H. S. Burgwyn, and many others who were competent, educated men, loyal to Clingman and his brigade.

In July 1862, Clingman was given command of a brigade, and placed in charge of the defenses of North Carolina from Weldon to the Cape Fear River.[4] He almost had to build his brigade from scratch, and it was not complete until late in the year. Clingman had received approval from General D. H. Hill for 3,500 arms, and Colonel Josiah Gorgas, Confederate chief of ordnance, suggested that two regiments of infantry, Faison's and Radcliffe's, and another one "up on the country" and "several companies" of partisan rangers, be placed at Clingman's disposal.[5]

During the summer of 1862, the 55th and 56th North Carolina regiments were placed under Clingman's command.[6] Clingman soon learned that being a brigade commander was far different from being the colonel of a regiment, and he was faced with a variety of problems. The first problem was to notify the various individual regimental commanders that they had been placed in his brigade and were now under his command. Although Clingman had been appointed in May, some of the regimental officers had not been informed. An assistant adjutant general reported in August 1862 that one officer of the 55th Regiment had received the announcement of Clingman's new command, but that in the "excitement and confusion of the enemy's approach," he must have forgotten it, or simply "not paid sufficient attention to his business...."[7]

Eventually, the regiments came together and from the latter part of 1862 to the end of the war, the 8th, 31st, 51st, and 61st regiments of North Carolina infantry were part of Clingman's Brigade.

After the battle for the Neuse River Bridge, Major General S. G. French issued General Order No. 1, on December 18, 1862, which set out clearly the responsibilities of the brigade commanders. Article V stated that "Commanding officers will immediately put their commands in light marching order, and in the best possible condition, & keep constantly on hand three days cooked rations." Article VI stated that the brigade commanders were:

Fig. 23. Captain Edward White, assistant adjutant general, Clingman's Brigade staff. (Courtesy of Tod Thompson.)

XII. Problems of a Brigade Commander

...to see that Officers & men are habitually at their posts, no one should be allowed to be absent, except upon written leaves of the Brigade Commanders, & then only in cases of urgent necessity, commanders will by frequent roll-calls & other necessary & stringent precautions provide for the strict observance of orders.

Further, brigade commanders were ordered to "adopt & enforce the necessary regulations to prevent straggling on the march, & upon the battle field, the observance of such regulations being of paramount importance, must be effected by whatever means may be necessary."[8]

During the two years in which Clingman commanded the brigade, very little time was spent in actual combat or under siege. Two exceptions were the siege of Morris Island, near Charleston, South Carolina, from July to late November 1863, and the siege of Petersburg, Virginia, from July to September 1864. The men of his brigade were involved in several major battles which lasted more than one day each, such as New Bern, Cold Harbor, Drewry's Bluff, and Bermuda Hundred.

Thus, Clingman spent much of his noncombat time in routine duties such as assigning men to picket duty, supervising marches and drills, and in moving from one place to another. There were countless daily tasks to be accomplished and orders to be issued to insure that those tasks were done by a large group of men. Little things that had to be done almost daily often required more time than the actual battles, but it was the little things that often determined the results of the battle. The old saying is pertinent:

>...a little neglect may breed mischief ...for want of a nail the shoe was lost; for want of a shoe the horse was lost; and for want of a horse the rider was lost...[9]

Carried to the extreme, it is the little

Fig. 24. Captain Edward White's Confederate uniform. (Courtesy of Tod Thompson.)

things, such as the loss of a nail, that can result in the loss of a war.

Initially, Clingman was uncertain about many things involved with the administration of the brigade. Although a lawyer and politician by profession, Clingman's education enabled him to familiarize himself with military regulations and get down to the basics of the administration of his brigade. The orders which were issued to his regimental commanders and to men of his brigade have been preserved at Duke University. The order books have been designated for this work as "Order Book 1" and "Order Book 2." They are housed at Duke University. For typed copies of these orders, see Appendix A and Appendix B, respectively.

Most of the orders were handwritten by his assistant adjutant general, Edward White. Other correspondence in the Southern Historical Collection at Chapel Hill gives insight into just how a brigade was operated. These two collections are invaluable in that they provide a wealth of information about the inner working of a Confederate brigade.

Close analysis of the orders issued by Clingman paints a graphic picture of camp life, and provides the details of the many problems in a brigade of the Confederate States Army that had to be dealt with and solved by the general in command. How he solved those problems was dictated in part by military regulation, and in part by his own abilities and his ideas of what proper conduct should be. His ability to handle those problems influenced, in large measure, the performance of his brigade.

The two order books differ in both size and content. Order Book 1 consists of 39 pages and covers the period from November 25, 1862, to October 22, 1864. It contains announcements of staff appointments, notices of drill times, deadlines for reports, and regulations regarding permission to leave camp, as well as orders from higher authorities. The orders are written and signed by Assistant Adjutant General Edward White, and most state that they were done by the command of Clingman as the brigadier general commanding. A few of the orders have Clingman's name only, especially correspondence addressed to Confederate officials in Richmond or commanders of higher rank.

The first entry in Order Book 1 announces Clingman's appointment as brigadier general, lists the appointment of the men who were to be the officers of the brigade, and also names the regiments which had been placed under his command. Clingman then informed his men that they were to be stationed at Camp Whiting near Wilmington.[10] Many of the orders, especially those in Order Book 1, appear to be repetitions of orders received by Clingman from his superiors which were, in turn, relayed by him to his subordinates and men in the ranks.

Order Book 2 contains 114 pages and consists of orders and correspondence about specific problems. From these order books, it appears that Clingman conveyed directives from his superiors to his men promptly, clearly, and concisely. He followed up on orders, also, frequently reprimanding his officers for negligence in carrying out commands, or for their failure to submit reports promptly. Order Book 2 also contains many orders relating to matters pertaining specifically to the men in his brigade, such as disobedience, desertion, disorderly conduct, leaves of absence, promotions, and staff positions.

Of note is the fact that orders and correspondence are missing during the periods of time in which the brigade was in actual combat. For example, there are no orders during the weeks spent defending Battery Wagner in the summer of 1863. Again, in 1864 there is a lapse of six weeks from April 14 to May 31, the time in which the brigade was involved in several major battles in Virginia at Drewry's Bluff and Bermuda Hundred. Similarly, there were no orders after the second battle at Cold Harbor began on June 1, 1864, until the brigade established headquarters at Petersburg on July 19.

Clingman quickly learned that communications between himself and the regiments of his brigade required couriers, and he requested that two or three reliable men be assigned to him for that purpose.[11] He also tried to get an engineer assigned to his brigade, but was informed by Major General John Pemberton that none was available.[12]

In order for the regiments to function as a brigade, a brigade headquarters had to be established, and a brigade staff appointed. The staff officers consisted of an assistant adjutant general, an assistant inspector general, a quartermaster, an ordnance officer, and an aide-de-camp. On November 25, 1862, notice was given the various regiments of the brigade that Captain Edward White was to serve as assistant adjutant general. Various staff changes were subsequently recorded in the order books.[13]

Administrative Staff Changes

Over the period of its existence, there were many staff changes in Clingman's Brigade. Some changes in command were due to resignation, others were due to illness, injury, or death of the officers. Charles C. Clark tendered his resignation as captain of the 31st Regiment when he was elected to the North Carolina legislature, and because his family were refugees from New Bern and needed him to assist in their relocation.[14]

As the war continued and more and more staff vacancies occurred, Clingman preferred to fill those positions with men whom he knew and trusted, men from his own former congressional district, or relatives and friends. Hal Puryear, one of Clingman's nephews, was appointed aide-de-camp after he had already served 18 months as a volunteer and private in the ranks.[15] Captain William H. S. Burgwyn was recommended to Clingman for the post of assistant adjutant general in July 1864. He later served as assistant inspector general.[16] Burgwyn got General M. W. Ransom to recommend him to General Clingman for the post of inspector general of Clingman's Brigade.[17] Vacancies in the ranks were filled from the ranks by men who were entitled to promotion by reason of seniority.[18]

Clingman established specific hours at brigade headquarters to take care of brigade business. At brigade headquarters, such matters as requests for leave were submitted, reports of various kinds could be turned in, and complaints voiced, but only during the hours of 9 A.M. to 2:30 P.M. "No business, unless of importance, will be attended to, except during those hours." Permits to leave camp were to be issued only from 9 to 10 A.M.[19]

Administrative Paperwork

There was a "mountain" of paperwork required to keep records on the men of the brigade. A "Supply Order" dated June 22, 1863, lists the need for forms for muster and pay rolls for the troops, muster rolls for field staff and band, muster rolls for those in the hospital, company morning reports, field returns, and company monthly returns.[20] Numerous forms and reports were to be turned in to Clingman's headquarters and then forwarded to division headquarters or headquarters of the Confederacy at Richmond. General Order No. 2 directed regimental commanders to see that the "necessary reports of their commands" were sent to Clingman's headquarters promptly on the "13th and 29th" of each month to show the strength and condition of the regiments.[21] Clingman was very particular about the way in which reports and other official communications were submitted to him. These reports were to be written "on letter paper and not on fools cap paper, the letter must be folded in three equal folds parallel with the writing" and endorsed across the fold with the "post or station and date of letter, Name and rank of writer, Analysis of contents."[22] On February 25, 1863, Clingman insisted that "no communication will be considered at or forwarded from these Headquarters unless written with ink upon letter paper, and properly endorsed."[23]

Turning Raw Recruits into Soldiers

Changing men from raw, inexperienced troops into seasoned, well-trained, battle-hardened veterans was not an easy task, but that transition had to be accomplished. The ability of the brigade to function as an effective fighting unit in battle under fire was developed slowly by the endless drills and experience on the battlefield. The brigade and regimental officers had to gain the respect and confidence of the men. Obedience was a prime concern, probably even more so than concern for food and shelter. If the men learned to obey orders in times of noncombat, then their ability to follow orders on the battlefield increased. Their very survival or the survival of others might very well hinge upon the ability to obey orders.

When Clingman first began putting together his brigade in the fall of 1862, he ordered that the brigade be drilled twice daily, except on Sunday.[24] Shortly before the battle at the Neuse River bridge, drill time for the men was increased and commanding officers were specifically ordered to be on the field with their men during drills.[25] Major James H. Hill, chief of staff, and Captain N. P. Tansell, assistant inspector general, devoted a "portion of each day (Sunday excepted) to the instruction of the regiments" of Clingman's Brigade "in the school of the battle line."[26] After the brigade's first battle in December 1862, drill time was again increased,[27] and any regimental officers not attending drills on the field with the men were to be reported.[28] Drills kept the men occupied, developed their ability to obey orders, and was good physical activity.

When the brigade moved to James Island near Charleston, South Carolina, "Schools of Instruction" were established in each regiment, conducted by the senior officers. The studies were to be based on Hardee's *Rifle and Light Infantry Tactics*. Each day the instructor was to drill the brigade and the various companies in "movements taught [them] the preceding day." No deviation from the "letter of the tactics either in command or execution" was to be allowed. Weekly progress reports were to be turned in to General Clingman with "a table showing all the absences and the reasons therefore."[29] When Colonel J. V. Jordan, commander of the 31st Regiment, failed to establish a school of instruction, he was called upon to explain why.[30] Some of the field officers were also slack in attending drill along with their men. Clingman stressed the importance of drill, and expressed his hope "that in the future no such cause of complaint will be given."[31] Another officer, Colonel H. M. Shaw of the 8th Regiment, was reprimanded for allowing his regimental officers to attend drill "without side arms or belts."[32]

Considered a part of training, dress parade was required as per items #334 and #335 of the *Regulations for the Army of the Confederate States*.[33] Dress parade was also a means to boost troop morale and to inspire public confidence and confidence in the men themselves. Clingman was "surprised" to learn that the "customary dress parades" had been discontinued after the brigade moved to Petersburg, Virginia, in January 1864. He directed Colonels Shaw and Jordan to resume dress parade immediately and not to discontinue them except in "bad weather."[34]

Furloughs, Passes, and Permission for Leaves of Absence

One of the pressing problems when Clingman assumed command of the brigade was the matter of furloughs. Clingman wrote General D. H. Hill to ask how applications for furloughs were to be processed. "I suppose I must send all applications for furlough to your headquarters, no matter how urgent the case."[35]

While the brigade was stationed near Wilmington, the men wanted permission to go into town, but this privilege had to be curtailed because of complaints voiced by local citizens of injury to private property. To solve this problem, Clingman ordered that "not more than one officer and two privates" be permitted to leave at any time from each company.[36]

Health and Welfare

Attention to the health and well-being of the men was a constant concern. It was essential that the men had arms and ammunition, blankets, and food. Sickness reduced the number of effective troops. Yellow fever was always a threat and was prevalent in the Wilmington area in 1862. Clingman was even stricken with the dreaded disease.[37] When the brigade was first sent to James Island, near Charleston, South Carolina, there was "much sickness and many deaths due to malaria," the result of the island's proximity to swamps and marshes.[38] A circular was issued on July 4, 1863, which ordered all men in the brigade to be vaccinated.[39] At the suggestion of the brigade surgeon, Clingman issued several orders regarding food sold to the men by outsiders. One order prohibited the sale of "pies, cakes and other foods" within a two-mile radius of the camp, which was located near Wilmington. However, Clingman encouraged the sale of vegetables to the troops by local citizens.[40]

Even finding a camp site for the troops could present a problem. Friction arose between the 8th and the 31st regiments because the 8th had picketed their horses on ground assigned to the 31st Regiment for a campsite. Clingman had to order Colonel Shaw of the 8th Regiment to move his horses elsewhere.[41]

While the men needed wood for many activities involved in camping, private property was to be respected. Clingman issued an order that the men were not to cut any more wood where they were camped.[42]

Daily Activities/ Work Details

Much of the time the men were in camp and not on the battlefield was spent in anticipation of and preparation for actual combat. They built and strengthened fortifications. They did picket and guard duty. While at Camp Whiting, 200 men were required daily to work to "complete the lines about Wilmington."[43] Twenty-five men were needed to construct "rifle pits on the county road" near Wilmington.[44] These and other requests for manpower were handled by General Clingman. He constantly received requests for men with special talents to work at various jobs. Two men with experience "driving four horse teams" were ordered from Colonel Hector McKethan's 51st Regiment.[45] While at Camp Whiting, 25 men, including blacksmiths, were detailed for special duty.[46] Two men were detailed from the 51st Regiment "to act as couriers" and the quartermaster was ordered to furnish them with "horses, saddles, and bridles."[47] Clingman ordered Colonels Shaw and Allen to send the names of "seafaring men" in their commands."[48] A Corporal Jarvis was requested to report for duty as a "butcher."[49] While in Charleston during the summer of 1863, Clingman's Brigade was ordered to construct "new batteries for 24 pounder or 32 pounder guns."[50]

In every new situation, routines for guard duty and special detail had to be established.[51] Guards were needed to protect roads and bridges and to guard equipment and supplies. Guards were requested for funeral escorts[52] and to put out fires.[53]

Problems with Civilians

The civilian population caused many problems for the Confederate Army and also for Clingman's Brigade. While he was in charge at Weldon, North Carolina, in December 1863, Clingman received reports that the express company officers had been "buying up provisions in the District and sending them off without proper authority." He requested that the provost marshal look into the matter and to "seize all supplies being sent off without authority...."[54] Another order was issued to prevent "corn, pork, forage, etc." from being removed from the area "by private parties, without special authority...." To gain that permission, "private parties" were required to certify that the supplies were for the specific use of their families and were not to be sold. To prevent inflation, citizens were not allowed to purchase items at a price higher than that which was being paid by the Confederate government.[55] One man went over Clingman's head and got permission from Governor Zebulon B. Vance to "remove supplies." Undoubtedly, many were using the cover of transporting supplies to communicate with the enemy in eastern North Carolina, and Clingman directed that a note of warning be included when he was required to issue such a permit. "You will use every precaution to prevent your teamster or others whom you may employ from communicating in any way with the enemy."[56]

Guards stationed at a private residence were reported to have "torn down fences," which they used for shelter and to fuel campfires. Clingman ordered the fencing restored.[57] Some guards who were members of the 51st Regiment reportedly stopped some civilians and took potatoes and other foods from them. If that type of action was repeated, Clingman promised that the offenders "would be severely punished."[58]

Moving an Army

Whenever the brigade was ordered to move, there were hundreds of details to attend to. On June 10, 1863, the brigade was ordered to move from North Carolina to Charleston, South Carolina. This necessitated a tally of men and equipment, and detailed reports were requested from each regimental commander as to the number and kind of arms and accouterments, and their condition; the number of rounds of ammunition in boxes; the number of tents and other camp equipment; the amount and kind of baggage; the number of public and private horses available, and their condition; the number of mules; the number of men in each company, and the names of the officers, their rank, and if absent, why. The quartermaster was asked to submit a report on the balance of supplies he had on hand, as well as the amount of stores received and issued during the preceding week, together with a list of articles needed by each regiment.[59]

Discipline

Discipline was contingent on obeying orders promptly and Clingman was insistent in this requirement. In May 1863, he noted the discipline of the brigade was generally "good," but regretted a "want of punctuality and promptness in the movement of regiments." He emphasized that "Time is an element of the greatest importance in military movements." He pointed out that many battles had been lost because "troops failed to move promptly to the position assigned them." He encouraged the "habit of promptness on ordinary occasions," as the only means by which troop movement on the battlefield could be executed with any measure of success. He specifically directed the commanders of the regiments to assure promptness in troop movements.[60]

Regardless of how he tried, Clingman was not always successful in enforcing discipline among his troops. A report to division headquarters in 1863 described the discipline in one regiment as having been "sadly neglected, the officers neither exacting, or receiving the proper respect due them." The report further stated that the lieutenant colonel of the regiment was "absent without leave," and the colonel and major were not "well versed in their duties as commanding officers." That the colonel and major were derelict in their duties was evident from the condition of the arms. The troops had been armed with "altered Springfield muskets" and "altered Richmond Rifles," but because of the "insufficiency of the officers," the weapons were almost "unfit for service." The report blamed the officers for never having instructed their men in their "first duties" as soldiers.[61]

While one regiment was criticized, the 31st Regiment won a favorable inspection in January 1863. It was noted that this regiment had been instructed "to be respectful to their Superior officers." Their guns and accouterments were in "excellent order," and the colonel and lieutenant colonel of the regiment appeared to be familiar with their duties as commanding officers.[62]

Offenses and Punishment

The performance of the required duties necessary to maintain an army and put it in the field required strict discipline. The tasks were not always agreeable to the men. Disobedience was a common problem, and offenders were subject to arrest for even minor offences. Drunkenness, a common problem, often led to disorderly conduct, and sometimes even desertion. To prevent these problems, Special Order No. 8 authorized the provost marshal to "seize immediately all spirituous liquor found in the possession of persons" known to be in the habit of selling it. Such confiscated liquor was ordered to be given to the medical director, who could use it in the hospital or have it destroyed, as he saw fit.[63] Colonel H. M. Shaw of the 8th Regiment reported to Clingman that a "Mr. Hopkins keeps a very disorderly house" and that he sold "spirits to soldiers" and that some men were engaged in a fight at the Hopkins house, and a soldier of the 8th Regiment was "badly cut."[64] That same day, Clingman ordered a detachment to search the house of a man suspected of selling liquor. The detachment had orders to destroy any liquor found and to arrest the man if he was discovered selling liquor again.[65]

A guard posted at a house used by Clingman for his headquarters "struck his bayonet into a horse" which belonged to the homeowner. Clingman ordered the guard arrested and an inquiry into the matter.[66]

Guards were frequently derelict in performing their duties. As early as August 1862, Clingman issued orders to his regimental commanders for them to regularly visit those men on guard to see that they did not neglect their duties.[67] After learning that guards had been negligent in guarding a bridge over Wappoo Creek near Charleston, South Carolina, Clingman ordered that "one sentinel be posted at each end of the two bridges, and that they continue at all times to walk their posts." He further commented on the failure of the guards to note the absences of soldiers "until after dress parade," and he directed the officers in charge to report such absences promptly.[68]

On a lighter note, it was believed that some guards either stole soap or allowed others to steal the soap. These guards were confined in the guard house pending further investigation.[69]

Clingman, an officer and a gentleman himself, expected his soldiers to behave as gentlemen should. When a subordinate officer permitted his men to "strip themselves for the purposes of bathing" while in the presence of ladies, Clingman demanded a report of the incident and a statement from the officer. The general would not condone "disgraceful conduct" such as bathing in the nude even in the hottest months.[70]

On another occasion, several officers attended a "public ball at the house of a prostitute" and returned to camp at "a late hour of the night."[71]

When two men from the 8th Regiment were not granted passes to go into town, they forged them. An investigation was ordered, and Privates Thomas Morris and John Knight were arrested. They were charged with "forgery" and found guilty. Both Privates were confined to the guardhouse and were to be "severely punished" for this offense.[72] Morris was under arrest during January-February 1864. He rejoined his unit before June 1, 1864, in time for the battle at Cold Harbor. He was captured there, and removed to the Federal prison at Elmira, New York, where he died of "chronic diarrhea."[73] Private Knight continued in the service and was wounded on Morris Island on July 30, 1863. He rejoined his company before November 2, 1863, and continued to be present until he was reported "missing" at Fort Harrison in September 1864.[74]

Penalty for Desertion

Adjutant and Inspector General S. Cooper stated emphatically in his General Order No. 110, dated December 22, 1862, that the "52d Article of War" directed that:

> …any officer or soldier who shall misbehave himself before the enemy, run away, or shamefully abandon any fort, port or guard, which he or they may be commanded to defend, or speak words inducing others to do the like, or shall cast away his arms and ammunition, or who shall quit his post or colors to plunder and pillage, every such offender being duly convicted thereof shall suffer death, or such other punishment as shall be ordered by the sentence of a general court martial.[75]

While few Confederate deserters were actually shot in Clingman's Brigade for desertion, many were punished by flogging (39 lashes in one case).[76] Clingman's order books record only one execution, that of Private M. Clayton, of Company D, 8th Regiment, shot for desertion on March 21, 1864, near Petersburg.[77] However, he may have been granted a reprieve. According to information in *North Carolina Troops: 1865–1865*, Private Monroe Clayton enlisted at age 29 on August 11, 1861. After being captured on Roanoke Island, paroled and exchanged in August 1862, Clayton was present "until he deserted at Sullivan's Island, Charleston Harbor, South Carolina, August 15, 1863." He was reported under arrest and was held in the "guard house" at Petersburg, Virginia, from January to February 1864. However, he reportedly had rejoined his company before June 1, 1864, when he was captured at Cold Harbor, Virginia. He was imprisoned at

Point Lookout, Maryland, before being transferred to Elmira, New York, where he died on October 6, 1864, of "chronic diarrhea."[78] The spotted military career of Private Monroe Clayton is not at all unusual in the records of thousands of Confederate soldiers in this as well as other regiments— a period of being present, taking part in battles, then deserting to go home, later returning to the regiment, then perhaps being wounded or ill and sent to a hospital, with a return to duty, only to be captured and die in a northern prison.

Undoubtedly, Clingman was not as tough as he could have been on the men who deserted. Typical of the military service of many of the Confederates overall is the case of William A. Inman, Company H, 61st Regiment, North Carolina Troops. Inman, a resident of Brunswick County, North Carolina, enlisted at about age 25 in Wake County on October 1, 1862, for the duration of the war. However, he must have had second thoughts about his enlistment and did not show up for duty. A month later, on November 2, he was reported absent without leave. Finally, Inman reported for duty on February 21, 1863, and was placed in the guardhouse under arrest during March and April. He was reported "sick in hospital" at Wilmington during the months of May and June. Then again he was reported absent without leave at Charleston, South Carolina, through July and August 1863. Again, Inman was reported present during the months of September and October 1863. However, he deserted near Kinston, North Carolina, on December 13, 1863, but was caught, arrested and imprisoned at Petersburg from January to April, 1864. Again, Inman returned to duty, and he remained with the troops and took part in the fighting at Fort Harrison. There, on September 30, 1864, he was wounded in the "shoulder, back and eyes by a bursting cannon." He had recovered enough to return to duty by November 1, 1864, and was listed as present through December 1864. Inman was a lucky fellow, and is known to have survived the war. Somehow, he had avoided being executed for desertion, and was never wounded seriously enough to cause death.[79]

Several soldiers were noted in Clingman's order books as having been imprisoned and sentenced to hard labor. One man who was found guilty by a court-martial was sentenced to suffer corporal punishment before being put to hard labor on the fortifications at Wilmington.[80] Those who were caught after deserting were often confined in local jails while charges were being brought.[81]

Clingman could be lenient. Lt. Charles T. Guy, of Company I, 51st Regiment, was ordered released and returned to duty with his company. In a letter to Lieutenant Colonel Hobson, General Clingman expressed the hope "that the punishment, tho slight, will have the effect contemplated and that Lieut. Guy will in future be attentive and observant of all duties which he may be called upon to perform."[82]

Feuding Between Officers

Colonel James Dillard Radcliffe, of the 61st Regiment, and his men had been on General Evans' left on the south bank of the Neuse River near Kinston with three detached companies. This was the first action that the 61st Regiment had taken part in.[83] Out of ammunition, the 61st was forced to fall back across the bridge.[84] When they reached the bridge the men of the 61st Regiment saw it had been set on fire, and many men were injured attempting to cross it. The fight at the bridge resulted in a Union victory and 3 men of the 61st Regiment were killed, 13 wounded, and 69 captured, including Radcliffe, on December 14, 1862. Captain Edward Mallett, Company C, 61st Regiment, charged Radcliffe and several other regimental officers with drunkenness "on Duty," and "neglect of duty" on the battlefield, as well as "cowardice." There was some evidence that Radcliffe had been drinking, but the charges were dismissed by a one-man court of inquiry.

Clingman was of the opinion, as was the district commander, Major General D. H. Hill, that the charges against Radcliffe "should be forwarded, without delay, for the consideration of the authority competent to act upon them."[85] Not satisfied, Mallett took his charges directly to Hill, who threw them out. Radcliffe then ordered Mallett to be arrested. Hill, learning of the arrest, ordered Mallett released. Not to be outdone, Radcliffe swore that he would "call M[allett] to a personal account" after the war had ended. Discontent continued between the two men and when Mallett was appointed major of the regiment on August 10, 1864, Radcliffe resigned. Radcliffe stated in his resignation letter that "disagreements and unpleasant differences of long standing between myself and Field officers [have destroyed] the harmony of my command."[86] Radcliffe never did get to exact his revenge because Mallett, who had risen in the ranks to lieutenant colonel of the regiment, was killed at Bentonville on March 21, 1865.[87]

Desertion and Declining Morale

The fight at Fort Harrison on September 30, 1864, had a demoralizing effect on the men of Clingman's Brigade. On December 3, 1864, Captain Nathan W. Ramsey wrote to Brigadier General Clingman, who was still out recovering from his leg wound, that many members of the brigade were deserting to the enemy, and urged him to return. Ramsey stated emphatically: "If you do not return, I git it as my private opinion, that at least One Hundred (100) will go to the Enemy in less than Thirty (30) Days."[88] Colonel Hector McKethan urged Clingman to disregard Ramsey's reports because "Capt Ramsey was reported to Div. Head Qrs. for neglect of duty," and stated that General Robert E. Lee had ordered a court to "investigate the matter."[89]

As the war progressed it became harder and harder to keep the brigade fully manned. Clingman reported on June 25, 1863, that most of the companies of his regiments were below the minimum number. He was anxious to have his brigade "full" and asked his superiors that Major T. Brown Venable be sent to Raleigh to obtain conscripts.[90]

As desertion increased, security measures were tightened. A circular was issued on February 11, 1863, to regimental commanders to "re-establish the proper guard around their camps."[91] The problem of desertion became acute, and Clingman began to distrust men requesting to go home for any reason. He complained in April 1863 that too many medical furloughs were being granted to men of his brigade. He unrealistically believed that no one able to leave the hospital should be sent home for health reasons, because, as he saw it, the climate of the camp on James Island was "as healthy as any other that can be found." He thought the men could convalesce just as rapidly there as at home. This view did not endear him to his men. However, he reasoned, that the men, once at home, probably would not return "when they ought to do so." Clingman was even so bold as to suggest that the practice of granting furloughs to anyone in his brigade should be stopped.[92]

Clingman made many attempts to

arrest and punish those who had deserted, beginning in August 1862, when he first ordered a detail from the 55th and 56th regiments to arrest deserters from the regiment "wherever found."[93]

Desertion and unauthorized absences continued despite all precautions and despite the severe punishment meted out to deserters who were unlucky enough to be caught.[94] The problem was not confined to enlisted men and conscripts; a number of officers were also recorded as being absent in May 1863 when Clingman requested an accounting.[95] Lieutenant J. W. McAllister, of Company A, 51st Regiment, was one of those absent without leave, and he was charged with "absence without leave, disobedience of orders, conduct prejudicial to good order and military discipline," and others. McAllister, from New Hanover County, who had previously served as a captain in the 23rd Regiment of North Carolina Militia, was "dismissed from service on August 24, 1863.[96]

While Clingman's Brigade was stationed near Wilmington, desertion increased because many of the men were from nearby counties. Some of those counties had been under Union control for most of the war, and there was much Union support among those living in those counties. When some men of the 51st Regiment went home on leave and did not return, Clingman appealed to Governor Zebulon B. Vance to send the "proper officials to the homes of the men to get them back to their regiment."[97]

One soldier was arrested for enticing others to desert. Captain Wharton of the 8th Regiment was ordered placed under arrest for "leaving camp without permission and inducing his subordinates to go with him."[98] Another man who had deserted to the Yankees, but who had returned to the lines, was viewed by Clingman as "intelligent" and "quite eloquent," but was probably dishonest. Clingman ordered that this deserter be questioned as to the location and purpose of the Yankees before sending him to Major Charles Pickett at Petersburg for further questioning and before charges for desertion were brought against him.[99]

Some soldiers tried to get out of the army by legal means. Sergeant Edward B. Koonce, Company K, 61st Regiment, tried to get out of military service by obtaining a job as a mail carrier. While Clingman was in Weldon, North Carolina, he was served with a writ of habeas corpus to produce the soldier. Recognizing a ploy to get released from military duty, Clingman suggested to Major Charles Pickett that the soldier in question be given a leave of absence of "ten days to enable him to go to Raleigh and have the matter adjudicated." Since the man was already in the military before obtaining the civilian job, Clingman believed that if the soldier failed to return after his 10-day leave was up, he should be declared a deserter. However, Clingman was willing to submit the matter to his commanding general for his consideration.[100]

Clingman saw military service as taking precedence over any civilian service. Others, such as Chief Justice Richmond M. Pearson, regarded personal liberty as more important than either, and since Pearson had interpreted the Confederate conscription laws as unconstitutional, the judge was able to obtain the release of many men from military duty by writs of habeas corpus.[101]

Some recent statistical studies have established that there was one deserter for every nine enlistments in the Confederate Army. North Carolina furnished the largest number of troops, but it also had the largest number of deserters (23,694). An absentee rate of 21 percent at the begining of the war around 1862 increased to 51 percent by December 1864.[102]

On January 30, 1863, a total of 606 men were absent from the four regiments of Clingman's Brigade. This number included deserters, men absent without leave, men absent with leave or on sick leave, and men on parole as exchanged prisoners.[103] In addition to those six hundred, the ranks were depleted by battle casualties which had not been refilled. The 8th Regiment reported it needed 378 men to bring its number up to the standard. The 51st Regiment needed 332 men.[104] The 31st Regiment needed 549 men to fill its ranks.[105]

Evidence that desertion increased in Clingman's Brigade, as it did in other units, as the war progressed can be noted in the frequent orders relating to the establishment of courts-martial from March 1863. There were several orders for the appearance of witnesses and prisoners.[106] General William D. Pender remarked that by August 1863, "desertions from General Clingman's Brigade" were increasing daily. He commented that the result of desertion was that "Lawlessness prevades the country...."[107] This increase in desertion was after the men of Clingman's Brigade had lived in "Hell" and suffered the horrors of defending Battery Wagner on Morris Island.

The problems confronting a brigadier general were numerous, time-consuming, and perplexing. Solving those problems took time and effort. Decisions had to be made daily, and often they had to be made quickly. Although an educated man, Clingman, with no military preparation or experience, tried to cope with the multiple problems of commanding a brigade to get his men into condition for a confrontation with the enemy, and to help them survive when that encounter came.[108] Whatever the men lacked in the way of training and discipline which resulted in their failure to obey orders was reflected as a criticism of Clingman himself, who, in the final analysis, was responsible for the actions of his brigade both on and off the field of battle.

Notes

1. Livermore, p. 32.
2. "Organization of the Armies in the Civil War," http://www.civilwarhome.com/armyorganization.html.
3. After the war, Edward White removed from North Carolina to St. Louis, Missouri, where he became a police court judge. White died at age 47 from tuberculosis, according to a descendant, Tod Thompson.
4. General Order No. 35, General D. H. Hill to General Thomas L. Clingman, July 29, 1862, Clingman Papers, Southern Historical Collection, Wilson Library, University of North Carolina, Chapel Hill, North Carolina. Hereinafter designated Clingman Papers, SHC.
5. Telegram, Thomas L. Clingman to Josiah Gorgas, August 24, 1862, Clingman Papers, SHC.
6. Colonel P. F. Faison, 56th Regiment, to Thomas L. Clingman, August 14, and August 18, 1862; Special Order No. 7, Thomas L. Clingman to John K. Connally of the 55th Regiment, August 15, 1862, Clingman Papers, SHC.
7. J. R. Cole, Assistant Adjutant General, to Edward White, Assistant Adjutant General, August 26, 1862, Clingman Papers, SHC.
8. General Order No. 1, Graham Daves, A. A. G., French's Division, December 18, 1862, Thomas L. Clingman Papers, SHC.
9. Ben Franklin's work *Preface: Courteous Readers*, cited in *Bartlett's Familiar Quotations*, 15th rev. ed., Emily Morison Beck, ed., (Boston: Little, Brown & Co., 1980), p. 347.
10. General Order No. 1, Headquarters near Wilmington, November 25, 1862, Order Book 1, in Thomas L. Clingman Papers, Manuscript Collection, Duke University, Durham, North Carolina. Hereinafter cited as Order Book 1.
11. Thomas L. Clingman to Major James H. Hill, December 2, 1862, Clingman Papers, SHC.
12. Major J. A. Pemberton to Thomas L. Clingman, September 9, 1862, Clingman Papers, SHC.
13. General Order No. 4, January 17, 1863, Order Book 1.
14. Captain Charles C. Clark to Brigadier General Thomas L. Clingman, Camp Whiting, North Carolina, December 11, 1862, Clingman Papers, SHC.
15. Thomas L. Clingman to General Samuel Cooper, December 21, 1863, Order

Book 2, in Thomas L. Clingman Papers, Manuscript Collection, Duke University, Durham, North Carolina. Hereinafter cited as Order Book 2.

16. W. H. S. Burgwyn, "Clingman's Brigade," Clark, III, p. 486.

17. Letter from Brig. Gen. M. M. Ransom to Brig. Gen. T. L. Clingman, December 20, 1863, cited in William H. S. Burgwyn, *A Captain's War* (Shippensburg, Pa.: White Mane Publishing Co., 1994), pp. 111–112.

18. General Order 3, March 20, 1863, Order Book 1.

19. General Order No. 7, February 27, 1863, Order Book 1.

20. Edward White to Major J. W. Hill, June 22, 1863, Order Book 2.

21. General Order No. 2, November 25, 1862, Order Book 1.

22. General Order No. 6, January 26, 1863, Order Book 1.

23. General Order No. 8, February 25, 1863, Charleston, South Carolina, Order Book 1.

24. General Order No. 2, November 25, 1862, Order Book 1.

25. General Order No. 4, December 12, 1862, Order Book 1.

26. Special Order No. 34, December 11, 1862, Major General W. H. C. Whiting to General Thomas L. Clingman, Clingman Papers, SHC.

27. General Order No. 7, December 24, 1862, Order Book 1.

28. General Order No. 6, December 25, 1862, Order Book 1.

29. General Order No. 2, James Island, South Carolina, March 20, 1863, Order Book 1.

30. To Col. J. V. Jordan, 31st Reg., James Island, South Carolina, March 26, 1863, Order Book 2.

31. General Order No. 5, Paragraph II, III, Clingman Papers, SHC.

32. To Col. H. M. Shaw, Camp Whiting, December 1, 1862, Order Book 2.

33. Confederate States of America, War Department, *Regulations for the Army of the Confederate States, 1863*, 2nd ed. (Richmond: J. W. Randolph, 1863), p. 35.

34. To Col. H. Shaw, 8th Reg., and Col. J. V. Jordan, 31st Reg., January 3, 1864, Order Book 2.

35. *O.R.*, IX, Ser. I, p. 477, Thomas L. Clingman to General D. H. Hill, August 7, 1862.

36. To Major Moore, Comdg. 3rd N.C. Battalion, July 9, 1863, Order Book 2.

37. Quartermaster, Wilmington, North Carolina, to Thomas L. Clingman, December 12, 1862, Clingman Papers, SHC; Colonel William Lamb to Thomas L. Clingman, December 7, 1862, Clingman Papers, SHC.

38. Burgwyn, "Clingman's Brigade," p. 484.

39. Circular, July 4, 1863, Order Book 2.

40. Henry P. Rhette, Surgeon, 8th Regiment, North Carolina Troops, to Captain Edward White, Camp Whiting, January 2, 1863, Clingman Papers, SHC; Circular, February 3, 1863, Order Book 2, and General Order No. 8, May 29, 1863, Order Book 1.

41. Edward White to Colonel H. M. Shaw, December 7, 1862, Order Book 2.

42. Edward White to colonel of one of the regiments in Clingman's Brigade, December 18, 1863, Order Book 2.

43. Edward White to Colonels Shaw, Allen, and Jordan, from Camp Whiting, December 10, 1862, Order Book 2.

44. Edward White to Colonels Jordan, Shaw, McKethan and Radcliffe, Camp Whiting, January 14, 1863, Order Book 2.

45. Edward White to Colonel Hector McKethan, James Island, South Carolina, April 10, 1863, Book 2.

46. Edward White to Colonel H. M. Shaw, 8th Regiment, Camp Whiting, November 27, 1862, Order Book 2.

47. Thomas L. Clingman to Major James H. Hill, from Camp Whiting, December 5, 1862, Order Book 2.

48. Edward White to Colonels H. M. Shaw and W. H. Allen, December 5, 1862, Order Book 2.

49. Edward White to Colonel J. V. Jordan, 31st Regiment, December 18, 1863, Order Book 2.

50. *O.R.*, XXVIII, Ser. I, Pt. II, p. 2828.

51. Circular, March 12, 1863, Order Book 2; and order from Edward White, March 13, 1863, Order Book 2.

52. T. Brown Venable to Colonel J. D. Radcliffe, 61st Regiment, May 8, 1863, Order Book 2.

53. Edward White to Lt. Col C. B. Hobson, 51st Regiment, May 28, 1863, Order Book 2.

54. Thomas L. Clingman to Provost Marshal J. H. Irving, December 8, 1863, Order Book 2.

55. Thomas L. Clingman to Colonel H. M. Shaw, December 11, 1863, Order Book 2.

56. Edward White to Mr. T. B. Satterthwaite, at Wilson, N.C., December 11, 1863, Order Book 2.

57. Edward White to Colonel J. D. Radcliffe, 61st Regiment, June 17, 1863, Order Book 2.
58. Edward White to Hector McKethan, 31st Regiment, January 24, 1863, Order Book 2.
59. General Order No. 10, Edward White to all Regimental Commanders of Clingman's Brigade, June 10, 1863, Order Book 1.
60. General Order No. 7, May 12, 1863, Order Book 1.
61. Lieutenant L. M. Butler, Inspecting Officer, Wilmington, North Carolina, January 11, 1863, to Thomas L. Clingman, Clingman Papers, SHC.
62. Lieutenant L. M. Butler, Inspecting officer, to Captain Mallery P. King, Clingman Papers, SHC.
63. Special Order No. 8, Thomas L. Clingman to provost marshal, August 16, 1862, Clingman Papers, SHC.
64. Col. H. M. Shaw to Brig. Gen. T. L. Clingman, Camp Whiting, December 9, 1862, SHC.
65. Edward White to Colonel H. M. Shaw, Camp Whiting, December 9, 1862, Order Book 2.
66. Edward White to Colonel, in regard to James Hawks, Craft House, near Charleston, South Carolina, February 25, 1863, Order Book 2.
67. Special Order No. 3, August 10, 1862, Clingman Papers, SHC.
68. General Order No. 4, James Island, South Carolina, April 9, 1863, Order Book 1.
69. Edward White to Col. Hector McKethan, 51st Regiment, James Island, South Carolina, March 25, 1863, Order Book 2.
70. Edward White to Col. Hector McKethan, June 7, 1863, Order Book 2.
71. Major J. M. Clinton to Colonel H. M. Shaw, December 9, 1862, Clingman Papers, SHC.
72. Edward White to Col. H. M. Shaw, James Island, South Carolina, March 31, 1863, Order Book 2; Edward White to Col H. M. Shaw, March 31, 1863, Order Book 2.
73. Manarin and Jordan, IV, p. 570.
74. Manarin and Jordan, IV, p. 569.
75. General Order No. 110, by S. Cooper, adjutant and inspector general, Richmond, Virginia, December 22, 1862, to S. W. Melton, major, and A. A. G., Goldsboro, N.C., Thomas L. Clingman Papers, Southern Historical Collection, University of North Carolina, Chapel Hill, North Carolina.
76. Clement Eaton, *A History of the Southern Confederacy* (New York: The Macmillan Co., 1954), p. 272.
77. General Order No. 3, Petersburg, Virginia, March 21, 1864, Order Book I.
78. Manarin and Jordan, IV, p. 553.
79. Manarin and Jordan, XIV, p. 731.
80. Edward White to Col. Hector McKethan, Camp Whiting, North Carolina, January 9, 1863, Order Book 2.
81. Edward White to Col. J. V. Jordan, Camp Whiting, North Carolina, January 9, 1863, Order Book 2.
82. T. Brown Venable to Lt. Col. Hobson, 51st Regiment, Wilmington, North Carolina, May 13, 1863, Order Book 2.
83. Ramsey, "Sixty-First Regiment," in Clark, III, pp. 503–507.
84. Ramsey, Clark III, pp. 508–509.
85. Edward White to Col. J. D. Radcliffe, Wilmington, North Carolina, May 22, 1863, Order Book 2.
86. Manarin and Jordan, XIV, pp. 500–600, footnote 16.
87. Manarin and Jordan, XIV, p. 651.
88. N. W. Ramsey to Thomas L. Colingman, December 3, 1864, Clingman Papers, Duke University, Durham, North Carolina.
89. Hector McKethan to Thomas L. Clingman, December 6, 1864, Clingman Papers, Duke University, Durham, North Carolina.
90. Thomas L. Clingman to James H. Hill, A. A. G., June 26, 1863, Order Book 2.
91. Circular, February 11, 1863, Order Book 2.
92. Thomas L. Clingman to Colonel J. V. Jordan, April 14, 1863, Order Book 2.
93. Edward White, A. A. G., to Colonel P. F. Faison, 56th Regiment, August 14, 1862; and Edward White to colonel of the 55th Regiment, August 15, 1862, Clingman Papers, SHC.
94. Edward White to Lt. Col. C. B. Hobson, Wilmington, North Carolina, May 24, 1863, Order Book 2.
95. T. Brown Venable to Col. Hector McKethan, Wilmington, North Carolina, May 24, 1863, Order Book 2.
96. Edward White to Lt. Col. C. B. Hobson, Commander 51st Reg., May 24, 1863, Wilmington, N.C.; and Manarin and Jordan, XII, p. 279.
97. Thomas L. Clingman to Governor Z. B. Vance, from Charleston, South Carolina, March 19, 1863, Order Book 2.
98. Edward White to Col. H. M. Shaw, Camp Whiting, North Carolina, December 12, 1862, Order Book 2.

99. Thomas L. Clingman to Maj. Charles Pickett, from Weldon, North Carolina, December 11, 1863, Order Book 2.

100. Thomas L. Clingman to Maj. Charles Pickett, December 26, 1863, Order Book 2.

101. James Albert Hutchens, "Richmond Mumford Pearson: Founder of Richmond Hill Law School," in Frances H. Casstevens, ed., *Heritage of Yadkin County* (Winston-Salem: Hunter Publishing Company, 1981), p. 55. In 1864 Pearson decided that the antisubstitute bill passed by the Confederate Congress, which ended the practice of having a substitute serve in the place of a conscript, was unconstitutional. He tried to discharge all who had been taken into the Confederate Army under this act. Congress was prompt in responding to Pearson's obstructions by suspending the writ of habeas corpus in cases where men were trying to avoid military service. See also, Robert G. H. Kean, *Inside the Confederate Government: The Diary of Robert Garlick Hill Kean,* ed. Edward Younger (New York: Oxford University Press, 1857), pp. 55, 137–138.

102. Eaton, p. 271.

103. Report by T. Brown Venable, January 30, 1863, Clingman Papers, SHC.

104. Report of Major J. W. Hamlin, 8th Regiment, and Hector McKethan, 51st Regiment, January 30, 1863, Clingman Papers, SHC.

105. Report of Colonel J. V. Jordan, January 30, 1863, Clingman Papers, SHC.

106. Thomas L. Clingman to Major J. J. Lucas, James Island, South Carolina, March 19, 1863, Order Book 2; Edward White to Captain Mallory P. King, James Island, South Carolina, March 27, 1863, Order Book 2; Edward White to Cols. Jordan, Shaw, Radcliffe, and Hobson, June 2, 1863, Order Book 2; Edward White to Col. J. D. Radcliffe, June 13, 1863, Order Book 2; and Edward White to Col. J. D. Radcliffe, June 17, 1863, Order Book 2.

107. *O.R.*, II, Ser. IV, p. 770, C. D. Melton to John S. Preston, Columbia, South Carolina, August 25, 1863.

108. *O.R.*, XVIII, Ser. I, p. 786, General W. H. C. Whiting at Wilmington, North Carolina, November 26, 1862, to Major General French at Petersburg, Virginia.

CHAPTER XIII

Evaluation and Summary

> *My duty is to obey orders.*
> — Thomas Jonathan "Stonewall" Jackson (1824–1864)

Some historians judge Clingman and Clingman's Brigade too harshly. Richard J. Sommers, in his book on the siege of Petersburg, described Hoke's Division as a "nonhistoric unit thrown together only during the crisis of the Bermuda Hundred Campaign," and its brigades as "decidedly uneven in quality. Thomas L. Clingman's North Carolinians, singularly unfortunate, had been badly pummeled in virtually all their battles from Roanoke Island to Globe Tavern." Sommers saw Clingman's being wounded and forced out of command on August 19, 1864, as a "step in the right direction." He also incorrectly described Hector McKethan, who assumed command of the Brigade as an "inexperienced junior colonel" who "gave little indication of being able to raise its fortunes."[1] Sommers' sentiments have been repeated in other works, such as his comments written for the "Foreword" to *A Captain's War: The Letters and Diaries of William H. S. Burgwyn, 1861–1865*, in which he described Clingman's Brigade as "below average."[2]

As to Sommers' views, Clingman's Brigade was not even formed until months after the defeat of the 8th and 31st Regiments on Roanoke Island. The 51st Regiment was organized April 13, 1862, and the 61st Regiment in August 1862. So the assertion that Clingman's Brigade, as a whole, suffered defeat from Roanoke Island to the end of the war is entirely fallacious.

Likewise, Colonel Hector McKethan was *not* an "inexperienced junior colonel," but a seasoned, respected officer who had seen action from the first battle of the war, at Bethel Church, and who had been in charge of the 51st Regiment since the battle for the Neuse River Bridge in December 1862.

By the time that Clingman's Brigade became a part of Hoke's Division, what men remained were the seasoned survivors of battles, including the siege of Battery Wagner on Morris Island.

If those men did not always behave as "knights in shinning armor," it may have been because many of the engagements in which Clingman's Brigade was involved were characterized by insufficient numbers of troops, delays in sending reinforcements, conflicting reports on enemy movement, failure of unseasoned troops to carry out commands, and confusion as to who was in command.

The strength and effectiveness of Clingman's Brigade steadily decreased as the war progressed. From an initial strength of approximately 4,000 men, by September 10, 1864, the brigade was down to 1,121 "present effective for the field" out of a total of

3,021 men (which included both present and absent).³ This number declined by March 17, 1865, to 49 officers and 536 men "present for duty."⁴

Neuse River Bridge, Near Goldsboro, North Carolina, December 1862

The fiasco at the Neuse River Bridge in December 1862 is a prime example of the deficiencies present in the Confederate army by the end of the second year of the war. At the railroad bridge over the Neuse River near Goldsboro, the forces at Clingman's command were not large enough to withstand the greater numbers of Federal troops. This was complicated when the expected support from Evans was late in arriving.⁵

Clingman's job was to hold both bridges—the railroad and the county road bridge of the Neuse River near Goldsboro—but his force was insufficient to defend even one of them against the larger number of Federal troops. He positioned his men correctly near the bridges, but was overrun by the superior numbers of Federals and their deadly artillery fire.⁶ Clingman saw that he did not have enough men to hold the railroad bridge, and he had ordered their retreat. He then had them reform for a flank attack on the enemy.

In addition to losing the bridge and allowing the Federals to burn it, in the confusion of the retreat the 52nd Regiment was fired upon by the 51st Regiment, who mistook them for the enemy. That confusion resulted when General Evans arrived and took over command from Clingman. Evans disregarded Clingman's orders for the 51st and 52nd Regiments to wait until he could bring the men around for a flank attack. Evans, without waiting for Starr's Battery to get into position, ordered the troops to advance at once. The Confederates were met with heavy fire from Federal artillery and had to retreat. The flank attack launched by Clingman's 8th and 61st was launched but it was too late to renew the frontal attack.

Colonel William A. Allen, the commander of the 51st Regiment, resigned because of his part in this incident, and command passed to Hector McKethan.

Judge Thomas C. Fuller, in command of Starr's Battery, commended Clingman's conduct and stated there was no braver man during the "hour of fiercest battle." He noted that Clingman "rode up and down the line on horseback, absolutely without fear, giving his commands: 'Fire slowly, men, keep it up.'"⁷ Historian John H. Wheeler noted that Clingman was "distinguished for his defense of Goldsboro ... which he saved from a superior force under Foster...."⁸

The mix-up at the Neuse River Bridge was, in part, the result of the tardiness of General Evans in coming to the support of Clingman's men. Evans, who had been defeated at White Hall, had retreated to Goldsboro, where Clingman was positioned. Evans had been advised to go there as quickly as possible by rail. The cars were delayed, however, until after 11 o'clock, by which time Clingman had been forced to withdraw.

Evans was criticized in several of the regimental histories and accused of "reckless disregard for the lives of his troops."⁹ Although the men of the brigade sided with Clingman and blamed Evans, the "legislature and others at Raleigh" blamed Clingman for allowing the bridges at Goldsboro "to be burned by the enemy...." He and his troops were blamed for the damage the Federal forces did to the railroad tracks around Goldsboro as well. He believed that "certain members of the Legislature and others at Raleigh were censuring" him for permitting the bridges at Goldsboro to be destroyed.¹⁰ Clingman wished to write a public vindication of his brigade, and Governor Zebulon Vance urged him to do so. However, Clingman was informed by General Smith that the Secretary of War " in Richmond declined to allow my report to be published."[11]

Clingman then suggested that perhaps Vance might publish the story for him, and he reminded Vance of a conversation they had had shortly before the battle, when there was another "brigade in Goldsboro within three miles of the Railroad Bridge." Clingman believed if those troops had been moved to his support, he could have defended the bridges. While Clingman did not wish to make charges against anyone, he believed that if those facts were published, "censure would fall on some other officers." Clingman concluded that "if anyone is to suffer on that account, it should be the guilty rather than the innocent men…."[12] However, nothing further was ever published, and Clingman and his brigade were never vindicated. This is, perhaps, the beginning of the tarnished reputation Clingman's Brigade would carry throughout the war and beyond.

The whole situation might have ended differently. The Federal troops withdrew almost as suddenly as they had appeared. One report said their withdrawal was because of a lack of ammunition. Had the Confederates known this, they might have pressed an assault.

Morris Island, South Carolina, July-August, 1863

The contest for control of Morris Island became one of endurance on both sides. For the most part, the men of Clingman's Brigade performed admirably under unbelievable conditions in the defense of Battery Wagner on Morris Island. The one incident that stained the honor of the brigade was the failure of the men of the 31st Regiment to man the parapets. At the time this occurred, the little sand fort was under the command of General Taliaferro.

The failure of the 31st Regiment was of little consequence, however, because the men of the 51st Regiment rushed to take their places instead, and prevented a takeover by the Federals.

The men of the 31st Regiment were criticized by many for their lack of courage. In answer to that criticism, one member of the 31st Regiment wrote to the editor of the *Weekly Raleigh Register* defending the loyalty of the men of his regiment. He accused W. W. Holden of slandering them in his paper, the Raleigh *Standard*.[13]

To counteract this blot on the brigade was the heroism of one man, Robert Winship Stedman, of the 61st Regiment, who ran to an abandoned gun, aimed, and fired it at a passing Yankee gunboat. An artillerist, Stedman's aim was accurate and he hit the enemy vessel.[14] (More on the heroic Robert Winship Stedman can be found in Chapter XI, entitled "Heroes, Cowards or Fools.")

Perhaps the men of the 8th Regiment suffered the most. In a report to Captain W. F. Nance, Brigadier General Clingman stated: "The hardest service was performed by the Eighth North Carolina Regiment, commanded by Colonel Shaw, which after several days' duty in Battery Wagner outside of the bomb proofs, and all the while exposed to the enemy's shot and shell, with no other protection except that offered by the comparatively low parapet on the right of the work, was obliged to spend the eighth day in the sand between Battery Wagner and Fort Gregg, and there, with a portion of the Fifty-fourth Georgia Regiment, commanded by Lieutenant Colonel Rawls, and part of the Sixty-first North Carolina under Captain Mallett, was exposed to an extraordinary fire from the fleet."[15] During the 58-day siege, the 8th Regiment of Clingman's Brigade spent a total of 21 days on duty at Battery Wagner.[16]

The "hard service" rendered by the men of Clingman's Brigade cannot be topped in any other situation during the entire war. While the numbers were not as great as those in battles at Gettysburg, Spotsylvania, or Cold Harbor, the "fierce fighting and heroism at [Battery] Wagner was not excelled upon any battlefield in the war."[17] Against the larger numbers of Federal troops, and the heavy, constant bombardment from both land and sea, the most the Confederates could hope for was to delay the loss of Morris Island until the fortifications on James Island and Sullivan's Island could be completed. This, as Beauregard had planned, was carried out effectively, and the city of Charleston was able to hold out until the closing months of the war.[18]

Strategically, the Federal assault on Morris Island was considered a failure. It was costly in numbers of men lost by the Federals. However, once the island was captured, the major objective was achieved. Fort Sumter was rendered ineffective, and Charleston Harbor was closed to blockade-running and troop movement to and from Charleston. However, some Confederates, under the command of General Clingman, remained until late in the fall of 1863 on Sullivan's Island, "a very dangerous place"[19] but one that was essential to the defense of Charleston.[20] From an exposed position on Sullivan's Island, Clingman and his command rendered great service by firing on passing monitors and other Federal gunboats.[21]

New Bern Expedition, 1864

The New Bern Expedition was doomed to fail from the moment the Confederates encountered the enemy at Batchelder's Creek, since the necessary element of surprise was lost at that point. Had Hoke's forces overcome the opposition at Batchelder's Creek and moved immediately to New Bern, the story might have had a different ending. As it was, the Federal pickets guarding the creek alerted the Federal troops in the city and reinforcements were brought in, aided by General Seth Maxwell Barton's failure to cut the railroad and telegraph lines.

Burgwyn, of Clingman's staff, said that the attack on New Bern did not occur because they were waiting for Barton to attack the city from his side of the Trent River. According to Burgwyn, once General Pickett got in touch with General Barton, he then ordered Clingman's Brigade to fall back to the Kinston side of the Core Creek about thirteen miles from New Bern.[22]

It does appear that Clingman was "left out on a limb." Had he continued to hold his position and waited for reinforcements, his troops surely would have sustained heavy casualties. Unknown to Clingman, the assault had been called off when it was learned that the other branches of the expedition had failed to achieve their goals. Some of those goals had not been attained because the force was divided into smaller groups, none of which had sufficient numbers to overcome the greater enemy forces they encountered. Thus, poor timing and the failure of several of the attacking Confederate forces to carry out their tasks and converge as planned, made any further action by Hoke's forces futile. An ambitious project that could possibly have succeeded was abandoned in failure.[23]

It appears that Clingman and his men did their job, but when others failed in their objectives, everyone blamed someone else. In reality, this assault, from different angles with its force divided, was uncoordinated. Inadequate or inaccurate information about the number and placement of fortifications and the terrain, a lack of communication, a failure to carry out objectives in a timely manner, and the assumption that a very tired army who had marched all night could perform their best made this advance against New Bern a failure when it could have succeeded.

Pickett blamed Hoke and said,

> "...it was impracticable for General Hoke to force a passage till after daylight. This he did in most gallant style. At this time the enemy, reinforcing heavily by railroad and trying to rake our lines with the guns on the steam iron-clads, they attempted to turn my right flank with these reinforcements. I threw Corse forward to drive them in, which he did handsomely, and Clingman, with his two regiments, following General Hoke. After effecting the crossing the enemy were hotly pursued, but having no cavalry, and the men much worn by the long night's march, and not having been allowed fires, we were unable to press our advantage...."

Pickett made excuses for the failure to take New Bern by saying that he found "the ground in my front swept by half a dozen forts, one of them mounting seven rifle guns, with which they fired at pleasure over and into our line of battle. Had I had the whole force in hand I have little doubt that we could have gone in easily, taking the place by surprise." He further warned against trying to take New Bern or Washington (North Carolina) "until the iron-clads are done."[24]

Hoke was more honest. He described how his brigade had halted to meet any enemy advancing from the town, and Clingman was ordered to cross the Trent Road to prevent the return of the enemy from Deep Gully, but "not knowing the country, he failed to reach the road, which was extremely unfortunate, as during the evening, at different times (500) five hundred infantry and (400) four hundred cavalry, passed into the town panic-stricken leaving their camps in wild confusion." Hoke mentioned that Barton had failed to reach his destination, but modestly remarked, "Being [a] junior officer, it does not become me to speak my thoughts of this move." Hoke did think that they could have succeeded, and that the enemy had been at least "thoroughly routed and demoralized." "The Work could have been done, and still can be accomplished. I have recruited my brigade somewhat since I have been in the State, and I am sanguine about increasing it a good deal. My men are in good health and fine spirits." Hoke optimistically reported that his troops did not see "our campaign as a failure, as the real object was not known to them, and the capture of several rich camps pleased them wonderfully." Hoke reported that he had put men to work to repair the gunboat.[25]

Barton stated that the scouts, spies, and mapmakers reported that there were "no other fortifications than those abandoned by our troops at the capture of Newbern." He was unprepared to meet with such unsurmountable obstacles (additional forts) to gain the south bank of the Trent River, which he thought unprotected. Because of the manned fortifications, Barton was forced to detour by Evan's mill, which added 11 miles to the distance between his men and Pickett's.[26] Barton knew he was being blamed for the failure of the capture of New Bern, and he requested a court of inquiry, and General R. E. Lee agreed that it should be granted.[27] That court of inquiry was never actually granted, however, and even though Barton, while under Ransom's command at the Wilderness, was again criticized for a "lack of cooperation," his regimental commanders sent a petition to the Confederate government in Richmond setting forth their confidence in him.[28]

Plymouth, North Carolina, April 20, 1864

Although only the 8th Regiment of Clingman's Brigade took part in this battle, it truly was a Confederate victory and a feather in the cap for Brigadier General Robert F. Hoke. "In this brilliant victory, the Eighth Regiment attached to Ransom's Brigade, did its full duty and bore a distinguished part."[29] Here, the men of the 8th Regiment redeemed themselves for their defeat and capture on Roanoke Island in 1862. But that victory was not without costs. The 8th Regiment reported 154 killed and wounded, about a third of those engaged in the battle. Historian Ludwig stated in his regimental history that the charge ordered against Fort William "was reckless and unnecessary. It was made under the flush of victory, not by the order of the commanding general. The fort, being surrounded, would have had to surrender anyhow, as it did a few hours afterward."[30]

Drewry's Bluff, Virginia, May 16–19, 1864

Major General Robert F. Hoke, in his report of the action on May 16, reminded Commanding General Beauregard that he had warned of the "strength of the enemy" in front of Corse and Clingman's brigades in "both position and force," and Hoke had suggested that "great credit" be given those commanders for their actions. Both Corse's and Clingman's brigades were small, but they "did their duty well." Hoke noted that his brigade commanders "entered into the move with spirit, and rendered every co-operation."[31] In a later account of the battle, Hoke alluded to "some misunderstanding of the officer who conducted those forces" so that they were improperly placed.[32]

Beauregard had planned to avoid the danger of a frontal attack on Hoke's men by a flank move, but, according to Hoke, the planned move was "in no portion of the line accomplished," and as a result, Hoke's losses were very heavy. Losses in Clingman's and Corse's brigades were "necessarily heavy," because of the frontal attack.[33]

Beauregard did credit the actions of Corse and Clingman and their men with some success, because the enemy did not regain the ground they had lost.[34]

While Drewry's Bluff is generally considered a Confederate victory, A. A. McKethan, historian for the 51st North Carolina Regiment of Clingman's Brigade, believed that they could have captured Butler's entire army, if the Confederate forces at Petersburg had cooperated.[35] Two sections of the movement had worked well, but Confederate General W. H. C. Whiting, who had been ordered to push from the rear, failed to do so and "spoiled what would else have been a brilliant and decisive action."[36]

This battle, like many in which Clingman's Brigade was involved, has not been given major attention either by peers or later historians. General George E. Pickett remarked on the fighting at Drewry's Bluff in a speech to some Confederate veterans in 1891 that "very little has been said—much less than of any battle of its magnitude and importance which occurred throughout the war." He noted that no "regular report from the Confederate side, except the brief statements of Beauregard, Ransom or Hoke, has ever reached the public...." Charles T. Loehr, commenting on Pickett's speech, concluded that the events at Drewry's Bluff broke "Butler's right wing," which prevented the Union general from moving against either Richmond or Petersburg as Grant had planned for Butler to do.[37] However, President Davis did commend the 31st and 51st

Regiments for their performance as one of the "most gallant charges" he had ever witnessed. A Richmond paper described those same charges as "most gallantly made, eliciting high compliments from both Generals Hoke and Clingman."[38]

Critics of Clingman and his men tend to overlook these "gallant charges" when they portray Clingman's Brigade as a bunch of losers throughout the entire war.

Bermuda Hundred, May 16, 1864

At Bermuda Hundred, Clingman's Brigade was ordered with Corse's Brigade to attack Butler's line. This was successful and Butler's lines were broken and the Union general retreated to Bermuda Hundred, where he was "bottled up."

Cold Harbor, May 31–June 9, 1864

The engagement on June 1 was one of the hardest-fought battles of the entire war. The men of Clingman's command were hit hard, and every staff officer, including Clingman, was wounded. One-third of the command fell in the field. Colonel Murchison and Major Henderson of the 8th Regiment were among those injured. Yet, even though Radcliffe and his men refused to obey orders and move out of the trenches, Clingman's Brigade managed to move men and defend their position and hold their ground.

According to Clingman, his brigade was "deprived suddenly of its support," while at the same time it was attacked "in front, on its left flank and from its rear, at close quarters and by vastly superior numbers, [and] it was neither panic-stricken [n]or beaten." He maintains that his brigade, even after fighting continuously for three hours, and after losing "more than one-third of its strength," recovered "all its ground and repulsed its assailants."[39] Accusations that the lines of his brigade and those of Wofford's "were both broken" were denied by Clingman in a letter to a Richmond newspaper.

> This attack [on June 1] was repeatedly and signally repulsed with great loss to the enemy on my entire front. Near our left where they came in columns their dead were much thicker than I have ever seen them on any battlefield.... There was, however, at the beginning of the engagement a brigade from another State than my own, stationed on our left. This brigade did give way, and while the contest was going on in our front, the enemy in large force occupied the ground on our left flank and rear. After we had repulsed the last attack in front, and the men were cheering along the line, the Eighth regiment, which formed my left, was suddenly attacked on its left flank and rear. The woods there being thick and the smoke dense, the enemy had approached within a few yards and opened a heavy fire on the rear of the Eighth as well as its left.... It, by facing in two directions, attempted to hold its position, and thus lost about two-thirds of its numbers."[40]

Clingman praised the men of the 61st Regiment who came to the aid of the 8th, and stated that his brigade, together with the 27th Georgia, had driven back the Federal flank attack, and "still held its entire front of the works."[41]

The men of Clingman's Brigade did fight bravely in a difficult position, but seemed to have been blamed for the failure of other troops.

The position at Cold Harbor, though casualties were heavy, was preserved. This was one battle the Yankees regretted having fought. On June 4, 1864, the Army of the Potomac launched an attack on the Confederate lines manned by inferior numbers, but in the process, the Federal forces lost 10,000 men in twenty minutes. After the fighting ceased, it was not until June 7 that a truce was arranged, and by then "all but two of the wounded Federals had died."[42]

Petersburg, Virginia, June 10–August, 1864

On June 16, 1864, when the Union batteries mounted two heavy assaults on the Confederate lines, and both were repulsed. The brigades of Clingman and Martin were used to close a breach in Wise's line.[43] Wise had abandoned his position "in panic without firing a gun," his men leaving their works unprotected. Each subsequent Federal attack was repulsed by the men of Clingman's Brigade. Through Clingman's efforts "every third man" was placed in front of that position of the works in possession of the enemy. The fighting continued, somewhat unequally, until Ransom's Brigade arrived. With those reinforcements, the Confederates were able to retake the lost position. Clingman's men got little credit for their efforts. A Petersburg newspaper reported, however, that "Hoke's division stood last night like a rock wall and saved the city. They may be overrun, but no power on earth can drive them from a position." Clingman's aide, Hal Puryear, showed the paper to General Hoke, who remarked: "They should have said Clingman's Brigade, for no other troops of my command were engaged."[44] Because they were at Petersburg when the Federal assault began, Clingman and his men did an invaluable service, and prevented the lines from being overrun, but credit for that effort was given to others.

Clingman and his brigade became embroiled in controversy but this time over who "saved Petersburg" from the Federal assault of June 16–17. Although there was evidence that one of General Wise's regiments (the 34th Virginia) did not do their duty, it was proven untrue that "Wise's Brigade abandoned" its position without "firing a gun," as alleged by Captain William H. S. Burgwyn of Clingman's staff. Most agree that Wise's men did fall back, but under orders, and most of them "fought well thereafter." Burgwyn claimed that Clingman's Brigade had "held Grant's army in check" alone, unaided by any other regiments, until Ransom's Brigade arrived, and had, thereby, "saved" Petersburg from capture. Clingman contributed to the debate by objecting to the claim of Colonel John Thomas Goode, who commanded Wise's Brigade during the fighting at Petersburg on these days, that his brigade, assisted by Ransom's, had "saved Petersburg." Clingman wrote a letter to the Raleigh *Daily Confederate* which contradicted Goode by saying that since "Gen. Ransom's did not advance up to them until about 11 o'clock, did it not occur to you that some [other] troops were engaged during these four hours?"[45]

As had happened after the battle for the Neuse River Bridge, Clingman's Brigade was embroiled in a controversy which involved "poor battlefield performance" or "failure to receive credit for a good one." It seems that here, his men performed admirably, but that others took the credit due them.

Again, in the dangerous situation caused by the explosion of the Federal mine under the Confederate lines, Clingman and his men were there to help staunch the flow of Federal soldiers into the Confederate works. The Federal mine had been constructed under the Confederate lines at Bushrod Johnson's position. When the explosion occurred, the only Confederate divisions in the trenches were those of Hoke and Johnson.[46] Clingman's 8th and 61st regiments were among those who assisted in repulsing the enemy during three successive attempts to take the Confederate lines after the explosion.[47]

Globe Tavern, August 19, 1864

In this action, 2,100 Federal prisoners were taken, and many were killed or wounded. Clingman's Brigade captured "three times as many prisoners" as they had men in the battle. However, Clingman was wounded and was out of the military action until shortly before the surrender at Greensboro on April 26, 1865.[48]

Clingman's failure to remain behind lines and take proper precautions for his own safety resulted in his being shot in the leg and becoming unable to command his regiment for most of the remainder of the war. Certainly, the brigade suffered without his leadership. However, the end result would have been the same whether Clingman had remained in command or not.

Fort Harrison, September 30, 1864

The failure to take Fort Harrison was a blow to the Confederacy. Although the fort needed to be retaken, it was an almost impossible task. Several officers had warned against it and attempted to get General Lee to change the plan of attack.

Major General Robert F. Hoke thought the attack should not even have been made. He believed it "impracticable," and would result in very heavy casualties without accomplishing anything. He believed that, rather than attempting to take the fort by storm, Lee should establish a new line of defense, about 200 yards away from the fort.[49]

Even Lee's artillery chief, Edward Porter Alexander, saw that it was a "hopeless task" to attempt to drive superior forces out of a strongly defended work.[50]

Colonel McKethan, now brigade commander, and other officers at Fort Harrison saw before them "the impossibility of success and the heavy loss that we must sustain," and they protested against the assault.[51] Hector McKethan's brother, Second Lieutenant A. A. McKethan, reasoned that any attempt to recapture the fort "under such circumstances was a mistake," and a "terrible blunder."[52] However, their protests fell on deaf ears, and the men bravely moved forward to their deaths. Clingman's Brigade suffered heavily for their obedience.

Captain W. H. S. Burwgyn attributed the failure to take the works at Fort Harrison to Field's Division's inability to "drive the enemy or turn their right flank and to General Kirkland's and Hagood's Brigades not charging on the right and to Colquitt's Brigade not supporting us." Burgwyn estimates that his brigade, Clingman's, lost "at least two-thirds killed, wounded, and prisoners, and I fear three-fourths."[53]

Certainly, Clingman's Brigade lost many more men than any other regiment at the site. Bad timing undoubtedly played a key role, but if the advice of Hoke and others had been taken, such heavy casualties might have been avoided.

Colonel Hector McKethan felt personally responsible for the loss of so many lives in his brigade. However, the attack was not his decision, and he had to follow orders. Those in command were responsible for the attack, its failure, and the subsequent loss of lives. After the disastrous battle at Fort Harrison, McKethan became depressed and never recovered his health.

Fort Fisher, March 1865

Although Clingman's Brigade, as part of Hoke's Division, were stationed at Sugar

Loaf near Fort Fisher, their effectiveness was curtailed by General Braxton Bragg. General Bragg was believed to be as incompetent as Union general Butler, and certainly, he was not the best person for the job of defending Fort Fisher.

After the fall of Fort Fisher, from the prison camp at Fort Columbus on Governor's Island, General Whiting asked that an investigation be made of Bragg's conduct of the defense of Fort Fisher. Bragg's leadership was questioned, as was the fact that he "made no effective effort to use Hoke's division to hit the Federal rear during the land attack on Fisher."

Whiting, who died shortly after the battle in his Yankee prison, attributed the loss of Fort Fisher "solely to the incompetency, the imbecility and the pusillanimity" of Braxton Bragg. He accused Bragg of not meeting the enemy forces who were attacking Fort Fisher on land because he (Bragg) "was afraid." Whiting also noted that after the Federal naval bombardment had ceased, the 6,000 Confederates in the fort had continued to fight for six more hours, while Bragg sat within 2½ miles with "6,000 of Lee's best troops, three batteries of artillery and 1,500 reserves." Bragg was "held in check by two negro brigades while the rest of the enemy assaulted and he didn't even fire a musket."[54]

This opinion was shared by other Confederates. D. A. Buie surmised: "Had Genl. Bragg let Genl. Hoke attack the enemy when he asked him to do so," then Fort Fisher would still be in Confederate hands. Another stated that Hoke should have attacked the enemy "whether he could carry the works or not." Another expressed the opinion that Bragg had had "bad luck wherever he has been and always will, he is too fond of retreating or too fearful of being taken by the enemy."[55]

However, the Union forces were determined to take the fort, and close the port of Wilmington. With the resources at their disposal, and with Bragg in command, it was a foregone conclusion that they would succeed.[56]

Bentonville, March 19–21, 1865

The final battle of the War Between the States was fought between the exhausted remnant of a once-proud Confederate army, and the superior forces of Slocum and Howard with Sherman on the way.

Hoke's Division, who comprised a third of Johnston's army, was the first group on the battlefield at Bentonville. Hoke's men entrenched along the Goldsboro Road, and his artillery were successful in blocking the troops of Brevet Major General Jefferson C. Davis and Brigadier General William Carlin. Repeated Federal assaults were repulsed.[57]

Although Braxton Bragg was supposed to be in charge of the battle because of his rank, actually Hoke was directing the action. However, true to form, Bragg intervened and caused trouble, not once but twice. According to Daniel W. Barefoot in his biography entitled *General Robert F. Hoke: Lee's Modest Warrior*, the first time was when he ordered reinforcements to help Hoke early in the day on March 19. When Union general Slocum sent forward reinforcements on March 19, Bragg got nervous and applied to Johnston for reinforcements. As a result Confederate general Hardee was ordered to send men to assist Hoke. However, the reinforcements, in the form of McLaw's Division, were delayed and arrived just in time to see Hoke repulse the enemy "after a sharp contest of half an hour, at short range." Therefore, the advantage that could have been gained was lost because the battle had ended before McLaw's men arrived. McLaw's men were then held in reserve the balance of the day.[58]

On the second occasion, Bragg ordered Hoke to carry out a frontal attack. Hoke reluctantly complied and came into conflict with Morgan's entire line. General Hagood blamed Bragg for the heavy casualties and the failure to win the battle, and proclaimed that the "loss in our division at least would have been inconsiderable and our success eminent had it not been for Bragg's undertaking to give a tactical order upon a field that he had not seen."[59]

General Joseph E. Johnston blamed himself for not having sent Bragg "back to Raleigh on the 18th."[60] However, regardless of Bragg's poor direction, the final outcome was already decided. Even if Hoke had succeeded in driving Slocum's men from the field, Sherman was on his way. The Confederates were outnumbered, and soon when the elements of Sherman's army were reunited, Johnston's Confederates found themselves almost surrounded. The Confederate forces moved on to Smithfield. The war was swiftly drawing to a close.

Here at Smithfield, Brigadier General Thomas L. Clingman joined Joseph Johnston. Clingman visited with Hoke and some of the men of his brigade, then asked Johnston if he could have the "honor of commanding the rear guard of the army." Johnston saw that Clingman could not even walk from the leg wound he had received in August 1864.

Clingman reportedly begged General Johnston:

> Sir, much has been said about dying in the last ditch. You have left with you here thirty thousand of as brave men as the sun ever shone upon. Let us take our stand here and fight the two armies of Grant and Sherman to the end, and thus show to the world how far we can surpass the Thermopylae of the Greeks. [61]

Johnston's reply has been recorded various ways, but its meaning has always clearly been negative. "General, if they were all like you, I would do it, but there are many young men here who have a future, and I ought not to sacrifice their lives.[62] Other sources quote Johnston as saying: "I am not in the Thermopylae business."[63]

Johnston did not intend to carry the war any further. After surrendering at the Bennet House on April 26, the remaining Confederate forces with Johnston's army were paroled at Greensboro, North Carolina, on May 1, 1865. Johnston, along with Clingman, surrendered. The parole lists were signed by Major Generals Daniel H. Hill and Robert F. Hoke, and by Brigadier Generals Thomas L. Clingman, W. W. Kirkland, and Lawrence S. Baker.[64] All the other general officers from North Carolina at that time were "either dead, or wounded, prisoner or on detached service."[65]

Thus ended four years of bloody struggle. The fighting unit known as Clingman's Brigade had some successes and some failures. While they were not able to prevent the burning of the Neuse River Bridge at Goldsboro in 1862, this first encounter with the enemy taught them some valuable lessons: that things don't always go as planned, that cooperation and communication are vital, that war is not a game but deadly reality, and that timing is a crucial element. They learned that it took more than courage to win against the superior forces and firepower of the enemy. They also learned that whenever there was a failure, someone was made the "scapegoat" and had to take the blame, whether guilty or innocent.

Clingman himself was subject to orders from his superiors. He did not always agree with their decisions. However, he tried his best to obey orders and see that his men did so also. His actions and those of his men were often subject to outside forces beyond their control.

The brigade was frequently in a position where defensive action was all that was possible. He and his men showed great courage on the battlefield in every instance except three: (1) on Morris Island when some of the men of the 31st Regiment refused to man the parapets at Battery Wagner; (2) at the crossroads at Old Cold Harbor when a company of the 51st regiment refused to fire; and (3) during the main battle at Cold Harbor when the men of the 61st Regiment refused to leave the trenches as ordered.

In the first incident, Clingman was on Sullivan's Island and not with his troops to see that they obeyed. Yet, men of the 51st reversed the actions of the 31st Regiment when they answered the call for volunteers and mounted the parapets to save the day. At Cold Harbor, an officer of the brigade failed to obey commands, and when Fitzhugh Lee's Cavalry retreated, Clingman's men were left to face Sheridan's troops alone. In the third instance, the brigade was attempting to cope with simultaneous attacks from both the front and rear, and Clingman was unaware for a time that one of his regiments had failed to move out of the trenches to attack the enemy.

Clingman's Brigade performed admirably at Petersburg, Drewry's Bluff, Bermuda Hundred, and along the Weldon Railroad. Clingman's Brigade was successful in holding the lines at Petersburg on July 17 until reinforcements could arrive. They suffered for many days in the trenches at Petersburg, and were there when the Federal mine exploded. They endured the sweltering heat and stench within the bombproof of Battery Wagner,

Fig. 25. Confederate General Joseph E. Johnston, taken between 1860 and 1865. Brady National Photographic Art Gallery, Washington, D.C. (Library of Congress)

and braved the deadly fire when up on the parapets of the little fort. They obeyed orders and, as a result, forfeited their lives in the assault at Fort Harrison, while their officers, who had tried to prevent the useless slaughter, watched helplessly as their men fell.

Some of the units of Clingman's Brigade helped in the retaking of Plymouth and in the defense of Wilmington and Fort Fisher. What few were left performed as seasoned veterans in the last battle at Bentonville.

Clingman, at least, was proud of the

troops of his state and, especially, his own brigade. He never passed up an opportunity to brag on those brave men:

> Our late great contest was mainly fought by infantry, and no other State furnished so large a force of that arm as did North Carolina. Mr. Davis himself in no respect partial to us, told me in 1864 that our regiments were better kept up than those of any other State. Nor did any other State lose so many men in battle.[66]

Clingman viewed the recent conflict with awe and great respect:

> Our late war developed all that was most striking in ancient or modern warfare.... But, nothing that England's soldiers ever did, surpassed the unshaken courage of our North Carolina Confederates under the most formidable assaults on more than one occasion, when attacked again and again, at the same time in front and flank, by more than ten times its number, one of its brigades remained unbroken.

Clingman was forever awed by the grandeur of the *charge*, a maneuver his brigade had performed many times.

> ...the most striking feature of the late war was the Confederate charge. The student will remember that at Marathon the Athenians for the first time made a wild dash against the mass of their enemies.... This mode of fighting had, however, gone into disuse in the world for centuries, and was revived only in our day by the Confederate soldiers when after the seven days' fight at Richmond ... the people in Europe could have no idea of the effect of a charge extending over a length of three miles. Our friend, General D. H. Hill, if present, could tell us all about this. Often as I witnessed this charge, I never saw it fail to break and carry down the force against which it was directed.[67]

Clingman also said in his speech at Charlotte during the centennial celebration that he had often felt regret, as had many other Confederates, that he had not "fallen in battle."[68] Such was the character of Brigadier General Thomas Lanier Clingman and the troops he led into battle, known as Clingman's Brigade.

Despite some of the blunders made by some officers and regiments, Clingman's Brigade did not leave behind such a terrible record. When all is said and done, this brigade was probably no better or no worse than any other brigade that served its state and the Confederacy through four years of unbelievable hardships and life-threatening peril. That they endured at all is commendable. Through all the battles, the forced marches, the cold, the hunger, it is a wonder that any were alive at the end of the war. One simply cannot imagine the agony, the fear, the pain, the heartbreak of seeing friends, comrades and brothers die before one's eyes as they did so very often.

In spite of it all, the men of Clingman's Brigade remained true and obeyed their orders to the best of their ability. In some cases they performed brilliantly; in other cases, they merely tried to survive. Let us hope that they will be remembered for their efforts.

Notes

1. Sommers, p. 116.
2. Burgwyn, *A Captain's War*, p. xi.
3. *O.R.*, XLII, Ser. I, Pt. II, p. 1244, "Strength of the forces of infantry and artillery stationed near Petersburg, Va., General G. T. Beauregard commanding, September 10, 1864, as shown by inspection reports."
4. *O.R.*, XLVII, Ser. I, Pt. II, p. 1424, "Abstract from field return of Hoke's Division for March 17, 1865."
5. John H. Robinson, "Fifty-Second Regiment," in Clark, *Histories or the Several Regiments*, III, pp. 229–232; *O.R.*, XVIII, Ser. I, pp. 118–119; and Manarin and Jordan, IV, pp. 516–517.
6. Manarin and Jordan, IV, pp. 515–516. Neither the regimental history of the 61st Regiment nor John G. Barrett in his *The Civil War in North Carolina*, pp. 145–147, places the 61st

Regiment at the Neuse River railroad bridge with General Clingman until late in the afternoon of December 17, 1862. Clingman mentions Devane and the 61st, but he may have more correctly meant a portion of the 61st Regiment or the 40th Regiment. See *O.R.*, XVIII, Ser. I, pp. 117–119 for Brigadier General Clingman's report of the action.

7. Burgwyn, "Clingman's Brigade," p. 484.
8. Wheeler, *Reminiscences and Memoirs,* p. 73.
9. Robinson, p. 231.
10. Thomas L. Clingman to Governor Zebulon B. Vance, January 28, 1863, Zebulon B. Vance Papers, North Carolina Department of Archives and History, Raleigh, North Carolina.
11. Clingman to Vance, January 28, 1863.
12. Thomas L. Clingman to Governor Zebulon B. Vance, January 28, 1863, Zebulon B. Vance Papers, North Carolina Department of Archives and History, Raleigh, North Carolina.
13. *The Weekly Raleigh Register*, 9 Sept. 1863.
14. Ashe, *History of North Carolina*, II, p. 832.
15. *O.R.*, LIII, Ser. I, pp. 297–298, T. L. Clingman to Capt. W. F. Nance, September 25, 1863.
16. Ludwig, pp. 392–295.
17. Burton, p. 151.
18. Samuel A. Ashe, "Life at Fort Wagner," *Confederate Veteran*, XXXV (1927), 256.
19. *O.R.*, XXIX, Ser. I, Pt. II, pp. 761–762, Thomas L. Clingman to W. H. C. Whiting, September 28, 1863.
20. *O.R.*, XXVIII, Ser. I, Pt. II, pp. 423, 431, October 23, 1863.
21. *O. R.*, XXVIII, Ser. I, Pt. II, pp. 500–501, Thomas L. Clingman to W. F. Nance, November 12, 1863.
22. Burgwyn, *A Captain's War,* p. 120.
23. Williams, "Fifty-Fourth Regiment," p. 274.
24. Major General G. E. Pickett to General S. Cooper, February 15, 1864, *Southern Historical Society Papers*, IX, 3–4.
25. Brigadier General Robert F. Hoke, "Report of General Hoke," February 8, 1864, *Southern Historical Society Papers*, IX, 6–7.
26. General Barton, "Report of General Barton," February 21, 1864, *Southern Historical Society Papers*, IX, pp. 9–10.
27. Endorsement by General R. E. Lee to "Report of General Barton," February 21, 1864, *Southern Historical Society Papers*, IX, 11.
28. Boatner, p. 49.
29. Burgwyn, "Clingman's Brigade," in Clark, IV, p. 488.
30. Ludwig, "Eighth Regiment," p. 401.
31. *O.R.*, XXXVI, Ser. I, Pt. II, p. 238, "Report of Major General Robert F. Hoke," May 25, 1864; and *O.R.*, XXXVI, Ser. I, Pt. II, pp. 236–238.
32. R. F. Hoke, "Battle of Drewry's Bluff, May 16, 1864," *Southern Historical Society Papers*, XII (1884), 227–229.
33. *O.R.*, XXXVII, Ser. I, Pt. II, p. 238.
34. Beauregard, "The Defense of Drewry's Bluff," pp. 202–203.
35. McKethan, p. 211.
36. Kean, *Inside the Confederate Government: The Diary of Robert Garlick Hill Kean,* p. 14.
37. Charles T. Loehr, "Battle of Drewry's Bluff," Richmond *Times,* October 25, 1891; rpt. *Southern Historical Society Papers*, XIX (1891), 100–101.
38. Bryan and Meadows, "Thirty-First Regiment," pp. 515–516.
39. Clingman, "Second Cold Harbor," p. 205.
40. Hill, *Confederate Military History: North Carolina*, IV, pp. 252–253.
41. *Ibid.*, p. 253.
42. Miller, Cold Harbor picture caption, III, p. 87.
43. Barefoot, p. 205.
44. Burgwyn, "Clingman's Brigade," in Clark, IV, pp. 493–495.
45. *Daily Confederate* (Raleigh), July 18, 1864, cited in Manarin and Jordan, XIV, p. 625, footnote 89.
46. Hill, p. 266.
47. Hill, p. 269.
48. Burgwyn, "Clingman's Brigade," IV, p. 495.
49. Barefoot, p. 223.
50. *Ibid.*
51. *Ibid.*
52. *Ibid.*
53. Burgwyn, *A Captain's War,* p. 153.
54. Barrett, pp. 279–280.
55. Barrett, p. 280.
56. Barefoot, p. 241.
57. Barefoot, pp. 295–296.
58. Barefoot, p. 296.
59. Barefoot, pp. 298–299.
60. Barefoot, p. 296.
61. Burgwyn, "Clingman's Brigade," p. 449; and Clingman, "Charlotte Speech," p. 112.
62. Clingman, "Charlotte Speech," p. 112.
63. Tucker, p. 180.

64. *O.R.,* XC, Ser. I, pp. 1601–1666; and Ashe, "North Carolina," *Confederate Veteran,* XXXVII (1929), p. 175.

65. Brooks, p. 502.

66. Clingman, "Davidson Speech," in Clingman, *Speeches and Writings,* p. 49.

67. Clingman, "Charlotte Speech," in Clingman, *Speeches and Writings,* pp. 111–112.

68. Clingman, "Charlotte Speech," in Clingman, *Speeches and Writings,* p. 112.

APPENDIX A

Clingman's Order Book 1— General Orders Issued by Brigadier General Thomas Lanier Clingman

The two original Order Books are held at Duke University, Durham, North Carolina, and are used with permission. The first book contains general orders for Clingman's Brigade issued by Brigadier General Clingman 1862–1864 from Camp Whiting and Wilmington, North Carolina, and Sullivan's Island, South Carolina. The second book (see Appendix B) contains specific brigade orders issued by Clingman and letters written by him.

Head Quarters
Near Wilmington
Nov. 25, 1862

General Order
No. 1

In compliance with orders, the undersigned hereby assumes command of the Brigade Corps and of the 8th, 31st, 51st, and 61st Regiments, N.C. Troops.

The following Staff officers are as announced.

Captain Edward White   Assist. Adjt. Gen.
Lieutenant A. M. Eunice   Aide de Camp & Actg. Brigade Quartermaster

The Commissioned Officers of the Brigade will be hereafter known and assigned as "Camp Whiting."

[Signed] T. L. Clingman,
Brig. Genl.

Head Quarters
Camp Whiting
November 25, 1862

General Order
No. 2

I. In compliance with instructions from District Head quarters, the Regiments of this Brigade will be drilled at Skirmish, Company or Battalion will drill twice a day (Sunday excepted) during the following hours:
From 9 to 11 A.M.
From 2 to 4 P.M.

II. Commanding officers will send to this office promptly on the 13th and 29 before the last days of each month, reports showing the strength and condition of their Regts.

They will also forward immediately those Headquarters statements setting forth the condition and efficiency of their command, the number of small arms and the amount and kind of ammunition (serviceable) and a certified list of the commissioned officers with date of commission or appointment of each.

III. The men of the Regiments of this Brigade will not be permitted to go beyond the limits of their camp, except on Regimental business with written authority from the Officer in Command or in charge of a non-commissioned officer where necessary.

By Command of
Brig. Gen. Clingman
Edward White, A. A. General

Head Quarters
Camp Whiting
Dec. 6th 1862

General Order
No. 3

Commanding Officers of Regiments in this Brigade will forward, without delay to this office lists of the names of all deserters from their Regiments, stating the companies to which they belong and the place where they are supposed to be.

By Command
Brig. Gen. Clingman
Edward White
A. A. G.

Head Quarters Camp Whiting
Dec 12th 1862

General Order
No. 4

Hereafter in lieu of Past General Order No. 2 from thee Head Quarters, respecting drill, the following will be observed:
Commanding officers of Regts will hereafter command in the field lying between these Head Quarters and the Mill Road, prepared for Battalion drill, all the field officers attending, at 10 A.M. every morning.
Skirmish and company will commence at 2½ P.M. daily.

By Command
Brig. Gen. Clingman
Edward White, Asst. Adj. Gen.

Hdq. Clingman's Brigade
Dec 22, 1862

General Order
No. 5

Until further order the Regiments of this Brigade will be in the field immediately beyond the county bridge at 9½ A.M. daily for Battalion drill.

By Command of Brig. Gen. Clingman
Edward White
A. A. G.

Hdq. Clingman's Brigade
December 25, 1862

General Order
No. 6

Hereafter Brigade & Battalion drill will begin at 9½ A.M. and the Regts will be drilled at company drill from 2 to 3½ P.M. All the officers attend thee drills and the commanding officer of each Regiment will report to these HdQtrs the names of such Field or Company officers as failed to attend.

By Command of
Brig. Gen. Clingman
Edward White
A. A. G.

Hd. Qtrs. Clingman's Brigade
Dec. 24, 1862

General Order
No. 7

Hereafter the hours for drill in this Brigade will be as follows:
Company drill from 7 to 9 A.M.
Brigade drill from 10 A.M. to 12 M.
Battalion drill from 2½ to 4½ P.M.

By Command of
Brig. Gen. Clingman
Edward White
A. A. G.

Hd. Qrs. Clingman's Brigade
Dec. 27th 1862

General Order
No. 8

I. The Regiments of this Brigade will be put on the march for Wilmington tomorrow morning at 8 A.M.

In order to accomplish this, Commanding officers will see that their men, beginning at a very early hour cook all the rations now on hand.

Any Regimental company who has not already drawn his provisions will do so tonight.

One days rations additional will be drawn by the Brigade company and as no opportunity will probably occur for drawing again during the march the rations must be carefully husbanded.

II. Regimental commanders are particularly required to use their utmost endeavors to prevent straggling on the march. Each Regiment will be followed by a rear guard detailed with special reference to their reliability & under charge of a good officer with orders to see that straggling is not permitted except in cases where the Regimental surgeon shall give written permission. At night & morning rolls will be called absentees marked, reported to Regimental Hd.Qrs. and properly and promptly punished.

Those who are pronounced by the Surgeon unable to march will be left in camp in charge of competent & reliable officers, one of whom, the senior in rank, will report tomorrow at Dept. Hd. Qrs. Goldsboro for instructions.

The necessary cooking utensils will be left with them.

    By Command
    Brig. Gen. Clingman
    Edward White
    A. A. G.

    HdQrs. Clingman's Brigade
    Dec. 28th 1862

General Orders
No. 9

II. The Orders of March for today will be
1st 8th Reg. N C. Troops
2nd 31st " " "
3rd 51st " " "
4th 61st " " "

The whole wagon train will come in rear of the Brigade one wagon from each Regiment will be put at the disposal of the Brigade Commissary.

III. The detail from this Brigade on duty at the R. R. Bridge will be at once recalled to be rear-guard for the 41st will bring up the rear of the wagon train.

    By Command of Brig. Genl. Clingman
    Edward White
    A. A. G.

    Hd Qrs. Clingman's Brigade
    Dec. 28th 1862

General Orders
No. 10

II. The March will be resumed tomorrow morning at 7½ o'clock promptly in the following order
1st 31st Regt N.C. Troops
2nd 51st " " "
3rd 61st " " "
4th 8th " " "

III. The pioneer corps of the entire Brigade under charge of a competent commissioned officer from the 31st Reg. Will start at 7 o'clock A.M. and keep in advance of the Brigade repairing the road wherever necessary.

III. The surgeons train will go in front of the troops.

    By Command of
    B. G. C.
    Edward White
    A. A. G.

    Hd. Qrs. Clingman's Brigade
    Dec. 29, 1862

General Order No. 11

The march will be resumed tomorrow morning at 7½ o'clock in the following order
1st Brigade wagons
2nd 51st Regt. N.C. Troops
3rd 61st " " "
4th 8th " " "
5th 31st " " "

The pioneer corps will be sent in advance under charge of a commd. officer from the 51st Reg.

    By command of
    Brig. Gen. Clingman
    Edward White
    A. A. G.

    Hd. Qrs. Clingman's Brigade
    Dec. 30th 1862

General Order No. 12

The order of March for tomorrow will be
1st Wagon train
2nd 61st Reg. N C. Troops
3rd 8th " " "
4th 31st " " "
5th 51st " " "

The hour for starting will be at 7½ A.M. The pioneer corps will go in advance under charge of a commd. officer from the 61st Regt.

    By command of
    Brig. Genl. Clingman
    Edward White A. A. G.

    Hd. Qrs. Clingman's Brigade
    Dec. 30th 1862

General Order No. 13

Commanding officers of the Regts will see that their men cook tonight all the rations they have on hand. All cooking utensils that can be used and shoes & other Quarter Master stores issued will be sent to the Rail Road at Lackey's [?] depot under charge of one man from each Regt.

By command of
Brig. Gen. Clingman
Edward White
A. A. G.

Hd. Qrs. Clingman's Brigade
Dec. 31st, 1862

General Orders
No. 14

The march will be resumed tomorrow morning at 7 o'clock in the following order
1st 8th Reg. N.C. Troops
2nd 31st " " "
3rd 51st " " "
4th 61st " " "

The wagon train will start at 6 A.M. promptly. The pioneer corps will be in charge of a commd. Officer from the 8th Regt.

By command

Hd. Qrs. Clingman's Brigade
January 1st 1863

General Order
No. 15

The March will be resumed tomorrow morning 7½ o'clock in the following order
1st 31st Reg. N.C. Troops
2nd 51st " " "
3rd 61st " " "
4th 8th   " " "

The pioneer corps will be but a short distance in front of the brigade under charge of a commd. Officer form the 31st Regt.

By command of
Brig. Gen. Clingman
Edward White A. A. G.

Hd. Qrs. Camp Whiting
January 2nd 1863

General Order
No. 1

Commanding Officers of Regts of their brigade will see that such men of their commands as were absent last night without permission required to do all the necessary police duty and labor under charge of a commanding officer until further ordered.

By command of Brig. Gen. Clingman
Edward White
A. A. G.

The names of all commd. Officers absent without leave will be reported at once to the Hd. Qrs.

E. W., A. A. G.

Head Quarters Camp Whiting
January 3, 1863

General Order
No. 2

General Order No. — Hd. Qrs. Clingman's Brigade, December 24, 1862
Respecting hours for drill is rescinded

Hereafter the Regts of this brigade will be on the field lying between these Hd. Qrs. And the Mill Pond at 10 A.M. daily for battalion drill.

The Regts will be drilled in company and skirmish drill from 2½ to 4½ P.M.

II. Men organized to do police duty and labor for absence without leave, under General Order No. 1, January 2nd 1863, from these Hd Qrs will be required in addition to attend Regimental and Company drills, and perform ordinary guard duty.

III. The following Staff officers are announced: Major T. B. Venable, P.A. C. S. Inspector General

Lieut. Woodbury Wheeler P. A. C. S. Ordnance Officer

They will be obeyed and respected accordingly.

IV. All General orders heretofore published to this Brigade from District Hd Qrs and from this office, will continue in force.

V. Commanding officers will see that necessary reports of their commands are sent in to this office by 10 A.M. daily.

VI. Regimental commanders will as soon as practicable muster their Regts. for payment stating in the certificate attached to the rolls the reason why the muster was not made on the 31st Dec.

Requisitions for such Muster & Pay Rolls as are required must be made at once in this office.

By command of
Brig. Gen. Clingman
Edward White
A. A. G.

Head Quarters Camp Whiting
January 14th 1863

General Order
No. 3

1st Lieut. Woodbury Wheeler, A___ P. A. C. S. Is hereby announced as Aid-de-Camp to the

Brig. Gen. Commdg. He will be obeyed & respected accordingly.

Lt. Wheeler will perform the duties of ordnance officer until relieved by an officer assigned to the Brigade for that duty.

          By command
          Brig. Gen. Clingman
                Edward White A. A. Genl.

          Hd. Qrs. Camp Whiting
                January 17, 1863

General Order
No. 4

Major A. M. Erwin P.A.C.S. is announced to this command as Brigade Quarter Master on the Staff of the Brig. Gen. Commdg. He will be obeyed and respected.

          By Command
          Brig. Gen. Clingman
             Edward White
               A. A. G.

          Hd. Qrs. Camp Whiting
                January 23, 1863

General Order No. 5

The attention of Comdg. Officers of the Regts of this Brigade is called to Genl. Order No. 3 from Hd quarters of Major Gen. Smith and Gen. Order No. 7 of Division Hd. Qrs., Wilmington, strict compliance with which is required and will be enforced.

The Provost Guard for this Brigade will be constituted as follows:

One Captain, one Sergt, one Corporal, and twenty-five (25) men from the 51st Regt.

One 2nd Lieut., one Sergt, one corporal and twenty-five (25) men from the 31st Regt.

One Jr. 2nd Lieut, one Sergt, one corporal and twenty-five (25) men from the 61st Regt NCT.

The officers will be selected with reference to their reliability and capability of performing the duties required of them.

          By command of
          Brig. Gen. Clingman
             Edward White
               Asst. Adj. Gen.

          Hd. Qrs. Camp Whiting
               Jany. 26th 1863

General Order
No. 6

I. The attention of Regimental commanders of this Brigade is called to those sections of the "Army Regulation" relating to orders and corresppondence and to General Order No. 3 Regt & Insp. Genl.'s office Richmond of date January 9th 1863 relating to the same subject.

Hereafter all official communication forwarded and through this office must be written, when practicable, on letter paper and not on note or fools cap paper. The letter must be folded in three equal folds parallel with the writing and endorsed across the fold which corresponds with the top of the sheet in the following manner.

    <u>Post or Station and date of Letter</u>
    <u>Name and rank of writer</u>
    <u>Analysis of Contents</u>

II. Commanding officers forwarding communications will see that they are addressed to the proper staff officers and will endorse upon them an expression of opinion, either in approval or disapproval.

III. Further information on this subject will be given at this office if desired.

          By command of
          Brig. Gen. Clingman
             Edward White A.A.G.

          Hd.Qrs. Clingman's Brigade
          Crafts House near Charleston
                February 27, 1863

General Order
No. 7

I. Until further ordered, the hours for drill in this Brigade will be:

For Battalion drill from 9 to 11 A.M.

For Company & skirmish drill from 2½ to 4½ P.M.

II. Regimental commanders will at once establish color lines in front of their camps and keep the arms of the Regts stacked upon the line.

III. Special attention is called to General Order No. 182 from General Gist's Hd. Qrs.

IV. Office hours at these Hd.Qrs. will be from 9 A.M. to 2½ P.M.

No business, unless of importance, will be attended to, except during those hours.

Permits to leave camp will be signed between the hours of 9 & 10 A.M. These permits must be collected by the adjutants of Regts. and sent by one man to these Hd. Qrs.

V. Capt. N. B. Moses is announced to the command as Volunteer Aide-de-camp on the Staff of Brig. Genl. Comdg.

By Command
Brig. Gen. Clingman
Edward White
A. A. Genl.

Head Quarters Clingman's Brigade
Craft's House near Charleston, S.C.
February 25th 1863
General Order
No. 8

I. Hereafter no communication will be considered at, or forwarded from, these Head Quarters unless written with *ink*, upon *letter paper*, and properly endorsed.
Endorsements must in all cases be made upon the fold corresponding with the top of the sheet as will be seen from the enclosed form.
Paper coming to these Head Quarters not prepared in accordance with the above, will invariably be returned for correction.
II. Immediate requisitions will be made upon the Brigade Quarter master for the regulation allowance of stationery for each Regiment and company.
III. Regimental morning reports must be sent to this office before 10 A.M. and weekly reports by 8 A.M. on Wednesday of each week.
IV. Regimental commanders will forward immediately to these Hd. Qrs. lists of all Commissioned officers of their Regts. giving names, dates of appointments, where born, and from what state appointed.
V. The following staff officers are announced to the Brigade
1st. Lieut. S. A. Ashe, CSA Ordnance officer
1st   "   Woodbury Wheeler, Actg. Brigade Inspector

By Command
Brig. Gen. Clingman
Edward White
A. A. G.

Head Quarters Clingman's Brigade
Sullivan's Island, October 8, 1863
General Order
No. 9

Lieut. S. W. Maurice, Actg. P.A.C.S., is announced to the Brigade as Ordnance Officer on the Staff of the Brig. Gen. Comdg. He will be obeyed and respected.

By Command
Brig. Genl. Clingman
Edward White
Ass. Adj. General

Head Quarters Western Div. James Island
Heyward House March 12th 1863
General Order
No. 1

I. In compliance with Genl. Orders No. 5, Hd. Qrs. McLeods House, the undersigned assumes command of the Western Division James Island.
II. The following Staff is announced:
Captain Edward White, Asst. Adj. Genl.
Major A. M. Erwin, Brigade Quarter Master
1st Lieut. T. R. Blake,   Brigade Commissary
1st Lieut. Woodbury Wheeler, Actg. Asst. Inspr.-Genl.
1st Lieut. Sam'l. A. Ashe, Ordnance Officer
Capt. M. B. Moses, Vol. Aide-de-camp

By Command
Brig. Genl. Clingman
Edward White
Asst. Adjt. Genl.

Hd.Qrs. Clingman's Brigade
James Island, March 20, 1863
General Orders No. 2

I. In accordance with Genl. Orders No. 6 Hd. Qrs. James Island & St. Andrews, the following regulations for drills & school of instruction are hereby ordered. There will be two regular drills each day, one in the A.M., and one in the school of the company from 3 to 4:15 P.M.
II. Schools of Instruction are ordered in each Regiment. The Sr. officer present will instruct the field officers, excepting the officer next in rank to himself, his company commander, and the adjutant in the school of the Battn on each day from 11 to 12 A.M. The officer second in rank will at the same hour be charged with the instruction of the Lieuts not comdg. companies, the adjutant will from 2 to 3 P.M. instruct the non-comd. Officers paying particular attention to the School of the Guides.
III. The studies will be conducted regularly through <u>Hardees</u> tactics, <u>without omitting any subjects</u>.
At such rates as the Instructor deems proper, and on each day the Battn & Companies, at their respective drills will at <u>least once</u>, perform the <u>movements</u> taught the preceding day, in the school of Instruction. In the Drills no deviation will be allowed from the letter of the Tactics either in command or execution.
IV. A weekly report will be made to these Hd. Qrs. of the progress in studies with a table

showing all the absences and the reason therefor.

> By Command
> Brig. Gen. Clingman
> Edward White
> A. A. Genl.

Head Quarters Western Div.
James Island
March 20, 1863

General Order
No. 3

In compliance with instructions from Brig. Genl. Gist, Regimental and Battalion commanders in this Div. will forward without delay, to this office statements of all vacancies in companies of their commands, showing how each vacancy occurred and giving the name of the officer entitled to promotion by reason of seniority.

> By command of
> Brig. Gen. Clingman
> Edward white, A. A. Genl.

Head Qrs. Western Division
James Island April 9, 1863

General Orders
No. 4

The Brig. Genl. Comdg. has learned with regret that negligence has been exhibited in the guarding of the bridges over the Wappoo Creek.

It is therefore directed that one sentinel be posted at each end of each of the two bridges (two for each) and that they continue at all times to walk their posts. It has been reported that soldiers having permission to be about until dress parade frequently remain about until after that time and that no notice is taken of it by the guard. Hereafter when this is the case, the officer in charge will retain the permit and report the fact promptly to the Field officer of the day, who will in turn report it to these Hd. Qrs. and the offender whether officer or soldier will be immediately punished.

The officer of the guard at the two bridges as well as the non-coms. Officers will be held strictly responsible for the execution of this order and also for the delivery to his successor.

> By Command of
> Brig. Gen. Clingman
> Edward White, A. A. Gen.

Headquarters Clingman's Brigade
Wilmington NC May 1st 1863

General Order
No. 5

The Brig. Gen. Comdg. takes pleasure in communicating to the brigade the Special Orders of the Gen. Commanding this Department and also of the immediate Division Commander. A compliment from one so distinguished and so widely known in the world as General Beauregard, who has so recently on two occasions reviewed this Brigade, ought to stimulate us to the highest executions to merit a continuance of such praise.

Though while in this Department we have not had an opportunity to meet the enemy, yet it has been a source of gratification that by our presence here we have been able to reciprocate the prompt and efficient aid rendered by the gallant troops of South Carolina & Georgia when our own state was threatened by a large hostile force. It has been our good fortune too while here to witness the signal defeat of the boasted invincible iron clad armada of the Yankee government. Having met with great kindness here, having been both relieved from outpost and other fatiguing duty, ample leisure has been afforded for improvement in drill and discipline, when therefore it may be our fortune again to meet the Robbers and murders who are endeavoring to exterminate us in order that they may occupy our country, it is to be hoped that the action of this Brigade will be such as to satisfy the expectation of every North Carolinian and merit the applause from brave and noble compatriots throughout the Confederacy.

> [signed] T. L. Clingman
> Brig. Genl.

Headquarters Clingmans Brigade
Wilmington, NC May 5th, 1863

General Order
No. 6

Regimental Commanders of the Brigade will forward promptly to these Hd. Qrs. the following returns.

On the 6 & 11th of each month a field return with blanks furnished from this office

On the 26th a monthly return, the table of alterations exhibiting the changes which may have occurred in the command during the month.

By command of Brig. Gen. Clingman
Edward White
Asst. Adjt. Genl.

Headquarters Clingmans Brigade
Wilmington, NC May 12th, 1863

General Order
No. 7

The Brigadier General commanding while gratefied with observing the general good discipline of the Brigade, regrets to have noticed in several instances a want of punctuality and promptness in the movement of Regiments.

Time is an element of the greatest importance in military movement. Many battles have been lost and won because troops failed to move promptly to the position assigned them. When a thing is ordered to be done at a particular time, it is not a compliance unto the order if it is done at a later period. It is only by a habit of promptness on ordinary occasions that troops are able to execute important movements on the field of battle with such expeditions and as to ensure success.

The Brigadier General therefore hopes that in his thus calling the attention of the colonels and all other officers to this subject they will so direct the movements of those under their commands as to insure the necessary degree of promptness and dispatch.

By Command Brig. Genl. Clingman
T. Brown Venable
Maj., A. A. G.

HeadQuarters Clingmans Brigade
Wilmington, NC, May 29th, 1863

General Order
No. 8

The attention of the Brig. Genl. Comdg has been called by the Surgeon to the increase of sickness in the Brigade produced by the use of pies, cakes and other food of like description by the men.

In order, as far as practicable, to remedy this evil, the sale of such articles of food to the troops is positively prohibited, and commanding officers are required to see that they are not kept for sale within two miles of the camp.

The use of vegetables will conduce very much to the health of the troops, and their sale will be not only permitted but encouraged.

By Command of
Brig. Genl. Clingman

Edward White
Asst. Adj. Genl.

Head Quarters Clingmans Brigade
Near Wilmington, June 10th 1863

General Order
No. 9.

In consequence of frequent complaints made by citizens of this vicinity of injuries to private property by the troops of this Brigade, the Brig Genl Comdg finds it necessary to order that the Cols. Comdg the several regiments will see that no one leaves his company without written permission from the commander of the company and not more than one officer and two privates will be allowed to be absent from each company.

Fatigue parties or detail for regimental business will always be held strictly accountable for the conduct of those under his command. All leaves to go to Wilmington will be obtained at these Head Quarters, except that each Col. can detail, if necessary, two men daily to go there on business for the regiment.

Soldiers will not be permitted to go into the water for bathing or any other purpose except under charge of a comd officer, who will see that they do not remain in more than twenty (20) minutes at a time.

By Command, Brig. Gen. Clingman
Edward White, A. A. Genl.

Headquarters Clingmans Brigade
June 10th, 1863

General Order
No. 10

Regimental commanders will forward on Friday of each week to Major T. B. Venable, Asst. Inspt. Genl., the following report, viz.

Number and kind of arms and accouterments
Condition
No. of rounds of ammunition in boxes
No. of rounds of ammunition in reserve
No. of tents and other camp and garrison equipage
Amount and kind of baggage
Wagons and trains (serviceable)
  "   "   (Unserviceable)
No. of public horses
  "   " private   "
Condition of horses
No. of mules
Strength of each company — No. of officers

and No. of enlisted men. Officers, names, rank and why absent. Report of balance in hands of A. Q. M. and A. C. S. Report of stores received and issued during the week by A. Q. M. Articles needed by Regt.

By Command of
Brig. Genl. Clingman
Edward White
A. A. Genl.

Head quarters Clingmans Brigade
June 26, 1863

General Order
No. 11

The Regts. of this Brigade will be mustered and inspected on the 30th inst by the following officers:
8th N.C. Troops and detached companies of artillery
by Colonel James D. Radcliffe
31st Reg N C Troops by Colonel H. M. McKethan
51st   "   "   Lt. Col. C. W. Knight
61st   "   "   Colonel H. M. Shaw

By Command
Brig. Gen. Clingman
Edward White
A. A. Genl.

Head Quarters Clingmans Brigade
Sullivan's Island, S.C.
October 7, 1863

General Order
No. 12

Hereafter the Regts of this Brigade will be drilled daily not less than three hours, in Battalion and company drill.

Battalion drill will begin at 9 A.M. and all officers and men fit for duty, except those especially ordered on other duty, must be present.

Company drill will begin at 3 P.M. and in addition to having all the men and company officers present will be superintended by one at least, of the Field officers of the Regt.

These drills will be commenced tomorrow. When a Regt has been on picket duty at night it will be excused from drill during the next day.

By Command
Brig. Genl. Clingman
Edward White, A. A. Genl.

Head Quarters Clingmans Brigade
Sullivan's Island, October 8, 1863

General Orders
No. 13

Lieut. S. W. Maurice, Actg. P. A. C. S. is announced to the Brigade as Ordnance Officer on the Staff of Brig. Genl. Comdg. He will be obeyed and respected.

By Command
Brig. Gen. Clingman
Edward White
A. A. Genl.

Head Quarters
Weldon, N.C.
December 5, 1863

General Order
No. 14

In compliance with orders, the undersigned assumes command of the district heretofore commanded by Brig. Gen. Ransom.
The following Staff is announced.

Capt. Edward White   Asst. Adj. Genl.
Major A. M. Erwin   Quarter Master
1st Lieut. F. R. Blake Aide-de-Camp
Capt. P. Du Heamme   Ordnance Officer
" H. B. Lane   A. C. S.

(Signed) T. L. Clingman
Brig. Genl.

Hdq. Clingmans Brigade
December 17, 1863

Gen. Ord.
No. 15

I. It is the wish of the Brig. Genl. Comdg that while the Brigade is in this vicinity, no private property shall be interfered with. Comdg officers will therefore use their utmost exertions to prevent the destruction of fencing or any other species of private property by their men.

II. Permits to visit the city may be granted at the rate of one man from each company and four officers from each Regiment daily. All permits must be countersigned at these Hd. Qrs. And will expire at retreat.

By Command of
Brig. Gen. Clingman
Edward White
A. A. Genl.

Headquarters Clingman's Regt.
December 30th 1863

General Order
No. 16

The regular bi-monthly muster and inspection of the troops of this Brigade for payment will take place at 10 o'clock A.M. tomorrow, each Regiment being mustered by its commanding officer.

The mustering officers will conform in all respects with the requirements of the Army Regulations, forwarding their reports to these Hd. Qrs with the least practicable delay.

By Command of
Brig. Genl. Clingman
Edward White
A. A. Genl.

Head Quarters Clingmans Brigade
January 2nd 1864

General Order
No. 1

On and after Monday 4th inst there will be a daily drill of two hours duration from 10 o'clock A.M. to 12 o'clock P.M. Battalion drill will take place each alternate day and the intermediate days will be occupied in company and skirmish drill.

A strict attendance by all commissioned officers, except those regularly excused, will be required.

By Command of
Brig. Gen. Clingman
F. R. Blake
A. A. Gen.

Head Quarters Clingman Brigade
Near Petersburg March 11, 1864

General Order
No. 2

The following Staff officers are announced to the Brigade.

Captain F. R. Blake   Asst. Insp. Genl.
1st Lieut. H. S. Puryear   Aide-de-Camp

They will be obeyed and respected accordingly.

By command of Brig. Gen. Clingman
Edward White
Asst. Adjt. Gen.

Head Quarters Clingmans Brigade
Near Petersburg VA
March 21, 1864

General Order
No. 3

The execution of Private M. Clayton Co. D, 8th Regt., N.C. Troops sentenced to die for desertion, will take place in the presence of the 8th & 51st Regt. At 11 A.M. on Wednesday, the 23 inst in the open ground lying east of the Camp of the 57th Regt.

The Comdg. Officers of the 8th Regt. Is charged with the ___ connected with the execution.

By Command of Brig. Genl. Clingman
A. A. Genl.

Head Quarters Clingmans Brigade
Oct 25th 1864

CIRCULAR

In compliance with instruction from Hd. Qr. 1st Army Corps, it is ordered that hereafter no wood will be cut in rear of the lines. It must be obtained between the lines and the pickets.

A rigid compliance with this order is enjoined upon all Comdg officers and all offenders will be severely punished.

By command of
Col. H. McKethan
Edward White
A. A. Genl.

Appendix B

Clingman's Order Book 2 — Specific Orders

Hdq. Camp Whiting
Nov. 26 1862

To Col. Shaw, 8th NCT
and Maj. McKethan
Col.

The Brig. Gen. Comdg directs that you furnish at once to this office a list of the names of all the men in your Regiment who are seafaring men stating the company of each.

Very respectfully your obt.
Servt.
Edward White
A. A. Genl.

Hdq. Camp Whiting
November 27 1862

To Col. H. M. Shaw, 8th
Colonel:

The Brig. Genl. Comdg. directs that you forward a detail of one non-commissioned officer and twenty-five men who will report at once to Captain C. M. Styron, Depot quarter Master at Wilmington.

Send some Blacksmiths among them.

I am — very Resp. Your obd. Servant
Edward White
A. A. Genl.

Hdq. Camp Whiting
Nov. 27, 1862

Major

The Brig. Genl. Comdg directs that you have your Regiment prepared for inspection tomorrow morning at 10 A.M.

Edward White
A. A. G.

Hdq. Camp Whiting
Dec 1st 1862

To: Col. W. A. Allen, 51st N C Troops
Colonel:

I have the honor to call your attention to the following extract from a note from Major James H. Hill, Asst. Adjutant Genl., Cape Fear District.

The Brig. Genl. Comdg. directs me to call your attention to Pars. II and III Gen. Order No. 5 and to say that he observed no Field Officers present at drill in the 51st Regt.

Genl. Clingman expresses the hope that in future no such causes of complaint will be given.

Edward White
A. A. G.

Hdq. Camp Whiting
Dec 1 1862

[To Col. H. M. Shaw]
Colonel

I have the honor to call your attention to the following extract from a note from Major James H. Hill, Asst. Adjt. Genl., Cape Fear District.

"The Brig. Genl. Comdg. directs me to call your attention to Pars. II and III General Order No. 5 and to say that all the officers of the 8th Reg. Were on drill without side arms or belts."

Genl. Clingman expresses the hope that in future no such causes of complaints will be expressed.

Edward White
A. A. Genl.

HeadQuarters
Camp Whiting
Dec 5 1862
[To Major J. H. Hill]
Major

I have the honor to request that Private G. W. Highsmith of Capt. Newkirk's company may be detailed to report to me as orderly. He has been acting in that capacity with Genl. Raines.

I am, Major, Very Respectfully
Your Obt. Servt.
[signed] T. L. Clingman
Brig. Genl.

Hdq. Camp Whiting
Dec 5, 1862
[To Major James H. Hill]
Major:

I have the honor to report that I have detailed from the Regt. two men to act as couriers at these Head Quarters and I therefore request that the Quarter Master may be ordered to furnish them as soon as practicable, with horses, saddles, and bridles.

[signed] T. L. Clingman
Brig. Genl.

Hdq. Camp Whiting
Dec 5, 1862
[To Col. Shaw, Col. W. H. Allen]
Colonel

The Genl. Comd directs that you forward without delay to this office statements showing the number and kind of arms and the amount and kind of ammunition on hand in your Regt.

You will also send in at once a list of the names of the seafaring men in your command.

Edward White, A.A. Genl.

Hdq. Camp Whiting
Dec 7, 1862
[To Colonel W. A. Allen, 51st Regt.]
Colonel

In compliance with orders from District Head Quarters you will furnish a detail of one subaltern, two non-commissioned officers and fifty (50) men to report without delay to Capt. C. M. Styron, Depot Quarter Master, Wilmington.

Edward White, A. A. Genl.

Hdq. Camp Whiting, Dec 7, 1862
[To Colonel H. M. Shaw, 8th Reg.]
Col

The commanding officer of the 31st Regt represents that on account of the horses of your Regt being picketed on part of the ground assigned him by Genl. Clingman this morning he cannot find room sufficient for his camp.

You will please therefore make such disposition of your horses as will enable him to occupy the ground.

Edward White
A. A. G.

Head Quarters
Camp Whiting
December 8 1862
[To Colonels H. M. Shaw
and W. H. Allen]
Colonel

The Brig Genl Comdg directs that you be on the field lying between these Head Quarters and the Mill pond with your Regiment prepared for review at 9 A.M. tomorrow.

The Brigade will be reviewed by Genl. Whiting.

Edward White
A. A. Genl.

Hd Qrs Camp Whiting
Dec 9th 1862
[To Col. H. M. Shaw]
Colonel

The Brig. Gen. Comdg directs that you send a commissioned officer with a file[?] of men from your Regt to the house of the man Hopkins spoke of in your note of this evening with instructions to destroy all the liquor found in his possession and inform him that he will be put under arrest if found selling it again.

Edward White
A. A. Genl.

Hd. Qrs. Camp Whiting
Dec 10th 1862
[To. Colonels Shaw, Allen, and Jordan]
Col

The Brig Gen Comdg directs that you order an inspection of your Regiment this evening for the purpose of ascertaining how many men are without blankets.

You will report the results as soon as ascertained.

     Edward White, A.A.G.

     HdQuarters
     Camp Whiting
     Dec 10 1862

[To Colonels Shaw, Allen, and Jordan]
Colonel

The Brig Gen Comdg directs that until further ordered, you furnish a daily fatigue detail of two hundred men with the proper command and non-com. officers to assist in completing the lines about Wilmington.

They will report to Lieut. Obercahain at Wilmington at 8 A.M.

     Edward White, A. A. G.

     Head Qrs
     Camp Whiting
     Dec 12 1862

[To Colonel H. M. Shaw, 8th Regt.]
Colonel

The Brig. Gen. Comd directs that Capt. Wharton of your regiment be immediately put under arrest and that your adjutant be instructed to draw up charges against him. The only offence cognizable by a court martial which he has been guilty of seems to be leaving camp without permission and inducing his subordinates to go with him.

     Ed White
     A. A. Gen.

     Camp Whiting Dec 14 1862

[To Colonel H. M. Shaw, 8th Regt.]
Colonel

The Brig Gen Comdg directs that the Rifles now in possession of co. "G" of your Regiment be immediately turned over to Co. "B" for whom they were evidently originally intended. Co. "B" will in like manner turn over its arms to Co. G.

He also directs that you effect such exchange of arms among the companies as well, as far as practicable can then uniformly [be accomplished].

     Edward White

     Hd Q Camp Whiting
     Dec 14 1862

[To Colonel H. M. Shaw, 8th Regt.]
Colonel

In reply to your letter of the 12th instance respecting the difficulty that exists in regard to the payment of your Regiment, the Brig Genl. Comdg. directs that you muster the Regiment at once and state in this certificate appended to the rolls the circumstance causing the delay of the muster. Nothing else will be necessary to ensure the payment.

     Edward White, A. A. G.

     Hdq. Camp Whiting
     Dec 14 1862

[To Colonel H. M. Shaw, 8th Regt.]
Colonel

In reply to your letter of yesterday asking how you shall proceed to procure conscript for your Regt. The Brig. Genl. Comdg. directs that you make requisition for such numbers as you may require and forward it to these Head Quarters for approval. He will then endeavor to procure them for you.

     Edward White, A. A. G.

     Hdq. Camp Whiting
     Jany. 8th 1862[3]

[To Colonel J. V. Jordan]
Colonel

The Brig. Genl. Comdg. directs me to request that you will report without delay to these Hd Qrs. the cause of your absence from your Regt. since the 23rd of December and the authority by which you were absent.

     E. W.
     A. A. G.

     Camp Whiting
     Jan 8, 1863

[To Col. H. M. Shaw, 8th Regt.]

Col. The Brig. G. Comdg. directs that you furnish a daily detail of one commissioned officer and ten men to assist in throwing up a line of work on the South side of the plank road near the mill pond.

They will be on the ground to day at 10 o'clock and hereafter daily at 8½ o'clock A.M. You will also furnish a detail of one non-commissioned officer and twenty men to report immediately to Capt. Archer, Ordnance officer Wilmington.

     E. White
     A. A. G.

Camp Whiting
Jan 8, 1863
[To Colonels Jordan, McKethan, and Devane]
Col.

The Brig. G. Comdg. directs that you furnish a daily detail of one commissioned officer and ten men to assist in throwing up a line of work on the South side of the plank road near the mill pond.

They will be on the ground to day at 10 o'clock and hereafter daily at 8½ o'clock A.M. You will also furnish a detail of one non-commissioned officer and twenty men to report immediately to Capt. Archer, Ordnance officer Wilmington.

E. White
A. A. G.

Hd. Qrs. Camp Whiting
Jan 9 1863
[To Colonel Jordan]
Colonel

The Brig. Genl. Comdg. directs me to call your attention to the fact that the following named men of your Regt. are in confinement in the county jail charged with desertion but that as yet no charges against them have been forwarded through this office. These charges will be furnished as soon as practicable.
Private A. Sealy, Co. "A" 31st NC Troops
" Jerry Bass, " " " " "

Edward White
A. A. Genl.

Hd Qrs Camp Whiting
January 9th 1863
[To Colonel Hector McKethan, 51st Regt.]
Colonel

Enclosed I send you the proceeding of a General Court Martial in the case of Private John Hardy, Co. "G" 51st Regt NC Troops.

The Brig. Gen. Comdg. directs that the first part of the sentence relative to corporal punishment be immediately executed. Private Hardy will then be [sent] to the Provost Marshall at Wilmington to be put to hard labor at such part of the fortifications as the authorities there may direct.

The Genl also directs me to call your attention to the fact that the following men of your Regt. Are in confinement in the county jail at Wilmington charged with desertion but that as yet no charges against them have been forwarded through this office. These charges will be furnished as soon as practicable.
Private F. Blackburn, Co. K, 51st Reg, NC Troops
" A. Boswell, Co. "G"

Edward White, A. A. G.

Hdq. Camp Whiting
January 14 1863
[To. Colonel J. V. Jordan, H. M. Shaw, Hector McKethan, and Radcliffe]
Colonel

The Brig. Gen. Comdg. directs that you furnish a detail of one comd. Officer, one non-comd. Officer and twenty-five men to assist in constructing rifle pits on the county road.

The detail will be on the ground at 8 A.M. tomorrow. The officer will report at these Hd Qrs in passing.

Edward White
A. A. G.

Hd. Qrs. Camp Whiting
January 15 1863
[To Colonel H. M. Shaw, 8th Regt.]
Col.

The Brig. Genl. Comdg. directs me to enclose herewith statements from the Comdg. officers of the 31st, 51st, & 61st NC Regts. of the number of men necessary to fill up their Regts.

He desires that Capt. Bagby, detailed to procure conscripts for your Regt. may at the same time endeavor to obtain them for the whole Brigade.

Edward White, A. A. Genl.

Hd Qrs
Camp Whiting
January 16, 1863

CIRCULAR

Commanding officers of Regts. of this Brigade will hold their commands in readiness to move at a moments notice.

Five days' rations will be kept constantly on hand of which three days' will be cooked.

Each Regiment must have transportation for sixty rounds of ammunition to the man and two days rations.

By command of
Brig Genl Clingman
Edward White
A. A. Genl.

Head Quarters Camp Whiting
January 17th, 1863
[To Colonels Radcliffe, Shaw, Jordan]
Col.

The Brig. Genl. Comdg. directs that the following named men of your Regt sent to you yesterday by the Provost Marshall from Wilmington charged with [desertion?] _____ be kept at hard labor until in your opinion his offence is sufficiently punished.

J. W. Burchette, Co. "B" 61st Regt. NC Troops
W. H. Tomlinson " "D" " "
E. S. Ausley   " "   " "
J. W. Johnston   " "   " "
Rich'd Ausly   " "   " "
Jas. Hendley [?] " "   " "
Isham Ham Co. "D" 8th Regt.
James Hawks " "G" " "
Mike Ethridge Co. "H" 31st Regt.

Edward White
A. A. G.

Head Quarters Clingman's Brigade
Wilmington, January 13 [1863]
[To Colonel John Withers]
Col.

The letter of Maj. E. J. A. Palfrey, A. A. G. of Jan 4th has to day been received in which it is stated that the appointment of R. S. Gage is withheld as Commissary of my Brigade until it is known what has become of the former Commissary Maj. H. W. Miller. In reply I have to state that at his own request Maj. H. W. Miller was ordered to duty in a Brigade formerly commanded by G. B. Anderson, dea'cd. This was done as I was informed by order of the Commissary General at Richmond about the first of November last.

Though done without my knowledge and with some inconvenience to me at the time, I acquessed [sic] in it the more cheerfully because done at the insistence of the Major himself Col. Northope approved — however that as soon as I recommended another person he should be promptly commissioned. Supposing that the Department was aware of its own action, I did not regard it as proper for me to remind it of what had been done under its authority.

Robert A. Gage was recommended and has in fact been on duty with me since the 7th day of December last and I think in justice to him his commission should bear date from that period.

Very Respectfully yours
[signed] T. L. Clingman
Brig. Genl.

Hd Qrs Camp Whiting
Jan 22 1863
[To Capt. M. P. King, A. A. Genl., Wilmington]
Capt.

I have the honor to apply for information on the following points.

1st In the 51st NC Regt of my Brigade there are several Lieuts who have held their position in the Regt during the space of three or four months and have received commissions from the Gov. of North Carolina subject to confirmation by a Board of Examination. Funds are now in the hands of Quarter Master for the payment of the Regt but he refuses to pay these officers until their commissions have been confirmed. Will these officers be entitled to pay for their services as Lieuts. In the event that their commissions are not confirmed, are there no means by which they can draw pay form the funds now in the hands of the Quarter Master of the Regt.?

2nd Some time since Lt. Col. Allen then in command of the 51st Regt ordered an election to fill certain vacancies which had occurred, in compliance with which orders several officers were elected. Were these elections valid and will the officers elected retain their positions?

Your attention will greatly oblige me.

I am, Capt., Very Respectfully Yours
[signed] T. L. Clingman
Brig. Genl.

Hd Qrs Camp Whiting
Jan 24th 1863
[To Major Hector McKethan, 51st Regiment]
Major -

It has been represented to the Brig. Genl. Comdg. That the Guard from your Regt. at the Bridge on the plank road have on several occasions stopped wagons crossing the bridge and taken potatoes and other things from them.

The Genl. therefore directs me to call your attention to the fact and to say that if the offence be repeated and the offenders can be detected they will be severely punished.

Edward White
A. A. G.

Hd. Quarters Camp Whiting
Jan. 24th 1863

[To Cols. Radcliffe, Shaw, Jordan & McKethan]
Col.

The Brig. Genl. Comdg. directs me to notify you to have your command on the field opposite the encampment of the 8th Regt N.C. Troops, precisely at ten o'clock on Monday next (should the day be fair) for Battalion & Brigade drill.

F. Brown Venable
Major & A. A. & I. G.

Hdq. Camp Whiting
Jan 27 1863

Circular

Regimental Commanders will furnish <u>as soon as possible</u> to these Hd. Qrs. complete rosters of the commissioned officers of their Regiments.

They will also send in <u>immediately</u> official statements of any vacancies among the staff officers of this regiment.

By command of
Brig. Genl. Clingman
Edward White
A. A. G.

Hd Q. Camp Whiting
Jan 30 1863

Circular

Regimental commanders will furnish <u>without delay</u> to these Head Quarters statements showing the number and distribution of conscripts required to fill up their Regts to the prescribed standard.

By Command of
B. G. Clingman
Edward White

Hd Qr Camp Whiting
Feb. 3rd 1863

Circular

Attention is called to the enclosed report of the Senior Surgeon of this Brigade.

Regimental commanders will take immediate steps to exclude the persons referred to therein from their camps and to prevent as far as practicable the consumption of pies and other food of like description by the troops under their command.

By Command of
Brig. Genl. Clingman
Edward White, A. A. G.

Head Quarters Camp Whiting
Feby 5th 1863

[To Col. Shaw, 8th Reg.]
Colonel

The Brig. Gen. Comdg instructs me to say that you need no longer keep a guard at the bridge near your camp but directs that you detail a fatigue party to remove without delay the flooring and such other portion of the bridge as are liable to be flooded away.

Edward White

Hd Qr Camp Whiting
Feb. 11, 1863

Circular

Regimental commanders will immediately re-establish the proper guards around their camps.

By command of
Brig. Gen. Clingman
Edward White
A. A. G.

Hdqrs Camp Whiting
Feb 14th 1863

[To Major Hector McKethan, 51st Reg.]
Major

The Brig Genl. Comdg directs that until further ordered you will retain in your possession all letters that may be addressed to persons in Robinson [Robeson] County or that neighborhood and that you will prevent, as far as practicable, the men of your Regt becoming aware of the destination of the company about to proceed to that county.

He also directs that you detail all visitors from that vicinity who may now be in your camp.

Edward White

Hdq. Camp Whiting
Feb. 14th 1863

[To Col. Shaw, 8th Reg.]
Colonel

In compliance with the enclosed instruction from Gen. Whiting the Brig Genl Comdg directs that you will select from your Regt a company for guard duty, at North East.

You will be careful to detail for this duty one of the most reliable and efficient company commanders in your Regt.

The company will be provided with with

[sic] three days cooked rations and the commanding officer will report, this evening, at these Hd. Qrs. for instructions.

Edward White

Hd Qrs Clingman's Brigade
February 24th 1863

[To Col. Shaw, 8th Reg.]
Colonel

In reply to your note of this date respecting permits to visit Charleston, the Brig. Genl. Comdg directs me to say that as regards the men you may use your discretion, but permits must not be given to officers to be absent during drill hours, unless they are for some reason, exempt from drill.

Edward White

Head Quarters Clingman's Brigade
Crafts House near Charleston
Febr. 25 1863

Colonel

The Brig. Genl. Comdg directs that you have arrested private James Hawks of Co. I of your Regt. (Charged with having stuck his bayonet into a horse belonging to Capt Crafts owner of the house occupied as Head Quarters) and ascertain whether the charges be true.

Private Hawks was on guard at these Head Quarters yesterday.

Edward White

Hd Qrs. Clingman's Brigade
Gist's Division (Charleston)
Febr. 25th 1863

[To Gen. S. Cooper, Adjt. Genl.]
Gen.

I respectfully recommend for the position of aide-de-camp Capt. Frederick R. Blake. He is not now commissioned in the service but was formerly a Capt in my old Regt (25th N.C.) Prior to its reorganization. He is at present acting as a volunteer aid to Gen. Ripley and is in all respects well qualified for such a position. I have at present no aid, as Capt. Alfred M. Erwin my former aid has been promoted to the position of Quarter Master of my Brigade. I request that Capt. Blake may be commissioned without delay as his services are needed at this time.

[signed] T. L. Clingman
Brig. Gen.

Hd Qrs Clingman's Brigade
Crafts House near Charleston
Feb. 25th 1863

Circular

The Brig Genl Comdg has learned with much regret that some of the troops of this Brigade have committed several outrages at the depot of the Charleston and Savannah R. R.

Their conduct has been represented as disgraceful in the extreme, and if the perpetrators of the offences could be detected they would be severely punished.

In order to prevent, as far as possible, any repetition of the same thing, Regimental commanders will at once establish the proper guards around their camp and will see that no soldier is permitted to leave camp without special permission from themselves.

Any violation of this order will be visited with prompt and severe punishment.

By command of Brig. Gen. Clingman
Edward White A. A. G.

Hd Qrs Clingman's Brigade
Craft House near Charleston
[no date, but probably late February 1863]

Circular

Commanding officers of the Regts. will see that hereafter their commissaries report in person at these Hd Qrs to draw provisions and do not send their sergeants.

If a commissary is prevented from coming by sickness, absence of any other cause, a commissioned officer will be sent to represent him.

By command of
Brig. Gen. Clingman
Edward White, A. A. G.

Hdq. Clingman's Brigade
Craft House near Charleston, S.C.
February 27, 1863

Genl. Sam'l. Cooper
Adj. & Insp. Genl. C. S. A.
Genl.

I have the honor to represent that several applications have been made by Colonel H. M. Shaw, Comdg. 8th Regt. N.C. troops, for the appointment of Lieut. Walter Williamson 13th Regt NC Troops as Adjutant of this Regt.

Two of these applications passed through these Hd. Qrs. and were forwarded through the proper channels, but nothing has been yet heard from them.

I would therefore respectfully request that Lieut. Williamson be appointed and ordered to report as soon as possible, to Colonel Shaw.

[signed] T. L. Clingman
Brig. Genl.

Hd Qrs Clingman's Brigade
Savannah, Ga, March 8th 1863
Circular

Regimental commanders in this Brigade will hold Regts in readiness to march to Charleston this evening.

Three days cooked rations must be <u>at once</u> prepared.

By command Brig. Genl. Clingman
Edward White
Asst. Adjt. Genl.

Hd Qrs Western Division James Island
Heywards House March 12 1863
To Maj. J. J. Lucas
  Fort Pemberton
& Maj. Campbell
  West lines
" Major

The Brig. Genl. Comdg this Div. directs that you forward to this office with as little delay as possible, a complete list of the commissioned officers of your command, showing names, dates of appointment, where born and from what state appointed.

Edward White
A. A. Genl

Head Qrs. Western Division
James Island
Heyward House, March 12, 1863
Circular

Office hours at these Head Quarters will be from 9 A.M. to 2½ P.M.

Permits to visit the city will be signed between the hours of 9 & 10 A.M.

No business, unless of importance, will be attended to, except during the hours referred to.

Brig. Genl. Clingman
E. White, A. A. G.

Head Qrs. Western Division
James Island, Heyward House
March 13th 1863
Colonel

The Brig. Genl. Comdg directs that until further orders you send daily to these Hd. Qrs.

One (1) non-comd officer and six (6) men for guard daily.

Edward White, A. A. G.

Head Qrs. Western Div. James Island
March 14th 1863
Circular

The number of all Special Orders issued from these Hd. Qrs. since March 12th 1863 are changed as follows: S. O. No. 32 to 1, 33 to 2.

By Command of
Brig. Genl. C.
Edward White, A. A. G.

Hd Qrs. Clingman's Brigade
Near Charleston S.C. March 19th 1863
To Z. B. Vance
  Gov. Of N.C.
Sir,

I enclose to your excellency a list of men absent from the 51st Regiment, a portion of whom are doubtless staying at home without reason. The remarks opposite their several names will indicate their residencies [sic] as far as they are known and will perhaps enable the proper officers to arrest such as are now able to do duty. As you were kind enough to tell me that you would endeavor to have such persons returned to duty, I request that such orders may be issued to the several counties as may be necessary to cause such as are now well to return to duty.

Very respectfully
[signed] T. L. Clingman
Brig. Genl.

Head Qrs. Western Division
James Island
March 19 1863
To Major J. J. Lucas
Major:

The Brig. Genl. Comdg directs that you forward to this office as soon as possible, the name of one Captain from your command to be appointed member of a garrison court martial to be convened at the camp of your Battalion for the trial of Privates Hart & Wheaty.

You will also signify on what day it will be

agreeable to you for the court to commence its setting.

    Edward White, Asst. Adjt. Genl.

  Hd Qrs Western Division James Island
      March 19th 1863
[To Col. H. M. Shaw, 8th Regt.]
Colonel

I have the honor to enclose herewith a copy of a letter from Col. Roman, Insptor. Genl. signifying that he inspect a Regt of this Brigade on Saturday March 21st.

In compliance therewith, the Brig. Genl. Comdg. directs that you will have your Regt in readiness to be inspected at the appointed hour.

    Edward White, Asst. Adj. Genl.

    HdQrs Western Divi Jas. Isld.
      March 21st 1863
[To the Officers of the Guard
at the Bridge near Wappoo Creek]
Sir

Enclosed I send you a copy of an order in relation to the use of the new bridge near Wappoo Creek in accordance with which you will instruct the guard at that point. You will hand the order to the officer who will relieve you, as part of his instructions.

    Edward White
    A. A. G.

    Hd. Qrs. Western Div.
      James Island
      March 23rd 1863
[To Col. J. V. Jordan, 31st Reg.]
Colonel,

The Brig. Genl. Comdg directs me to notify you that Lt. Col. Roman, Inspr. Genl. will inspect your Regt. tomorrow morning at 10 o'clock.

    Edward White, A. A. G.

  Hd Qrs. West Div. James Island
      March 25, 1863
[To Col. J. V. Jordan, 31st Regt.]
Colonel

The Field officer of the day for yesterday has reported that the officer of the guard at the bridge was not relieved until one o'clock P.M.

As the officer of the guard yesterday was from your Regt. the Brig. Genl. Comdg directs that you report at once to these Hd Qrs., the reason for the delay.

    Edward White, A. A. G.

    Hd Qrs Western Div.
      James Island
      March 25, 1863
[To Colonel Hector McKethan, 51st Regt.]
Colonel

The Brig. Genl. Comdg directs that you confine at once in the guard house, Corpl. Geddie, Co. "I," Private B. P. Strickland, C. J. Summersett, Co. "G" and E. Grimsley, L. Grimsley, B. Grimsley, S. E. Privatt Co. "E" of your Regt. They constituted the guard at these Hd Qrs last night and through negligence permitted some one to steal some soap from the Commissary storehouse. The statement of the Corporal implies that one of the guard is the guilty party, you will therefore thoroughly investigate the matter keeping the men in the meantime, in confinement.

    Edward White, A. A. G.

    Hd Qrs Western Div
      James Island
      March 26, 1863
[To Col. J. V. Jordan, 31st Regt.]
Colonel

The Brig. Genl. Comdg has understood that you have not yet established "schools of instruction" as required by Genl. Order No. 2.

He therefore directs me to inquire if this be the case, and if so, what your reasons are for having delayed to do so.

    Edward White, A. A. G.

    Hd Qrs. Western Div.
    James Island March 26 1863
[To Col. H. McKethan, 51st]
Colonel

The Brig. Genl. Comdg directs that you furnish a detail of ten (10) men to report on Friday and Saturday mornings at 10 A.M. to Capt. F. G. Be___, A. C. S., Dills Bluff for fatigue duty.

    Edward White, A. A. G.

  Hd Qrs Western Div — James Is.
      March 27th 1863
[To Mallory P. King, A. A. Genl.]

Captain

Yours of this date, enclosing charges and specifications against Private M. Austin and others has been received and in reply I have the honor to note that there is a Garrison Court Martial now in session at Fort Pemberton consisting of Capt. Gary Lucas Battn [?] and Lieut M. Arthur and Mansfield of my Brigade.

Unless you particularly desire a new Court, I will have the offenders brought for trial before the one already in session.

[Signed] T. L. Clingman
Brig. Genl.

Head Qrs. Western Div.
James Island
March 31, 1863
[To Col. H. M. Shaw, 8th Regt.]
Colonel

The Brig. Genl. Comdg directs that you confine in the guard house, Private Thos. Morris and Jno Knight of your Regt.

These men are charged with having forged a pass, and should be severely punished.

Further instructions will be sent.

[Edward White]
Asst. Adj. Genl.

Hd Qrs. Western Div Jas. Isd.
March 31st 1863
[To Col. H. M. Shaw, 8th Regt.]
Colonel

The Brig. Genl. Comdg directs that if upon investigation you have reason to believe that Private Morris and Knight were guilty of the forgery for which they were arrested this morning, you will have charges at once, preferred against them and sent to this office.

Edward White, A. A. G.

Head Qrs. Western Division James Island
April 8th 1863
[To Colonel J. V. Jordan, 31st Regt.]
Colonel,

In compliance with instructions just received your Regt. will be sent to report to Brig. Genl. Ripley in Charleston for temporary duty with Genl. Trapier [?].

You will start in light marching order, with two days cooked rations, at five A.M. tomorrow morning or sooner if necessary. You must report to Genl. Ripley at 7 A.M. promptly.

By Command of
Brig. Genl. Clingman
Edward White
Asst. Adjt. Genl.

Head Qrs. Western Div.—James Island
April 8th 1863
[To. Col. H. McKethan, 51st Regt.]
Colonel

The Brig. Genl. Comdg directs that you send at once one non-comd and six (6) men to relieve the guard from the 31st Regt. now on duty at the new bridge. The 31st will move at five in the morning.

You will also send fifty (50) men, to report to Capt. Rumborough at Elliott's cut, instead of thirty (30) as directed in Special Order No. 27.

I am Very Respectfully
Edward White, A. A. G.

Head Qrs. Western Div, James Island
April 8th 1863
[To Colonel H. M. Shaw, 8th Regt.]
Colonel

The Brig. Genl. Comdg directs that you send thirty (30) men to report to Capt. Rumborugh at Elliotts cut, instead of twenty five (25) as directed in Spl. Order No. 27 from these Hd. Qrs.

I am Col. Very Respectfully
Your Obt Servt.
Edward White
Asst. Adjt. Genl.

Head Qrs. Western Division
James Island April 10th 1863
[To Colonel Hector McKethan, 51st Regt.]
Colonel

The Brig. Genl. Comdg directs that you send immediately two men from your Regt. to report to Major Thos. S. Green, Q. M. at Col Gists Hd. Qrs. for temporary duty as teamsters.

You will select men who have had experience in driving four horse teams.

I am Col Very Respectfully\
Your Obt. Servt.
Edward White
Asst. Adjt. Genl.

Head Qrs. Clingman's Brigade
Gists Division April 14th 1863
[To. Brig. General Thomas Jordan,

Chief of Staff]
General

I respectfully desire to remonstrate against the action of the Examining Board of Surgeons. They are furloughing a large number of men from my Brigade so as to weaken it essentially. I am satisfied that at this season of the year, no one who is able to leave the hospital ought to be sent away from camp because at this period this locality is as healthy as any other that can be found and the convalescents will recover as rapidly here as at any other place, I think sooner, in fact, than if allowed to travel home. Those who recover at home seldom return when they ought to do so. The commanders of Regiments in my Brigade complain of the action of the Surgeons and from my own experience in the service, I feel confident that the Surgeons ought to be restrained. I earnestly request that the General in Command of this Department will see the propriety of arresting the evil and prohibit the furloughing of anyone under my command.

Very Respectfully
[signed] T. L. Clingman
Brig. Genl.

Head Qrs. Western Division
James Island April 14th 1863

[To Col. Hector McKethan, 8th Regt.]
Col.

The Genl Commanding directs me to make an inspection of the arms of your regiment. You will please have the different companies at their company grounds this morning immediately after Dress Parade ready for inspection.

I am Col. Very Respectfully,
T. Brown Venable

Head quarters Western Division
James Island April 18th 1863

[To Colonels Shaw, McKethan, Radcliffe]
Colonel

The Brig. Genl. Comdg. Directs that, at such time as may best suit you, you assemble the officers of your Regt, and read to them the report of the Inspection of the Regt recently made by Colonel Roman.

I am Col Very Respectfully
Your Obt Servt
Edward White
Asst Adjt Genl

Head Quarters Western Division
James Island Apri 21st 1863

[To. Colonel H. M. Shaw]
Colonel

The Brig. Genl. Comdg directs that you detail at once a corporal and two men to conduct the two men from Col. Stevens command, confined in your guard house last night, to the camp of their Regt.

The corpl. will report at these Hd. Qrs. Before starting.

I am Col. Very Respectfully
Your Obt Servt
Edward White
Asst. Adjt Genl.

Hd. Qrs. Western Division James Island
April 21st 1863

[To. Colonel C. H. Stevens,
Comdg. Secessionville, S.C.]
Colonel

Two men of your command were yesterday arrested by the officer of the guard at the Pontoon Bridge over Wappoo cut, for attempting to pass with forged permits.

Their names or at least the names assumed for the occasion were I. Sham___ and A. Hughes.

I had them confined in the guard house during last night and sent them to you today under guard.

In addition to the permits used by them I enclose also a number of passes used by officers and men of your command. From the memoranda of the officer of the guard you will observe that they all returned after the time specified.

I am Col., Very Respectfully,
Your Obt. Servt.
Edward White
Asst. Adj. Genl.

Head Quarters Western Division
James Island April 23 1863

[To Colonel H. M. Shaw, 8th Regt.]
Colonel

In compliance with instructions received from Hd Qrs James Island and St. Andrews Parish I have the honor to inform you that you have been temporarily assigned to the command of the Western Division James Island.

I am Col Very Respectfully

Your Obt. Servt.
Edward White
Asst. Adjt. Genl.

Head Quarters Western Division
James Island April 26th 1863
[To. Colonel J. V. Jordan, 31st Regt.]
Colonel

I enclose herewith the acceptance of the resignation of Lt. Col. E. R. Liles and Capt. C. B. Lindsay of your Regt.

The Colonel Comdg. directs that, in compliance with Genl. Order No. 24 Adjt Inspr Genl. Office March 5th 1863, you will immediately enroll these officers in such company or companies of your Regt as they may select.

If either or both of them are prepared to furnish substitutes, the substitutes may be accepted as soon as the enrollment is effected, and the officer or officers to [sic] furnishing, be given the proper discharge papers.

I am Very Respectfully
Edward White
Asst. Adjt. Genl.

Head Quarters Clingman's Brigade
Wilmington N Ca
May 6th 1863
[To Colonels Shaw, Radcliffe, Jordan, McKethan]
Col.

The Brig. Genl. Commanding directs me to call your attention particularly to the Genl. Orders No. 14 & 15 from Genl. Whiting Commanding District of Cape Fear herewith enclosed. The Brig. Genl. _____ relies upon the cooperation of all the officers in his command in the strict execution of these orders so necessary and proper and that both officers and soldiers will endeavor to treasure that good name and reputation of which they should be justly proud.

He directs me further to say that if in any case there should be a violation of these orders, the offender shall be promptly punished to the full extent of the military law.

I am Col.
With Great respect,
Your obt. Servant
T. Brown Venable
(Mgr. & AAG)

HdQrs—Clingman's Brigade
Wilmington 7th May 1863
[to Colonels Shaw, Jordan, McKethan & Radcliffe]
Col

The Brig Gen commanding directs me to call your attention to copies of circulars from Hd. Qrs. District of Cape Fear, Wilmington, N.C., dated Feby 1st & 4th, 1863, in relation to granting furloughs. He further directs that all applications be made out in strict compliance with these circulars otherwise they will not be granted.

I am, Col., Your Obt. Servant
T. Brown Venable
Maj. & A.A.G.

Head Quarters Clingman's Brigade
Wilmington NC May 8th 1863
Col [J. D. Radcliffe]

In accordance with orders from Maj. Genl. Whiting, the Brig. Genl. Commanding directs me to order you to have your regiment at the Depot of the Wilmington and Weldon R. R. At 12 o'clock A.M. today as a funeral escort to the remains of Col. Purdy of the 18th NC Vols.

T. Brown Venable
Maj. & A.A.G.

Hd Qrs Clingman's Brigade
Wilmington NC May 8 1863
Col [Shaw and Jordan]

The Adjutant General of North Carolina proposes to issue at an early day a second edition of the Army Register of North Carolina Troops and for this purpose wishes a roster of officers with date of commission, residence at time of entry into service and strength of Regiment.

The Brig. Genl. Commanding directs that you have made out such a return of your Regiment, in accordance with the printed blanks regularly furnished, and forward
  to Genl. D. G. Forde
    Asst. Genl. NC
    Raleigh

T. Brown Venable
Maj. A.A.G.

HdQ Clingman's Brigade
Wilmington May 8 1863
CIRCULAR

Office hours at these Head quarters will be from 9 A.M. to 2½ P.M.

No business unless of importance will be attended to unless during the hours referred to. Permits to visit the city may be granted by the commanding officers of Regiments to one commissioned officer, one non-commissioned officer and two privates from each company and for no longer times than one day to return in all cases by dress parade.

In all other cases they must be brought to these Head Quarters for approval.

 By command of
  Brig. Gen. Clingman
   T. Brown Venable, Maj. & A.A.G.

   Head Quarters Clingman's Brig.
    Wilmington NC May 9th 1863
Col.

The Brig. Genl. Commanding directs me that you have each day until further orders, detailed from your command one non-commissioned officer and three men to report to these Head Quarters for Guard duty — They are to report at Sunset and be relieved at 6 o'clock the following morning.

   I am, Col.
   Very respectfully
   Your obt. Servant
   T. Brown Venable
   Maj. & A.A.G.

   Head Quarters Clingman's Brigade
    Wilmington NC May 11th 1863
[To. Col. McKethan, 51st Reg.]
Col.

The Brig. Genl. Commanding directs me to order you to have sent immediately to these Head Quarters a list of all officers in your command who have been absent without leave since the command has been in this district. He further directs that your attention [be] called to General. Order No. 5. Goldsboro N Ca in regards to enlisted men who have overstayed their leave of absence.

   I am, Col. With great Respect
   Your obt. Servant
   T. Brown Venable
   Maj. & A. A. G.

   HQ Clingman's Brigade
    Wilmington NC May 12 1863
[To Cols. Shaw, Jordan, Radcliffe]
Col.

Pursuant to instructions from Head Quarters District Cape Fear the Brigadier General commanding instructs me to direct you to have detailed immediately from your commands one active and efficient Lieutenant, one Sergeant, two corporals and twenty-two privates to proceed to an adjoining county to arrest deserters and recusant conscripts.

This detail will be held ready to report at these Head Quarters at a moments notice with two days cooked rations.

   T. Brown Venable
   Maj. & A. A. G.

   Hd. Qr. Clingman's Brigade
    Wilmington, NC May 13th 1863
[Telegram]
Lt. Col. C.B. Hobson
 Comg. 51st Regt.
  Near Topsail

I telegraphed you yesterday to send Capt. W. S. Norment to report to me for duty in Robeson County. Why have you not obeyed the order. Send him immediately

   [signed] T. L. Clingman
   Brig. Genl.

   Hd. Qrs. Clingman's Brigade
    Wilmington NC May 13th 1863
[Lt. Col. Hobson, 51st Reg.]
Col.

The Brigadier General Commanding directs me to inform you that he has ordered the charges against Lieut. Charles T. Guy, Co. I, 51st Regt., NC Troops to be withdrawn and also directs that you have Lieut. Guy released and ordered to duty in his company.

The Brig. Genl. hopes that the punishment tho slight will have the effect contemplated and that Lieut Guy will in future be attentive and observant of all duties which he may be called on to perform.

   T. Brown Venable, Maj. & A.A.G.

   Hd. Qrs. Clingman's Brigade
    Wilmington NC May 13, 1863
[Cols. Shaw, Jordan, Radcliffe]
Col.

The Brigadier General Commanding directs that the detail made by his order on yesterday from your company report at these Head

Quarters tomorrow morning precisely at half past 5 o'clock, with two days cooked rations, knapsacks & blankets.

    T. Brown Venable
    Maj. & A. A. G.

    Hd. Qrs.
   Clingman's Brigade
  Wilmington May 15, 1863
[Cols. Shaw, Jordan, Radcliffe, Hopson]
CIRCULAR

Commanding officers of Regiments in this Brigade will furnish immediately to these Head Quarters a list of all men detailed from their commands, to places & duties, by whose order & for what time.

    T. Brown Venable
    Maj. & A. A. G.

   Hd. Qrs. Clingman's Brigade
   Wilmington NC May 20, 1863
[Radcliffe, 61st Reg.]
Col.

The Brig. Genl. Commanding directs that you have the same detail ordered from your command in special order No. 61 from these Head Quarters to report precisely at 9 o'clock on tomorrow (21st) at the four mile post on the plank road, to Capt. W. C. Strong for fatigue duty.

The General further directs me to say that he is informed by Capt. Strong that you failed to furnish the detail today promptly as ordered.

    T. Brown Venable
    Maj. & A. A. G.

   Head Qrs. Clingman's Brigade
   Wilmington NC May 22nd 1863
[Col. Radcliffe, 61st Reg.]
Colonel,

The Brig. Gen. Comdg directs me to inform you that it is his opinion, as well as, that of the Dist. Commander, that the charges preferred against you, by Capt. Edward Mallette, should be forwarded, without delay for the consideration of the authority competent to act upon them.

I enclose permission for Capt. Mallette to visit the city.

    Edward White
    A. A. G.

  Hd. Qrs. Clingman's Brigade May 23rd 1863
[Lt. Col. C. B. Hobson, Comd. 51st Reg.]
Colonel

In reply to your letter of yesterdays date respecting the detail of Private Bullock, the Brig. Genl. Comdg. directs me to say that it did not contain the information which he desired.

He has understood that, at the time of this detail, Bullock was undergoing punishment for some offence which he had committed, and he desires to know as soon as possible, what that offence was, and what was the nature and term of the punishment, in addition to which, the circumstances of the detail, and all other facts connected with the case, should be stated.

The Genl. wishes you to send to this office, a copy of the letter written you by Capt. Blake on this subject.

    Edward White
    Asst. Adj. Genl.

   Head Quarters Clingman's Brigade
   Wilmington N C May 24th 1863
[Col. J. V. Jordan, 31st Reg.]
Colonel

The Brig Genl Comdg directs that until further ordered, you furnish from your Regt the following details for guard duty to relieve those from the 8th Regt. now in duty as the prints indicated.

One non comd. officer and nine men to relieve the guard at the bridge on the county road. It shall be their duty to guard the Bridge, the mill dam, battery, and magazine near it.

One non comd. officer and twelve (12) men whose duty it shall be to guard the bridge on the plank road, the plank road battery and magazine and the magazine to the right.

One non-comd officer and three (3) men to report at these Head Quarters daily at sunset and be relieved at six o'clock next morning.

These details will be furnished immediately and instructions must be given to the details from the 8th when they are relieved, to rejoin their Regt at the outer lines.

   I am, Colonel, Very Respectfully
   Your Obt. Servant
   Edward White
   Asst. Adj. Genl.

   Head Quarters Clingman's Brigade
   Wilmington NC May 24th 1863

[To. Lt. Col. C. B. Hobson, Commander 51st Reg.]
Colonel,

The Brig. Genl. Comdg directs that you will cause to be prepared and forwarded to this office at once charges and specifications against Lieut. J. W. McAlister, Co. "A" of your Regt.

He has rendered himself liable to several charges.

Absence without leave, Disobedience of orders, conduct prejudicial to good order and military discipline, and others.

   I am, Very Resp. Yours
    Edward White
     A. A. Genl.

  Head Quarters Clingman's Brigade
    Wilmington May 28th 1863
[Lt. Col. C. B. Hobson, 51st Regt.]
Colonel,

In compliance with instructions from Major Genl. Whiting, you will send immediately a detail of one hundred and fifty men with their officers to report to Lt. Col. Thorbiurn, to assist in extinguishing the fire over the river.

   I am, Col., Very Respectfully
    Your Obt. Servant
     Edward White
      A. A. Genl.

  Head Quarters Clingman's Brigade
   Wilmington N.C. May 28th 1863
[Col. H. M. Shaw, 8th Regt.]
Colonel,

A conscript named Wm. H. Deal, sent by Col. Mallett for your Regt was today delivered at these Hd. Quarters. I gave a receipt for him in your name and had him turned over to the Provost Marshal.

The Brig. Genl. Comdg directs that you send in tomorrow one man to take charge of him and take him to camp. I enclose his papers.

   I am, Col., Very Respectfully
    Your Obt. Servant
     Edward White
      Asst. Adj. Genl.

  Head Quarters Clingman's Brigade
   Wilmington N.C. May 29th 1863
[Col. J. V. Jordan, 31st Regt.]
Colonel,

The Brig. Genl. Comdg directs that you furnish a detail of five carpenters to report without delay to Capt. Styron for temporary duty.

   I am, Col., Very Respectfully,
    Your Obt. Servt.
     Edward White
      Asst. Adj. Genl.

  Head Quarters Clingman's Brigade
      June 1st 1863
[Lt. Col. C. B. Hobson, 51st Regt.]
Colonel,

The Brig Genl. Comdg directs that Capt. J. M. Stanford of your Regt. be ordered to report at these Hd. Qrs. at 8 A.M. tomorrow morning for the purpose of taking charge of a fatigue party.

   I am, Col. Very Respectfully
    Your Obt. Servt.
     Edward White
      Asst. Adj. Genl.

  Head Quarters Clingman's Brigade
      June 1, 1863
[Col. J. V. Jordan]
Colonel,

The Brig. Gen. Comdg directs that the following named officers and men of your Regt who are witnesses and prisoners in cases to be tried before the G. C. M now in session at these Hd. Qrs be placed in attendance on the Court at 11 A.M. tomorrow.

Prisoners Private Jesse Blalock, Co. E 31st N C Regt.
Witness Lieut. J. H. Berry " " "

The Genl. further directs that you send a suitable man to report at 10 A.M. tomorrow to Lieut S. A. Ashe Judge Advocate, as orderly to the G C M now in session.

   I am Col Very Respectfully
    Your Obt Servt
     Edward White
      Asst. Adj. Genl.

  Head Quarters Clingman's Brigade
      June 1, 1863
[Cols. Radcliffe, Hobson]
Colonel,

The Brig. Gen. Comdg directs that the following named officers and men of your Regt. Who are witnesses and prisoners, in cases to be tried before the G. C. M. now in session at

these Hd. Qrs. Be placed in attendance on the court at 11 A.M. tomorrow.
Prisoners:
    Private W. A. Inman, Co. H, 61st Reg., N.C.
    Luke R. Cartrett   "   "
Witnesses:
        Capt. Wm. Lanier "   "   "
        [S. W.] Maultby   "   "   "
Private Jno. Thompson   "   "   "
  "   Daniel R. Gore   "   "   "
    Sanders Millican   "   "   "
    Dan'l M. Long, Co. G, 51st Reg.

          I am, Col., Very Respectfully
          Your Obt. Servt.
              Edward White
              Asst. Adj. Genl.

          Head Qrs. Clingman's Brigade
                            June 1, 1863
[Cols. Jordan, Radcliffe, Hobson]
Colonel,

The Brig. Gen. Comdg directs that you furnish a detail of twenty five (25) men for fatigue to report to Capt. J. M. Stanford, 51st NC Reg. At these Hd. Qrs. at 8 A.M. tomorrow morning.

          I am Col. Very Respectfully
          Your obt. Servt.
              Edward White
              A. A. Genl.

          Head Quarters Clingman's Brigade
                            June 1st 1863
[Cols. Radcliffe and Hobson]
Colonel

The Brig. Gen. Comdg directs that the following named officers and men of your Regt. who are witnesses and prisoners, in cases to be tried before the G. C. M now in session at these Hd. Qrs. be placed in attendance on the Court at 11 A.M. tomorrow.
Prisoners:
Private Wm. A. Inman, Co. H, 61st Regt., NCT
    "   Luke R. Cartrette   "   "   "
Witnesses:
    Capt. Wm. B. Lanier   "   "   "
        Maultsby   "   51st Reg. NCT
Private Jno. Thompson   "   "
  "   Danl. R. Gore   "   "   "
  "   Sanders Milligan   "   "   "
  "   Danl. M Long   " G   "

              Edward White
              A. A. Genl.

          Head Quarters Clingman's Brigade
                            June 2, 1863
[Cols. Jordan, Shaw, Radcliffe, Hobson]
Colonel,

The Brig. Genl Comdg. directs that the following named officers and men of your Regt. Who are witnesses and prisoners in the cases to be tried before the G. C. M. now in session at Wilmington, N.C. be placed in attendance on the court at 11 A.M. tomorrow.
Orderly:
    Sergt. Pickman   31st Regt. N.C.T.
Prisoner:
    Private J. Seatherwood, Co. G,   "
    "   Jas. J. Cameron, Co. E, 8th "   "
Witnesses:
    Capt. J. R. Murchison   "   "   "
    Sergt. E. A. Hendricks   "   "   "
    Private W. A. Godfrey   "   "   "
Prisoner:
    "   W. A. Inman, Co. H, 61st   "
    "   Luke A. Cartrett   "   H   "
Witness:
    Capt. W. B. Lanier   "   H   "
    Private Jno. Thompson   "   H   "
    Private Danl. R. Gore   "   H   "
    Private Danl. M. Long   "   H   "
    "   Sanders Mulligan   "   H   "
    Capt. Maultsby   "   H   "

I am Col. Very Respectfully, Your Obt. Servt.,
          Edward White, A. A. Genl.

          Head Quarters Clingman's Brigade
                            June 3, 1863
[to Major James H. Hill, A. A. G.]
Major

In compliance with instructions I have the honor to suggest the names of five commissaries.
    Private F. Bell, Co. B, 51st Reg. NC Troops
        K. Meritt
        A. McKenzie   "   I   "
        D. S. Morgan   "   D   "
        W. H. Hamilton"   E   "

          I am Major Very Respectfully
              Your Obt Servt
    [signed]   T. L. Clingman
              Brig. Genl.

            Hd. Qrs. Clingman's Brigade
                            June 4, 1863
[to Colonel Radcliffe]

Colonel,

The Brig. Genl. Comdg directs that until further ordered you send daily to these Hd. Qrs. a detail of one (1) non-comd. officer and three (3) men to report to Major R. S. Gage for guard duty.

    I am, Col. Very Respectfully
    Your Obt. Servt.
    Edward White
    A. A. Genl.

   Head Quarters Clingman's Brigade
       June 5th 1863
[To Colonel Jordan]
Colonel,

The Brig. Genl. Comdg directs that you send immediately to these Hd. Qrs. a guard of one non-comd. officer and three men.

You will hereafter furnish this guard daily they will report every evening at sunset and will be relieved from duty at six oclock every morning.

    I am Col Very Respectfully
    Your Obt. Servt.
    Edward White
    Asst. Adj. Genl.

   Head Quarters Clingman's Brigade
       June 7th 1863
[To Col. H. M. McKethan]
Colonel,

The Brig. Genl. Comdg directs me to say that it has been represented to him that Lieut Watson of your Regt., while in charge of the party repairing the bridge in front of Mr. Bradley's house, permitted his men to strip themselves for the purpose of bathing, notwithstanding the presence of ladies in the house.

He desires to know whether this be true, and therefore wishes you to cause Lieut. Watson to send this morning, to these Head Quarters a statement of the facts.

    I am Col. Very Respectfully
    Your Obt. Servt.
    Edward White
    Asst. Adj. Genl.

   Head Quarters Clingman's Brigade
   Near Wilmington N.C. June 12, 1863
Genl. S. Cooper
 Adjt. Inspr. General
  Richmond, VA

General

In compliance with Par: 2, Section II General Order No. 10, A. J. G. O. May 29th 1863, I have the honor to recommend Capt. J. B. Lee, A. C. S., 8th Reg, N.C. Troops, as the best qualified regimental commissary of his Brigade, for assignment to duty as the brigade commissary.

    I am General Very Respectfully
    Your Obt. Sevt.
    Edward White
    A. A. Genl.

   Head Quarters Clingman's Brigade
       June 12, 1863
[Col. Radcliffe, 61st Reg.]
Colonel

During last night a certain amount of bacon was taken from the commissary tent at these Hd. Qrs.

The guard was from your Regt and consisted of Corpl. Mount, Co. B, & Private Jesse Peel [Peal], Co. A., J. W. Bloodworth, Co. G, S. D. Richardson, Co. I.

The Brig. Genl. Comdg directs that you summons these men before you and investigate the matter; and if possible, ascertain whether the theft was committed by some outside party, or by some one of the guard.

You will report the result of your investigation to these Hd. Qrs.

    I am Col. Very Respectfully
    Your Obt. Servt.
    Edward White
    Asst. Adj. Genl.

   Hd. Qrs. Clingman's Brigade
       June 13, 1863
[to Major D. J. Hill, Assist Adjt. Genl]
Major

I have the honor to report that an order from your office requiring Captain Stanford and Lieut McArthur, 51st N.C. Regt. to be placed in attendance on the G.C. M. in session at Wilmington, at 10 A.M. today was received precisely at the hour indicated for their appearance before the court.

This will account for the delay which will occur in their compliance with the order.

    I am Major Very Respectfully
    Your Obt. Servt.
    [signed] T. L. Clingman, Brig. Genl.

Head Quarters Clingman's Brigade
June 13th 1863

[Colonel J. D. Radcliffe]
Colonel

In compliance with instructions from Major Gen. Whiting, the following named prisoners will be transferred from the guard house of your Regt. To the military prison in Wilmington where they will remain until after their trial before the G. C. M. now in session.

You will send them this morning under proper guard to Capt. Andrew's ____ comdt.

Private Rial Edmonds [Edwards], Co. B, Reg., N.C. Troops
" Emanuel Edwards " " "
" Richard Taylor " " "
" Alexander McDaniel " D "
" Oscar Connaway " K "
" Thomas Edwards " B "
" Lorton Gardner " H "
" Thomas Armstrong " G "

I am Col. Very Respectfully
Your Obt. Servt.
Edward White
A. A. Genl.

Head Quarters Clingmans Brigade
June 15th 1863

Major R. G. Gage
   Brigade Commissary
     Maj.

The Brig. Genl. Comdg. directs me to say that many complaints have been made by officers of this Brigade, that they find great difficulty in getting supplies from your department, and that you have refused to sell to them on any day except Tuesday & Friday of each week. He directs me to say that you must so regulate your department that officers can purchase on any day in the week that they may wish, and in any quantities, such commissary stores for their own use in camp which you may have on hand, and that he expects that you will keep always, when possible, a full supply of all articles that you can obtain from the nearest Post Commissary for supplying their wants.

He further directs that you will make no other regulation or rule by which either the officers or men are inconvenienced without first submitting these to him for approval.

I am Major with great respect
Your Obt. Servt.
Majr. A. A. G.

Head Quarters Clingmans Brigade
June 17th 1863

Circular

Hereafter Regimental Commanders will send morning reports to this office at 9 A.M. daily.

By Command of
Brig. Genl. Clingman
Edward White
A. A. Genl.

Hd. Qrs. Clingmans Brigade
June 17th 1863

[to Major D. H. Hill, A. A. G., Wilmington, NC]
Major

In compliance with circular from this Head Quarters Dist. Cape Fear June 13th 1863, I have the honor to enclose herewith descriptive lists of conscripts, received by Regimental and Company commanders under my command, since October 1862.

I am Maj. Very Respectfully
Your Obt. Servt.
T. L. Clingman
Brig. Genl.

Head Quarters Clingmans Brigade
June 17th, 1863

[D. H. Hill, A. A. G., Wilmington, NC]
Major

I have the honor to report that a communication from Lieut. Ashe, Judge Advocate, dated June 16th, respecting the non-appearance of Private Furmage 51st N.C. Regt. before the G. C. M. was received at 10 A.M. today. The cruiser who brought it from the 7 mile post. states that he started last night, but could not find his way hence.

The neglect of duty on the part of the cruisers at that point, will account, in a great measure, for the delay so frequently complained of.

I would suggest that, as the 8th N.C. Regt. is nearer to Wilmington than to this point, all regulations for prisoners and witnesses be sent direct, instead of through these Head Quarters.

I am, Major, Very Respectfully
Your Obt. Servt.
Signed T. L. Clingman
Brig. Genl.

Head Qrs. Clingmans Brigade
June 17th 1863
[to Col. Hector McKethan, 51st Reg.]
Col.

In your note explaining the delay in sending private Furmage before the G. C. M., you say I have seen but one (requisition) and that was promptly complied with.

On referring to the papers on file in this office I find that an order was sent to you on the 11th inst. to send private Furmage to Wilmington on the next day, 12th.

You say in your note that he was sent yesterday, the 16th.

Genl. Clingman insists to know why four (4) days were allowed to elapse before the order was complied with.

   I am, Colonel, Very Respectfully,
   Your Obt. Servt.
   Edward White
   A. A. G.

Head Quarters Clingmans Brigade
June 17th, 1863
[To. Col. J. D. Radcliffe, 61st Reg.]
Colonel

The Brig. Genl. Comdg directs me to say that information has reached him that the picket guard from your Regt. stationed near Dr. Berry's house, has torn down part of that gentleman's fencing using it for making shelters and for fuel.

He wishes you to send an officer, at once, to Dr. Berry's to inquire into the matter and, as far as practicable, to have the fencing restored.

He will report the results of his investigation to these Head Qrs.

   I am Colonel Very Respectfully
   Your Obt. Servt.
   Edward White
   A. A. Genl.

Head Qrs. Clingmans Brigade
June 17th, 1863
[To. Col. J. D. Radcliffe, 61st Reg.]
Colonel

The Brig. Genl. Comdg directs that the following named officers and men of your Regt., who are witnesses and prisoners, in the cases to be tried before the G. C. M. now in session at Wilmington N.C. be placed in attendance on the Court at 10 A.M. tomorrow promptly.

Prisoner:
 Oscar Connaway Private Co. K, 61st Reg., N.C.T.
Witnesses:
 Lt. Berock
 Sergt. Huggins
 Lt. Garrett
 Lt. Koonce
 Jas. Connaway, Private
 Wm. Riggs
 Harry Robeson, Private Co. H, 61st N.C.
 Jno. N. Griffin
Prisoner:
 Rial Edwards
Witness:
 Lt. David Reddith
 Sergt. Sharendel
Witnesses:
 Sergt Hill Co. "B" 61st Reg. N.C.T.
Prisoner:
 Rich'd Taylor
 Lt. J. J. Wilkins

   I am Col. Very Resptfully Yours,
   Edward White, A. A. G.

Head Quarters Clingmans Brigade
June 17th, 1863
[to Col. Hector McKethan, 51st Regt.]
Colonel

In compliance with a summons from the Judge Advocate of the G. C. M. now in session at Wilmington and with instructions from Maj. Genl. Whiting, you will be in attendance in the Court by 10 A.M. tomorrow.

   I am Col. Very Respectfully
   Your Obt. Servt.
   Edward White
   Asst. Adjt. Genl.

Head Quarters Clingmans Brigade
June 20th, 1863
[to Major J. A. D. McKay, 31st Regt.]
Major

In reply to your note of the 19th inst. relating your having passed the pickets from this brigade without a permit from these Hd. Qrs., the Brig. Genl. Comdg directs me to say that it is not at all satisfactory.

You know that an order requiring all permits to be countersigned at this office had now expired, and he thinks that one of your experience in the military service should also have known, that an order, once expired, continues in force until modified or rescinded by the authority issuing it, and that it is not necessary, to insure the validity of an order, that it shall be repeated from day to day.

    I am, Major, Very Respt.
    Your Obt. Servt.
    Edward White
    A. A. Genl.

    Head Quarters Clingmans Brigade
   Near Wilmington N.C. June 21st, 1863
General S. Cooper
 Adjt. Inspr. Genl.
 Richmond VA.
General:

Private S. E. Koonce, Co. I, 27th Regt., N.C. Troops, Cooke's Brigade, having been elected Senior 2nd. Lieut. of Co. K, 61st Regt., N.C. Troops of my Brigade, I respectfully request that he be ordered to report without delay to Colonel Jas. D. Radcliffe, Comdg. 61st Regt.

    I am General Very Respectfully
    Your Obt. Servt.
    [Signed] T. L. Clingman
    Brig. Genl.

    Head Quarters Clingmans Brigade
      June 22nd 1863
[to Major. J. W. Hill, A. A. G.]
Major

I require the following blanks for use in my Brigade. If you have them or any part of them, please send them by the courier.
 135 Muster & pay rolls, 45 muster rolls
 12 Muster rolls for field, staff and band
 12 Hospital muster rolls
 80 Company morning reports
 15 Field Returns
 16 Company monthly returns.

    I am, Major, Very Respectfully
    Your Obt. Servt.
    Signed T. L. Clingman
    Brig. Genl.

    Head Quarters Clingmans Brigade
      June 24th, 1863
Circular

Regimental Commanders will forward immediately to these Hd. Qrs. a list [of] officers to be examined by the examining Board which will convene at these Hd. Qrs at 10 o'clock A.M. tomorrow.

    By Command of
    Brig. Genl. Clingman
    Edward White
    A. A. Genl.

    Head Quarters Clingmans Brigade
      June 25th, 1863
Circular

Regimental Commanders will report at once to this office the names of all men of their commands on detached duty in the Engineers Department.

It is important that this order be complied with without delay.

    By Command of
    Brig. Genl. Clingman
    Edward White
    A. A. Genl.

    Head Quarters Clingmans Brigade
      June 26th, 1863
Major Jas. H. Hill
 A. A. Genl.
Major

You will have doubtless perceived from the reports of the Inspecting officers, that in most of the Regiments of my Brigade there are companies below the minimum number. These Regiments are so situated that they had no means of recruiting, as the counties, from which they were raised, in some instances, have been for a long time within the enemy's lines. I am anxious to have my Brigade full and wish to send Maj. T. Brown Venable to Raleigh and, if necessary, to Richmond and make efforts to get a supply of conscripts. I would be pleased if orders were sent down today for Maj. Venable to go immediately.

    I am Maj. Very Respt.
    Your Obt. Servt.
    [Signed] T. L. Clingman
    Brig. Genl.

    Head Quarters Clingmans Brigade
      June 29th, 1863
[to Col. Hector McKethan, 51st Regt.]
Colonel

The Brig. Genl. Comdg. directs that Private Jones Co. I of your Regt. be ordered to report daily at 8 A.M. to Capt. Strong, at Wrightsville, until further ordered.

He will be employed in putting up a

chimney and will be needed only for two or three days.

> I am Col. Very Respectfully
> Your Obt. Servt.
> Edward White
> A. A. Genl.

Hd. Qrs. Clingmans Brigade
July 3rd 1863
[to Major Jas. H. Hill]
Major

I have the honor to enclose herewith the names of thirty (30) men, to be transferred to the Engineer Department in accordance with Special Order No. 193. Post Hd. Qrs., also the names of seven men already on detached duty in the Engineer Dept.

In addition to these, three (3) men are to be furnished from Companies D., E., G. H, 51st Regt., N.C.T. now at Magnolia, and as these companies are not under my commad, I would suggest that an order be sent from your office, to Major McDonald, to furnish them.

> I am Major Very Respectfully
> Your Obt. Servt.
> [Signed] T. L. Clingman
> Brig. Gen.

Head Quarters Clingmans Brigade
July 4th 1863
Circular

All men in this Brigade who have not been vaccinated, must be vaccinated at once.

> By Comd. Of Brig. Gen. Clingman
> Edward White
> Asst. Adj. Genl.

Head Quarters Clingmans Brigade
July 4th 1863 11½ P.M.
[to Lt. Col. C. W. Knight, Comdg. 31st Reg, N.C. Troops]
Colonel

In compliance with instructions from Major Gen Whiting, Major McKay with five companies from your Regt will proceed to Wilmington tomorrow morning at daylight, to take the cars on the W & W Road, to go to Magnolia to reinforce Major Jackson, in command there.

This order must be promptly complied with, as cars will be ready for them, at the depot, at daylight, and it is important that they shall report to Maj. Jackson as soon as possible.

> By command of Brig. Gen. Clingman
> Edward White
> A. A. G.

Head Quarters Clingmans Brigade
July 4th 1863
[to Capt. Marsh, Comanding Detatchment]
Captain

Information having been received, that the enemy has started in a cavalry raid, in the direction of Warsaw, some apprehensions are felt, lest they may move this way, the Brig. Gen. Comdg therefore directs that you exercise great vigilance, and to prevent surprise, that you then forward a picket about two miles in advance of your detachment.

> I am Capt. Very Respectfully
> Your Obt. Servt.
> Edward White
> Asst Adj Gen

Head Quarters Clingmans Brigade
July 5th 1863
[to Colonel Radcliffe]
Colonel

The Brig Gen Comdg directs that you send immediately five companies from your Regt. in light marching order, under command of Senior Captain, to report to Major Gen. Whiting at Wilmington.

> I am Col Very Respectfully
> Your Obt Servt
> Edward White
> A. A. G.

Head Quarters Clingmans Brigade
July 5th 1863
[to Maj. Moore, Comanding Artillery Battery]
Major

I enclose herewith a copy of an order form Gen. Whiting, requiring Gen. Clingman to send a section of your command to N. E. R. R. Bridge to reinforce Capt. Badham [??] — he directs that the section be started as soon as possible.

> I am Major Very Respectfully
> Your Obt. Servt.
> Edward White
> A. A. G.

Head Quarters Clingmans Brigade
July 5th, 1863

[to Col. Hector McKethan, 51st Reg.]
Colonel

The Brig Gen Comdg directs that you send at once two companies, to reinforce the detachment at Stevens line.

On their arrival they will report to Major Harding who will command the whole.

I am Col Very Respectfully
Your Obt Servt
Edward White
A. A. G.

Hd Qrs Clingmans Brigade
July 5th 1863
[To Lt. Col. C. W. Knight]
Colonel

The Brig. Gen. Comdg directs me to say that your companies sent up this morning were too small.

You will send immediately a company of seventy five (75) men to report to Gen Whiting at Wilmington.

I am Col Very Respectfully
Your Obt Servt
Edward White
A. A. G.

Head Quarters Clingmans Brigade
July 5th 1863
[to Colonel Hector McKethan]
Colonel

The Brig Gen Comdg directs that you send immediately a company of one hundred (100) men to report to Gen Whiting at Wilmington.

I am Col Very Respectfully
Your Obt Servt
Edward White
A. A. G.

Head Quarters Clingmans Brigade
July 6th 1863
[to Capt. W. C. Strong, A. D. C., Wrightsville]
Captain

In reply to your note of this date, I have the honor to state that, a list of the names of the men referred to was sent to Dist. Hd. Qrs. on the 3rd inst.

I was under the impression that as the men were to be transferred from my brigade, the order transferring them would be issued from that office.

I have today ordered these to report to Capt. James.

I am Capt Very Respectfully
Your Obt Servt
[Signed] T. L. Clingman
Brig. Gen.

Head Quarters Clingmans Brigade
July 6th 1863
[to Capt. O. P. Meares, 61st Regt., through Col. Radcliffe]
Captain

The Brig Gen Comdg, having been informed that the funds for the payment of the Regt for the months of May and June are now ready to be turned over to you, directs that you make immediate application for a leave of absence, of such length as will enable you to file your bond.

He thinks it desirable that the Regt shall be paid as soon as possible.

I am Capt. Very Respectfully
Your Obt Servt
Edward White
Asst Adj. Gen.

Head Quarters Clingmans Brigade
July 7th 1863
[to Col. H. M. Shaw, 8th Regt.]
Colonel

Enclosed I send you an order assigning ten men to your Regt.

The Brig. Gen. Comdg directs that you send tomorrow morning, a guard to take charge of them as well as of the seven men confined in Colonel Radcliffe's guard tent.

As these men are represented to be desparate [sic] characters, you had better send a strong guard.

I am Col Very Respectfully
Your Obt Servt
Edward White
Asst Adjt Gen

Head Quarters Clingmans Brigade
July 9th 1863
[to Major Moore, 3rd N.C. Battn.]
Major

The Brig. Gen. Comdg directs that you send, without delay, to this office a complete list of the commissioned officers of your Battalion, giving date of appointment of each.

I am Major Very Respectfully

Your Obt Servt
Edward White
Asst Adjt Gen

Head Quarters Clingmans Brigade
July 9th [1863]
[to Major Moore, Comdg. 3rd N C Battn.]
Major

The Brig Gen Comdg directs me to call your attention to General Order No. 34 Dist Head Quarters, requiring all permits to visit town, for officers and men from this command, to be approved at this Hd. Qrs.

In connection with this, he directs me to say that you may give permits to your men, to go beyond the limits of your camp, not to exceed two from a company and for not longer than three hours at a time.

These permits must be in writing and in every case the time must be specific.

I am Major Very Respectfully
Your Obt Servt
Edward White
Asst Adjt Gen

Head Quarters Clingmans brigade
July 10th 1863
[Col. J. V. Jordan, 31st Regt.]
Colonel

The Brig. Gen. Comdg directs that you furnish a detail of one non-comd officer and six men for picket duty.

There should be several oarsmen among them, they will report without delay to Captain Blake at these Hd. Qrs.

I am Capt. Very Respectfully
Your Obt. Servt.
Edward White
Asst. Adj. Gen.

Head Qrs. Clingmans Brigade
July 10th 1863
Circular

Commanding officers will hold their commands in readiness to move at a moments notice.

Four days rations will be cooked immediately.

By Command of
Brig. Gen. Clingman
Edward White
Asst. Adj. Gen.

Head Qrs Clingmans Brigade
July 10th 1863 2 PM
[Col. Hector McKethan, 51st Regt.]
Colonel

The Brig Gen Comdg directs that you move immediately to Wilmington, with your whole available force in light marching order, knapsacks and blankets and three days rations.

I am Colonel Very Respectfully
Your Obt. Servt.
Edward White
Asst. Adj. Gen.

Head Quarters Clingmans Brigade
July 10th 1863 5.45 P.M.
[to Major H. Harding, Comdg. Detach. Stevens Line]
Major

The Brig Gen Comdg directs that you move immediately to Wilmington with all the men under your command. The whole brigade is ordered away and will get off during the night or in the morning.

Take with you as much cooked provisions as possible.

I am Major Very Respectfully
Your Obt. Servt.
[Signed] Edward White
A. A. Genl.

Head Quarters Clingmans Brigade
July 10th 1863
[to Col. Radcliffe, 61st Regt and Jordan, 31st Regt.]
Col.

The Brig Gen Comdg directs that you start from this camp with your whole available force at 7 A.M. tomorrow, and proceed directly to Wilmington.

You will move with knapsacks, blankets, and three or four days rations.

You will leave only the sick and convalescent in charge of your camp.

I am Col. Very Respectfully
Your Obt. Servt.
Edward White
Asst. Adj. Genl.

Head Qrs. Clingmans Brigade
July 10th 1863
[To the Officers of the Camp of the 51st Reg.]

Sir

The Brig Gen Comdg directs that all men of the 51st Regt. who have not been pronounced by the surgeon unfit to move, proceed to Wilmington tomorrow to go with the brigade.

Only the sick and convalescents must be left in charge of this camp.

I am Sir Very Respectfully
Edward White
A. A. G.

Head Quarters Clingmans Brigade
Charleston S.C. Juy 14th 1863

[Capt. Maultsby Comdg. Co. G, 51st Regt.]

Captain

The Brig Genl Comdg directs that you have your company at the wharf, near Genl. Ripleys Hd Qrs. at 4½ P.M. promptly, whence you will proceed direct to Morris Island and report to Col. H. McKethan, comdg 51st Regt.

I am Capt Very Respectfully
Your Obt Servt
Edward White
Asst. Adj. Genl.

Head Quarters Clingmans Brigade
Sullivans Island October 2nd 1863

Circular

It has been observed that there is often a great deal of unnecessary and inexcusable delay in furnishing details for fatigue or other duty when ordered from the Regts of this Brigade.

In order to remedy this and to ensure some degree of regularity, Comdg officers will observe the following regulation and official notice will be taken of any failure to do so.

When a detail is ordered the Regt. Commander will require the Orderly Sergts. of each Company from which men are detailed to report with them to the officer or non comd. Officer who is to have charge of the detail, the detail will then be marched in a body under command of the officer or non comd officer to the place where they are ordered to report.

The officer will report for instructions requiring his men to remain in ranks until he is directed what disposition to make of them.

The Brig. Genl. Comdg hopes it will not be necessary again to call attention to this subject.

By Command of
Brig. Genl. Clingman

Headquarters

Colonel

I am directed by Brig. Gen. Clingman comdg. At this point, to say that he does not think it necessary for your Regt of Home Guard to be kept longer in service. It may therefore be disbanded for the present.

I am Col Very Respectfully
Your Obdt. Servt.
Edward White
A. A. Genl.

[To: Bell — Enfield
Johnston — Weldon
Odom — Jackson
Conyers — Rocky Mount
Loyd — Tarboro
Durham — Wilson]

Head Quarters Weldon No. Ca.
Dec. 7th 1863

Major

I enclose you copies of some dispatches below since which I have heard nothing further. Yesterday. Genl. Ransom went down in accordance with my desire and his own wishes to Hamilton. I had previously sent the 51st, my strongest Regiment, there to aid and relieve the 24th (Clarke's) of his Brigade. It is Genl. Ransom's opinion as well as Col. Clarke's that one regiment is altogether insufficient to hold that line and hence if it could be spared it is very desirable that both these regiments should stay there. My next largest regiment is at Kinston, the 8th (Col. Shaw) and is rather too small a force for that point. I have here now only one regiment, the 31st, & 6 companies of the 61st, the other 4 companies being still with Gen. Whiting. Besides this I have moved so frequently that many are absent from my Brigade so that I regard it as insufficient for this extent of country. The Yankes have at Newberne I think six thousand men and not less than two thousand at Washington, Plymouth & other points. If active operations have ceased north of Richmond one may expect an increase of force on this line. It is desirable that there should be at least two Brigades in this State beside the troops under Genl. Whiting. Butler will, according to all I hear from him, attempt to get further into this state as soon as he is strengthened and that may have already occurred. The General can however judge better than I can, whether or not besides the force below there should not be three or four regiments here & at Goldsboro, to move promptly to meet any advance of the enemy.

Though I have received no expressed order to that effect I have assumed the same command that Gen. Ransom, whom I relieved, held.

    Very respectfully,
    [Signed] T. L. Clingman
    Brig. Genl.
Major Charles Pickett
A. A. General
Petersburg, VA

    Headquarters Weldon NC
    December 8th 1863
[Lt. Col. Pool, Cmdg at Goldsboro]
Colonel

I am directed by Gen. Clingman to say that he has been informed by the Supt of the W & W R. R. that certain supplies purchased for the use of the employees of the Rail Road, were stopped in transit at Goldsboro.

The order of Gen Barton on that subject was not intended to apply to provisions purchased elsewhere and passing through Goldsboro, and the Gen directs that hereafter all such be permitted to pass.

    I am Colonel Very Respectfully
    Your Obt Servt
    Edward White
    Asst Adjt Genl
Lt. Col Pool
Cmdg at Goldsboro

    Head Quarters Weldon NC
    December 8th 1863
Lieutenant

It has been represented to the Brig Genl Comdg that the officers of the express company are in the habit of buying up provisions in this District and sending them off without proper authority. The Gen therefore directs that you ascertain the facts, and seize all supplies being sent off without authority from these Hd. Quarters.

    I am Lieut, Very Respectfully
    Your obdt Svt
    Edward White
    A. A. Genl
Lieut A. H. Irving
Provost Marshal

    Hd. Qrs. Weldon N.C.
    December 9th 1863
Major

In reply to a telegraphic order requiring me to furnish the names of officers to compose a General Court Martial, I have the honor to suggest the following names.
Viz: -
Maj. J. A. D. McKay, 31st Reg., N.C. Troops
Captain R. J. McEachern, 51st " "
  S. J. Maultsby, " " "
  L. A. Henderson, 8th " "
  T. J. Garris " " "
  W. M. Stevenson, 61st " "
  Jas. W. Robinson " " "

1st. Lieut. J. A. Liles, 31st N.C. Regt. Judge Advocate

    I am Major Very Respectfully
    Your Obdt Servt
    [Signed] T. L. Clingman
    Brig. Genl.
Major C. Pickett
A. A. Genl.
Petersburg, VA.

    Head Quarters Weldon, N.C.
    December 10, 1863
Major

In compliance with orders, I have the honor to suggest the names of the officers, additional, for members of the General Court Martial.
Captain T. C. Miller, Wilmington Light Artillery
  " C. W. Slater

    I am Major Very Respectfully
    Your Obdt Servt
    [Signed] T. L. Clingman
    Brig. Genl.
Major Chas. Pickett
A. A. Genl
Petersburg VA

    Head Quarters Weldon, N.C.
    December 11, 1863
[Col. H. M. Shaw
Comdg. At Kinston]
Colonel

Your communication of the 8th has been just received, and in reply the Brig. Genl. Comdg directs me to say, that corn, pork, forage, etc., must not be removed from this district by private parties, without special authority from these Headquarters. In order to secure this authority it will be necessary for the parties to make certificate upon honor (in case of doubt, affidavit), that the supplies are for use of their families and not to sell and that they have not paid a greater price than that which is paid by the government, the certificate must in each case also state the size of the family and the quanity will be regulated accordingly.

All applications to send flags of truce must be made to these Headquarters. You are not authorized to send such flags for any purpose.

I enclose herewith copies of the orders relating to leaves of absence and furlough.

Please have the field return due on the 16th forwarded in time to reach here on that day.

> I am Col. Very Respectfully
> Your Obdt. Servt.
> Edward White
> A. A. G.

Head Quarters Weldon N.C.
December 11, 1863

[To Mr. T. B. Satterthwaite
Wilson, N.C.]
Sir

I have the honor to enclose herewith the permit to remove supplies, given you by Governor Vance, approved.

I am directed by Genl. Clingman to require that you will use every precaution to prevent your teamsters or others whom you may employ from communicating in any way with the enemy while engaged in removing your supplies.

> I am, Sir, Very Respectfully
> Your Obdt Servt
> Edward White
> A. A. Genl.

Head Quarters Weldon N.C.
December 11, 1863

[To Col. H. McKethan
Comdg. At Hamilton]
Colonel

The Brig. Genl. Comdg directs me to inform you that he has received orders to move with the whole Brigade to Petersburg.

You will therefore hold your Regt in readiness to move at a moments notice. Orders to move will be sent you at the proper time.

> I am Col. Very Respectfully
> Your Obdt. Servt.
> Edward White
> A. A. G.

Head Quarters Weldon N.C.
December 11, 1863

Major

I send Author Dennis, a deserter to the enemy, who has returned to our lines. The papers enclosed give some information about him. He is intelligent and not, I think, very honest. Yet I take it that his statements are probably true. He can give some information as to the condition of things below and as he has a turn for talking he can become quite eloquent in describing the purposes of the Yankees as to the means of subjugating us. By asking him what they say about their plans, etc. you can draw him out. Supposing that the General might like to make some inquiries of him, I send him up. I have instructed Capt. Miller to prepare charges against him for desertion should his trial be necessary.

I also enclose a dispatch from Col. Griffin which confirms his statement as to the conscription of Negroes, etc.

> Very Respectfully, etc.
> [Signed] T. L. Glingman
> Brig. Gen.

Major Chas. Pickett
A. A. General
Petersburg, VA.

Head Quarters Weldon, N.C.
December 12th 1863 10:30 A.M.

[To. Co. James D. Radcliffe, Comdg. 61st Regt.]
Colonel

A train will be at Garysburg one hour hence to convey your Regt to Petersburg.

Move immediately to the depot at that place with all your baggage and be as expeditious as possible in boarding the train and starting.

On arriving in Petersburg you will report for instructions to Major Gen. Pickett.

> By Command of Brig. Genl. Clingman
> Edward White, A. A. G.

Head Quarters Weldon NC
December 12, 1863

[To Col. H. M. McKethan, Comdg. 51st N.C. Regt.]
Colonel

I am directed by the Brig. Genl. Comdg. to communicate the following information and instructions. The Brigade has been ordered to Petersburg, and one Regt., the 61st has already moved. Genl. Ransom has been ordered to send one of his Regts. to relieve you. As soon as you are relieved by another Regt., you will move, without waiting for further orders, and will rejoin us at this place in Petersburg. You will not however move from your present position until you are either relieved or receive instructions to that effect.

    I am, Col., Very Respectfully
    Your Obdt. Servt.
    Edward White, A. A. Genl.

Head Quarters Clingman's Brigade
December 18th 1863
[Col. H. M. Shaw, Comdg. 8th N.C. Regt.]
Colonel

The Brig. Gen. Comdg. directs that Capt. A. V. Jarvis, Co. B, 8th N.C. Regt., be ordered to report, without delay, to Major Gage, C. S., for duty as butcher.

You will also send two (2) men, butchers if you have them. These men will continue on duty with Major Gage until relieved by him.

    I am, Col., Very Respectfully
    Your obdt. Servt.
    Edward White
    A. A. Genl.

Head Quarters Clingmans Brigade
December 18, 1863
[to Col. J. V. Jordan, Comdg. 31st N.C. Regt.]
Colonel

The Brig. Genl. Comdg directs that you send without delay, three men; butchers if you have them, to report to Major Gage, C. S.

These men will continue on duty until relieved by Major Gage.

    I am Col. Very Respectfully
    Your obdt. Servt.
    Edward White
    A. A. G.

Head Quarters Clingmans Brigade
December 18, 1863
Colonel

The Brig. Gen. Comdg directs me to say that no more wood must be cut in the piece of woods in which you are encamped.

Hereafter all the wood used by your Regt. must be hauled from in front of the line of works near these Headquarters, but corded wood must not be taken.

    I am Col., Very Respectfully
    Your obdt. Servt.
    Edward White
    A. A. Genl.

Head Quarters Clingmans Brigade
December 26, 1863
[to Major C. Picket, A. A. Genl.]
Major

Before I left Weldon, a writ of Habeas Corpus, was served on me requiring the production at Raleigh of Sergt. Edward B. Koonce of Company K, 61st Regt. of my Brigade. I informed the Sheriff that the said regiment was then near Petersburg, VA. It is claimed that said Koonce should be discharged from the service on the ground that he has since entering the service become a mail contractor. I do not regard this fact if it be true, as furnishing any ground for his discharge as he was already in the service. Nevertheless, I submit the matter to the General Comdg. the dept. with the suggestion if it meets his approbation that the said Koonce have a leave of absence of two days to enable him to go to Raleigh and have the matter adjudicated, and in the event of a failure to return at the end of that time or be considered a deserter.

    Respectfully, etc.
    [Signed] T. L. Clingman
    Brig. Genl.

Head Quarters Clingmans Brigade
December 28th 1863
[To. Col. J. V. Jordan, Comdg, 31st N.C. Reg.
Col. Whitson, Comdg. 8th N.C. Regt.]
Colonel

In compliance with orders from Dept. Hd. Qrs. the Col. Comdg. Directs that you hold your Regt. In readiness to move at a moments warning.

The men in light marching order and particular attention must be paid to the condition of arms and ammunition.

    I am Col, Very Respectfully
    Your obdt. Servt.
    Edward White
    A. A. Genl.

Head Quarters Clingmans Brigade
December 31st 1863
[To Cols. H. M. Shaw, and J. V. Jordan]
Colonel

I am directed by the Brig. Genl. Comdg to

say that unless the weather becomes fine in time to complete the regular muster & Inspection ordered for today you may postpone it until tomorrow.

    Very Respt.
    Edward White
    A. A. Genl.

    Head Quarters Clingmans Brigade
        December 31st, 1863
[to General S. Cooper, A. A. I. General, Richmond, VA]
General

I have respectfully to state that my Brigade is greatly in want of an Inspector, having been without one since last July when Major Venable was transferred at the time from it then at Charleston to Gen. Whitings Department. I respectfully request that Lieut. Frederick R. Blake be promoted to the rank of Captain and assigned as Inspector to this Brigade. He has been in the service during the entire war. He served with the rank of Captain in the 15th N.C. Regt. Under my command and was remarkable for his dilligence [sic] and efficiency in all respects. However on the reorganization of the Regiment, like many other first rate officers he was left out. He has nevertheless in some capacity continued in the service ever since and for nearly twelve months has been my aide-de-camp having been commissioned as Lieutenant. I regard him as being equal in merit to any officer in the service and as well entitled to promotion. I therefore earnestly request that he may receive the commission of Captain for the purpose indicated above.

Should he be thus promoted, I request that the place of Aid be filled by a commission of Lieut to Henry S. Puryear, who has served about eighteen months as a volunteer and a private in the ranks.

    Very Respectfully, &
    [Signed] T. L. Clingman
    Brig. Genl.

    Head Quarters Clingmans Birgade
        Jan. 3rd 1864
[to Col. H. Shaw, 8th N.C. Regt, and Col. J. V. Jordan, 31st N.C. Regt.]
Colonel

The Brig. Genl. Comdg directs me to say that he is much surprised to hear that since the Brigade has been encamped at this place, the customary Dress parades have been discontinued. He directs that they be immediately resumed and not again omitted except in bad weather or with his knowledge.

    I am, Col., Very Respectfully
    Your obdt. Servt.
    [Signed] F. R. Blake
    A. A. A. Genl.

    Head Quarters Clingmans Brigade
        January 3rd 1863 [1864]
[To. Col. J. V. Jordan, Comdg. 31st N.C. Regt.]
Col.

The Brig. Genl. Comdg directs me to say that your communication in relation to the wood has been received. He desires you to forward immediately to these Hd. Qrs. a report of the number of wagons and teams furnished to your Regt. by the Q. M. Dept.

    I am, Col., Very Respectfully
    Your Obdt Servt.
    [Signed] F. W. Blake
    A. A. A. Genl.

    Head Quarters Clingmans Brigade
        January 11th 1864
[To. Co. H. M. Shaw, Comdg. 8th N.C. Regt.]
Colonel

The Brig. Genl. Comdg directs me to say that after the 14th inst. commissary stores for your Regt must be drawn from Major Gage at these Head Quarters.

Capt. Grandy must include in his provision returns [of] all the sick of the Regt not in General Hospital or otherwise about.

    I am, Col Very Respectfully
    Your obdt. Servt.
    Edward White
    A. A. Genl.

    Head Quarters Clingmans Brigade
        January 13th 1863 [1864]
General S. Cooper
Adjt & Inspr. Genl.
Richmond, VA
General

I have the honor to enclose herewith copies of all the orders announcing the promotion of officers in my brigade.

    I am, Genl. Very Respectfully
    Your obdt Servt.
    [Signed] T. L. Clingman
    Brig. Genl.

Head Quarters Clingmans Brigade
January 13, 1864
[To Col. J. V. Jordan, Comdg., 31st N.C. Regt.]
Colonel

The Brig. Genl. Comdg directs me to enclose herewith a furlough used by private J. J. Wallace of your Regt. The figures indicating the number of days, have evidently been altered, and his account for commutation of rations has been made in accordance with them as they now stand. Whether private Wallace was himself guilty of making this alteration is not known but the Genl wishes you to investigate the matter at once, and if you have reason to believe him guilty, you will have him arrested and charges preferred against him.

    I am, Col., Very Respectfully
    Your obdt Servt
    Edward White
    A. A. Genl.

Head Quarters Clingmans Brigade
January 14 1864
Circular

Regimental Commanders will see that no wood is removed by the troops of their command, from the Encampment just vacated by the 51st N.C. Regt.

    By Command of
    Brig. Genl. Clingman
    Edward White
    A. A. Genl.

Head Quarters Clingmans Brigade
January 18 1864
[To Col. J. D. Radcliffe, Comdg. N.C. Regt]
Colonel

The Brig. Genl. Comdg directs me to enclose you the accompanying statement of Capt. Wallace, respecting the use to which the transportation furnished your Regt. has been put. In future you will see that this transportation is used only for the purpose specified in the regulations and orders on that subject.

    I am, Col., Very Respectfully
    Your obdt. Servt
    Edward White, A. A. Genl.

Head Quarters Clingmans Brigade
January 20, 1864
[To Capt. N. A. Ramsey, Pittsboro, N.C.]
Captain

In accordance with orders sent you by Genl. Whiting and instructions received from Maj. Gen. Pickett, the Brig. Genl. Comdg directs that you rejoin your Regt with as little delay as possible.

The Regt is now near Iron Station on the Norfolk and Petersburg Rail Road.

    I am, Capt., Very Respectfully
    Your obdt. Servt.
    Edward White
    A. A. Genl.

Head Quarters Clingmans Brigade
January 20, 1864
Circular

Hereafter the number of permits to visit the city, granted to officers of this Brigade, will not be limited, but must in every case be countersigned at these Head Quarters. The presentation at these Head Quarters of accounts for commutation of rations, by the men to whom the commutation is due, is prohibited. Commanding officers will forward them with their official papers, without however making any endorsement upon them.

    By Command of
    Brig. Genl. Clingman
    Edward White
    A. A. Genl.

Head Quarters Clingmans Brigade
January 21st 1864
[To Col. J. V. Jordan, Comdg. 31st Regt., N.C. Troops]
Colonel

Through the negligence of a guard from your Regt. consisting of Sergt. Watson, Co. H, Privates J. Pipkin, Co. K, J. Thompson, Co. E, J. Adams, Co. C., certain property belonging to the Commissary department was lost.

The Brig. Genl. Comdg therefore directs that these men be required to do fourteen days extra duty and with the exception of the Sergt to spend the time they are not so engaged, in the guard house.

    I am, Col., Very Respectfully
    Your obdt. Servt
    Edward White
    A. A. Genl.

Head Quarters Clingmans Brigade
January 31, 1864

Circular

Regimental Commanders will forward without delay to this office lists of the names of all men of their commands transferred to the Navy and to the Engineers dept and of all men on detached service showing where they are detailed and on what duty.

   By Command of
   Brig. Genl. Clingman
   Edward White
   A. A. Genl.

   Head Quarters Clingmans Brigade
      January 22nd 1864
[To. Co. J. V. Jordan, Comdg. 31st Regt. N.C. Troops]
Colonel

In compliance with orders from Major Gen. Pickett, you will have your Regt in readiness to move tomorrow morning to Iron depot on the Norfolk & Petersburg Road where you will relieve Lt. Col. Herbert, 7th C. S. Navy.

You will be informed at what time the train will be ready for you. You will move in light order, leaving behind a guard to take charge of your camp.

Col. Herbert will give you all the necessary instructions.

   I am, Col., Very Respectfully
   Your obdt. Servt
   Edward White
   A. A. Genl.

   Head Quarters Clingmans Brigade
      January 22 1864
Brig. Genl. Thos. Jordan
Chief of Staff, Charleston, S.C.
General

While I was on Sullivans Island, a General Court Martial was convened for the trial of certain men of my Brigade.

Many of these men have been confined in the guard house for several months and I would like to know the decisions of the court in these cases, in order that their sentences may be executed.

Below you will find a list of the names of the men who were tried.

 Private Jesse Lawson, Co., G, 51st N.C. Regt.
 Private A. Dawson, Co. G, 51st N.C. "
  " S. W. Prince " " "
  " W. W. Tearoe (Teaboe) " " "
  " M. Porter, Co. I, " " "
  " W. Page, Co. I " "
  " Jno. W. Carroll " "
  " S. H. Chestnutt, Co. K " "
  " S. W. Royal, Co. K " "
  " N. Parker " " "
 I. W. Ezzell, Co., B " "
 E. Armstrong, Co. B " "
 L. Merritt, Co. C " "
 R. Register, Co. C " "
 Daniel Faircloth, Co. E, 8th, N.C. Regt. "
 George Anderson, Co. G, 8th, N.C. "

   I am, Gen., Very Respectfully
   Your obdt. Servt.
   [Signed] T. L. Clingman
   Brig. Genl.

   Head Quarters Clingmans Brigade
      January 23rd 1864
[To. Col. J. V. Jordan, Comdg. 31st N.C. Regt.]
Colonel

The Brig. Genl. Comdg directs me to say that he has understood that certain officers of your Regt. have purchased from some of the men, shoes or other clothing drawn by them.

He wishes you to investigate the matter and if it is true, the names of the officers purchasing and the men who sold must be at once, reported to these Head Quarters.

You will positively prohibit transactions of this sort in the future.

   I am, Colonel, Very Respectfully
   Your obdt Servt
   Edward White
   A. A. Genl.

   Head Quarters Clingmans Brigade
      January 25, 1864
Circular

Regimental Commanders will forward <u>immediately</u> to this office lists of deserters and unauthorized absentees from their commands, giving their places of residence. These lists will be forwarded to Genl. Hoke.

No applications to send men to arrest deserters need be forwarded.

   By Command of Brig. Genl. Clingman
   Edward White
   A. A. Genl.

   Head Quarters Clingmans Brigade
      January 27, 1864
[To J. D. Radcliffe, 61st Reg.]

Colonel

You will please forward, without delay to these Head Quarters, a memorandum showing the dates of resignation of the following officers, Captains Croome, Marsh, Moore, Van Amringe, and Cox, also the date that Capt. Koonce was dropped. You will also state how the following officers left the Regt, whether by death or resignation, and the date.

Lieut. Higgins, Co. I; Haskins, Co. K; Harris, Co. F; Freddle, Co. G.

    I am, Col., Very Respectfully
    Your obdt Servt
    Edward White
    A. A. Genl.

  Head Quarters Clingmans Brigade
      January 27th 1864
[To Colonel H. McKethan, Comdg 51st N.C. Regt.]
Colonel

In compliance with instructions from Hed Qrs, Dept. N.C. the Brig. Genl. Comdg directs that you furnish from your Regt a detail of three (3) comd. officers, seven (7) non-comd. officers, and eighty (80) men for Provost duty in the City of Petersburg to relieve the 18th VA Regt.

The detail will report at Dept Hd. Qrs. at 9 oclock A.M. tomorrow.

    I am, Col., Very Respectfully
    Your obdt. Servt
    Edward White
    A. A. Genl.

  Head Quarters Clingmans Brigade
  Petersburg VA February 16 1864
[To General S. Cooper.]
General

I respectfully ask information which will enable me to act properly under the circumstances in which I am placed. I have been for some weeks past in command of two regiments of my Brigade, the other two having been detached and directed to report to Maj. Genl. Pickett. On yesterday, Maj. Gen. Pickett went with his staff to the vicinity of Goldsboro, six miles from which place I understand he has secured a house for his occupation, and that his Head Quarters were to be at Goldsboro or its vicinity.

On inquiring yesterday I learned that he had left one of his Staff, Capt. E. R. Baird at Petersburg to give orders, but had left no orders for me. Should there be an advance of the emeny from any point on James River or from the Black Water, I desire to know whether I am as the officer of highest rank in the district of country, to use the troops here to resist any movement of the enemy, or whether I am to be commanded by the Staff officer left here, or am to await orders from the Department Commander near Goldsboro. In other words I desire to know what is my duty here and what is the extent of my responsibility.

If Maj. Genl. Pickett having his Head Quarters one hundred and fifty miles distant can cause one of his Staff directly to command this District, he can I presume in like manner have Brig. Gen. Ransom commanded at Weldon and Brig. Gen. Hoke commanded at Kinston. I do not understand however that either of these officers is so treated, and as their rank is no higher than my own, while their commissions are of a junior date, I do not see any reason for such a discrimination.

At other points where I have been stationed, even where the General in command had no intention to change his Head Quarters, but was merely absent for a few days, the next in rank was instructed to discharge for the time the duties. While I hold a commission from the President I shall at all times obey with alacrity all such commands as come from proper authority if I know it, yet as my impressions are at variance with the action taken by Maj. Gen. Pickett, I have felt it my duty to make this statement. My wish is simply to ascertain whether in the event of any movement of troops being necessary in this immediate district, I am to direct it, or secondly whether I shall receive orders from the Staff officer, that has been left here by Maj. Gen. Pickett, or thirdly, am I to await orders in all instances from the Department Head Quarters. These inquiries are made with no desire either to assume or to avoid responsibility but merely to enable me to discharge properly the duties of my present position.

After determining to address this communicaiton to you, general, I received a communication from Capt. Baird of which a copy is enclosed to you with this note.

    Very Respectfully,
    Your most obdt. Servt.
    [Signed] T. L. Clingman
    Brig. Genl.

Head Quarters Clingmans Brigade
February 17, 1864
[Tol Col. J. V. Jordan, Comdg. 31st N.C. Regt.]
Colonel

The Brig. Genl. Comdg directs me to inquire whether it will be practicable for your Regt to alternate with the 61st in doing picket duty on the Blackwater without the necessity of changing the quarters of either Regt.

Please reply to this at once.

    I am, Col., Very Respectfully
    Your obt Servt.
    Edward White
    A. A. Genl.

Head Quarters Clingmans Brigade
February 20, 1864
[To Capt. E. R. Baird, Actg. Asst. Adjt. Genl. Petersburg, Va]
Captain

The following blanks are necessary for the use of my command. Please send them to me as soon as possible.

125 Muster & Pay Rolls, 45 Muster Rolls.
15 Hospital Muster Rolls, 15 Muster Rolls for Field Staff & Band
75 Descriptive Rolls. 57 Certificates of disability
50 Soldiers discharges, 57 Final Statements
20 Field Returns. 20 Monthly Returns

    I am, Capt. Very Respectfully
    Your obdt Servt
    [Signed] T. L. Clingman
    Brig. Genl.

Head Quarters Clingmans Brigade
February 21st 1864
[To Col. H. McKethan, Comdg 51st NC Regt.]
Colonel

I am directed by the Brig. Genl. Comdg to inform you that he has been ordered to make his Head Quarters at Iron Station. During his absence you will assume command of the ten [or two?] Regts at this point and will report direct to Dept. Hd. Qrs. At Petersburg.

We leave tomorrow morning.

    I am Col. Very Respectfully
    Your obdt Servt.
    Edward White
    A. A. Genl.

Head Quarters Clingmans Brigade
February 21, 1864
[To. Lt. Col. J. M. Whitson, Comdg. 8th N.C. Regt.]
Colonel

The Brig. Genl. Comdg directs me to inform you that he has been ordered to make his Head Quarters on the Blackwater.

During his absence, Col. McKethan will command the two Regts at this point. You will accordingly report to him.

    I am, Col., Very Respectfully
    Your obdt Servt.
    Edward White
    A. A. Genl.

Head Quarters Clingmans Brigade
February 22, 1864
[To Col. J. V. Jordan, Comdg. 31st N.C. Regt.]
Colonel

The Brig. Genl. Comdg directs me to inform you that Col. Radcliffe has been authorized to call upon you for sufficient force to relieve his Regt from Picket duty on the Black Water.

If he should make the application to you, you will, retaining _____

your present quarters, the requested force and will continue to do the picket duty until otherwise ordered from these Head Quarters.

    I am, Col, Very Respectfully
    Your obdt Servt.
    Edward White
    A. A. Genl.

Head Quarters Clingmans Brigade
March 8th, 1864

Brig. Genl. R. C. Gatlin
  Adjt. Gen. N.C.
  General

I have the honor to enclose herewith copies of the report of a Military Board appointed to examine candidates for appointment and promotion in the 8th North Carolina Regt. of my Brigade. Below you will find a list of the names of the officers examined. Please take such action in their cases as may seem to you proper, with as little delay as possible.

Captain J. N. Ramsey, Co. I, 8th N.C. Regt for promotion
  " L. R. Breece " E " " " "
Lieut. W. L. Townsend" C " " " "
  " L. N. Simmons " B " " " "
  " L. B. Holt   " I " " " "
  " John Baker   " H " " " "

"	E. A. Moye	"	G	"	"
"	D. J. Baker	"	E	"	"
"	A. H. Grandy	"	B	"	"
"	*Alexander Floyd	"	K 51st	"	"
"	F. F. Floyd	"	E	"	"
"	R. J. T. Hawes	"	A	"	"
"	Jordain Hughes	"	H	"	"
"	T. B. Lippitt	"	G	"	"

      I am, General, Very Respectfully
          Your obt Servt
         [Signed] T. L. Clingman
             Brig. Genl.

*Note: Alexander Floyd in this list should correctly read Alexander Elliott. See Louis H. Manarin and Weymouth T. Jordan, Jr., eds., *North Carolina Troops, 1861–1865: A Roster*, Volume XII (Raleigh: Division of Archives and History, 1990), p. 382.

      Head Quarters Clingmans Brigade
            March 8, 1864
[To. Col. H. McKethan, Comdg. 51st N.C. Regt.]
Colonel

I have the honor to inform you that the following named officers of your Regt have been recommended for appointment and promotion by the Military Board of which Lt. Col. Devane is President. The reports of the Board in their cases have been forwarded to the Adjt. Genl. of N.C. with the request that their commissions be sent them at once.
Lieut. R. J. T. Hawes, Co. A
"   F. F. Floyd   " E
"   T. B. Lippitt   " G
"   Alexander Elliott " K
[listed as Alexander Floyd in previous order.]
The report of the Board in the case of Lieut Jordan Hughes, Co. H is unfavorable, and I presume no commission will be given him.

      I am, Col., Very Respectfully
          Your obt. Servt.
           Edward White
            A. A. G.

      Head Quarters Clingmans Brigade
           March 8th, 1864
[To Colonel J. M. Whitson, Comdg. 8th N.C.T.]
Colonel

I have the honor to inform you that the following named officers of your Regt have been recommended for appointment and promotion by the Military Board of which Lt. Col. Devane is President. The report of the Board in their cases have been forwarded to the Adjt. Genl. of N.C. with the request that their commissions be sent them at once.
Capt. J. N. Ramsey, Co. I
"   L. R. Breece   " E
Lieut. W. L. Tounsend " C
"   L. N. Simmons " B
"   L. B. Holt   " J
"   John Baker   " A
"   E. A. Moye   " G
"   D. J. Baker   " E
"   A. H. Grandy   " B

      I am, Col., Very Respectfully
          Your obt Servt.
          Edward White
          A. A. G.

      Head Quarters Clingmans Brigade
          March 8th 1864
[To Col. H. McKethan, Comdg 51st N.C. Regt. and Col. J. M. Whitson, Comdg 8th N.C. Regt]
Colonel

The Brig. Genl. Comdg directs that you forward without delay to this office, a list of the casualties in your Regt. during the expedition to New Berne.

      I am, Col. Very Respectfully
          Your obt Servt.
          Edward White
          A. A. G.

      Head Quarters Clingmans Brigade
           March 8, 1864
Brig. Genl. Thos. Jordan
Chief of Staff, Charleston, S.C.
    General

I have the honor to acknowledge the receipt of the orders promulgating the proceedings of the General Court Martial convened on Sullivans Island in October last for the trial of certain prisoners of my Brigade.

      I am, Genl. Very Respectfully
          Your obt. Servt.
         [Signed] T. L. Clingman
            Brig. Genl.

      Head Quarters Clingmans Brigade
          March 10th 1864
[To. Col. J. D. Radcliffe]
Colonel

The Brig. Genl. Comdg directs that, in

obedience to a writ of Habeas Corpus served upon him for the person of Sergt. Edw. B. Koonce, Co. K, 61st N.C. Regt., you will send the said Sergt. Koonce immediately under charge of a commissioned officer to Richmond to appear before Judge Halyburton.

You will also send a written statement showing the day and cause of his being taken and detained in your Regt.

The officer will report at these Headquarters on his way to Richmond,

> I am, Col., Very Respectfully
> Your obt. Servt.
> Edward White
> A. A. G.

Head Quarters Clingmans Brigade
March 17, 1864

[To Major C. Pickett
A. A. Genl.
Dept of No. Car.]
Major

I have been prevented from complying with the order in the circular of the 21st ult from the fact that at the time it was received by me, one of the Regiments, the 8th, was detached from my command and it was not until this morning that I was able to obtain the statement of its casualties required. As I was instructed to "give a full list of casualties" and state particularly whether I "lost any prisoners" I was compelled to delay the report. In obedience to orders received during the previous night, on the morning of the 29th Jany, last, I with two Regiments of my Brigade, the 8th commanded by Col. H. M. Shaw and the 51st by Col. H. McKethan took the Rail Road trains for Kinston, N.C. at which place I arrived on the evening of the 30th and advanced five miles toward Newbern. In obedience to orders from Maj. Gen. Pickett on the next day I followed with my command Genl. Hoke's Brigade which was in the advance of the column and rested for a part of the night about twelve miles on this side of Newbern. Having been ordered to follow immediately Genl. Hoke's Brigade and support him at one o'clock on the morning of Feb. 1st, I moved forward with my command. Owing to the delay at Bachelor's Creek and to the darkness of the night, I with the part of my command passed the rear of Genl. Hoke's which was resting on the right side of the road. While in this position within two or three hundred yards of the creek, Col. Shaw who was with me at the head of his Regiment, was instantly killed by one of the enemy's shots from the opposite side of the creek. Most unfortunate casualty rendered it necessary that Lieut.Col. J. M. Whitson should assume the command of the Regiment. When at a later hour the passage of Bachelor's creek had been effected my command followed Genl. Hoke's closely until we reached the point where the railroad was intersected by the road along which we were advancing. I then received orders from Maj. Genl. Pickett to take the advance and move along the road to be followed and supported by Gen. Hoke's Brigade. I was wisely instructed to be particular in my guard against any attack that might be made on my left from the direction of the town of Newbern and Genl. Hoke having been primarily acquainted with the location there was instructed to accompany me. After moving along the road until within nearly a mile of the town my Brigade diverged to the right keeping a direction nearly parallel to the line of the enemy's fortifications on the front of the town.

The enemy were not encountered until we had advanced to a position within six or eight hundred yards of the Trent road. There they were in position with a regiment of Cavalry and some field artillery, supported also by what appeared to be a small force of infantry on their right and nearer to the city. Their cavalry dashed forward to charge in but were repulsed and defeated by the fire of my skirmishers without getting near enough to receive the volley of the Brigade. Their field pieces then opened on us chiefly with spherical case shot, but the men were directed to lie down and their [sic] being a slight swell in the ground in front little or no injury was sustained by us. Their cavalry started forward several times but whenever our line rose to its feet they halted and retired. Thinking it advisible [sic] to attack the enemy and drive them within the fortifications of the town and occupy the Trent road I requested Genl. Hoke to bring up his Brigade to my support, it being then nearly a mile to the rear. He returned for that purpose but after waiting nearly an hour without hearing from him, I sent two of my Staff in succession to request that at least a section of artillery should be brought up to my assistance. While in this position the heavy batteries of Fort Totten opened on us. As this fortress represented to be the strongest in the town of Newbern and armed with not less than fifteen guns of large caliber was not more than three quarters of a mile distant, and had a complete infilading fire on us, had their practice been good we must have sustained serious injury. In point of fact however their fire proved nearly harmless. After retaining this position for two or three hours, I was informed that the artillery could not be brought forward. Genl. Hoke did not come up with his Brigade and I was soon after ordered to retire. As in addition to the fire of the heavy batteries on our left we were confronted with the enemy's cavalry, field artillery and infantry. I withdrew my command slowly by sections and occupied successively such positions as would enable us to repel an attack if suddenly made by the cavalry. It gives me great pleasure to be able to state that though exposed both on the flank and front to artillery fire and threatened constantly with attack by the enemy's cavalry and infantry the troops under my command performed the movements ordered with as much coolness and precision as I ever saw them show when in drill.

After retiring I was instructed to occupy the ground in front of the rail road crossing within range of the enemy's fire from the fort and on each night of our bivouacking there. I sent forward for the distance of a mile strong detachments to guard against any attack that the enemy might make. In obedience to orders these detachments were withdrawn about two o'clock on the morning of the 3rd and my Brigade returned with the rest of the command to the vicinity of Kinston.

The casualties in my Brigade were small in number but the loss of Col. Shaw is deeply to be deplored. Equally remarkable for his attention to all the duties of his position and for coolness and selfpossession and courage in the field, I know no one filling a similar position whose loss would inflict a greater injury to the service than that sustained in his fall. The other casualties in his Regt., the 8th, are killed Private D. M. Barringer, Co. "K," wounded Sergt. W. Harris, Private J. Coe, Co. "I," and Private M. Sides, Co. "H." Missing Privates D. Carter, D. Faircloth, Co. "E," W. Parris, Co. "D" and M. Cosby, Co. "J." The losses in the 51st were Privates W. E. Pugh, Co. "C," Dixon Sessoms, Co. "K" wounded, missing Sergt. J. W. Croom, Co., Private D. Sumerlin.

In conclusion, I have to state that every officer and private seems to have acted creditably on all occasions.

    I have the honor to be
        Very Respectfully yours
    [Signed] T. L. Clingman
        Brig. Genl.

    Head Quarters Clingmans Brigade
        March 24, 1864
General S. Cooper
Asst. A. Inspt. Genl.
Richmond, VA
General

I have the honor to enclose herewith the reports of a Military Board appointed to examine certain candidates for promotion and appointment in the 31st & 61st N.C. Regts. of my Brigade. I would respectfully request that each of the reports be approved or disapproved as may seem to you proper and returned as soon as possible in order that the officer examined may know whether they are to continue on duty in their present capacities. Below you will find a list of the names of the officers examined.

Captain J. H. Robinson, Co. "A," 61st Regt. For promotion
Lieutenant W. F. Smith " " " "
" H. H. Raspberry " "E" " "
" J. D. Barnes " "F" " "
" A. D. Lippitt " "G" " "
" N. H. Fennell " " " "
" W. H. Joines " "I" " "
" S. E. Koonce " "K" " "
Captain J. T. Bradley " "B" 31st "
" J. W. Smith " "H" " "
Lieut.W. J. Bethea " "I" " "
" D. McL. Jones " "J" " "

    I am, General, Very Respectfully
      Your obt. Servt.
      [Signed] T. L. Clingman
        Brig. Genl.

    Head Quarters Clingmans Brigade
        March 24, 1864
General R. C. Gatlin
Adjt. Genl. N.C.
General

I have the honor to enclose herewith copies of the reports of a Military Board appointed to examine candidates for appointment and promotion in the 8th & 51st N.C. Regts of my Brigade.

Please take such action in their cases as may seem to you proper with as little delay as possible.

Below you will find a list of the officers examined.

Lieutenant J. R. McKethan, Co. E., 51st N.C. Regt.

"	J. H. Taylor	"	"J"	"	"
"	H. T. Houston	"	"C"	"	"
"	B. A. Gorman	"	"G"	"	"
"	J. T. Smith	"	"B"	"	"
"	T. W. Butt	"	"A"	8th	"

          [Signed]   T. L. Clingman
                      Brigadier General

        Head Quarters Clingman's Brigade
                        March 23rd 1864
[To Colonel J. V. Jordan
Comdg. 31st N.C. Regt.]
Colonel

I have the honor to inform you that the following named officers of your Regt. have been recommended for appointment, and promotion by the Military Board of which Lt. Col. Devane is President.

His report of the Board in their cases have been provided to the adjt. & Inspr. Genl. with the request that immediate action be taken on them.

    Captain J. T. Bradley, Co. B
       "   J. W. Smith,   "   H
    Lieut. D. M. L. Jones   "   I

The report of the Board in the case of Lieut. W. J. Bethea ___ is unfavorable and I presume no commission will be given him.

           I am, Col., Very Respectfully
           Your obt. Servt.
           Edward White
           A. A. Genl.

        Head Quarters Clingmans Brigade
                        March 23rd 1864
[To Lt. Col. Hobson,
Comdg. 51st N.C. Regt.]
Colonel

I have the honor to inform you that the following named officers of your Regt have been recommended for appointment and promotion by the Military Board of which Lt. Col. Devane is president. The reports of the Board in their cases have been forwarded to the Adjt. Genl. of N.C. with the report that commissions be sent them at once.

    Lieut. J. R. McKethan, Co. E.

"	J. H. Taylor	"	J
"	H. T. Houston	"	C
"	B. A. Gorman	"	G
"	J. T. Smith	"	B

           I am, Col. Very Respectfully
           Your obt. Servt.
           Edward White
           A. A. G.

        Head Quarters Clingman's Brigade
                        March 23rd 1864
[To Colonel J. M. Whitson
Comdg. 8th N.C. Regt.]
Colonel

I have the honor to inform you that the report of the Military Board of which Lt. Col. Devane is President, in the case of Lieut. T. W. Butt of your Regt is unfavorable. It has been forwarded to the Adjt. Genl. of N.C. but I presume no commission will be given him.

           I am, Col, Very Respectfully
           Your obt. Servt
           Edward White
           A. A. Genl.

        Head Quarters Clingmans Brigade
                        March 23rd 1864
[To Lt. Col. Devane
Comdg. 61st N.C. Regt.]
Col,

I have the honor to inform you that the following named officers of your Regt have been recommended for appointment and promotion by the Military Board of which Lt. Col. Devane is President. The report of the Board in their cases have been forwarded to the Adjt. & Inspr. Genl. with the report that immediate [action] be taken on them.

    Captain J. H. Robinson, Co. A.
    Lieutenant W. F. Smith   "   "

"	H. H. Raspberry	"	E
"	J. D. Barnes	"	F
"	A. D. Lippitt	"	G
"	N. H. Fennell	"	G
"	S. C. Koonce	"	H

The report of the Board in the case of Lieut. W. H. Joines is unfavorable and I presume no commission will be given him.

           I am, Col, Very Respectfully
           Your obt Servt
           Edward White, A. A. Genl.

        Head Quarters Clingmans Brigade
                        March 30th 1864
Major C. Pickett
A. A. Genl. Dept. N.C.
  Major

I have the honor to request that the

following blanks be furnished for the use of my command.
(45) Forty-five Muster Rolls
(125) One hundred and twenty five Muster & Pay Rolls
(40) Forty Company Monthly Reports
(10) Ten Regimental   "   "
(75) Seventy five Description Rolls

The Muster & Pay Rolls are required to muster the men who are present on the 1st of April in order that they may receive the bounty, due them at the expiration of six months provided they are not absent without leave during that period.

   I am, Major, Very Respectfully
   Your obt. Servt.
   [Signed] T. L. Clingman
   Brig. Genl.

  Head Quarters Clingman's Brigade
   Petersburg VA March 30th 1864
Circular

As it is very desirble that the cultivation of the lands shall not be in any way interferred [sic] with it is hereby directed that the officers and men of this Brigade, in passing to and fro in this vicinity, shall confine themselves to the roads and established paths and shall in no account ride or walk across fields in a state of cultivation.

   By command of
   Brig. Genl. Clingman
   Edward White
   A. A. Genl.

  Head Quarters Clingmans Brigade
     March 31st 1864
[To Col. H. M. McKethan
 " J. V. Jordan
Lt. " J. R. Murchison]
Colonel

In pursuance of orders from the Adm. Secy. of War, the Brig Genl Comdg directs that you send that you send, [sic] with a list of their names, such men of your Regt as are fitted for and desire to join, the Navy, to report at these Head Quarters at 9 A.M. tomorrow promptly. Nine (9) men are required from this Brigade and will be selected from those who volunteer.

   I am, Col., Very Respectfully
   Your obt. Servt.
   Edward White
   A. A. Genl.

  Head Quarters Clingmans Brigade
     April 4, 1864
[To Lt. Col Murchison,
Comdg 8th N.C. Regt.]
Colonel

The Brig Genl Comdg directs that the following named men, transferred from your Regt to the Navy by order of the Sec. of War, be ordered to report to Master Mate L. D. Pitt.

Each one will be furnished with a descriptive list.

J. A. Nobles, Co. A, 8th N.C. Regt.
G. W. Hobbs " B   "
C. L. Hobbs " K   "
J. B. Snowden " B   "
Wm. Oneil " B   "
Mathias Paine " A   "
Am. Pratt " C   "
Jno. L. O'Daniel " B   "
Thos A. Kale " J   "

   I am, Col., Very Respectfully
   Your obt Servt.
   Edward White
   A. A. Genl.

  Head Quarters Clingmans Brigade
     April 4th 1864
[To Col. J. V. Jordan
Comdg. 31st N.C. Regt.]
Colonel

The Brig Genl Comdg directs that the following named men transferred from your Regt to the Navy by order of the Sec. of War be ordered to report to Master Mate L. D. Pitt.

Each man will be furnished with a descriptive list.

Jno. O. Donnel, Co. E, 31st N.C. Regt.
M. Farrell   F "   "

   I am, Col., Very Respectfully
   Your obt Servt.
   Edward White
   A. A. Genl.

  Head Quarters Clingmans Brigade
     April 8th 1864
Capt. E. R. Baird
A. D. C.
 Captain

In compliance with your request I have the honor to suggest the names of the following officers, to be detailed for duty on the Genl. Court Martial now in session in Petersburg.

Captain C. H. Barron Co. C, 8th N.C. Regt.
1st Lieut A. H. Gregory, Co. D " "
Captain S. M. Stanford " C " "
1st Lieut E. T. McKethan " K " "
Capt. Jos. Whitley " K " "
1st Lieut. J. D. Gatlin " G " "

    I am, Captain, Very Respectfully
       Your obt. Servt.
      [Signed] T. L. Clingman
        Brig. Genl.

    Head Quarters Clingmans Brigade
           April 9, 1864
Circular

Hereafter Regimental commanders will always state in their certificates upon applications for leave of absence for officers, whether the applicant has already received one leave under the provisions of Gen Order No 6 Dept of No. Ca.

No applications will be forwarded unless this statement is made.

       By Command of
      Brig Gen Clingman
       Edward White
        A. A. Genl.

    Head Quarters Clingmans Brigade
          April 14 1864
[To Col. J. V. Jordan
Comdg 31st N.C. Regt.]
Colonel

In compliance with orders from Major Genl Pickett you will move immediately with your Regt to Petersburg to take the train for Ivor. You will move with cooking utensils and knapsacks, nothing else. You will report at Gen. Pickett's Head Quarters for instructions.

No time is to be lost.

     I am, Col., Very Respectfully
       Your obt. Servt.
       Edward White
        A. A. Genl.

    Head Quarters Clingmans Brigade
Near Bermuda Hundred VA May 31st 1864
General S. Cooper
Ast. Insp. Genl.
Richmond, VA
    General

I have the honor to enclose herewith the copy of an order summarizing the promotion of certain officers of the Brigade.

    I am, Genl., Very Respectfully
      Your obt. Servt.
     [Signed] T. L. Clingman
       Brig. Genl.

    Head Quarters Clingmans Brigade
         July 19th 1864
General S. Cooper
Adjt. & Insp. Genl
   General

I have the honor to enclose herewith the copy of an order announcing the promotion of certain officers of this Brigade.

    I am, General, Very Respectfully
      Your obt. Servt.
[Signed]   T. L. Clingman
      Brig. Genl.

        Head Quarters
    Clingmans Brigade
     July 20th 1864
General S. Cooper
Asst. & Inspt. Genl.
   General

I respectfully recommend under the late Acts of Congress for the organization of the Staff Capt. Edward White for the appointment of Asst. Adj. Gen. to my Brigade with the rank of Major. Capt. White has been in the service more than two years and has been nearly that period serving in this capacity on my staff.

    I am, General, Very Respectfully
      Your obt. Servt.
   [Signed] T. L. Clingman
      Brig. Genl.

    Head Quarters Clingmans Brigade
       July 20th, 1864
General S. Cooper
   General

Under the late Act of Congress of the organization of the Staff, I respectfully recommend for appointment on my Staff, as Inspector with the rank of major Capt. F. R. Blake. Captain Blake has been in the service more than two years and has been for more than _____ _____ the Inspector of my Brigade. Though severely wounded at Cold Harbor on the first day of June last, yet he is recovering and and is expected soon to be able to do duty again.

     Very Respectfully.
   [Signed] T. L. Clingman
      Brig. Genl.

Head Quarters Clingmans Brigade
July 20th 1864

General S. Cooper
Adjt. & Insp. Genl.
 General

Under the late Act of Congress for the organization of the Staff I respectfully recommend Capt. W. H. S. Burgwyn, for the position of Asst. Adjt. General for my Brigade with the rank of Major. [balance of correspondence unreadable]

Head Quarters Clingmans Brigade
Near Petersburg VA July 28th [1864]

General S. Cooper
Adjt & Inspr. Genl.
 General

In compliance with General Order No. 44, A & I. G. O, current Series, I have the honor to submit the following report of officers of the General Staff Department on duty with my Brigade.

Capt. Edward White, Asst.	Adj. Gen.
" F. R. Blake "	Inspr.
Major A. M. Ervin "	Quartermaster
Major R. S. Gage	Commissary
Captain H. B. Law	Asst. "
1st Lieut. H. S. Puryear	Aide de Camp
P. Du Heaumme	Ordnance officer
Capt. W. H. Burgwyn	Act. A. D. C.

In addition to the above statement, I have to add that I desire to retain Captain Edward White as A. A. General and Major A. M. Ervin as Quarter Master, Major R. S. Gage as Commissary & Lieut. H. S. Puryear as Aide de Camp with rank of Captain. I also desire that under the last Staff Act, Capt. T. R. Blake be Inspector and Capt. W. H. S. Burgwyn be my Second A. A. Genl., and that Lieut. James C. Cooper be second A. D. C. with rank of Lieut.

 Very Respectfully
 [Signed] T. L. Clingman
  Brig. Genl.

Head Quarters Clingmans Brigade
August 24, 1864

Brig. Genl. R. C. Gaither
Adjt. Genl. Of No. Car.
 General

I have the honor to inform you that the position of Lieut. Colonel in the 8th N.C. Regt. has been rendered vacant by the death of Lieut Colonel J. R. Murchison who was wounded at Cold Harbor on the 1st Day of June and died on the 7th of the same month at the White house.

Major R. A. Baird is the officer entitled to promotion by reason of seniority. Should he be promoted Captain A. J. Rogers of Co. "D," will be entitled to the majority by reason of seniority. I enclose his application for promotion.

 Very Respectfully
 [Signed] J. V. Jordan
  Col. Comdg. Brig.

Appendix C

The Men Who Made Up Clingman's Brigade — Officers

Clingman's Brigade[1]

The brigade staff consisted initially of Captain Edward White, assistant adjutant general; Captain Frederick Blake, assistant inspector general; Major Alfred M. Erwin, quartermaster; "Major R. S. Gage," commissary; Lieutenant Du Heaume, ordnance officer and also an English Gentleman; and Lieutenant Hal. S. Puryear, aide-de-camp, a relative of Clingman's.

8th Regiment[2]

First Commander: Henry M. Shaw (colonel), of Currituck County, not only a physician, but also a former member of the United States Congress, was elected colonel of this regiment.

Field Officers: Rufus A. Barrier (major, lieutenant colonel)
James W. Hinton (major, lieutenant colonel)
Henry MacRae (major)
John R. Murchison (major, lieutenant colonel)
William J. Price (lieutenant colonel)
Andrew J. Rogers (major)
James M. Whitson (major, lieutenant colonel, colonel)
Edward C. Yellowley (major)

31st Regiment[3,4]

First Commander: John V. Jordan, of Craven County, was elected colonel of the 31st Regiment when it was organized on September 19, 1861.

Field Officers: Daniel G. Fowle (lieutenant colonel), Wake County
Charles W. Knight (lieutenant colonel)
Edward R. Liles (lieutenant colonel)
John A. D. McKay (major)
Jesse Johnston Yeates (major), Hertford County
Peter Custis (surgeon), Craven County
W. J. Busbee (assistant surgeon), Wake County

51st Regiment[5]

First Commander: John L. Cantwell of Company G was elected colonel. Cantwell, from New Hanover County, resigned, as did his successor, Colonel William A. Allen from Duplin County. In July 1863, Major Hector McKethan, from Cumberland County, was promoted to colonel and continued in this capacity until the end of the war.

Field Officers: William A. Allen (lieutenant colonel)
Caleb B. Hobson (lieutenant colonel)
James R. McDonald (major)
Hector M. McKethan (major, lieutenant colonel, colonel)

61st Regiment[6]

First Commander: James D. Radcliffe was elected colonel in September of 1862, when the regiment was organized. He had formerly served as a colonel in the 18th North Carolina Troops. Radcliffe resigned in October 1864 and was replaced by William S. DeVane from Sampson County, who had been the lieutenant colonel. When DeVane was promoted, Major Edward Mallett moved up to lieutenant colonel. According to Burgwyn, Mallett was one of the best and bravest officers in the entire brigade. He served throughout the war until he was killed at the battle of Bentonville on March 19, 1865.

Field Officers: William S. DeVane (lieutenant colonel, colonel)
 Henry Harding (major)
 Edward Mallett (major, lieutenant colonel)

Notes

1. Burgwyn, p. 482.
2. Sifakis, p. 96.
3. Sifakis, p. 129.
4. Bryan and Meadows, p. 507.
5. Sifakis, pp. 150–151.
6. Sifakis, pp. 160–161.

Appendix D

Miscellaneous Letters

SUBJECT OF LETTER: Burgwyn's father inquiring after his son's conduct while on Clingman's staff

Head Quarters of Clingman's
Brigade near Petersburg
June 25, 1864

[To Col. H. K. Burgwyn,
 father of W. H. S. Burgwyn[1]]
My dear Col.

After long delay your letter reached me in the trenches where I have been for more than fifty days. I have delayed answering it for a week or two in the hope that I might get to some place where I could write with ink but believe it altogether uncertain when I can do that.

You wish me to state particularly what has been the conduct of your son Capt. [W. H. S.] Burgwyn while on my Staff. This it gives me great pleasure to do. He has always shown himself intelligent energetic and efficient. While at Newberne I had an opportunity of seeing that he carried out orders with the same alacrity in danger that he did out of it. In the campaign in this state he was equally courageous and prompt. In the charge on the enemy at Drury's Bluff which decided the contest and defeated the entire army of the enemy though made with only two of my Regiments, he was in the front rank of the attack. Both then and at Bermuda Hundred he rendered good service. At the latter place, he became so unwell that I ordered him to the rear. Nevertheless, I was surprised when I went through Richmond just after we had gotten through a severe fight on the evening of the 31st of May in which with only three regiments of my Brigade and some Cavalry two Corps of the enemy were held in check and that position saved. He came to me in the night though so feeble that I endeavored to induce him to go to the rear. He insisted in lying with me on the ground that night and next day was in the hard struggle of June 1st in which my Brigade defeated the enemy in front and though attacked in flank and rear because Wofford's Georgia Brigade ran away from our left still held its ground and saved to Genl. Lee's Army that most important position. Capt. Burgwyn was very active in assisting to form the new line of battle and while advancing with it to the attack, I learned afterwards, was wounded. I must have been within a few yards of him at the time on the right of the line, but owing to the confusion and noise of the occasion and the many duties that devolved on me I was not aware of the accident to him at the time. It was not until we had retaken our position that I learned from Col. McKethan that he had been wounded near him and sent to the rear. While I deeply regret the injury to him, yet I trust he will soon be able to return to the field. I learn that the new Staff Bill gives me two Adjt. Genls. And I shall be pleased to give him one of them if he cannot do better.

As I have formerly told him I will give him the preference over anyone else if he should prefer to return to me which I hope he will be able soon to do.

As to your other son, I know not what temporary employment I could give him that would suit him and hence as he is so soon to return to school again had he not better remain at home.

I have written this note finally amid the hissing of bullets and the roar of artillery. I have not been out of the trenches for any length of time for more than fifty days. If you think proper you can have this copied with ink. I do not know when it will reach you. _____ the mails onward interrupted. I shall always be pleased to hear from you and to serve you if I can.

In haste,

Yours truly &C.
T. L. Clingman
Brig. Genl.

Letter from Brigadier General Thomas Lanier Clingman to Captain Edward White[2]

Panther Creek, N.C. Sept. 7th, 1865

My dear Capt.

After being detained three months on the road your letter of the 23rd of May reached me. I am much gratified to hear that you reached home in health. Though better myself than when we parted I am still unable to walk without some support from a stick. In time, I shall probably be well.

Though since you wrote you doubtless have heard little through the papers from this state. I have little to add in the way of news for conditions here is not very different I presume from that of your state. There has been a considerable change of feeling among the people however since the close of the war when there was, as you know, a strong union and peace party that the course of the authorities of the United States [word crossed out] has precidenced [sic] a strong feeling of dissatisfaction with that party. The former peace men express much more discontent and hostility than the original secessionists. In fact though there are no outbreaks yet, the hostility to the power of the U.S. seems to be more general than it was. This is owing as much to the activity of the military stationed here as to the other causes. The crops here except the wheat are very abundant.

You state that you think of going abroad. Should you intend to do so it will give me great pleasure to testify to your good character as a gentleman and excellent conduct as an officer. You were connected with my Brigade as Asst. Adj. General from July 1862 to the close of the war and during that whole period your conduct both in the office and in the field was in the highest degree satisfactory and praiseworthy. On all occasions you cheerfully encountered both famine [?] and danger and except while temporarily disabled by a severe wound you were always at your best.

Wheresoever you may go, I hope you will meet with that success and good fortune which you so well deserve.

For myself I am at present waiting the course of events being as for _____ excluded from the amnesty both as an ex-senator and as a Brig. Gen. Puryear is well, but from that other members of the staff, I have heard nothing since we parted.

I shall always be happy to hear from you and will be gratified to serve you in any way that may be offered to me.

Very truly yours

T. L. Clingman
(Late) Brig. Gen.

To. Capt. Edward White, A. A. Gen. of Clingman's Brigade

Letters to and from Hector McKethan, originals in the Edwin Robeson MacKethan Papers, #4298, Southern Historical Collection, Wilson Library, University of North Carolina at Chapel Hill.

Camp Whiting[3]
Dec 13th 1862

[To Hector McKethan from
Lieutenant Colonel William A. Allen[4]]

My Dear Major

The General sent over ten men soon after you left and I went & saw the Board of Examiners. The order[?] was five and myself. The Board expressed many regrets at your not being present and Maj. Hill said he was sure of meeting you after the conversation he had with you yesterday. The Gen'rl, however, seemed exceedingly affable and he and myself put in all sorts of plausible pleas for you and the matter passed off. Their examination of me was pretty rigid, though very pleasant. The formations in column by companies & divisions, closing in mass and the changes of front were the points expressed [on] which the examination was based. I have a new mode of forming a square from Maj. Hill with which I am very much pleased. I will explain it to you when you come. They examined pretty particularly also about the advancing in line of battle. I am perhaps no competent judge of how I stood. I suppose about mediocre. The Capt will begin to Drill the Brigade on Monday next.

The news about Kinston is rather exciting. I should not be surprised if you join us in that locality unless you return very soon. The abolitionists are evidently threatening that place. That course will be presumed [and] is not yet indicated. No new orders.

Very truly,
Wm. A. Allen

Camp Whiting[5]
Feb. 5, 1863

[Hector McKethan to his
brother Edwin Turner McKethan[6]]

Dear Ed

I have nothing to write but realy [sic] lack for something to do. It has been raining all day and I have seldom spent such a long dull day. No mail north or south and nothing worth reading in this Journal. As I predicted the Geo.[rgia] & SC [South Carolina] troops are ordered off and are going as fast as possible and I understand the 61st Reg. of our Brigade goes tomorrow and was elected I suppose, because Radclif is in SC and was stationed down near Charleston a long time last summer.

Whether any man of us will go is uncertain but I think not for some boddy [sic] must be keeped [sic] here. I am quite willing to stay where I am for the present. The Yanks will make a dish ___ effort if they do attack Charleston and will have a blood time of it. Charleston is nearly as important to them as Richmond. Should the fight last long we may be sent for no telling, Lt. Murphy goes up home tomorrow to see his sister, Mrs. Devane who is very ill. If he will also try to fill up his company as he learned that the conscripts are to be examined in Sampson on Monday next, but don't know whether all meet at Clinton or at the head Qrts of the different regiments, if so you might do something in Mington [?] and could easily go by Uncle Jameses. Murphy says for you to come to Clinton and go foraging with him his address will be Clinton he will not be off long. I wish all our company could be filled with good men for a few hard fights might thin us out mightly. I sent three weeks ago by one of Gen'l Whiting the names of any officer from each co. to go home to fill up company, but as yet no detail has been made in this Brigade, and I fear we will get but few men.

I have urged on Clingman with all my power the importance of it, but Whiting will sign nothing and will let no one off over any pretext whatever. I have heard nothing of Pa yet and thought I would send your money by him. Please do say if you can tell what I have sent home and how much Pa sent me as I wish to keep an account of it. I have drawn 8 months this pay as Major $1250 and my month as Capt $130 making $1380 and certainly have sent much of it home but can form no idea, but my letters if Rufid [?] would show. When I get my commission as Col will get $190 per month and can certainly save some then but it is time enough when I get it to calculate on that. Have not heard a word from Raleigh since Clingman wrote to Genl. Martin, hope to hear everyday and am a little impatient but don't see why I should be uneasy. I should think Pa would finish up all his Buggy and light material and trim with whatever he can get for you know there is but little trimming about some buggies, say a Pump Handle, Light tire can be used on the ambulances if the fillys are made heavy & can be beveled to fit the tires; sheep skin would make good tops for cushions. Skipper in Sloan's company wants a knapsack like those we make. See Peter Hale & find if all our old Co had are gone if not ask him to send me one and if all gone send one any way for Skipper he is our cook and a clean fellow. You had better stay until you get perfectly well. I see some one advertises trace chains in the Journal. W. H. McRary & Co I think in paper about a wk ago, close up all old acts. And see how the Jas. Sunday matter stands. It is in awful fix and I can proove that that Sunday admitted to me his act was not correct. You will find it in the acts. He charged us with all Harness and often neglected to Cr when paid and if never paid one should not loose as we did not run all the risks and make no profit. W McL McKay is largely in our debt and his matter should be settled and he too will get into us if Pa dont look sharp. He wishes to charge an awful fig. For defending Tom ___ Banks & some one else we employed and did but little. You will find many other such cases first off from year to year because troubilsom [sic] and if Pa or I am to die never could be settled. How about the Parson McNair & L McKellar notes would it not be better for us to pay them while money is plenty and have the matter all in our own hands if there is no honorable way to evade them and I dont think there is Col Alex Murchison is another hard old act & should be settled some how The act of the McCallum children too should be examined & is in a bad fix some day the children may call for a showing & then who can make it.

Dont hurry back stay until you are perfectly well. Tell Guss[7] I suppose he has forgotten entirely how to write and Ma should make him study every night. Dont let him have too much money and make him set down all expenditures. Dont let him get articles at the stores and have them charged it will ruin any boy. Try to teach him the value of money and industry but dont expect to do all this in a day. He has too much spirit to be checked to sudenly and might rare up & fall over backwards like my horse. Howe about Bullet & the price of corn &. Send me the $5 in specie if you can get it even at 2 for one. No more tonight

Your Brother
Hector

Camp Whiting⁸
Feby 4/63

[Hector McKethan to
 brother Edwin McKethan]
Dear Ed

I sent by Anderson my old cape of which I wish a vest made and sent me as early as you can. I have the buttons and will use one sett [of] 7 on both vests. Send my Black horse back as soon as he gets well as it will cost me nothing to feed him here and corn is high although when you send anything hereafter let me know the prices and put in enough to cover the costs & charges. I have heard nothing of Pa yet if he comes back this way will be here in a few days. By the paper today I see Charleston is to be attacked if true troops will be sent from here but I doubt if our Brigade goes but no telling. I have not a particle of other news now. May hear something by morning.

Your Bro.
Hector
Over

I wish you to get and send me $5 in specie by Hidie if it can be got. I borrowed today $5 in specie to purchase a nice hat and if I had paid Confederate money would of have had to pay $15. They charge three for one on the Store Tell Hidie we will be paid off again in a few days.
I collected of Rockwell your pay for two months up to Jan. 1863 $160 One Hundred & Sixty dollars will send first chance. Tis awful cold tonight.

Camp Whiting⁹
Wednesday
Dec 14 [1864]

[Hector McKethan to father,
 Alfred Augustus McKethan, Sr.]
Dear Pa

We are ordered to be ready to move at short notice and only reliable information of the advance of the enemy. I am all ready and my Reg was never in better trim. We lack nothing unless it be a few guns that are in bad orders and would like to exchange others. Rev. Colin Shaw¹⁰ reported for duty today & will be of value to us all as he has had 12 ms. Experience and is fitt for any position and will be invaluable to the Reg as an adviser in camp & on field. All the boats & every man under 45 are being pressed in today for the emergency — when or which way we move no one in Reg knows. I send today in Capt. McDonald's trunk my overcoat (have another), 1 pr boots (too small), & 1 pr shoes (that Ed can have cost me $4 and overcoat $25). Also 1 pr pants. You can call on Lieut [?] for them. Petition we[nt] to the Genl today signed by all the officers for me for Col and another signed by 27 officers (all except A & B & the Capt of D) for Sloan & Norment.

Your son H McKethan

My new boots will do first rate I think unless too short. Our mess takes at cost all we get from home. We have a fine mess — Stout officers — Hidie Rockwell & Rev C. Shaw. Underwood forwarded his resignation a week ago for reason that he wishes time to attend to his father & brothers estates. Capt McD sent in his today — he is badly hurt because he did not get a single vote — Neither will be accepted in my opinion without surgeons certificates. Ed had better send certificate every ten days.

H.

Report of Inspection of the 31st N.C. Regiment by Lt. L. M. Butten, C. S. A.¹¹

Division Head Quarters
Wilmington, N.C.
Jany 12th 1863

Capt. Mallery P. King, A. A. Genl.
Capt.

In pursuance to Special orders No. 2 of these Hd. Qrs. I have the honor to make the following report of an Inspection of the 31st Regt N.C. Vols. Col. J. V. Jordan Comdng.

Field Officers Col J. V. Jordan   Present
"   "   Lt. Col. E. R. Liles   "
"   "   Maj. J. J. Yates   Resigned
              Company officers
Co. C.   Capt. N. J. Long   on sick leave
"   A   Brevt. 2nd Lieut. J. L. Everitt absent without leave

Discipline

Apparently very good. It is very evident that this Regt. has been instructed to be respectful to their Superior officrs. The Col. and Lt Col. appear acquainted with their duties as commanding officers.

General Appearance	Good
Material of the Regt.	Fine
Clothing	Tolerable

Arms. This Regt is armed with Belgian Rifles, Enfield Rifles and altered muskets. Belgian Rifles 160 Enfield Rifles 29 Altered Muskets 678. The arms are very good, and kepted in excellent order. Showing that the company officers understand their duty. The accretrements [sic] are kept in excellent order. The ammunition is in good condition and the Regt is supplied with 78 rounds to the man.

The Adjutants office

The adjutant is well versed in his duties. His Books are well kept & he thoroughly understands his business.

Hospital

This Regt has no Hospital. The sick are sent to the City, the Surgeon is off on duty in the city in the Medical Board of Examiners.

Quartermaster and Commissary

The latter has resigned and Lieut Liles of Co. B, acting in his place. The former on leave for the purpose of obtaining his bonds. Quarter-Master Sargent acting for him. I have the honor to be

Very Respectfully
Your Obt. Servt.
(Signed) L. M. Butler
Inspecting Officer

Notes

1. Original letter in W. H. S. Burgwyn Papers, Department of Archives and History, Raleigh, North Carolina. Col. H. K. Burgwyn, an old friend of Clingman's, was the father of W. H. S. Burgwyn, on Clingman's brigade staff.

2. Courtesy of Tod Tompson, a descendant of Edward White.

3. From William A. Allen to Hector McKethan, 13 December 1862, in the Edwin Robeson MacKethan Papers #4298, Southern Historical Collection, Wilson Library, University of North Carolina at Chapel Hill.

4. Lieutenant Colonel William A. Allen, previously a 2nd Lieutenant of 1st Company C, 12th Regiment, N.C. Troops (2nd Regiment N.C. Volunteers), was appointed captain in Company C, 51st Regiment on February 11, 1862. He was appointed a Lieutenant Colonel on April 30, 1862, and transferred to the field and staff of the 51st Regiment. He was present until he resigned on January 5, 1863, because of "imputation[s] against my character" and also because of "rheumatism." Allen was being court-martialed at this time for entering camp at Rockfish Church "intoxicated," on the night of December 30, 1862, and for using "the most abusive and insulting language to Major Hector McKethan" that night. He also challenged Major McKethan "to fight him with pistols." This letter was written before the unfortunate incident which resulted in Allen's court-martial and his subsequent resignation, which was accepted on January 19, 1863. Manarin and Jordan, XII, pp. 276, 299,

5. From Hector McKethan to his brother Edwin Turner McKethan, 5 February 1863, in the Edwin Robeson MacKethan Papers #4298, Southern Historical Collection, Wilson Library, University of North Carolina at Chapel Hill.

6. Edwin Turner McKethan served as 1st lieutenant in Company K, 51st Regiment, N.C. Troops, part of Clingman's Brigade. He was born February 8, 1840, in Cumberland County. Edwin was reported "absent sick" from November 7, 1862, through February 28, 1863, but returned to duty during March and April 1863. He continued present for active duty until September-October 1864, when he was reported to be sick in a Fayetteville, N.C. hospital. He went on furlough in November 1864 and retired to the Invalid Corps December 13, 1864. See Manarin and Jordan, North Carolina Troops, 1861–1865: A Roster, XII, p. 382.

7. Hector McKethan's younger brother, Alfred Augustus "Gus" McKethan, Jr., was born in 1847. See "Descendancy Chart for James McKethan," at http://mason.math.tntech.edu/jasmck3.htm. Augustus A. McKethan, Jr., enlisted April 28, 1864, in Company K, 51st Regiment, North Carolina Troops. He was wounded in Virginia in June 1864, but was able to return to duty by September. He was appointed 3rd Lieutenant on November 4, 1864, and transferred to Company B, 51st Regiment, North Carolina Troops. Gus McKethan was with the regiment at the surrender and was paroled at Greensboro on May 1, 1865. Manarin and Jordan, XII, pp. 289, 387.

8. From Hector McKethan to his brother Edwin Turner McKethan, 4 February 1863, in the Edwin Robeson MacKethan Papers #4298, Southern Historical Collection, Wilson Library, University of North Carolina at Chapel Hill.

9. From Hector McKethan to his father, Alfred Augustus McKethan, Sr., 14 December 1864 (?), in the Edwin Robeson MacKethan Papers #4298, Southern Historical Collection, Wilson Library, University of North Carolina at Chapel Hill.

10. Colin Shaw, a Presbyterian chaplain, served in the 18th Regiment, N.C. Troops (8th Regiment, N.C. Volunteers), before transferring to the 51st Regiment around January 1, 1863. However, he resigned on October 27, 1863, because "the condition of my family

is such as to require my personal attention which cannot be longer delayed without serious loss." Manarin and Jordan, XII, p. 277.

11. Lt. L. M. Butler, Inspecting Officer to Capt. Mallery P. King, A. A. Genl., Division Head Quarters, Wilmington, N.C., January 12th, 1863, in Thomas L. Clingman Papers, Southern Historical Collection, Wilson Library, Chapel Hill, North Carolina.

Bibliography

Primary Sources

Manuscripts and Miscellaneous Papers

Auburn University, Auburn, Alabama
  James H. Lane Papers
Clingman, Thomas L. "The Tobacco Remedies—The Greatest Medical Discovery." North Carolina Collection, Wilson Library, University of North Carolina, Chapel Hill, North Carolina.
Manuscript Collection, Duke University, Durham, North Carolina.
  Charles Lanman Papers
  Thomas Lanier Clingman Papers
  Charles Van Noppen Papers
National Archives, Washington, D.C.
  Record Group 109, Regimental Returns and Field and Staff Muster Rolls
North Carolina Department of Archives and History, Raleigh, North Carolina.
  Paul B. Barringer Papers
  W. H. S. Burgwyn Papers
  Asa J. Daniels Papers
  Thomas Lanier Clingman Papers
  John Wright Family Papers
  Zebulon B. Vance Papers
Southern Historical Collection, University of North Carolina, Chapel Hill, North Carolina.
  Clingman-Puryear Papers
  Thomas Lanier Clingman Papers
  William Lucius Faison Papers
  Edwin Robeson MacKethan Papers
  David Outlaw Papers
  William S. Pettigrew Papers

County Records

Buncombe County, North Carolina, Deeds, Register of Deeds' Office, Asheville, North Carolina.
Rowan County, North Carolina, Deeds, Register of Deeds' Office, Salisbury, North Carolina.
Rowan County, North Carolina, Wills, Clerk of Court's Office, Salisbury, North Carolina.
Surry County, North Carolina, Wills, Clerk of court's Office, Dobson, North Carolina.

Published Sources

Public and Official Records

Absher, Mrs. W. O. *Abstracts of Surry County, North Carolina, Deed Books A, B, and C (1770–1778)*. Easley, S.C.: Southern Historical Press, 1981.
Absher, Mrs. W. O., and Mrs. Robert K. Hayes. *Abstracts of Surry County, North Carolina, Court Minutes*, I. Privately published, n.d.
Biographical Directory of the American Congress 1774–1971. Washington, D.C.: Government Printing Office, 1971.
Confederate States of America, War Department. *Regulations for the Army of the Confederate States, 1863*. 2nd ed. Richmond: J. W. Randolph, 1863.
Congressional Globe, XIII–XXIV, 1843–1861.
Cook, Gerald Wilson. "List of Taxable Property in Surry County, North Carolina, for the Year 1812." In *The Descendants of Claiborne Howard*. Cholone, Republic of Vietnam: privately published, 1960.
Crow, Mr. and Mrs. Judson, comp. *McDowell County, North Carolina, Land Entry Abstracts*, Vol. No. 1, 1843–1869. Spartanburg, S.C.: The Reprint Co., 1982.
Laws of North Carolina—1822, Chapter CX.

Linn, Mrs. Stahle, Jr. *Abstracts of Wills and Estate Records of Rowan County, North Carolina, 1753–1815, and Tax Lists of 1759 and 1778.* Salisbury, N.C.: privately published, 1980.

"Marriage Bonds of Goochland County." *William and Mary Quarterly*, Series I, VI–VII (1897–1899), pp. 98–106.

North Carolina, Adjutant General's Department. *Muster Rolls of the Soldiers of the War of 1812: Detached from the Militia of North Carolina in 1812 and 1814.* 1851; rpt. Winston-Salem, N.C.: The Barber Printing co., Inc., 1926.

Official Records of the Union and Confederate Navies in the War of the Rebellion. 30 vols. Washington, D.C.: United States Government Printing Office, 1880–1927.

Potter, Dorothy W. *1820 Federal Census of North Carolina.* Vol. LI, Surry County, North Carolina. Privately published, 1971.

Saunders, William L., ed. *The Colonial Records of North Carolina.* 10 vols. Raleigh, N.C.: Joseph Daniels Printing Office, 1880–1905.

The War of the Rebellion. A Compilation of the Official Records of the Union and Confederate Armies. 70 vols., 130 parts. Washington, D.C.: United States Government Printing Office, 1880–1905.

Writings, Diaries, Speeches, and Correspondence

Anderson, R. H. "Official Diary of First Corps, A. N. V., while Commanded by Lt.-General R. H. Anderson from June 1st to October 18, 1864." *Southern Historical Papers*, VII, 1879, pp. 504–512.

Brooks, Aubrey Lee., ed. *The Papers of Walter Clark.* 2 vols. Chapel Hill, N.C.: University of North Carolina Press, 1948.

Brooks, Benjamin F. *Private and Official Correspondence of Benjamin F. Butler During the Period of the Civil War.* 5 vols. Privately published, 1917.

Burgwyn, W. H. S. *A Captain's War.* Shippensburg, Pa.: White Mane Publishing Co., 1994.

Chestnut, Mary. *Mary Chestnut's Civil War.* Ed. C. Van Woodward. New Haven, Conn.: Yale University Press, 1981.

Clingman, Thomas L. *Selections from the Speeches and Writings of Honorable Thomas L. Clingman of North Carolina with Additions and Explanatory Notes.* 2nd ed. Raleigh: John Nichols, Book and Job Printer, 1878.

Clingman, Thomas L. "Address—Delivered at Davidson College, June 25, 1875. *Selections from the Speeches and Writings of Honorable Thomas L. Clingman of North Carolina with Additions and Explanatory Notes.* 2nd ed. Raleigh, N.C.: John Nichols, Book and Job Printers, 1878, pp. 39–53.

Clingman, Thomas L. "Speech: Delivered at the Charlotte Centennial, May 20, 1875." *Selections from the Speeches and Writings of Honorable Thomas L. Clingman of North Carolina with Additions and Explanatory Notes.* 2nd ed. Raleigh, N.C.: John Nichols, Book and Job Printers, 1878, pp. 110–112.

Clingman, Thomas L. "Volcanic Action in North Carolina: Lecture Delivered before the Washington Philosophical Society, May 1874." *Selections from the Speeches and Writings of Honorable Thomas L. Clingman of North Carolina with Additions and Explanatory Notes.* 2nd ed. Raleigh, N.C.: John Nichols, Book and Job Printers, 1878, pp. 78–83.

DeLeon, T. C. *Four Years in Rebel Capitals.* Mobile, Ala.: The Gossip Printing Co., 1890.

Edmondston, Catherine D. *Journal of a Secesh Lady: The Diary of Catherine Ann Devereaux Edmondston.* Eds. Beth G. Crabtree and James W. Patton. Raleigh, N.C.: North Carolina Department of Cultural Resources, 1979.

Ellis, John W. *Papers of John Willis Ellis.* 2 vols. Ed. Nobel J. Tolbert. Raleigh, N.C.: North Carolina Department of Archives and History, 1964.

Freeman, Benjamin H. *The Confederate Letters of Benjamin H. Freeman.* Ed. Stuart T. Wright. Hicksville, N.Y.: Exposition Press, 1974.

Freeman, Douglas S., ed. *Lee's Dispatches.* New York: G. P. Putnam's Sons, 1957.

Girard, Charles. *Visit to Confederate States in 1863: Memoirs Addressed to Napoleon III.* Trans. William S. Hoole. 1864; rpt. Tuscaloosa, Ala.: Confederate Publishing Co., 1962.

Graham, William Alexander. *Papers of William Alexander Graham.* 6 vols. Eds. J. G. De Roulhac Hamilton and Max R. Williams. Raleigh, N.C.: North Carolina Department of Cultural Resources, 1973–1976.

Henderson, C. F. R. *The Civil War: A Soldier's View.* Ed. Jay Luvaas. Chicago, Ill.: University of Chicago Press, 1958.

Hoke, R. F. "Battle of Drewry's Bluff, May 16, 1864, Report of General R. F. Hoke." *Southern Historical Society Papers* XII (1884), 227–229.

Johnson, B. R. "Operations from the 6th to the 11th of May, 1864 — Report of General B. R. Johnson." *Southern Historical Society Papers*, XII (1884), 274–282.

Johnston, Frontis N., ed. *The Papers of Zebulon B. Vance*. 2 vols. Raleigh, N.C.: North Carolina Department of Archives and History, 1963.

Jones, Iredell. "Letters from Fort Sumter." *Southern Historical Society* Papers, XII (1884), 253–258.

Jones, John B. *Rebel War Clerk's Diary*. 2 vols. Ed. Howard Swiggett. 1866; rpt. New York: Old Hickory Bookshop, 1935.

Jones, Samuel. *The Siege of Charleston*. New York: The Neal Publishing Co., 19__.

Kean, Robert G. H. *Inside the Confederate Government: The Diary of Robert Garlick Hill Kean*. Ed. Edward Younger. New York: Oxford University Press, 1957.

Lee, Robert E. *Wartime Papers of Robert E. Lee*. Eds. Clifford Dowdy and Louis H. Manarin. Boston: Little, Brown and Co., 1961.

Lord, Walter, ed. *The Fremantle Diary, being the Journal of Lieutenant Colonel James Arthur Lyon Fremantle, Coldstream Guards, on his Three Months in the Southern States*. Boston: Little, Brown and Company, 1954.

Pender, William D. *The General to His Lady (The Civil War Letters of William Dorsey Pender to Fanny Pender)*. Ed. William W. Hassler. Chapel Hill, N.C.: University of North Carolina Press, 1965.

Pickett, George. "Report of General Pickett." *Southern Historical Society Papers*, IX, No. 1 (1881), 1–11.

Pressley, John G. "Diary of Lieutenant Colonel John G. Pressley." *Southern Historical Society Papers*, XIV (1886), 35–62.

Ross, Fitzgerald. *Cities and Camps of Confederate States*. Ed. Richard B. Harwell. 1865; rpt. Urbana, Ill.: University of Illinois Press, 1958.

Rowland, Dunbar. *Jefferson Davis, Constitutionalist. Letters, Papers and Speeches*. 10 vols. Jackson, Miss.: Mississippi Department of Archives and History, 1923.

Yancey, William L. *Memoranda of the Late Affair of Honor Between Honorable T. L. Clingman, of North Carolina, and Honorable W. L. Yancey, of Alabama*. Washington, D.C.: by the author, 1845.

Secondary Sources

General Works

Abbott, Lyman, et al., eds. *The National Cyclopaedia of American Biography*. 30 vols. New York: James T. White and company, 1897.

Alumni Office of the General Alumni Association. *The University of North Carolina at Chapel Hill Directory*. Durham, N.C.: Seeman Printery, Inc., 1954.

Andrews, J. Cutler. *The South Reports the War*. Princeton, N.J.: Princeton University Press, 1970.

Appleton's Cyclopedia of American Biography. 6 vols. New York: Appleton & Co., 1887.

Arthur, John Preston. *Western North Carolina: A History 1730–1913*. 1914; rpt. Spartanburg, S.C.: The Reprint Company, 1973.

Ashe, Samuel A'Court. *History of North Carolina*. 2 vols. Raleigh, N.C.: Edwards and Broughton Printing Company, 1925.

Barefoot, Daniel W. *General Robert F. Hoke: Lee's Modest Warrior*. Winston-Salem, N.C.: John F. Blair, Publisher, 1996.

Barrett, John G. *The Civil War in North Carolina*. Chapel Hill, N.C.: University of North Carolina Press, 1963.

Battle, Kemp P. *History of the University of North Carolina: From Its Beginnings to the Death of President Swain, 1789–1868.*

Beck, Emily Morison, ed. *Bartlett's Familiar Quotations*. 15th rev. ed. Boston: Little, Brown & Co, 1980.

Blum, John M., Edmund S. Morgan, Willie Lee Rose, et al. *The National Experience: A History of the United States*. 3rd Ed. New York: Harcourt Brace Jovanovich, 1973.

Boatner, Mark M., III. *The Civil War Dictionary*. Revised ed. New York: Vintage Books, 1991.

Boykin, James H. *North Carolina in 1861*. New York: Bookman Associates, 1961.

Brumfield, Lewis Shore. *Thomas Lanier Clingman and the Shallow Ford Families*. Yadkinville, N.C.: Typescript, privately published, 1989, pp. 1–157.

Buchard, Peter. *One Gallant Rush: Robert Gould Shaw and his Brave Black Regiment*. New York: St. Martin's Press, 1965.

Burton, E. Milby. *The Siege of Charleston 1861–1865*. Columbia, S.C.: University of South Carolina Press, 1970.

Casstevens, Frances H., ed. *Heritage of Yadkin County, North Carolina*. Winston-Salem, N.C.: Hunter Publishing Co., 1981.

Clark, Walter. Ed. *Histories of the Several Regiments and Battalions from North Carolina in the Great War, 1861–1865, Written by Members of the Respective Commands.* 5 vols. Goldsboro, N.C.: Nash Brothers, 1901.

Concise Dictionary of American Biography. New York: Charles Scribner's Sons, 1964.

Connor, R. D. W. *History of North Carolina.* 6 vols. Chicago, Ill.: Lewis Publishing Company, 1919.

Crosse, Melba C., comp. *Patillo, Pattillo, Pattullo, and Pittillo Families.* Fort Worth, Tex: American Reference Publishing Co., 1972.

Denny, Robert E. *The Civil War Years: A Day-By-Day Chronicle.* New York: Random House, 1991.

Dupuy, R. Ernest, and Trevor N. Dupuy. *Compact History of the Civil War.* New York: Hawthorn Books, Inc., 1960.

Eaton, Clement. *A History of the Southern Confederacy.* New York: The Macmillan Co., 1954.

Evans, Clement A., ed. *A Confederate Military History.* 12 vols. Atlanta, Ga.: Confederate Publishing Co., 1899.

Foote, Shelby. *The Civil War: A Narrative.* 3 vols. New York: Random House, 1958–1963.

Freeman, Douglas S. *Lee's Lieutenants: A Study in Command.* 3 vols. New York: Charles Scribner's Sons, 1942–1944.

Grant, Daniel L. *Alumni History of the University of North Carolina.* 2nd ed. Durham, N.C.: Christian and King Printing Co., 1924.

Hamilton, J. G. De Roulhac. *History of North Carolina.* 3 vols. Chicago, Ill.: The Lewis Publishing Co., 1919.

Henderson, Archibald. *North Carolina: The Old North State.* 5 vols. Chicago, Ill.: The Lewis Publishing Co., 1941.

Hendrick, Burton J. *Statesmen of the Lost Cause.* Boston: Little, Brown & Co., 1939.

Hollingsworth, J. G. *History of Surry County or Annals of Northwest North Carolina.* Privately published by the author, n.p., 1935.

Hoole, William S. *Lawley Covers the Confederacy.* Tuscaloosa, Ala.: Confederate Publishing Co., Inc., 1964.

Horn, John. *The Petersburg Campaign: The Destruction of the Weldon Railroad, Deep Bottom, Globe Tavern, and Reams Station, August 14–25, 1864.* 2nd ed. Lynchburg, Va.: H. E. Howard, Inc., 1991.

Hughes, Nathaniel Cheairs, Jr. *Bentonville: The Final Battle of Sherman & Johnston.* Chapel Hill, N.C.: University of North Carolina Press, 1996.

Hummel, Elizabeth H. *Hicks' History of Granville County, North Carolina.* Oxford, N.C.: Coble Printing Co., 1965.

Jeffrey, Thomas E. *Thomas Lanier Clingman: Fire Eater from the Carolina Mountains.* Athens, Ga.: The University of Georgia Press, 1998.

Johnson, Allen, and Dumas Malone, eds. *Dictionary of American Biography.* 16 vols. New York: Charles Scribner's Sons, 1958.

Johnson, Clint. *Touring the Carolinas' Civil War Sites.* Winston-Salem, N.C.: John F. Blair, Publisher, 1966.

Kerr, Mary H., comp. *Warren County, North Carolina, Records.* 3 vols. Granville-Warren Committee of the National Society of the Colonial Dames of America in North Carolina, n.p., 1967, typed.

Kitchum, Richard M., ed. *The American Heritage Picture History of the Civil War.* 2 vols. New York: American Heritage Publishing Co., Inc. 1960.

Lanman, Charles. *Biographical Annals of the Civil Government of the United States.* 2nd ed. New York: M. Morrison, 1887.

Lefler, Hugh Talmage, and Albert Ray Newsome. *The History of a Southern State: North Carolina.* 3rd ed. Chapel Hill, N.C.: University of North Carolina Press, 1975.

Livermore, Thomas L. *Numbers and Losses in the Civil War.* Bloomington, Ind.: Indiana University Press, 1957.

Mcallister, D. S. *Genealogical Record of the Descendants of Col. Alexander McAllister of Cumberland County, N.C.; Also of Mary and Isabella McAllister.* Richmond, Va.: Whitney and Shepperson, Printers, 1900.

Manarin, Louis H., comp. *Guide to Military Organization and Installations in North Carolina 1861–1865.* Raleigh: North Carolina Confederate Centennial Commission, 1961.

Manarin, Louis H., and Weymouth T. Jordan, Jr., eds. *North Carolina Troops, 1861–1865: A Roster.* 14 vols. Raleigh, N.C.: North Carolina Department of Archives and History, 1966–1998.

Miller, Francis T., ed. *The Photographic History of the Civil War.* 10 vols. New York: Castle Books, 1957.

Moore, John W. *Roster of North Carolina Troops in the War Between the States.* 4 vols. Raleigh, N.C.: Ashe and Gatling, 1882.

National Society Daughters of the American

Revolution. *DAR Patriot Index.* Washington, D.C.: National Society Daughters of the American Revolution, 1967.

Pleasants, Henry, Jr., and George H. Straley. *Inferno at Petersburg.* Philadelphia: Chilton Company, 1961.

Powell, William S., ed. *Dictionary of North Carolina Biography.* 2 vols. Chapel Hill, N.C.: University of North Carolina Press, 1979.

Rutledge, William E., Jr. *An Illustrated History of Yadkin County, 1850–1965.* 1st ed. Yadkinville, N.C.: Privately published by the author, 1965.

Sandburg, Carl. *Abraham Lincoln: The War Years.* 4 vols. New York: Harcourt, Brace & Co., 1939.

Seitz, Don C. *Famous American Duels.* New York: Thomas Y. Crowell, 1929.

Sifakis, Stewart. *Compendium of the Confederate Armies: North Carolina.* New York: Facts on File, 1992.

Sitterson, J. C. *The Secession Movement in North Carolina.* Chapel Hill, N.C.: University of North Carolina Press, 1939.

Sloan, John A. *North Carolina in the War Between the States.* Washington, D.C.: Rufus H. Darby, 1883.

Sommers, Richard J. *Richmond Redeemed: The Siege at Petersburg.* New York: Doubleday and Co., Inc., 1981.

Sondley, Foster A. *A History of Buncombe County.* 2 vols. Asheville, N.C.: Advocate Printing Company, 1930.

Stanley, Donald W., Hazel R. Hartman, and Anne E. Sheek. *Forsyth County, North Carolina, Cemetery Records*, vol. II. Winston-Salem, N.C.: Hunter Publishing Co., 1976, 340.

Trefousse, Hans L. *Ben Butler: The South Called Him Beast!* New York: Octagon Books, 1974.

Trudeau, Noah Andre. *The Last Citadel: Petersburg, Virginia, June 1864–April 1865.* Boston: Little, Brown & Company, 1991.

Wakelyn, Jon L. *Biographical Dictionary of the Confederacy.* Westport, Conn.: Greenwood Press, 1977.

Warner, Ezra J. *Generals in Gray.* Baton Rouge, La.: Louisiana State University Press, 1959.

The Wayne County Historical Association, Inc. and the Old Dobbs County Genealogical Society. *Heritage of Wayne County.* Winston-Salem, N.C.: Hunter Publishing Co., 1982.

Webster's Biographical Dictionary. Springfield, Mass.: G. & C. Merriam Co., 1970.

Wheeler, John H. *Historical Sketches of North Carolina from 1584 to 1851.* 1851, rpt. Baltimore: Regional Publishing Co. 1964.

Who Was Who in America: Historical Volume, 1607–1896. Chicago: Marquis Who's Who, 1967.

Wright, Marcus J. *General Officers of the Confederate Army.* New York: The Neal Publishing Co., 1911.

Memoirs

Alexander, E. P. *Military Memoirs of a Confederate.* New York: Charles Scribner's Sons, 1912.

Battle, Kemp P. *Memoirs of an Old-Time Tar Heel.* Ed. William James Battle. Chapel Hill: University of North Carolina Press, 1945.

Capers, Ellison. "South Carolina." In *A Confederate Military History.* Ed. Clement A. Evans. 12 vols. Atlanta, Ga.: Confederate Publishing Co., 1899.

Cheshire, Joseph Blunt. *Nonnula.* Chapel Hill, N.C.: University of North Carolina Press, 1930.

Davis, Jefferson. *The Rise and Fall of the Confederacy.* 2 vols. New York: D. Appleton, 1881.

Eggleston, George C. *A Rebel's Recollections.* 5th ed. Bloomington, Ind.: Indiana University Press, 1959.

Ford, Arthur Peronneau and Marion Johnstone Ford. *Life in the Confederate Army Being Personal Experiences of a Private Soldier in the Confederate Army; and Some Experiences and Sketches of Southern Life.* New York: The Neale Publishing Company, 1905.

Grant, U. S. *Memoirs and Selected Letters.* 2 vols in 1. New York: The Library of America, 1990.

Grant, U. S. *Personal Memoirs of U. S. Grant.* 2 vols. New York: Charles L. Webster and Co., 1892.

Hill, D. H., Jr. "North Carolina." In *A Confederate Military History.* Ed. Clement A. Evans. 12 vols. Atlanta, Ga.: Confederate Publishing Co., 1899.

Howe, W. W. *Kinston, Whitehall and Goldsboro Expedition,* December 1862. D. Appleton and Co., 1874.

Johnston, Joseph E. *Narrative of Military Operations.* New York: D. Appleton and Co., 1874.

Logan, Mrs. John A. *Reminiscences of a Soldier's Wife.* New York: Charles Scribner's Sons, ca. 1913.

Long, A. L. *Memoirs of Robert E. Lee: His Military and Personal History Embracing a Large Amount of Information Hitherto Unpublished.* New York: J. M. Stoddart & Co., 1886.

Pollard, Edward A. *The Lost Cause: A New Southern History of the War of the Confederates.* New York: E. B. Treat & Co., 1867.

Roman, Alfred. *The Military Operations of General Beauregard in the War Between the States, Including a Brief Personal Sketch and a Narrative of His Services in the War with Mexico, 1846–1848.* 2 vols. New York: Harper & Brothers, 1884.

Sorrell, G. Moxley. *Recollections of a Confederate Staff Officer.* 1905; rpt. Nashville, Tenn.: Mclowat-Mercer Press, Inc., 1958.

Wheeler, John H. *Reminiscences and Memoirs.* 1884, rpt. Baltimore: Genealogical Publishing Co., 1966.

Articles and Pamphlets

A[ugustus], H[enry]. J[arratt]. "General Thomas L. Clingman." *University of North Carolina Magazine,* New Series XVIII, No. 4 (April 1901), 166–170.

Ammen, Daniel. "Du Pont and the Port Royal Expedition." In *Battles and Leaders of the Civil War.* Eds. Robert U. Johnson and Clarence C. Buel. 1887; rpt. Secaucus, N.J.: Castle, 1982, I, 687–689.

Arthur, Billy. "The Cure-All of General Clingman." *State* L (July 1982), 9–10.

Ashe, Samuel A. "Life at Fort Wagner." *Confederate Veteran,* XXXV (1927), 254–256.

Ashe, Samuel A. "North Carolina in the War Between the States," *Confederate Veteran,* XXXVII (1929), 170–175.

Bartholomew, Robert H. "Tar Heal Fought Duel with Foe in Congress: Clingman Met Yancey in 1845. *Journal & Sentinel* (Winston-Salem, North Carolina), 29 June 1952.

Barton, General. "Report of General Barton." In *Southern Historical Society Papers,* IX (1881), 9–10.

Bassett, John S. "The Congressional Career of T. L. Clingman," *The Trinity Historical Records,* IV (1900), 48–63.

Beauregard, G. T. "The Defense of Charleston." In *Battles and Leaders of the Civil War.* Eds. Robert U. Johnson and Clarence C. Buel. 1887; rpt. Secaucus, N.J.: Castle, 1982, IV 1–23.

Beauregard, G. T. "The Defense of Drewry's Bluff." In *Battles and Leaders of the Civil War.* Eds. Robert U. Johnson and Clarence C. Buel. 1887; rpt. Secaucus, N.J.: Castle, 1982, IV 195–205.

Beauregard, G. T. "Four Days of Battle at Petersburg." In *Battles and Leaders of the Civil War.* Eds. Robert U. Johnson and Clarence C. Buel. 1887; rpt. Secaucus, N.J.: Castle, 1982, IV 540–544.

Beauregard, G. T. "Swift Creek." *Southern Historical Society Papers,* XXVIII, 321–322.

Biggs, Sarah. "Clingman's Dome Named After Dueling Dentist." *Journal & Sentinel* (Winston-Salem, North Carolina), July 10, 1955.

Birdsong, James C. "Sketch of the Thirty-First Regiment." In *Brief Sketches of the North Carolina State Troops In the War Between the States.* Raleigh, N.C.: Josephus Daniels, State Printer and Binder, 1894, p. 121

Brock, R. A., ed. "The Career of T. L. Clingman," reprinted from the Philadelphia *Times. Southern Historical Society Papers,* XXIV, 1896.

Bryan, E. K., and E. H. Meadows. "Defense of Fort Wagner." In *Histories of the Several Regiments and Battalions from North Carolina In the Great War, 1861–1865, Written by Members of the Respective Commands.* Ed. Walter Clark. Goldsboro, N.C.: Nash Brothers, 1901, V, pp. 161–167.

Bryan, E. K., and E. H. Meadows. "Thirty-First Regiment." In *Histories of the Several Regiments and Battalions from North Carolina In the Great War, 1861–1865, Written by Members of the Respective Commands.* Ed. Walter Clark. Goldsboro, N.C.: Nash Brothers, 1901, II, pp. 506–520.

Burgwyn, W. H. S. "Clingman's Brigade." In *Histories of the Several Regiments and Battalions from North Carolina In the Great War, 1861–1865, Written by Members of the Respective Commands.* Ed. Walter Clark. Goldsboro, N.C.: Nash Brothers, 1901, IV, pp. 479–500.

Burgwyn, W. H. S. "Thirty-Fifth Regiment." In *Histories of the Several Regiments and Battalions from North Carolina In the Great War, 1861–1865, Written by Members of the Respective Commands.* Ed. Walter Clark. Goldsboro, N.C.: Nash Brothers, 1901, II, pp. 589–628.

Cahill, Carl. "New Evidence Supports Marshall Ney Legend." *State* (Dec. 1987), 30–31.

Cameron, John D. "Thomas Lanier Clingman," *University of North Carolina Magazine,* VIII (1889), 249–257.

Casstevens, Frances H., ed. "The Puryear Family." *Heritage of Yadkin County, North Carolina.* Winston-Salem, N.C.: Hunter Publishing Co., 1981. p. 396.

Casstevens, Frances H., ed. "Thomas Lanier Clingman: General, Statesman, Explorer." In *Heritage of Yadkin County, North Carolina.* Winston-Salem, N.C.: Hunter Publishing Co., 1981, pp. 560–561.

Clark, Walter. "Brigade Organization." In *Histories of the Several Regiments and Battalions from North Carolina In the Great War, 1861–1865, Written by Members of the Respective Commands.* Ed. Walter Clark. Goldsboro, N.C.: Nash Brothers, 1901, IV, pp. 434–442.

"Clingman, Thomas Lanier." In *Who Was Who In America: Historical Volume, 1607–1896,* rev. ed. 1967, p. 180.

Clingman, Thomas L. "Davidson Speech." In *Selections from the Speeches and Writings of Honorable Thomas L. Clingman of North Carolina with Additions and Explanatory Notes.* 2nd ed. Raleigh: John Nichols, Book and Job Printer, 1878, pp. 39–53.

Clingman, Thomas L. "Farming and Cookery: Letter to Col. John D. Whitford, Editor, State Agricultural Journal, May 15, 1875." In *Selections from the Speeches and Writings of Honorable Thomas L. Clingman of North Carolina with Additions and Explanatory Notes.* 2nd ed. Raleigh: John Nichols, Book and Job Printer, 1878, pp. 87–90.

Clingman, Thomas L. "Religious and Popular Orators: An Address Delivered at the Commencement of the University of the South." In *Selections from the Speeches and Writings of Honorable Thomas L. Clingman of North Carolina with Additions and Explanatory Notes.* 2nd ed. Raleigh: John Nichols, Book and Job Printer, 1878, pp. 23–30

Clingman, Thomas L. "Second Cold Harbor." In *Histories of the Several Regiments and Battalions from North Carolina In the Great War, 1861–1865, Written by Members of the Respective Commands.* Ed. Walter Clark. Goldsboro, N.C.: Nash Brothers, 1901, V, pp. 197–205.

Clingman, Thomas L. "Water Spouts." In *Selections from the Speeches and Writings of Honorable Thomas L. Clingman of North Carolina with Additions and Explanatory Notes.* 2nd ed. Raleigh: John Nichols, Book and Job Printer, 1878, pp. 68–77.

Cook, Charles M. "Fifty-Fifth Regiment." In *Histories of the Several Regiments and Battalions from North Carolina In the Great War, 1861–1865, Written by Members of the Respective Commands.* Ed. Walter Clark. Goldsboro, N.C.: Nash Brothers, 1901, III, pp. 287–312.

Courtnay, William A. "Fragments of War History Relating to the Coastal Defense of South Carolina 1861–1865 and the Hasty Preparation for the Battle of Honey Hill, November 30, 1864." *Southern Historical Society Papers,* XXVI (1898), 62–87.

Edwards, Dunreath Jarratt. "Augustus Henry Jarratt, Sr." In *Heritage of Yadkin County.* Ed. Frances H. Casstevens. Winston-Salem, N.C.: Hunter Publishing Co., 1981, p. 584.

Fayetteville Independent Light Infantry, "Confederate Memorial Program," Cross Creek Cemetery, Fayetteville, North Carolina, May 10, 1991.

Ferguson, Garland S. "Twenty-Fifth Regiment." In *Histories of the Several Regiments and Battalions from North Carolina In the Great War, 1861–1865, Written by Members of the Respective Commands.* Ed. Walter Clark. Goldsboro, N.C.: Nash Brothers, 1901, II, pp. 291–297.

"Garrard's Raid on Mount Olive." In The Wayne County Historical Association, Inc., and the Old Dobbs County Genealogical Society. *Heritage of Wayne County.* Winston-Salem, N.C.: Hunter Publishing Co., 1982, p. 17.

"Gen. Clingman Dead, The Noble Former Senator and General Passed Away in the State Hospital of the Insane—Sketch of His Eventful Life." *Union Republican,* Winston-Salem, North Carolina, November 11, 1897.

Gilchrist, Robert C. "Confederate Defense of Morris Island." *Charleston Year Book,* 1884. Charleston, S.C.: City of Charleston, 1884, 350–402.

Gillmore, Quincy A. "The Army Before Charleston in 1865." In *Battles and Leaders of the Civil War.* Eds. Robert U. Johnson and Clarence C. Buel. 1887; rpt. Secaucus, N.J.: Castle, 1982, IV, p. 55.

Graham, John W. "The Capture of Plymouth." In *Histories of the Several Regiments and Battalions from North Carolina In the Great War, 1861–1865, Written by Members of the Respective Commands.* Ed. Walter Clark. Goldsboro, N.C.: Nash Brothers, 1901, V, pp. 175–195.

Graham, Robert D. "Fifty-Sixth Regiment." In *Histories of the Several Regiments and Battalions from North Carolina In the Great War, 1861–1865, Written by Members of the Respective Commands.* Ed. Walter Clark. Goldsboro, N.C.: Nash Brothers, 1901, III, pp. 313–404.

Grimes, Alice D. "I'm Going to be President." *State*, II (Sept. 1934), 22–23.

Hagood, Johnson. "Gen. P. G. T. Beauregard: His Comprehensive and Aggressive Strategy, Drewry's Bluff and Petersburg." *Southern Historical Society Papers*, XXVIII (1890), 318–336.

Harleston, John. "Battery on Morris Island, 1863." *South Carolina Historical Magazine*, LVII (Jan. 1956), pp. 143–152.

Hill, Daniel H. "Lee's Attacks North of the Chicahominy." In *Battles and Leaders of the Civil War.* Eds. Robert U. Johnson and Clarence C. Buel. 1887; rpt. Secaucus, N.J.: Castle, 1982, II, pp. 347–362.

Hoke, Robert F. "Battle of Drewry's Bluff." *Southern Historical Society Papers*, XII (1884), 227–229.

Hutchens, James Albert. "Richmond Mumford Pearson: Founder of Richmond Hill Law School." In *Heritage of Yadkin County.* Ed. Frances H. Casstevens. Winston-Salem, N.C.: Hunter Publishing Company, 1981, pp. 177–180.

Ireson, Pat. "Sofley Home Huntsville Landmark." *Yadkin Enterprise* (Jonesville, N.C.), 13 Aug. 1969.

Johnson, John. "The Confederate Defense of Fort Sumter." In *Battles and Leaders of the Civil War.* Eds. Robert U. Johnson and Clarence C. Buel. 1887; rpt. Secaucus, N.J.: Castle, 1982, IV, pp. 23–26.

Kearney, H. Thomas. "Clingman, Thomas Lanier." In *Dictionary of North Carolina Biography.* Ed. William S. Powell. Chapel Hill, N.C.: University of North Carolina Press, 1979.

Kerr, Jane P. "Brigadier-General Thomas L. Clingman." *The Trinity Archive*, XII, No. 6 (March 1899), 388–396.

Lawrence R. C. "General Thomas Clingman." *State* XII (April 1945), 6–8, 21.

Loehr, Charles T. "Battle of Drewry's Bluff." *Richmond Times*, October 25, 1891; rpt. *Southern Historical Society Papers*, XIX (1891), 100–111.

Ludwig, H. T. J. "Eighth Regiment." In *Histories of the Several Regiments and Battalions from North Carolina In the Great War, 1861–1865, Written by Members of the Respective Commands.* Ed. Walter Clark. Goldsboro, N.C.: Nash Brothers, 1901, I, pp. 386–415.

McKethan, A. A. "Fifty-First Regiment." In *Histories of the Several Regiments and Battalions from North Carolina In the Great War, 1861–1865, Written by Members of the Respective Commands.* Ed. Walter Clark. Goldsboro, N.C.: Nash Brothers, 1901, III, pp. 203–221.

McMahan, Martin T. "Cold Harbor." In *Battles and Leaders of the Civil War.* Eds. Robert U. Johnson and Clarence C. Buel. 1887; rpt. Secaucus, N.J.: Castle, 1982, IV, pp. 213–220.

Moore, T. C. "Tenth Regiment." In *Histories of the Several Regiments and Battalions from North Carolina In the Great War, 1861–1865, Written by Members of the Respective Commands.* Ed. Walter Clark. Goldsboro, N.C.: Nash Brothers, 1901, IV, pp. 221–221.

Murphy, Walter ("Pete"). "Thomas Lanier Clingman." *State*, XI (Oct. 1943), 4–5.

"The Opposing Forces at Fort Fisher, N.C." In *Battles and Leaders of the Civil War.* Eds. Robert U. Johnson and Clarence C. Buel. 1887; rpt. Secaucus, N.J.: Castle, 1982, IV, p. 661.

Pickett, G. E. "Letter to General S. Cooper, February 15, 1864." In *Southern Historical Society Papers*, IX (1881), 6–7.

Pickett, George. "Report of General Pickett." In *Southern Historical Society Papers*, IX, No. 1 (Jan. 1881), 1.

"The Poindexter Family." *The Virginia Magazine of History and Biography*, XIX (1911), 215–218.

Poindexter, Hattie. "George Poindexter (Poingdestre)." In *Heritage of Yadkin County.* Ed. Frances H. Casstevens. Winston-Salem, N.C.: Hunter Publishing Company, 1981, pp. 550–551.

Poindexter, Howard, and Frances H. Casstevens. "The Pledge Family." In *Heritage of Yadkin County.* Ed. Frances H. Casstevens. Winston-Salem, N.C.: Hunter Publishing Company, 1981, p. 550.

Ramsey, N. A. "Sixty-First Regiment." In *Histories of the Several Regiments and Battalions from North Carolina In the Great War, 1861–1865, Written by Members of the Respective Commands.* Ed. Walter Clark. Goldsboro, N.C.: Nash Brothers, 1901, III, pp. 502–514.

Robinson, John H. "Fifty-Second Regiment."

In *Histories of the Several Regiments and Battalions from North Carolina In the Great War, 1861–1865, Written by Members of the Respective Commands*. Ed. Walter Clark. Goldsboro, N.C.: Nash Brothers, 1901, III, pp. 222–223.

Rose, George M. "Sixty-Sixth Regiment." In *Histories of the Several Regiments and Battalions from North Carolina In the Great War, 1861–1865, Written by Members of the Respective Commands*. Ed. Walter Clark. Goldsboro, N.C.: Nash Brothers, 1901, III, pp. 685–701.

Rosenberg, Morton M. "Thomas Lanier Clingman." *Encyclopedia of Southern History*. Eds. Avery O' Craven and Dewey W. Granthan, Jr. Baton Rouge, La.: Louisiana State University Press, 1979, p. 243.

Seabrook, William. "The White House — the H. H. Sofley Home." In *Heritage of Yadkin County*. Ed. Frances H. Casstevens. Winston-Salem, N.C.: Hunter Publishing Company, 1981, pp. 80–81.

Sharpe, Bill. "Yadkin County." *State*, XXXII (Nov. 1964), 8–23.

Smith, William Farrar. "Butler's Attack on Drewry's Bluff. In *Battles and Leaders of the Civil War*. Eds. Robert U. Johnson and Clarence C. Buel. 1887; rpt. Secaucus, N.J.: Castle, 1982, IV, p. 211.

Thomas, William M. "The Slaughter at Petersburg." *Southern Historical Society Papers*, XXV (1897), 222–230.

Tucker, Glenn. "For Want of a Scribe." *North Carolina Historical Review*, XLIII (April 1966), 174–185.

Van Deusen, Glyndon G. "Some Aspects of Whig Thought and Theory In the Jacksonian Period." *American Historical Review*, XLIII, no. 2 (January 1958), 318–322.

The Wayne County Historical Association, Inc. and the Old Dobbs County Genealogical Society. "The Civil War." In *Heritage of Wayne County*. Winston-Salem, N.C.: Hunter Publishing Co., 1982, p. 17.

The Wayne County Historical Association, Inc. and the Old Dobbs County Genealogical Society. "First Dudley." In *Heritage of Wayne County*. Winston-Salem, N.C.: Hunter Publishing Co., 1982, p. 12.

Willcox, Orlando. "Actions on the Weldon Railroad." In *Battles and Leaders of the Civil War*. Eds. Robert U. Johnson and Clarence C. Buel. 1887; rpt. Secaucus, N.J.: Castle, 1982, IV, pp. 568–573.

Williams, J. Marshall. "Fifty-Fourth Regiment."

In *Histories of the Several Regiments and Battalions from North Carolina In the Great War, 1861–1865, Written by Members of the Respective Commands*. Ed. Walter Clark. Goldsboro, N.C.: Nash Brothers, 1901, III, pp. 267–285.

Unpublished Works

Barringer, Paul B. "Reminiscences." Unpublished paper, North Carolina Department of Archives and History, Raleigh, North Carolina.

Casstevens, Frances H. "The Military Career of Thomas Lanier Clingman." M.A. thesis, University of North Carolina at Greensboro, Greensboro, North Carolina, 1984.

Gilbert, Clarence N. "The Public Career of Thomas L. Clingman." M.A. thesis, University of North Carolina, Chapel Hill, North Carolina, 1947.

Jackson, A. T. "Personal Reminiscences of the Civil War." Civil War Collection Box 71, Folder I, page 2, Division of Archives and History, Raleigh, North Carolina.

Jarratt, Augustus H., Sr. "The Family History." Unpublished manuscript, Yadkin County Public Library, Yadkinville, North Carolina.

Malone, Mrs. C. E. "General Thomas L. Clingman." Unpublished paper, North Carolina Department of Archives and History, Raleigh, North Carolina.

Siegmann, Marlene D. "Thomas Lanier Clingman: Political Pilgrim." M.A. thesis, Wake Forest University, Winston-Salem, North Carolina, 1964.

Wills, George. "Thomas Lanier Clingman." Unpublished paper, Charles Van Noppen Papers, Duke University, Durham, North Carolina.

Internet web pages

Bradshaw, Tim. "Battle Flag of the 51st North Carolina Troops." http://www.geocities.com/Pentagon/Bunker/5870/flag.html.

Fox, W. F. *Fox's Regimental Losses*. Albany, NY: Albany Publishing Co., 1888. Electronic version at http://www.civilwarhome.com/foxspref.htm.

Mason, Alice. "Alice Mason's Genealogy Page." http://mason.math.tntch.edu/alice.htm.

Mason, Alice. "Descendency Chart for James McKethan.'" http://mason.math.tntech.edu/jasmck3.htm.

Mason, Alice. "Obituary, 'Death of Col. McKethan." http://www.mason.math.tntech.edu/mason/d0003/g0000014.htm.

"Organization of the Armies of the Civil War. http://www.civilwarhome.com/armyorganization.html.

Newspapers

Asheville (North Carolina) *News*, October 28, 1852; July 18, 1860.

(Charlotte, North Carolina) *News & Observer*, October 25, 1908.

(Charlotte, North Carolina) *Western Democrat*, August 18, 1863.

(East Bend, North Carolina) *Yadkin Valley Pilot*, July 6, 1916.

(Jonesville, North Carolina) *Yadkin Enterprise*. August 13, 1969.

(Laurinburg, North Carolina) *Enterprise*, November 9, 1881.

(Philadelphia, Pennsylvania) *Times*, October 10, 1896.

(Raleigh, North Carolina) *North Carolina Standard*, November 28, 1849; February 6, 1850.

(Raleigh, North Carolina) *Semi-Weekly Standard*, January 16, 1858; February 17, 1858.

Salem (North Carolina) *People's Press*, 1861–1864.

(Salisbury, North Carolina) *Watchman & Old North State*, September 25, 1868.

Weekly Raleigh (North Carolina) *Register*, August 13, 1811; 1845–1863.

(Winston-Salem, North Carolina) *Journal & Sentinel*, July 10, 1955; June 29, 1959; May 23, 1965.

(Winston-Salem, North Carolina) *Union Republican*, November 11, 1897.

Index

Numbers in *italics* refer to photographs.

Abbott's Brigade 92
Adams, E. J., Pvt. 219
Adams, James M., Maj. 83
Administrative duties 153
Albemarle, C.S.N. ironclad 56
Alexander, Edward P., Brig. Gen. 81
Alford, Vice Chaplin 112
Allen, William A., Lt. Col. 34, 111, 112, 230
Allen, William A., to Hector McKethan 233
Ames' Division 62
Anderson, G. B., deceased 195
Anderson, George 220
Anderson, R. H., Maj. Gen. 67
Appomattox River 72
Archdale, NC 96
Armstrong, E. 220
Armstrong, Thomas, Pvt. 208
Army of Northern Virginia 48
Army of the Potomac 66
Ashe, Samuel A. 17, 186
Atkin, Thomas W. 27
Ausley, E. S. 195
Ausley, Rich'd 195
Ayer's Division 79

Bachelor's Creek 224
Baird, E. R., Cap. 221
Baker, D. J., Lt. 222
Baker, John, Lt. 222
Baker, Lawrence S., Brig. Gen. 176
Barber, George W., died 107
Barber, William, Pvt. 100
Barefoot soldiers, 61st Regiment 145
Barnes, J. D., Lt. 225
Barnhardt, J. R., colorbearer 104
Barrier, Rufus A., Lt. Col. 96, 230
Barron, C. H., Capt. 228
Batchelder's Creek 53, 101, 116

Battery Gregg 36
Battery Wagner 2, 5, 35–47, 100, 123
Battles: *1862–63* 31–48; *1864* 52–84; *1865* 90–96
Beauregard, P. G. T., Gen. 22, 35, 38, 40, 60, 62, 96
Bell, F., Pvt. 206
Bentonville, NC 93, 118, 128, 175–176
Bermuda Hundred 59, 60, 65, 172
Berock, Lt. 209
Berry, Dr. 209
Berry, J. H., Lt. 205
Berry's house 209
Best Station, NC 107
Bethea, W. J., Lt. 225
Bethel Regiment 133
Blacksmiths 191
Blackwater River 52
Blake, Captain 71
Blake, Frederick R., 1st Lt. 186, 190, 197, 228, 229, 230
Blalock, Jesse, Pvt. 205
Bloodworth, A. J. W. 207
"Bottled-Up" Butler 65
Boyd's Landing 24
Bradley, J. T., Capt. 225
Bradley, Mr. 207
Bradshaw, Tim 118
Bragg, Braxton, Gen. 56, 90, 93, 175
Bragg, Thomas, Gov. 13, 26
Branch, Lawrence O'B., Gen. 25
Breckinridge, John C. 25
Breece, L. R. 222
Brice's Creek 53
Brigade problems 149–162
Bryan, E. K., Adjt. 109
Bryan, E. K., 1st Lieut. 41
"Buffaloes" 52
Buie, D. A. 175

Buncombe County, NC, elections 143
Burchette, J. W. 195
Burgwyn, W. H. S., Capt. 54, 63, 131, 134, 138–140, 229, 232
Burney, William J., Pvt. 112
Burnside Expedition 31, 56
Busbee, W. J., Asst. Surgeon 230
Bush Hill, NC 96
Butler, Benjamin F., Maj. Gen. 59, 64, 81, 90, 128
Butt, T. W., Lt. 225

Cally, J. B., Capt. 99
Cameron, Jas. J., Pvt. 206
Camp Ashe 35
Camp Beauregard 24
Camp Clingman 24
Camp Davis 24, 121
Camp Lamb 120
Camp Macon 98
Camp Mangum 99
Camp Radcliffe 120
Camp Ransom 25
Camp Whiting 99
Cantwell, Edward, Col. 28, 111
Cantwell, John L., Col. *114*, 230
Cape Fear River 90
Carpenter, James, death 145
Carpenter, Wyatt, death 145
Carroll, Jno. W. 220
Cartrett, Luke R., Pvt. 206
Casualties: Bentonville 95; Drewry's Bluff 65; Fort Fisher 93; Fort Harrison 84; mine, July 30, 1864 77; Neuse River Bridge 34; Petersburg 80–81; Port Walthall 61; Roanoke Is. 99; 61st Regiment 128; Swift Creek 61; Wagner 7/18/1863, 40, 108, 112, 113; Ware Bottom Church 66
Charleston Harbor 5, 35–47

249

Index

Charleston, SC 107–108, 112, 122; ruins 45
Cheshire, Joseph Blunt 57
Chestnut, Mary 13, 17
Chestnutt, S. H. 220
Chief Donnahoo 9
City Point Road 60
City Point, VA 59, 65, 108
Civilian problems 156
Clay, Henry 14
Clayton, M., Pvt. 190
Clifton, Henry, J. 38–39
Clingman, Alexander 8
Clingman, Jacob 8, 10
Clingman, Peter 8, 10
Clingman, T. L. 1–3, *3, 8,* 12–19, 22–28, 140–145; 176; report Cold Harbor 69; to Edward White 233; to Col. H. K. Burgwyn 232–233; to Mrs. H. M. Shaw 101; to Hector McKethan 84; wounded 117
Clingman Tobacco Cure Company 143
Clingman/Yancey duel 141
Clingman's Brigade 2, 27, 65, 66, 68, 75, 78, 90, 93, 96, 102, 108, 111, 123, 125, 132, 166–178
Clingman's Dome 12
Clingman's Order Book 1 181–190
Clingman's Order Book 2 191–229
Cobb, Howell 25
Cold Harbor, second battle 66, *67,* 103, 117, 124, 172–173
Coldstream Guards 37
Colquitt, A. H., Gen. 40
Colquitt's Brigade 63, 78, 83, 109
Colt, Capt., wounded 100
Confederate Congress 18
Confederate Senate 26
Connaway, Oscar, Pvt. 208, 209
Cooke, James W., Capt. 56, 57
Core Creek, NC 111
Cornwallis, Lord 11
Corse's Brigade 63, 102
Cotton, Thomas, death 145
Countermine, Confederate 76
Covert, Nicholas L., death 145
Crater, the, Petersburg 76
Crawford's Division 79
Cummings Point 37
Curtis, Peter, Surgeon 230

Daily activities 155
Davis, Jefferson, Pres. 2, 18, 27, 35, 47, 57, 63, 90, 108
Dawson, A., Pvt. 220
Deal, Wm. H. 205
Dearing, St. Clair, Lt. Col. 23, 25, 53
Deep Bottom Run 79
Deep Gully 55, 107
Department of North Carolina 26
Desertion, penalty for 158–159

Devane, William S., Col. 70, 94, 121, 230, 231; wounded 128
Dills Bluff 199
Discipline 156
District of Pamlico 26
Donnell, Jno. O. 227
Dortch, William T. 18
Dress parade 154
Drewry's Bluff 2, 59, 60, 62, 108, 116, 124, 171–172
Dudley Station, NC 31
Duel 15
Dugger, Lt. 104
Du Heamme, P., Capt. 189, 118, 229, 230
Dunlop's Farm 116
Dushane's Brigade 79

Early's Division 68
Eaton, Clement 72
Edwards, Emanuel, Pvt. 208
Edwards, Rial 209
Edwards, Thomas, Pvt. 208
8th Regiment: history 98–105; NC troops 32, 58, 75, 95, 96
Elliott, Alexander 222
Ellis, John W., Gov. 17–18
Enfield Blues 133
Ervin, A. M., Maj. 185, 189, 229
Ethridge, Mike 195
Evans, Nathan G., Brig. Gen 31, 32, 33, 121
Ewell's Corps 68
Ezzell, I.W. 220

Faircloth, Daniel 220
Fayetteville Arsenal 17
Fayetteville Independent Light Infantry 132
Fayetteville, NC 137
Fennell, N. H., Lt. 225
Ferguson, Garland 23
Ferrell, M. 227
Field, Charles W., Gen. 81
Fields, Elias, death 145
Field's Division 81
51st Regiment: history 111–118; NC troops 32, 61, 64, 69, 81, 95, 96, 114
52nd Regiment, NC troops 32
54th Regiment, Mass. 40, 113
55th Regiment, NC troops 150
56th Regiment, NC troops 150
Flag, 51st regimental 116
Floyd, Alexander, Lt. 222
Floyd, F. F., Lt. 222
Floyd, John Buchanan 25
Folly Island, SC 39
Foot, Henry, Sen. 13
Ford, Arthur 42
Fort Anderson 53
Fort Bartow 106
Fort Blanchard 106
Fort Burnham *82*
Fort Clifton 61

Fort Delaware 140
Fort Fisher, NC 90, *91,* 104, 117, 128, 174–175
Fort Harrison, VA 81, *82,* 103, 109, 127, 174
Fort Huger 106
Fort Marshall 43
Fort McAllister, GA 107
Fort Moultrie 42
Fort Sumter 17, 35, *46*
Fort Totten 224
Fort William 102
40th Regiment, NC Troops 96
Fortifications, Petersburg 74
Foster, John G., Gen. 31, 111, 121
Foster's Mill 116
Fowle, Daniel G., Lt. Col. 106, 230
Freeman, Douglas S. 3
Fremantle, Arthur Lyon 37
French, S. G., Maj. Gen. 34, 150
Furloughs, passes 155
Furmage, Private 208, 209

Gage, R. S., Maj. 229, 230
Gage, Robert A. 195
Gardner, Lorton, Pvt. 208
Garrett, Lt. 209
Garris, T. J., Capt. 215
Gatlin, J. D., 1st Lt. 228
Gatlin, R. C., Gen. 225
Geddie, Corp. 199
Gillmore, Quincy, Maj. Gen. 38, *39,* 44, 116
Gillmore's X Corps 60
Globe Tavern 79, 127, 174
Godfrey, W. A., Pvt. 206
Goldsboro, NC 4, 32–35, 118
Gore, Daniel, R., Pvt. 206
Gorgas, Josiah, Col. 150
Gorman, B. A., Lt. 225
Gracie's Brigade 65
Graham, R. F., Col. 40
Graham, William A. 12
Grandy, A. H., Lt. 222
Grant, U.S., Maj. Gen. 59, 65, *72,* 92
Graves, Thomas L., Sgt. 124
Green, Nathanael, Gen. 11
Green, Thos. S., Maj. 200
Greensboro, NC 96
Gregg, Maxey, Brig. Gen. 37
Gregory, A. H., 1st Lt. 228
Griffin, Jon. N. 209
Grimes' Brigade 68
Grimsley, B. 199
Grimsley, E. 199
Grimsley, L. 199
Guilford Court House 11
Gunter, William, death 145
Guy, Charles T., Lt. 159

Hagood, Johnson, Gen. 40
Hagood's Brigade 60, 84
Ham, Isham 195
Hamilton, W. H. 206

Index

Hancock's II Corps 125
Hardee's infantry 94, 118
Hardee's tactics 186
Harding, Henry, Maj. 230
Harleston, John, Pvt. 38, 40
Harrell, Thomas, Pvt., killed 100
Harriet's Chapel 121
Harrison, George P., Col. 40
Hawes, R. J. T., 222
Hawks, James 195
Health and welfare 155
Henderson, L. A., Capt. 215
Hendley, Jas. 195
Hendricks, E. A., Sgt. 206
High Point, NC 129
Hill, A. P., Gen. 79
Hill, Daniel H., Maj. Gen. 28, 93, 118, 150, 176
Hill, Gabriel H., Maj. 106
Hill, James H., Maj. 191, 192
Hill, Sgt. 209
Hill's Point 106
Hilton Head, SC 24
Hines' Mills 121
Hinks, Edward W., Brig. Gen. 65
Hinton, James W., Maj. 230
Hobbs, C. L. 227
Hobbs, G. W. 227
Hobson Caleb B., Lt. Col. 101, 159, 203, 230
Hoke, Robert F., Brig. Gen. 48, 52–53, 67, 71, 170, 176; promotion 58
Hoke's Division 48, 60, 63, 64, 68, 90, 93, 96, 101, 102, 118, 125
Holcombe's Legion 33
Holden, William W. 27, 168
Holland, William A., Maj. 96
Holmes, Theophilus H., Gen. 26
Holt, L. B., Lt. 222
Houston, H. T., Lt. 225
Howard, Oliver O., Gen. 95
Howell's Brigade 66
Huggins, Sgt. 209
Hughes, Jordain, Lt. 222
Hunton's Brigade 71
Huntsville, NC 8

Inman, W. A., Pvt. 206
Ivor Station 52, 108, 116

Jackson's Corps 149
James Island, SC 5
James River 62
Jarvis, T. J., Capt. 62
Johnson, Bushrod 60, 125
Johnson, J. D. 108
Johnston, J. W. 195
Johnston, Joseph E. Gen. 22, 93, 96, 109, 176, *177*
Joines, W. H., Lt. 225
Jones, D. McL., Lt. 225
Jones, Private 210
Jordan Farm 108

Jordan, J. V., Col. 106, 230
Junior Reserve Brigade 94

Kale, Thos. A. 227
Kautz' cavalry 62
Keith, L. M., Col. 40
Kershaw's Division 69
Kilpatrick's cavalry 94
King, M. P., Capt. 195
King, Mallery P., Capt., report 235–236
Kinlock, Willis 108
Kinston, NC 2, 93, 121
Kirkland, W. W., Brig. Gen. 176
Kirkland's Brigade 84
Knight, C. W., Col. 66, 96, 230
Koonce, Edward B., Sgt. 161
Koonce, S. E., Lt. 209, 210, 225

Lamb, William, Col. 90
Lane, H. B., A.C.S. 189
Lane's Brigade 68
Langley, Lt., killed 102
Lanier, Jane Pattillo 9
Lanier, Wm. B., Capt. 206
Law, H. B., Capt. 229
Lawson, Jesse, Pvt. 2 20
Leaves of absence 155
Lee, Fitz, Maj. Gen. 67–68
Lee, H. C., Col. 34
Lee, J. B., Capt. 207
Lee, Robert E., Gen. 1, 7, 24, 26, 35, 67, 72, 81–82
Lee, W. H. F., Maj. Gen. 67
Lewis, John M., Pvt. 125
Liles, E. R., Lt. Col. 202, 215, 230
Lincoln, Abraham, Pres. 92
Lincoln, Benjamin, Gen. 8
Lippitt, A. D., Lt. 225
Lippitt, James W., Capt. 96
Lippitt, T. B., Lt. 222
Long, Daniel M., Pvt. 206
Longstreet's Corps 68
Lossing, Benson J. 128
Ludwig, H. T. J. 98, 105

Mahone's Division 103
Maline, Mrs. J. E. 144
Mallett, Edward, Capt. 126, 160, 168, 230, 231; wounded 128
Malvern Hill, VA 117
Manassas, VA, first battle 22, 24
Martin, James G., Adj. Gen. 22
Martin's Brigade 68
Mauice, S. W., Lt. 186
Maultby, S. W. 206
McArthur, J. A., Lt. 114
McArthur, Lt. 207
McDaniel, Alexander, Pvt. 208
McDonald, J. H., Maj. 41
McDonald, James R., Maj. 230
McEachern, Robert J., Capt. *114*, 215
McKay, John A. D., Maj. 211, 215, 230

McKenzie, A. 206
McKethan, A. A., 2nd Lt. 83, 103, 113, 171
McKethan, Alfred Augustus, Jr. 132
McKethan, Alfred Augustus, Sr. 132
McKethan, E. T., 1st Lt. 228
McKethan, Hector, Col. 5, 28, 34, 41, 61, 64, 66, 83, 84, 111, 113, *114*, 131, 132, *133*, 230; takes command 117; to A. A. McKethan, Sr. 235; to Edwin T. McKethan 234–235
McKethan, J. R., Lt. 225
McKethan's troops 127
McLaw's Division 175
McRae, Henry, Maj. 230
Meade, George G., Gen. 67
Meadows, E. H., Sgt. 109
Mechanicsville, VA 67
Merritt, K., Pvt. 206
Merritt, L. 220
Military districts 4
Miller, H. W., Maj. 195
Miller, T. C., Capt. 215
Millican, Sanders, Pvt. 206
Mine, Federal 76
Mitchell, Elisha, Dr. 12
Morale, declining 160–160
Morehead City, NC 53
Morgan, D. S. 206
Morris Island, SC 2, 5, 35–47, 100, 112, 122, 168–169; casualties 123–124
Morrow, William H., M.D. 137
Moses, N. B., Capt. 185
Mount, Corp. 207
Mount Mitchell 12
Mount Olive Station, NC 32
Mount Pleasant, SC 107
Moye, E. A., Lt. 222
Mumps 122
Murchison, J. R., Lt. Col. 66, 206, 229, 230
Murphy, W. F. Capt. *114*
Muse, Howard 118

Nance, W. F., Capt. 42, 168
Neuse River Bridge 4, 31, 34, 121, 167–168
New Bern Expedition 52–56, 169–170
New Bern, NC 24
"New" Cold Harbor 66
Ney, Michel, Marshal 11
Ney, Peter Stuart 11
Noble, Steven W., Capt. 96
Nobles, J. A. 227
Norment, W. S., Capt. 203
North Carolina Troops 22

O'Daniel, Jon. L. 227
Offenses and punishment 157–158
"Old" Cold Harbor 66

O'neil, Wm. 227
Outlaw, Davis 14

Page, W. 220
Paine, Mathias 227
Paine's Division 92
Parker, N. 220
Patrick, Wiliam H., Lt. 96
Pattillo, Henry, Rev. 9
Pattillo, Jane 9
Peck's Division 34
Peel, Jesse, Pvt. 207
Perkins, Francis J., wounded 102
Petersburg, VA 59, 72–79, 116; siege of, 117, 173–174
Pettigrew, William S. 14
Pickett, Charles, Maj. 161, 215
Pickett, George, Gen. 47, 52, 171
Pickman, Sgt. 206
Pierce, Franklin, Pres. 15
Pilkinton, J. A., death 145
Pipkins, J., Pvt. 219
Pleasants, Henry 76
Pledge, Elizabeth 9
Pledge, William 9
Plymouth, NC 56–58, 171
Poe, Terry, death 145
Poindexter, Ann 8
Poindexter, Francis 9, 10
Poindexter, Jane Frances 8
Poindexter, Thomas 9
Pool, S. D., Col. 32
Port Walthall Junction 59, 60
Porter, David Dixon, Adm. 91
Porter, M. 220
Pratt, Am. 225
Price, William. J., Lt. Col. 230
Prince, S. W., Pvt. 220
Privatt, S. E. 199
Puryear, Elizabeth C. 12
Puryear, Hal S., 1st Lt. 3, 75, 190, 229, 230
Puryear, Richard C., Mrs. 12
Putnam, H. S., Gen. 40

Radcliffe, James D., Col. 66, 68, 122, 126, 159–160, 230
Ramsey, Junius N., Capt. 62, 222
Ramsey, Nathan, Capt. 39, 120, 123, 145
Ransom, Robert, Gen. 26, 98, 216
Ransom's Brigade 26, 53
Raspberry, H. H., Lt. 225
Ream's Station 81
Reddith, David, Lt. 209
Regimental company designations 149
Register, R. 220
Reilly, James, Maj. 92
Richardson, S. D. 207
Riggs, Wm. 209
Ripley, R. S., Brig. Gen. 25
Roanoke Island 99
Roberts, William Paul 26
Robeson, Harry, Pvt. 209

Robinson, Jas. W., Capt. 215
Rockfish Church 112
Rockwell, H. C., Capt. 114
Rogers, Andrew J., Maj. 230
Royal, S. W. 220
Rutledge, Henry M. 23

Sanford, Captain 207
Savannah, GA 122
Scales' Brigade 68
Schools of instruction 154
Seatherwood, J., Pvt. 206
Seymour, Truman, Gen. 40
Shallow Ford 11
Sharendel, Sgt. 209
Sharpe, George H., Col. 66
Shaw, Henry M., Col. 54–55, 101, 107
Shaw, Robert S., Col. 40, 113
Shepherd, Charles Upham 12
Sheridan, Phil, Gen. 68
Sherman, William T., Gen. 93, 109
Simmons, L. N., Lt. 222
Six Mile House 79
61st Regiment: history 120–129; NC troops 69, 96
63rd Georgia Regiment 113
Slater, C. W., Capt. 215
Sloan, George, Capt. 114
Smallpox vaccination 122
Smith, Gustavus W., Maj. Gen. 1, 32
Smith, J. T., Lt. 225
Smith, J. W., Capt. 225
Smith, W. F., Lt. 225
Smithfield, NC 93
Smith's XVIII Corps 60
Snowden, J. B. 227
Sondley, Foster A. 7
Southport, NC 111
Southwest Creek 93, 121
Spear, Samuel Perkins, cavalry 79
Spotsylvania, VA 59
Spring Bank, NC 107
Spring Green 120
Staff changes 153
Stanford, S. M., Capt. 228
Starr's Battery 33
Stedman, Robert Winship, Lt. 123, 131, 135–137, 168
Stevens, W. H., Lt. Col. 32
Stevenson, W. M., Capt. 215
Stokes, Montford, Gov. 11
Stono River, SC 122
Strickland, B. P., Pvt. 199
Strong, George C., Gen. 38
Sturtevant's Battery 108
Sugar Loaf Hill 92, 118
Sullivan's Island, SC 5, 39, 42, 123
Summersett, C. J. 199
Sumter, steamer 43
Swaim, David L. 2, 11
Swift Creek 59, 61

Taliaferro, William B., Gen. 40, 133
Taney, Roger B., Chief Justice 13
Tarboro, NC 47, 116
Taylor, J. H., Lt. 225
Taylor, Richard, Pvt. 208, 209
Taylor, W. H. , A.A.G. 67
Tearoe (Teaboe), W. W. 220
Terry, Alfred H., Gen. 92, 128
Terry's Brigade 56
Terry's Expedition 90
Terry's Provisional Corps 92
13th Battalion, NC troops 33
31st Regiment: history 106–109; NC troops 41, 69, 95
36th Regiment, NC troops 96
Thompson, Jon., Pvt. 206, 219
Thompson, Lt., wounded 102
Thompson, Monroe, death 145
Tilman's Brigade 61
Tomlinson, W. H. 195
Toombs, Robert A. 25
Townsend, W. L., Lt. 222
Trench warfare 78
Trent River 52
Troop movement 156
23rd Regiment, South Carolina 33
25th Regiment, NC Troops 23
27th Georgia Regiment 70

University of North Carolina 11

Vance, Zebulon Baird 2, 13
Venable, T. Brown, Maj. 160

Wagner, Battery, casualties 123, 124
Wagner, Thomas M., Lt. Col. 37
Ware Bottom Church, VA 66
Warren's V Corps 79, 127
Washington, NC 31
Watson, Sgt. 219
Webster, Nathan, death 145
Weitzel, Godfrey, Maj. Gen. 92
Weldon, NC 56
Weldon Railroad 79
Wentworth, Mary 9
Wessell's Brigade 34
Wheeler, Woodbury, 1st Lt. 186
Whig Party 14–15
White, Edward, Capt., A.A.G. 28, 71, *150*, *151*, 189, 228, 229
White Hall, NC 31, 107
White House 10
Whitford, J. N. Col. 53
Whiting, William H. C., Gen. 47, 92, 175
Whitley, Jos., Capt. 228
Whitson, James M. Maj. 230
Wilderness, battle of 59, 66
Wilkins, J. J., Lt. 209
Williamston, NC 116
Wilmington, NC 35, 100, 104, 121
Wilmot, David 13
Wilmot Proviso 13
Wilson, Willis, died 107

Winder, John Henry 26
Wise, Henry A., Brig. Gen. 25, 106
Wise's Brigade 73
Wise's Forks 93, 104, 118
Wofford's Brigade 72

Womack, Jefferson, death 145
Wood, John Taylor, Com. 54
Work details 155

Yadkin River 9
Yancey, William L. 15

Yancey and Clingman duel 15
Yates, Jesse J., Maj. 106, 230
Yellowley, Edward C., Maj. 230

www.ingramcontent.com/pod-product-compliance
Lightning Source LLC
Chambersburg PA
CBHW081548300426
44116CB00015B/2794